Italian Americans on Screen

MEDIA, CULTURE, AND THE ARTS

Series Editors: Theresa Carilli and Jane Campbell, both of Purdue University Northwest

Media, Culture, and the Arts explores the ways cultural expression takes shape through the media or arts. The series initiates a dialogue about media and artistic representations and how such representations identify the status of a particular culture or community. Supporting the principles of feminism and humanitarianism, the series contributes to a dialogue about media, culture, and the arts.

Recent titles in the series:

Italian Americans on Screen: Challenging the Past, Re-Theorizing the Future, Edited by Ryan Calabretta-Sajder and Alan J. Gravano

Sontag and the Camp Aesthetic: Advancing New Perspectives, Edited by Bruce E. Drushel and Brian M. Peters

Locating Queerness in the Media: A New Look, Edited by Jane Campbell and Theresa Carilli

Gender, Race, and Social Identity in American Politics: The Past and Future of Political Access, Edited by Lori L. Montalbano

Italian Americans on Screen

Challenging the Past, Re-Theorizing the Future

Ryan Calabretta-Sajder
and Alan J. Gravano

LEXINGTON BOOKS
Lanham • Boulder • New York • London

Published by Lexington Books
An imprint of The Rowman & Littlefield Publishing Group, Inc.
4501 Forbes Boulevard, Suite 200, Lanham, Maryland 20706
www.rowman.com

6 Tinworth Street, London SE11 5AL

British Library Cataloguing in Publication Information Available

Library of Congress Cataloging-in-Publication Data is Available

ISBN 978-1-7936-1154-3 (cloth)
ISBN 978-1-7936-1156-7 (pbk)
ISBN 978-1-7936-1155-0 (electronic)

Dedicated to my father, Dennis G. Sajder (1949–2019), with whom I spent many hours watching and "analyzing" film. It is thanks to him that I developed such a fierce work ethic, and is why I am so passionate about my research and teaching.

To my father, Alan Alfonso Gravano (1941–2011), who instilled in me a passion for movies at an early age. My continued fascination with Rocky Balboa has been growing since that momentous day in November 1976, when Dad took me to the theater to watch *Rocky*. It is to him that I dedicate this collection, especially the chapter on the *Creed* series, with all my love and eternal gratitude.

Contents

Acknowledgments   ix

Introduction   1
   Ryan Calabretta-Sajder and Alan J. Gravano

Part I: What is Italian American Cinema?

1 What is Italian about Sofia Coppola?: Tracing Ethnicity in
   Third-Generation Feminist Cinema   13
   Colleen M. Ryan

2 Edible Ethnicity: Italian American Representations, Cinematic
   Style, and Ethnic Commodification in Stanley Tucci's and
   Campbell Scott's *Big Night*   37
   Jonathan J. Cavallero

3 Questioning the Italian American Palooka: Race and Disability
   in the *Rocky* and the *Creed* Series   59
   Alan J. Gravano

Part II: Blurring the Lines between Italian and American on Screen

4 The Italian Pursuit of Hollywood: *Pursuit of Happyness*
   (Muccino, 2006)   81
   Mary Ann McDonald Carolan

5 Comedies of Identity: Italian Cinema and Television Narrating
   Italian Americans   95
   Giuseppe Sorrentino

Part III: *Re*-Viewing Italian Americana on Screen: Reception and Reflections

6 Who's Laughing at Whom? Masculinity, Humor, and Italian
   American Lives on Mainstream Television: *Friends*   117
   Ryan Calabretta-Sajder

7 Tony Soprano Meets Furio Giunta: Italian Americans and
   "Real" Italians in *The Sopranos*   141
   Francesco Chianese

Part IV: Italian Newspapers, Italian Cinema, and 2.0 Media

8 *Il Bambino in Pericolo*: Serializing Italian American Futurity 163
   Sarah H. Salter

9 *Cinema Paradiso*: Toronto's Italian Language Cinemas and
   Distribution Networks   183
   Jessica Leonora Whitehead and Paul S. Moore

10 Conversing about National Attributes Online: The Case of Italy
   and the United States   211
   Giacomo Sproccati

Index   229

About the Contributors   239

Acknowledgments

A scholarly work never stands on its own, but rather builds upon its foundational past. In this manner, we hope that this manuscript will "challenge" some past interpretations and theoretical models and "re-theorize" them to create new and exciting discourses in the present and future. We understand that this book would not be possible without those creative scholars who, in their present, were willing to confront the status quo. In particularly, we are indebted to the monographs and edited collections that paved the way for our book: Peter Bondanella's *Hollywood Italians: Dagos, Palookas, Romeos, Wise Guys, and Sopranos* (2004) and Anthony Julian Tamburri's *Re-Viewing Italian Americana: Generalities and Specificities on Cinema* (2011). In addition, several others informed our work: *Mediated Ethnicity: New Italian-American Cinema* (2010) edited by Giuliana Muscio, Joseph Sciorra, Giovanni Spagnoletti, Anthony Julian Tamburri and *From the Margin: Writings in Italian Americana* (1990, 2000) edited by Tamburri, Paolo A. Giordano, and Fred L. Gardaphé, and *Screening Ethnicity: Cinematographic Representations of Italian Americans in the United States* (2008) edited by Anna Camaiti Hostert and Tamburri. This volume also pays tribute to the theoretical background present in Robert Casillo's *Gangster Priest: The Italian American Cinema of Martin Scorsese* (2007).

We would like to extend our particular appreciation to Ben Lawton for allowing us to update his Select Filmography from *Beyond the Margins* and updating it. In the day, it was a critical publication.

In putting this book together, we have incurred numerous debts to others. We owe our thanks to the series editors, Jane Campbell and Theresa Carilli, for deeming our project worthwhile and providing feedback on several chapters as well as the editors Nicolette Amstutz and Jessica Tepper. We are indebted to colleagues who took the time to carefully read, edit, and offer suggestions. We thank Eugene L. Arva, Donnamarie Kelly, Michela Perna, Mercedes Rooney, and Anthony Julian Tamburri for always being available to read through another version of the "final draft." The fact that we can count on you means the world to us.

Introduction

Ryan Calabretta-Sajder and Alan J. Gravano

In *Italian Americans on Screen: Challenging the Past, Re-Theorizing the Future*, we hope to augment the existing scholarship on Italian American cinema and media. The premise of this book questions the earlier formulations regarding the field, and in some cases modifies definitions as a way to expand the scope. In addition, in the introduction we review several seminal works that precede ours and deserve context within these pages. In essence, our opening serves as a short history of Italian American film scholarship to those unfamiliar, while, at the same time, remaining critical of it.

In his comprehensive work, *Gangster Priest: The Italian American Cinema of Martin Scorsese,* Robert Casillo argues that "Scorsese is without a doubt the chief exemplar of Italian American cinema, for which the main criterion is that a director of Italian American descent treat his ethnic group in and of itself on screen."[1] Although Casillo makes space for few exceptions, citing, for example, Tennessee Williams's *The Rose Tattoo*, he maintains that Delbert Mann's *Marty* lacks a proper ethnic treatment of *Italian Americanità* due to the director's ethnic background.[2] Casillo's insight on Scorsese has become foundational for the reading of many of the Italian American director's films, and this volume will not put into question Scorsese's place within Italian American cinema and media studies. Instead, the contributors aim to engage with Casillo's traditional definition of Italian American cinema and media studies. As pointed out in this book's acknowledgements, Italian American cinema and media studies is indebted to a plethora of scholars who have paved the road before us. Scholars such as Peter Bondanella, Casillo, Thomas Ferraro, Fred Gardaphé, Giuliana Muscio, Ben Lawton, and Anthony Julian Tamburri[3] have all pushed the field forward, while inviting junior colleagues into the discourse, and supporting us personally and professionally with this and other projects. The authors in this collection, however, intend to wrestle with past scholarship and introduce new theoretical models potentially applicable not only to media studies but to literary criticism.

This collection of essays challenges, or at least, reconsiders Casillo's definition of Italian American cinema as that in which Italian American directors portray Italian American characters. More specifically, this study intends to reformulate Casillo's theory, rather by opening up, analyzing, and updating what "Italian American director" and "Italian American subject" can mean. In many regards, it returns to Ben Lawton's foundational essay, "What is Italian American Cinema?" and further expands the inquiry needed to approach this quite fluid, interdisciplinary field.[4] In doing so, scholars claim a place for Italian American cinema and media studies in the contemporary intersectional (race, class, gender, and sexuality) debates about ethnic identity. Given the ever broader, competing, and, at times, conflicting concepts of migration in culture and media studies—from exile and diaspora, page to screen, and theory to application—this project conjoins prior scholarship and theoretical underpinnings with new sociocultural hermeneutic approaches to newspaper, online media, television, and film.

As Italian American studies examine parallels and adopt affinities with the concept of "diaspora," scholars have broadened their discourses on the interconnections between Italy and the new home(s) of many migrants in North America. The very specific notion of "Italian American filmmakers" telling stories about "Italian American subjects" has thus given way to a much more complicated understanding of ethnic spaces, identities, and movements among immigrant groups as portrayed in cinema and other media.

Considering the role of Italian Americans on screen, numerous scholars including Casillo,[5] and more recently Anthony Julian Tamburri, have pointed out,

> As one rehearses a history of Italians and Italian Americans in three major mediatic forms, what becomes apparent is that Italian and Italian Americans are by no means a lacking entity in cinema, music, or television, nor have they ever been, be it from the perspective of their actual presence or simply their mere representation in films portrayed by others.[6]

This insightful and somewhat surprising observation is an important starting point for a work that aspires to "Challenge the Past and Re-Theorize the Future," as the subtitle of the volume suggests. The presence of Italian Americans both on and behind the scenes has been well documented, even though we would argue that a serious critical study of Italian Americans behind the scenes, with the exception of a few noted directors such as Francis

Ford Coppola, Martin Scorsese, and Quentin Tarantino, is conspicuously absent in both media and Italian American Studies.

Italian American cinema has focused on the topic of stardom in film studies, having investigated names from Rudolph Valentino to Sofia Loren, along with contemporary ones, such as John Travolta to Robert De Niro. Athough Bondanella attempts to analyze the representation of Italian Americans on screen by category, he seems to spend a significant amount of time discussing both actors, along with casting and producing.[7] His encyclopedic approach to Italian American cinema covers a considerable amount of academic ground, yet lacks theoretical backing. Where Bondanella's work flourishes is in his literary analysis and examination of genre.

Besides the realm of studies solely focused on Italian American cinema, a few similar works concentrate on the intersectionality of Italian and American cinema. Giorgio Bertellini scrutinizes various manners in which Italy and Italians are viewed in early American cinema, paying particular attention to the concept race.[8] Bertellini's work succeeds in its historical analysis marking the roots of stereotyping of Italians within the European backdrop and how, in fact, that representation then carried over into the American landscape. A year later, Flaminio Di Biagi contributes a cross-cultural analytical interpretation, first focusing on the representation of Italians and Italian Americans in Hollywood cinema and later exploring the depiction of Italian Americans in Italian cinema. Di Biagi, like many Italian American critics, underscores the concept of "in-betweenness" experienced by Italian Americans as presented on the big screen.[9] More recently, Mary Ann McDonald Carolan surveys various theoretical approaches in which the spectator meets a cross-pollination of cinematic styles, from direct adaptations to utilizing "foreign" cinema in one's own.[10] These three books additionally highlight the universality of cinema while deliberating the intersectionality of themes and cultural concepts.[11] The influence of Italian directors and films on Italian American directors and their pictures represents an important dialogue that continues to this day. Indeed, Italian directors such as Luca Guadagnino, Gabriele Muccino, and others have found success behind the camera in Hollywood.

When discussing the concept of Italian American media studies, we believe the field is grim. To our knowledge, there does not exist a true "companion" on the representation of Italian Americans on television. Outside the world of *The Sopranos,* which originally aired on HBO, little extensive critical attention has focused on the subject. This does not suggest that no one has worked on Italian American television; there are various articles published with Italian American journals, book collections, and some in media studies journals. However, the absence of a concise and organized encyclopedia, similar to Bondanella's *Hollywood Italians*, constitutes a large void within the field. We urge colleagues to consider filling this void, as it is important for parallel studies with cinematic representation and cultural stereotyping of Italian Americans, such a contribution would be foundational. Moreover, Italian American media studies must break free from the compulsive obsession with mafia images because, as Jonathan Cavallero points out,

> In recent years, groups such as the American Italian Defense Association and the National Italian American Foundation have protested the depiction of Italians in the HBO television series *The Sopranos* (1999–2007) while ignoring most contemporary presentations of Italian ethnicity and even applauding the depictions of Italians in television commercials for Ragu, radio advertisements for Spring PCS, and television programs such as the NBC series *Friends* (1994–2004). Such choices indicate a double standard on the part of these groups as they disparage the gangster but fail to provide the same degree of scrutiny for non-gangster Italian stereotypes. [12]

Not lost on the contributors is the fact that most noted auteurs are men (Coppola, Scorsese, and Tarantino), while only a few women in the profession (Sofia Coppola, Penny Marshall, and Nancy Savoca) have been treated to scholarship, but not as much as their male peers. These filmmakers demand attention from cultural and feminist studies as well as media and Italian American scholars as we move into the future.

We divided *Italian Americans on Screen* into four main sections: "What is Italian American Cinema?," "Blurring the Lines between Italian and American on Screen," "*Re*-Viewing Italian Americana on Screen: Reception and Reflections," and "Italian Newspapers, Italian Cinema, and 2.0 Media." Each part of the volume considers diverse representational politics of Italian Americans in the media, and there exists a philosophical progression from attempting to define Italian American cinema at large to analyzing ethnicity as presented through social media, which is rarely considered in the field of media studies.

In Part I: "What is Italian American Cinema?," Colleen Ryan examines the lack of research on the "Italianness" of Sofia Coppola. In "What Is Italian about Sofia Coppola? Tracing Ethnicity in Third-Generation Feminist Cinema," Ryan traces the way artistic allusions and ethnic sensibilities in Coppola's films intersect with her celebration of female voice and perspective. Ryan aims to liberate rather than constrain the auteur, by distinguishing her as an understudied prototype, alongside other women directors of Italian descent, whose films creatively combine discourses on gender, class, ethnicity, sexuality, age, and other forms of identity. Ryan maintains, specifically as Coppola's characters' search for a new life or new belonging, that the audience experiences a "feeling of Italianness" in her work. Meanwhile, Jonathan J. Cavallero contextualizes the Italian American actor, Stanley Tucci, who was tired of being cast in the roles of Italian American gangsters (like Lucky Luciano in *Billy Bathgate*) and Middle-Eastern terrorists (like Khamel in *The Pelican Brief*). He wanted to play complex characters who were not easily defined by their ethnic background. In "Edible Ethnicity: Italian American Representations, Cinematic Style, and Ethnic Commodification in Stanley Tucci's and Campbell Scott's *Big Night*," Cavallero examines food as a metaphor to understand the dynamics of the American Dream and the ways capitalistic pressures such as the bank force assimilation and erasure, and leads to the erosion of traditional ethnic values. To conclude Part I, Alan Gravano investigates non-Italian American filmmakers and films such as John G. Avildsen's *Rocky*, Ryan Coogler's *Creed*, and Steven Caple Jr.'s *Creed II*. In "Questioning the Italian American Palooka: Race and Disability in the *Rocky* and *Creed* Series," Gravano attempts to modify Casillo's definition of Italian American cinema as "works by Italian-American directors who treat Italian-American subjects." In addition, he applies Fiona Kumari Campbell's terms of the normate individual and "the aberrant, the unthinkable, quasi-human hybrid and therefore non-human" to characters such as Donnie, Bianca, and Amara Creed, Ivan and Viktor Drago, and Rocky Balboa.[13] Three types of marginalization—ethnic, racial, and sensory disabilities—occur in these films. Thus, Italian American identity adds to the discourses of access and privilege around African American and disabled bodies. The section combines film theory with other cultural studies theories to formulate new interpretations of classic films and directors.

In Part II: "Blurring the Lines between Italian and American on Screen," Mary Ann McDonald Carolan analyzes the longstanding and widespread influential relationship between Italian and American filmmakers. In "The Italian Pursuit of Hollywood: *Pursuit of Happyness*," Carolan examines Gabriele Muccino, who directed *The Pursuit of Happyness* (2006). Muccino's film traces the trajectory of an African American underdog from the margins to the pinnacle of American society. In addition, Carolan considers race and genre as factors in the reception abroad of films that tell essentially Black stories. In "Comedies of Identity: Italian Cinema and Television Narrating Italian Americans," Giuseppe Sorrentino scrutinizes the parallel development of two identities in the course of recent Italian history. On the one side, the Italians who "stayed" after the Unification of Italy (1861) and participated in the nation-building process, plagued by numerous political and social setbacks. On the other side, the Italians who "left," bringing with them their *Italianitá*, and contributing extensively, through their identity, to the cultural, social, economic, and political progress of the United States. Sorrentino analyzes the complex dynamic of the parallel development of these "two Italies" by concentrating on various filmmakers, movies, and television (Ettore Scola, Carlo Vanzina, and Mario Monicelli) and their representation of Italian American immigrants. This section explores the intersectional nature of cinema from both filmic and theoretical perspectives, underscoring the importance of applying established cultural studies approaches to Italian American cinema.

In Part III: "*Re*-Viewing Italian Americana on Television: Reception and Reflections," Ryan Calabretta-Sajder studies the representation of Italian and Italian American characters in the ten-season run of the NBC hit sitcom, *Friends*. In "Who's Laughing at Whom? Masculinity, Humor, and Italian American Lives on Mainstream Television: *Friends*," Calabretta-Sajder analyzes the various relationships in *Friends* and examines how the character of Joey Tribbiani represents the *inetto*, a man who is incapable of consummating a relationship, and how he remains the ethnic outsider of his friends' group, especially in terms of a romantic relationship. He also considers how Joey's character perpetuates the negative stereotypes of Italian Americans since *Happy Days*. Switching from a series with one token Italian American character to another filled with an ensemble cast, *The Sopranos* depicts the lives of an Italian American family living in New Jersey whose patriarch runs a criminal enterprise. Critics have described *The Sopranos* as one of the most sophisticated and realistic American TV shows, and has provided one of the most complex media representations of the Italian American character. Producer David Chase does not confine his representation within the borders of New Jersey and neighboring New York, but engages in a comparison with contemporary Italy. Francesco Chianese retraces Tony Sopranos's journey to Naples in the *Commedatori* episode (Season 2, Episode 4). Tony's experience of Italy was not limited to that single episode, and his journey did not end by coming back to New Jersey; he brought home a new series of doubts, questioning his beliefs, his values, his certainties, specifically the ones concerning the Italian family culture. In "Tony Soprano Meets Furio Giunta: Italian Americans and the 'Real' Italians in *The Sopranos*," Chianese shows how Furio Giunta plays the role of the Lacanian Real upon his arrival in the apparently happy New Jersey Italian American community. Furio forces Tony and Carmela to negotiate their myth of the Italian family and reconsider the ideal and nostalgic image of Italy abroad as it has been handed down through generations. Although different in their approaches to Italian American media studies, both pieces consider representations and stereotyping related to Italian Americans on television.

In Part IV: "Italian Newspapers, Italian Cinema, and 2.0 Media," Sarah Salter examines how the first daily Italian-language newspaper in the United States, *Il Progresso Italo-Americano*, used seriality to develop specific Italian American sociopolitical narratives tied to social responsibility and reproduction. Before television, before film, the newspaper brought sensational news in narrative form to the *colonia* (colony and community). As newspapers exploited the pedagogical opportunities of seriality, they produced and reproduced cultural values tied to civic norms. In "*Il Bambino in Pericolo*: Serializing Italian American," Salter applies to media theories of serialization and attention to the social implications of sensationalism to probe how tabloid exploits about a famous American political family were leveraged to suit the needs of a 19th century ethnic newspaper and its audiences. Navigating between imaginative sympathy and sensationalist revelation, the chapter instills in readers a sense of civic responsibility partaking simultaneously of romantic associations and realist intercessions. Using Lee Edelman's influential discussion of "reproductive futurism," Salter offers an early perspective on how newspapers addressed Italian migrant communities as they grew together from distinct enclaves to share long-term collective investments in US identities and struggles. Meanwhile, in Toronto, Canada, newly arrived Italian-speaking immigrants after WWII organized new routines within immigrant enclaves and helped reshape the face of Canada's commercial and cultural landscape, including entertainment industries. An ascendant postwar film industry in Italy coincided with the relative decline of mainstream Hollywood moviegoing in Canada. Dozens of Toronto movie theaters closed or sought new audiences in the face of competition from television, at the same time as tens of thousands of people newly arrived from Italy were seeking entertainment in their mother tongue. Jessica Leonora Whitehead and Paul S. Moore in "Cinema Paradiso: Toronto's Italian Language Cinemas and Distribution Networks" analyze movie advertising from three decades of the *Corriere Canadese* to demonstrate how Italian-language films provided a flourishing movie culture for Italian enclaves in Toronto. Part of a distinctly secular, commercial routine of middle-class consumption, moviegoing in Italian offered a type of unofficial multiculturalism allowing people to retain diasporic cultural ties to popular culture and mass entertainment. In total, more than two dozen Italian-language cinemas operated at least briefly between the early 1950s and the late 1980s, a time when the proportion of people with Italian as mother tongue grew to more than 10 percent of the city's population. Many of the Italian cinemas in Toronto were long-standing, profitable businesses fully integrated into larger, mainstream cinema chains and corporate structures. Finally, in "Conversing about National Attributes Online: The Case of Italy and the United States," Giacomo Sproccati investigates a 2015 BuzzFeed video "Questions Americans have for Italians" and *La Stampa*'s response. He applies various new media theory (Guo-Ming Chen, Marino Livolsi, and Robert Shuter) to this communication across national boundaries arguing that online media allow for incomplete dialogue as evidenced in Buzzfeed's "Questions Americans have for Italians" and *La Stampa*'s response "Our Answers to Buzzfeed's Questions on Italians." Thus, Buzzfeed and *La Stampa*'s videos fail to complete the conversational cycle like that of the slower and more traditional face-to-face correspondence; however, despite the incomplete cycle, new media still can construct a national sense of belonging in an online community.

In short, *Italian Americans on Screen* does not intend to fill the vast gaps we have noted within the general field. Rather, we hope this collection generates a discussion about Italian American cinema and media with some of the existing scholarship. Beyond the scope of dialoguing with the past, this collection aims to introduce *some* unique theoretical models in smaller doses to address specific questions concerning Italian American cinema and media studies. Through this approach, the editors and contributors hope to add to the building blocks of existing scholarship, and continue to enrich the ambitious debate in the field.

In American cinema, Frank Capra, Francis Ford Coppola, and Martin Scorsese represent the establishment, and the editors purposefully opted not to focus on these directors. While each director has Italian heritage and some, such as Scorsese, continue to explore Italian American subjects most notably *The Irishman* (2019), film, newspaper, online media, and television in particular, require more theoretical inquiries of Italian American characters such as Columbo or the Fonz played by non-Italian American actors. In addition, in order to continue to legitimize the field, graduate students and junior faculty are invited to build on the foundation provided by those who have come before them. In this sense, *Italian Americans on Screen* is just another beginning on the long journey ahead of us.

NOTES

1. Robert Casillo, *Gangster Priest: The Italian American Cinema of Martin Scorsese* (Toronto: University of Toronto, 2006): 383.

2. Ibid., 383.

3. There are too many to list in the introduction, but our work builds on many scholars of Italian American cinema: Pellegrino D'Acierno, *The Italian American Heritage: A Companion to Literature and Arts* (New York: Garland, 1999); Francesca Canadé Sautman, "Women of the Shadows: Italian American Women, Ethnicity, and Racism in American Cinema," *Differentia: Review of Italian Thought* 6–7 (1994): 219–46; Frank P. Tomasulo, "Italian-Americans in the Hollywood Cinema: Filmmakers, Characters, Audiences," *Voices in Italian Americana* 7.1 (1996): 65–72; Rebecca West, "Scorsese's 'Who's That Knocking at My Door?': Night Thoughts on Italian Studies in the United States," in *Romance Languages Annual*, ed. Jeanette Beer, Charles Ganelin, and Anthony Julian Tamburri (West Lafayette, IN: Purdue Research Foundation, 1992).

4. Ben Lawton, "What is Italian American Cinema?," *Voices in Italian Americana* 6.1 (1995): 27–51.

5. Ibid., "Preface"

6. Anthony Julian Tamburri, *Re-viewing Italian Americana: Generalities and Specificities on Cinema* (New York: Bordighera Press, 2011): 13.

7. Peter Bondanella, *Hollywood Italians: Dagos, Palookas, Romeos, Wise Guys, and Sopranos* (New York: Continuum International Publishing Group, 2004).

8. Giorgio Bertelinni, *Italy in Early American Cinema: Race, Landscape and the Picturesque* (Bloomington: Indiana University Press, 2009).

9. Flaminio Di Biagi, *Italoamericani tra Hollywood e Cinecittà*, Genoa, Italy, Le Mani, 2010. See Tamburri (2011), pages 24–25 for an in-depth explanation of how the work functions on a cultural and semiotic level.

10. Mary Ann McDonald Carolan, *The Transatlantic Gaze: Italian Cinema, American Film* (Albany: SUNY Press, 2014).

11. For a robust overview of the previous scholarship related to Italian American cinema, see Anthony Julian Tamburri's "Italian Americans and the Media: Cinema, Video, Television" in *Re-Viewing Italian Americana: Generalities and Specificities on Cinema* (New York: Bordighera Press, 2011): 1–45.

12. Jonathan J. Cavallero, "Gangsters, Fessos, Tricksters, and Sopranos: The Historical Roots of Italian American Stereotype Anxiety," *Journal of Popular Film and Television* 32.2 (2004): 50–51.

13. Fiona Kumari Campbell, *Contours of Ableism: The Production of Disability and Abledness* (New York: Palgrave Macmillan, 2006): 6.

BIBLIOGRAPHY

Bertelinni, Giorgio. *Italy in Early American Cinema: Race, Landscape and the Picturesque.* Bloomington: Indiana University Press, 2009.

Bondanella, Peter. *Hollywood Italians: Dagos, Palookas, Romeos, Wise Guys, and Sopranos.* New York: Continuum International Publishing Group, 2004.

Campbell, Jane, and Theresa Carilli. *Challenging Images of Women in the Media: Reinventing Women's Lives.* Lanham, MD: Lexington Books, 2012.

———. *Locating Queerness in the Media: A New Look.* Lanham, MD: Lexington Books, 2017.

Carolan, Mary Ann McDonald. *The Transatlantic Gaze: Italian Cinema, American Film.* Albany, NY: SUNY Press, 2014.

Casillo, Robert. *Gangster Priest: The Italian American Cinema of Martin Scorsese.* Toronto: University of Toronto, 2006.

Cavallero, Jonathan J. "Gangsters, Fessos, Tricksters, and Sopranos: The Historical Roots of Italian American Stereotype Anxiety," *Journal of Popular Film and Television* 32.2 (2004): 50–51.

———. *Hollywood's Italian American Filmmakers: Capra, Scorsese, Savoca, Coppola, and Tarantino.* Urbana: University of Illinois Press, 2011.

Di Biagi, Flaminio. *Italoamericani tra Hollywood e Cinecittà.* Genoa, Italy: Le Mani, 2010.

Ferraro, Thomas J. *Feeling Italian: The Art of Ethnicity in America.* New York: New York University Press, 2005.

Gardaphé, Fred L. *From Wiseguys to Wise Men: The Gangster and Italian American Masculinities.* New York: Routledge, 2006.

Hostert, Anna Camaiti, and Anthony Julian Tamburri. *Screening Ethnicity: Cinematographic Representations of Italian Americans in the United States.* New York, NY: Bordighera Press, 2008.

Lawton, Ben. "What is Italian American Cinema?" *Voices in Italian Americana* 6.1 (1995): 27–51.

Muscio, Giuliana. *Napoli/New York/Hollywood: Film between Italy and the United States.* New York: Fordham University Press, 2019.

Muscio, Giuliana, Joseph Sciorra, Giovanni Spagnoletti, and Anthony Julian Tamburri. *Mediated Ethnicity: New Italian-American Cinema.* New York: John D. Calandra Italian American Institute, 2010.

Ruberto, Laura E., and Kristi M. Wilson. *Italian NeoRealism and Global Cinema.* Detroit: Wayne State University Press, 2007.

Ruberto, Laura E., Joseph Sciorra, and Anthony Julian Tamburri. *New Italian Migrations to the United States. Volume 2, Art and Culture since 1945.* Urbana: University of Illinois Press, 2017.

Tamburri, Anthony Julian. *Re-viewing Italian Americana: Generalities and Specificities on Cinema.* New York: Bordighera Press, 2011.

Tamburri, Anthony Julian, Paolo Giordano, and Fred L. Gardaphé. *From the Margin: Writings in Italian Americana.* West Lafayette, IN: Purdue University Press, 2000.

Part I

What is Italian American Cinema?

Chapter One

What is Italian about Sofia Coppola?

Tracing Ethnicity in Third-Generation Feminist Cinema

Colleen M. Ryan

Sofia Coppola is an award-winning director working in Hollywood and at its fringes, making "smart cinema" or "Indiewood"-type films.[1] While she is perhaps best known for the Oscar winning *Lost in Translation* (2003), Coppola's first feature, *The Virgin Suicides,* dates back to 1999, and her most recent film, *The Beguiled* (2017) won for Best Director in Cannes.[2] Currently, Coppola's *On the Rocks*, is in pre-production for A24 and Apple. A digital project, *On the Rocks* will be the newest addition to Coppola's semi-autobiographical works, this one showcasing a "larger-than-life playboy father" (Bill Murray) on an adventure with his daughter in New York.[3]

In addition to being the worldly descendent of cineastes and winemakers, then, and far beyond her identity as the critically condemned Mary Corleone of *The Godfather, Part III*, Sofia Coppola is an Italian American filmmaker in her own right, and one of very few who are both female and internationally renowned.[4] Yet, despite the endless media reviews and ever-growing bibliography on her individual films and opus as a whole, Sofia Coppola has not, to date, been studied for her "Italianness." That is, while some critics, like Giovanna Grassi have picked up on her Italian style—*c'è qualcosa di molto italiano nel carattere e nel gusto visivo di Sofia Coppola*—no existant study takes fully into exam Coppola's biological, cultural, or iconographic status as an Italian American, nor for the distinctive marks of, or allusions to, Italian culture and ethnicity in her films.[5] This chapter aims to address what may be a moot point, an overlooked question, or a white elephant in the room. What is Italian about Sofia Coppola? What signs, themes, and practices in her art and persona bespeak her Italian heritage(s)? How do the traces of ethnicity in Coppola's films intersect with her tutelage of female voice and perspective? My scope is not to fit Coppola, as artist, into specific qualifying or constraining categories. Rather, like Mary Jo Bona and Helen Barolini, who claim a tradition and give voice to women's dreams, or like Edvige Giunta who "rescue(s) the work of some Italian American women authors from any over-simplification and distortion that the use and misuse of 'Italian American' may (have) bestow(ed)," I wish to liberate Coppola from the predominantly male, first- and second-generation paradigms of Italian American cinema, and to claim a space for her, along with the other women directors of Italian descent, where discourses on gender, class, ethnicity, sexuality, age, ability and other forms of identity intersect.[6] It is at the crossroads of such discourses, specifically among her characters' searches for new life and belonging, that we grasp the signs and sensibilities that "feel Italian" in her work.[7]

Coppola is not only an Italian name, but also a representative of artistic legacy and a cultural product. Beyond the Italian spelling of Sofia, the filmmaker's first and last name put together automatically denote something Italian, if not ancestry, creative legacy, and upper-crust Hollywood royalty, directly. Sofia is the daughter of Francis Ford and Eleanor.[8] Francis was, in turn, son of maestro Carmine Coppola, a renowned flautist born in New York City. And Carmine, in turn, was the son of Agostino Coppola and Maria Zasa, born in the Naples area of Italy. From the paternal side, then, Sofia continues the lineage of artists and performers, but this lineage also means that she is a direct descendent of the quintessential Italian American director and the archetypal Italian American film trilogy. It means she belongs to the in-group of global and Napa Valley winemakers.[9] It means that she grew up traveling the world and among the sets of Hollywood's greatest films and most formidable celebrities. Finally, for our purposes, and certainly among many other things, too, it means she was born and baptized an Italian American on screen—she was the infant Anthony Corleone in *The Godfather, Part I*—and died an Italian American on screen—as Michael Corleone's beloved daughter, Mary, in *The Godfather, Part III*.

Would Sofia Coppola called by any other name smell as sweet, then? Why, of course. She is an award-winning director in her own right for films which, for the most part, do not treat Italian American subjects per se, and thus does not echo her father's work or imitate his signature. Rather, Coppola develops and expresses an aesthetic taste and feminist position that make gender, sexuality, age, and class more central to her oeuvre. But whether we study Sofia's works in light of her biological roots and *Godfather* ties, or her family's star power and access to financial backing in the industry, or whether we analyze her films for their unique storylines, camerawork, characters, and themes, the director's ethnically declined familial-cultural and professional origins inflect the vision that she herself brings to the screen.

In an important 1996 article titled "Moments in Italian America Cinema," Robert Casillo details a narrow concept of the ethnic film directors, for which Sofia Coppola could never be considered: "Strictly speaking," he wrote,

> this definition applies to works by Italian American directors who treat Italian American subjects. It would thus exclude the works of [even] Frank Capra, Vincente Minnelli, and Gregory La Cava, all of whom "enjoyed distinguished careers in Hollywood" but whose works "do not treat specifically ethnic subject matter."[10]

Indeed, these first- and second-generation directors of the 1950s took a marked distance from their childhood immigration experiences. Like Casillo, Vito Zagarrio interprets such detachment as indicative of a hardship and despair that were still too vivid, too close, and thus, in the case of Capra at least, still threatening.[11] At the same time, both scholars suggest that a closer look at the works of these pre- and postwar directors reveals thematic undercurrents such as economic struggle, family loyalty, mistrust of outsiders, or hopes and dreams, all of which reflect the migrant experience.[12]

Following Casillo and his qualifying features, namely biological roots and direct treatment of ethnic subject matter, it would appear futile to consider third-generation, Hollywood dynasty daughter, Sofia, a significant voice for Italian American cinema.[13] She, who grew up in privileged, cosmopolitan settings, and she who never knew economic hardship? And, she whose well-branded persona does not *adapt to* cultural trends but, rather, *sets* them? How could her director's eye and big-screen handicraft convey a diasporic vision? While it is often the case that third- or fourth-generation Italian Americans enjoy enough emotional distance from the difficulties of their forebears to look back on the culture of origins through a critical lens and relate their "feeling Italian" to their ancestors' pasts, Rudolph Vecoli, citing both Herbert Gans and Richard Alba, reminds us that for many of these generations, "ethnicity has become muted, voluntary, and private." In other words, rather than act to celebrate and ensure the vitality of their cultural origins, today's generations are more likely, thanks to "massive educational and occupational mobility," to value similarity over difference.[14]

Though Coppola has only addressed Italian culture head-on in one film (*Somewhere*, 2010), recurrent themes such as marginality, despondency, foreignness/culture shock, or even the wealthy classes' dilemmas (rather than that of working-class's hardship) uncloak the gilded world of the "star" persona to accentuate emotional hardship and fundamental drives such as human connection, self-affirmation, and belonging. Much in the same way Vecoli once championed Italian American studies' "intellectual and emotional engagement not with a dead past but a living present," nearly three decades later, Coppola's work shows that ethnic filmmaking still constitutes a "dynamic, evolving form of adaptation . . . capable of taking on a variety of forms, and of being expressed in a range of behaviors, and of being revived."[15] Furthermore, her work gives credence to the idea that art is the primary means through which we can capture the now assimilated generations' ethnic experience. It is through art, writes Thomas Ferraro, and perhaps "only through art that we come to know and to deal with what it means to feel Italian still in America."[16]

> The phrase invokes cultural continuity over distance and across time, including the *mystique* of such continuity, without relying on the credentials of blood, so formulated, "feeling Italian" opens up the ranks (you don't have to be one to feel like one). . . . I know there's a loose-jointedness to the concept; that's the idea. It's an aesthetic, really: the play of ambiguity across the identity line, done well, is the *art* of feeling Italian in America.[17]

Contemporary artworks, in other words, reflect the real, lived, and fully assimilated experiences of the later generations, with hints and echoes, scents and allusions to the struggles and aspirations that once made emigrated Italians so distinct. Thus, when reviewers accuse Sofia Coppola of "whitewashing" her films or of limiting the scope of her works to the world she knows, one could invert the criticism to more constructively assert that Coppola recounts the world she knows, that of a third-generation Italian, sophisticated, internationally branded and artistically acclaimed woman who has not only realized the earlier American Dream through her family, but who, also, three generations in, personifies and problematizes the Dream in new ways.

The majority of the critical material we have on Coppola comes from the broader fields of film, media, and gender studies. While shorter pieces tend to treat single works, emphasizing Coppola's captivating aesthetics, affluent settings, or female themes, two full-length books of recent years have conceived Coppola's work as an oeuvre, thus attesting to her auteur status.[18] In *Sofia Coppola: A Cinema of Girlhood*, for example, Fiona Handyside (2015) situates Coppola between post-feminist and neo-feminist discourses, showing how, even in films with male protagonists, Coppola not only shifts our focus to young, female experiences, but also engages us in thinking about female agency.[19]

More recently still, Backman Rogers's monograph titled *Sofia Coppola: The Politics of Visual Pleasure* identifies the director as "resolutely feminist" and decries all claims that Coppola's cinema is surface-level fluff simply because it is pretty.[20] To the contrary, Backman Rogers shows how outward appearances are "deeply meaningful in Coppola's diegetic worlds." "If we cannot engage with the surface of the image as a provocation," she says, "we miss its signification entirely." This outer layer of things would naturally include Coppola's star status. Although it would seem, she writes, "that Coppola as a brand has become increasingly difficult to extricate from any consideration of the formal properties of her work, reading Coppola's films through the Coppola brand distorts their meaning entirely."[21] Consequently, Backman Rogers prefers to "examine Coppola as a creator, par excellence, of mood and beguilement through images that reveal, upon close reading, radical critiques of the gilded worlds in which her films are set."[22]

While part of Sofia Coppola's success clearly derives from her multitalented and internationally in-the-know status, part also originates from the Coppola name and reputation. Fiona Handyside nevertheless discourages the latter as a path for analysis. Unlike the *Godfather* trilogy, she says, "that made her father's name and in which she appeared on-screen," Sofia's films

> do not function as a reflection upon her Italian American ethnicity, other than perhaps via a theme of melancholia and nostalgia, *a Mediterranean "spleen" that infects* the protagonists of *The Virgin Suicides* (notably the girls are surrounded by the ritualized objects of the Catholic faith) and *Lost in Translation* (where the inevitable foreignness and loss of the émigré is projected onto the utter alienation of being outside of the Europeanised West).[23] [emphasis mine]

Thus, despite the echoes of Italianness one can discern in references to Fellini, for example, for Handyside such connections "in no way accent[s] her films as an expression of a diaspora in the way we may understand with the films by her father, Martin Scorsese or, Brian de Palma or Michael Cimino." Curiously, however, Handyside's metaphor for ethnicity as a body part (spleen) that injects foreign bodies into the system suggests that for Coppola, ethnic otherness exists within, it is intrinsic to one's system, and, therefore, influential (unless forcibly removed). Indeed, in the very next line, Handyside somewhat refutes the preclusion of an ethnic voice in Sofia's films by underscoring the central themes of the foreign versus the familiar, between the banal and the celebrity, and between everyday life and "the dream."

> Such a dialectic invites us to read the films both as acute appraisals of contemporary cultural mores and a quasi-autobiographical comment on the complexities of Coppola's own position as Italian American celebrity daughter and stylish cool fashion icon as well as director.[24]

The intricacies of Coppola's background, of her lived personal and professional experiences infiltrate and affect (or precisely, perhaps, *infect*) her work, as much as do other key elements of her identity—her being wealthy, being artsy, being worldly, or being womanly—thereby inflecting her voice and inspiring the brush-strokes of her vision.

Sociologist Takayuki Tsuda studies the resurgence of interest in ethnic heritage and ancestral homeland among contemporary fourth-generation Japanese Americans who have, from all social, economic, and cultural perspectives, completely integrated with the American mainstream. According to

Tsuda, "ethnicity does not follow linear trajectories over the generations where an initially strong minority identity gradually wanes as it is engulfed by the unrelenting assimilative pressures of mainstream society."[25] Furthermore, Tsuda maintains that although today's young people are still influenced by the ethnicity of their parents and relatives,

> each generation negotiates its own ethnic positionality in majority society in response to the complex dynamics of racialization, assimilation, and multiculturalism that constantly change over time. Therefore, the continued salience of ethnicity is just as much about active recovery of cultural heritage as it is about the persistence of original ethnic differences over the generations in the face of assimilation.[26]

Coppola, too, navigates a complex network of connections and different layers of meaning that both her ancestral and Hollywood heritages bear. At the same time, she fosters her own artistic identity through the stylistic choices she uses to develop discourses on family, wealth, love, beauty, and childhood from a refined and female perspective. As Jonathan Cavallero notes, "gender and class seem to be of more interest than ethnicity in Sofia Coppola's works, perhaps because she herself is more likely to be marked as different because of these two things."[27] To relate Coppola's ethnic positioning to Italian American and Italian diaspora studies more broadly, I will examine the *italianità*, or lasting signs and sensibilities of ethnicity—albeit generations away in time and place from the land of origins—through certain objects, homages, allusions, affective tones, and cultural values we locate in Coppola's films.[28]

ITALIANITÀ IN SOFIA COPPOLA'S CINEMA

There are many ways one can define or frame *italianità,* but there are few studies that explicitly treat what third- or fourth-generation female artists do with them. Theresa Carilli is an exception. In her chapter on Penny Marshall and Nancy Savoca, Carilli employs what Fred Gardaphé had previously identified as Italians' "two primary cultural codes": "*omertà*, the code of silence that governs what is spoken or not spoken about in public, and *bella figura*, the code of proper presence or social behavior that governs an individual's public presence."[29] In tracing the lineage of Italian female writers, Bona deems both *omertà* and *bella figura* to be crucial forces guiding behaviors and values. In the same light, Bona explores several additional codes and customs, among which the (patriarchal) order of and loyalty to the family; the cult of the Madonna and value of virginity; godparenthood or *compareggio*; fate or destiny; and *la via vecchia—the traditional way*, meaning a mode of moral reasoning when new cultures threaten.[30]

In what follows, I will show how some of these "signs of Italianness," particularly the primacy of the family and safety from the outsider as well as rigid codes for gender and sexuality, are constants across her films. I will also identify and briefly analyze some of Coppola's salutes to the ancestral homeland and homages she makes to Italian directors who have influenced her work.

THE VIRGIN SUICIDES (1999):
THE HERMETIC SEAL OF FAMILY CULTURE

The Virgin Suicides, adapted from Jeffrey Eugenides' 1993 novel, is a dark coming of age story, narrated by a group of anonymous neighborhood boys from the Detroit suburbs who, once infatuated with the beautiful Lisbon sisters, recall the events leading up to their deaths. First, thirteen-year-old Cecilia jumps from a window. A year later, fourteen-year-old Lux, fifteen-year-old Bonnie, sixteen-year-old Mary, and seventeen-year-old Therese all honor a group suicide pact on the same night. After the funerals, Mr. and Mrs. Lisbon sell their belongings and leave for a new, unknown destination. Twenty-five years later the grown narrators still lament the loss of their adolescent land express lingering perplexities.

Italian American sensibilities in *The Virgin Suicides* include the unquestionable order of the family; the cult of the Madonna; and *bella figura* or highly respectable outward appearances, as can be sustained or lost through virginity. To begin, the family is the only social system the Lisbon girls really know. Though until Lux's missed curfew on homecoming, the girls go to school, where their father is the math teacher, knows all the students, and can exert control over the girls' interactions. The school thus functions as an extension of the family, making the girls largely untouchable or inaccessible to onlookers. The closed family circuit may be safe, but it is psychologically suffocating, causing hopelessness, despair, and thoughts of death in the beautiful brood. As a result, a complex code of secrecy undergirds the girls' longing for freedom in the form of teenage love—a longing which flows as an undercurrent through the girls' lovelorn diary entries, tattoos with boys' names on their underwear, and the moods of contemporary music they hear. As the Lisbons laze about daydreaming, indoors or out, the five seem part of one same whole. So, just as secretive as their family life is, so is their pact to end their misery in unison.

Though Coppola does not assign the Lisbons an explicitly Catholic or Italian American identity in her film, she nonetheless portrays their tale as one of austere religion-based control over the sexual mores of the family's five beauties. These beautiful blond 1970s teens are expected to remain chaste, far beyond the norm for their day and age. At school and at home, they are five untouchable Madonna-like figures who illuminate the world with their beauty and hitherto guarded innocence, who attract the adolescent curiosity and worship of neighborhood boys, but who rot as their social-emotional growth as coming-of-age women is stunted. They are, in short, prevented from assimilating to the culture that surrounds them and that desires them, too. Worshipping the five girls are, in particular, five neighbor boys who watch them from afar, attend a party at their home, and who, when trying to save them from their family prison, inadvertently witness the girls' deaths. The impact of this intense, all-consuming childhood fascination lingers in the adult boys, as they narrate nostalgically about their inability to solve girls' mysteries.

Catholic/Christian references abound: in the form of excessive/extreme chastity, protected virginity, light, patriarchy, and martyrdom. Cecilia, in fact, the youngest of the girls, is the first to take her life. After one aborted attempt to drown in a bathtub with slit wrists, she jumps from her bedroom window to land on the pointed arrow-like iron poles that constitute the family fence or prison gate. Whether a St. Sebastian or a St. Cecilia, impassioned protector of her own virginity, Cecilia Lisbon commits an act of "extreme" agency that breaks the hermetic seal on this family system, symbolized by the neighbor boys infiltrating the household for a brief party or the removal of the iron fence after the party and Cecilia's death. Standing in contrast to the five girls are consistently the neighborhood boys whose point of view is quite literally "across the street," reminding us of the innocent adolescent libido running as undercurrent throughout the film and showing the Lisbon home to be an isolated enclave. Among the boys is one exotic figure and Italian American sign: Dominic Palazzolo.[31]

Dominic is dark-haired, dark-skinned, walks like John Travolta in *Saturday Night Fever*, has a foreign accent and is sexually, if ridiculously for his teen age, exuberant. He not only tries his luck on schoolgirl Diane (who refuses him), but also on Mrs. Lisbon during the party scene. Poking fun at the Latin lover stereotype, Coppola uses the ridiculous Dominic in contrast to the extreme chastity and possible ineptitude or sexual impotence of the family father. Mrs. Lisbon is attuned to young Dominic's performance, but, rather than laugh at the exaggerated behavior, she stiffens with discomfort and walks away. Curiously, just days before, the Italian boy had leapt from a window for this unrequited love, which foreshadowed Cecilia's actual death. In his case, he melodramatically declares that he won't be able to live without her during summer vacation, so he chooses death (albeit unsuccessfully) to end his misery. Ironically, Dominic lands in the bushes, popping up as if a mere movie stunt right after and assuming his cool guy leather- and sunglasses-clad persona as he walks away. His feigned suicide comes off as comical, even banal. In fact, the girls watching his dramatic gesture seem bored or indifferent. Cecilia's death will tarnish the Lisbon family's reputation. It will be discussed several times in the news and neighbors will observe and gossip about the state of affairs. But, as in Dominic's case, no one really cares. With the exception of the neighbor boy's narrative, indifference or disdain from the cultural outsider persists.

Another "bad boy" intruder in the hermetically sealed, female-gendered whiteness of this family, is the sexy, long- and dark-haired, and too-cool school athlete, Trip Fontaine. Trip slowly gains Mr. Lisbon's trust, enough to take Lux and her three remaining sisters to the homecoming dance. After Trip and Lux are named homecoming king and queen, the boy claims Lux's virginity, then abandons her on the football field which prefigures her demise. Though not Italian, Trip is a "rebel without a cause" figure who sheds light on the general state of middle-class American teens who gain status through outward appearances and social performances that reflect independence, financial stability, sexual prowess, and self-confidence. Trip, too, like Dominic, recalls Tony Manero, but one who has grown up and "made it." Coppola's film does not share the details of Trip's sexual experiences and financial backing, but depicts him as oppositional to and dangerous for the Lisbon family nucleus.[32] Trip's "dark" figure casts a grave shadow over the initially pure light of Lux (the names alone) and her sisters' innocent sexual curiosity. Though Coppola briefly endows Lux with an objectifying and desiring gaze (slow-motion camera on Trip and close shots of his features as she stares at him in class), this empowerment is short-lived and illusory, as the journey outside the rigidly circumscribed enclave or family sphere will have disastrous repercussions.

The camera angles and points of view, as well as the close shots of faces and bodies that Coppola uses throughout *The Virgin Suicides*, emphasize wistful gazing as an expression of desire for a life (or love) outside the realm of the patriarchal home. The girls watch the boys from afar, as if the latter were players on a world stage to which they do not belong. Conversely, the boys watch the girls, as if angels from a realm above and beyond their grasp or worth. Coppola privileges the long and medium shot to engulf her young, inhibited characters in the hues and tones of their physical and emotional environments, but punctuates the flow of separate, forbidden, or untouchable lives with extreme close shots making the partially obstructed perspectives and strong sense of unrequited desire for "the other" common to all.

SOMEWHERE (2010): HOMAGE TO THE
HOMELAND AND A CRISIS IN MASCULINITY

Nearly a decade later, the oppressive presence of the father and order of the family model are almost entirely subverted in *Somewhere*, a film in which the dad is not awful, per se, but is at the very least "a bit confused and helpless, accident prone," and the mother is largely absent.[33] *Somewhere* is a semi-autobiographical story about an Italian American actor's meaningless existence at the Chateau Marmont hotel in Los Angeles, until an extended visit with his daughter awakens the thirty-something man from his numbed emotional state. This new, daily encounter with eleven-year-old Cleo, amidst vapid Hollywood and Italian show business people, awakens Johnny Marco's paternal sensitivities, compelling him to reckon with his unhappiness. Checking out of the chic hotel, Johnny takes his car "to end of the road," where he leaves the key in the ignition and walks away.

In tracing ethnicity in Coppola's films, three generations removed from the immigrant experience, *Somewhere* is an interesting case because it starts with a reference to Italy, via the distant sight and distinctive sound of a sports car doing laps in a desert-like setting. We do not know who is driving, we do not know where we are, but we do learn quickly that what we see and hear— over and over—is a black Ferrari. The driver, thus, is wealthy, bored, self-isolating, and has a taste for Italian brands and design. Back in his hotel room/home, this sense of alienation persists. Whether he walks into a VIP "house party" in his own room (hosted by friends) or calls private pole dancers to perform in his room, Coppola's male protagonist is lacking energy and drive, motivation and purpose.

The people and actions around him eventually indicate that he is a successful actor—Johnny Marco—loved by everyone in the United States and abroad. Johnny's almost-teen daughter, Cleo, will unexpectedly come to live with him for the duration of a summer, catalyzing reflection and change in both characters. Symbolically, father and daughter travel to Italy to receive the *Telegatto* Award for Johnny's most recent film. In Italy, Hollywood culture with Italian television culture merge, comprising Coppola's meta-commentary on the industry. Whether at home or abroad, alone or accompanied, the fast-paced, glitzy realm of show business, the allure of VIP status, and even the awards (another self-referential nod for Coppola) constitute a superficial and empty existence.

Johnny Marco himself is an Italian sign. He resembles the Marcello Mastroianni figure in several of Fellini's films—particularly Guido Anselmi of *8½*—as he encounters different women from different moments in his life, but cannot create a meaningful bond with any of them. Whether they be Cleo's mother, former girlfriends and co-stars, party date hookups, or even hired dancers—Johnny Marco is, for the most part, the inept male and ineffectual Latin Lover. Though he acts quite virile and is visibly desired by many women, Johnny's actual performance (social, parenting, and sexual) signals deficits in emotion and energy. As Jacqueline Reich in *Beyond the Latin Lover*, notes,

> The *inetto* articulates the traditional binary opposite of the masculine, as it is constructed in Italian culture and society, and as it relates to sexuality: the cuckold, the impotent and the feminized man. Rather than active, the *inetto* is passive; rather than brave, he is cowardly; rather than sexually potent, he is either physically or emotionally impotent. His shortcomings and failings are in direct opposition to the prescribed masculine norms deeply rooted in Italian culture.[34]

Though Johnny does engage sexually (and successfully, we presume) with an Italian actress while in Italy (Laura Chiatti); it is because she nearly shames him in public for not pursuing her, arriving later that night for a rendezvous in his suite. She lingers in a bathrobe at the family breakfast table the next morning, having to contend, like Johnny, with Cleo's disapproving gaze.

Not only does *Somewhere* destabilize the rigid codes of family order and sexuality, but it also calls to question the concept of *bella figura* for a third- or fourth-generation Italian American who confronts the culture of origin with the culture of arrival and assimilation.

Once immersed in the ancestral homeland, for example, Johnny stands out for his unkempt look and appears relatively clueless both about customs and his not fitting in. For one, he maintains his unkempt American look posing for pictures with his less-than-pleased co-star while wearing jeans, a casual shirt hanging out, and messy hair. Second, Johnny fumbles ineptly with the language barrier, while the exuberant and highly (if not overly) functioning female journalist and talk show host outshine Johnny with their English and presences. Whether during hotel interviews or on national television, Johnny can only murmur stock phrases such as "buona sera" and "grazie a tutti." Although one would think all of the fast-paced and glitzy VIP fanfare would be routine for Johnny Marco, he is visibly *spaesato* or uncomfortable in the spotlight and other paparazzi-teeming spaces.

By contrasting the fast, flashy world of media and television with the womb-like comfort of Johnny's luxury sweet, Coppola conveys that this father would rather cocoon with his daughter—to swim or watch television—than partake in the chaos outside it. Indeed, one of the closest moments of father-daughter bonding occurs when, both jetlagged and restless, they "act American" watching sitcom reruns and eating ice cream in bed. Tellingly, this scene is an Italian American hybrid, as they order gelato from room service—some of each flavor—and the show they watch dubbed is *Friends*. The sitcom choice is subtle but strategic, as it stars another Italian American actor-in-crisis (the always struggling and only unpartnered member of the gang) Joey Tribbiani.[35] This is the night before the dizzying, hypersexualized *Telegatto* Award event which, though fascinating for father and daughter, proves to be "too much" and the two surreptitiously flee in a taxi for the airport the next day.[36]

The remnants of this "Italian moment" and bonding between father and daughter, and their generations, will be recalled at the end of the film once Cleo returns to her mother. Newly alone, Johnny cooks himself a spaghetti dinner. Whether due to fond memories of Cleo or because the dish is totally lacking in Italian taste, the spaghetti scene precedes Johnny's break with the past. He moves out of the hotel, takes his Ferrari for one last ride, and then literally abandons it. That is, he walks away from that one symbol that encapsulated his wealth and status.

Coppola also interweaves *italianità* (ethnic signs) in *Somewhere* through her salutes to at least three Italian directors. First, toward the end of filming in 2009, Coppola revealed that this film was in some ways a tribute to maestro Fellini, particularly for his exploration of the dark and constraining sides of show business in *Toby Dammit* (1968).[37] She also concedes the use of autobiographical material, since her own trip to Italy at age eleven, with father Francis, inspired the development of Johnny and Cleo's relationship. Second, *Somewhere* reflects the alienating tones and ambivalent moods established by maestro Michelangelo Antonioni, particularly in his trilogy of discontent: *L'avventura* (1960); *La notte*; and *L'eclisse* (1962). In these films, long takes feel almost like real-time takes, disorienting the viewer/spectator beyond the disorientation that issues forth from viewing silent protagonists blend in anonymously with bland, if alluring, abstract spaces.[38]

Based on the final scene, the film also recalls the unsettling conclusion in Pier Paolo Pasolini's *Teorema* (1968). In this masterwork, Massimo Girotti is the wealthy father of an upper-crust Milanese family plus servant, all of whom enters into a spiritual crisis when a Christ-like character arrives, engages sexually with each and then leaves. At the end of the film, this bourgeois *pater familias* leaves his executive position at a thriving factory, enters the train station, disrobes completely and starts walking away. In the final scene he is in the desert, where, naked, he treks in the sand, in long shots and close shots until he walks toward the camera, opens his mouth, and lets out a bestial cry. The final shot shows him from behind as he continues walking, and we still hear his cry. Likewise, in the final sequence of *Somewhere*, Johnny takes that symbolic Ferrari and heads from the vibrant city to the desert scape lying just beyond it. Therefore, he symbolically detaches from the materialistic world and his outward identity, namely his car as he stops, leaves the keys in the ignition, and walks off. Here, Coppola first captures Johnny Marco in a long shot from behind to suggest uncertainty in his direction. Then, she captures him in a medium shot, where he cracks a smile before the closing credits and end music cut the scene.[39]

The final sequence grants a circular shape to the film opening and closings. Sights and sounds of macho Latin lover sex-symbol bad-boy Ferrari once again derail our expectations. Rather than the closed-circuited race track, rote and meaningless at the start of the film, here at the end Coppola chooses to break the quasi deadbeat-if-also-rich-and-famous-dad cycle, creating the possibility of an opening for more authentic living.

Once out of the car, keys no longer in hand, Johnny starts walking in a linear fashion, toward a destination unknown. At first, we watch him from behind but next, and finally, we view him and he views us head on, cracking a faint smile as if to suggest that Cleo's love had indeed kindled change.

THE BEGUILED: A FEMINIST REVISION OF ITALIAN SENSIBILITIES

Another film that recalls and subverts the pillars of patriarchy is Coppola's adaptation of Thomas P. Cullinan's novel (1966) reinterpretation of Don Siegel's macho and male-victimizing Southern Gothic feature starring Clint Eastwood (1971), *The Beguiled*.[40] The film tells the story of Miss Martha Farnsworth, head of the Farnsworth Seminary for girls, in 1864 Virginia. With all the men and slaves gone, just five female students and one teacher, Edwina Morrow, remain. The youngest of these, Amy, stumbles on Yankee Corporal John McBurney while picking mushrooms one day. She brings him to the school where he falls unconscious and where the headmistress, intrigued, decides he can stay.

As Miss Martha tends to McBurney's wounds, Miss Edwina and all of the school girls grow attracted to the "exotic" male McBurney. They hide him from soldiers and let him stay on as a gardener when he starts to heal, until one night when he asks Edwina to await him in her room, but goes to promiscuous teen Alicia's room instead. When Edwina discovers him with Alicia, she thrusts him away. McBurney falls down the stairs, losing consciousness and breaking his bad leg, which the ever-calm Miss Martha swiftly decides must go. When McBurney wakes the next day to this devastating vision, he cries out that the women are punishing him because they all want him like a piece of meat. Fearing retaliation, they lock him up, but Alicia gets him a key. The corporal then breaks free, finds Miss Martha's gun, and begins wielding his authority. Desperate for peace and for John, Edwina locks herself back in with him and offers him sex. Meanwhile, Martha and the girls plot McBurney's death. Unbeknownst to him and to the enamored Edwina, they serve poison mushrooms at dinner and McBurney soon dies. The next day the seven women drag his body to the road in a bag. Like cats with a mouse, these desirous felines let the soldier into the house for a while to play and then mangled his body and put him out with the trash.

Coppola made this film almost as a dare. A friend asked her to see Siegel's film and challenged her to tell the story from a female perspective.[41] Surely drawn to the tale of women's solidarity and to the aesthetic potential of the mystical moss-lined South, Coppola made her film, starring Nicole

Kidman and some of her "regulars" (Kirstin Dunst, i.e., Lux Lisbon, and Elle Fanning, i.e., Cleo Marco), emphasizing female agency. Though there are no explicit Italian signs in this Civil War thriller, as in *The Virgin Suicides*, there are Italianate themes and codes of conduct that we can perceive and interpret in that key.

Whether by blood or clan, *l'ordine della famiglia* and *la serietà* that command female comportment and chastity exist with a clear hierarchy and pervade the seminary environment. As in *The Virgin Suicides*, so in *The Beguiled,* the closed-circuit family community compels strong bonds of loyalty. It allows outsiders in, only with the greatest suspicion. Therefore, it is a key moment of agency when Miss Martha's authority goes unchecked or when she falls prey to curiosity. By letting this one (half dead, but nonetheless sexual other) male outsider in, she risks compromising the family's integrity. Different from *The Virgin Suicides* girls, however, Coppola's *The Beguiled* women are not helpless. They are self-sufficient, capable agents operating under Miss Martha's command, honoring the deeply rooted patriarchal order of things. In the absence of men, Miss Martha assumes the role of the father, but completely feminizes the tasks and the outward manner in which the school's daily business gets done. With the collaboration-turned-complicity of the six young women in her care, Martha will attend to daily chores, entertain tastefully, and then maim, deceive and, finally, kill their guest.

Additional examples of Italianate sensibilities in this film can be perceived through the cultural codes of chastity, *bella figura*, and silence or secrecy. As per Southern decorum in the 19th century, wealthy white plantation ladies were "God-fearing" people and their public display of solid morals and graceful hospitality were equally important. Predictably, then, we see the Farnsworth Seminary women praying before meals and conducting prayer services in their candlelit chapel every evening. Clearly, they uphold strict religious values, including monogamy and virginity until marriage. Thick into war-time, though, in the absence of husbands, fiancés, or even courtship and the future prospect of marriage, the schoolhouse smacks of sexual repression. Thus, when a handsome man falls into their hands, none is too eager to turn him over to the troops and all begin to vie for his attention. The angel/whore dichotomy that burgeoned in Lux, after being deflowered by Trip, returns as a trope in *The Beguiled* through the fiery sexuality of Alicia whose unseemly behavior quickly erodes the women's bonds and risks besmirching the whole clan.

There are at least two more elements in this most recent of Coppola's features worth mention in this study of ethnic signs and sensibilities. The first is the revision of prototypical cowboy Clint Eastwood in Siegel's seventies film with the foreign hottie Collin Farrell, who brought both war film and hostage film experience to the project. By re-proposing a film that starred

Spaghetti Western-famed Eastwood, Coppola conjures and then subverts another Italian film genre on which she places the stamp of her female gaze and aesthetic tastes. This Yankee soldier could have been foreign simply as "a northerner," but instead, McBurney has an accent and a story—a story of migration and assimilation. In other words, Coppola replaces the Spaghetti Western icon with an Irish immigrant who is fighting as a mercenary. Therefore, he is a double outsider and perhaps doubly other, doubly "dangerous," (and doubly desirable) for this reason. Using the American cowboy in the Italian wild west is tantamount to using the Irish immigrant in the American Civil War South. With this brushstroke, Coppola replaces Leone's "The Good, the Bad and the Ugly" brand with something more like "The Suspicious, the Sexual, and the Savvy."

Another intriguing element in considering Coppola's treatment of ethnicity is her widely criticized decision, despite or because of her Cannes victory, to eliminate the black female slave figure of Mattie (Tullman)/Hallie (Siegel) as well as the biracial identity of the second-in-command Edwina figure. Conversely, Mattie Tullman's novel and Hallie in Siegel's film are both pivotal figures for the community of women living alone and the first that the mutilated McBurney threatens to rape. Thanks to flashback scenes in these earlier works, through which Mattie/Hallie recalls a sexually abusive white master from her past, the black woman musters the courage to tell the sex-starved Yankee that the only way he will ever have her is dead. Accused on many fronts of whitewashing her adaptation to reflect the white, privileged world in which she lives (rather than portraying the crude realities of racial oppression in the Civil War South), Coppola told critics that she did not want to "brush over such an important topic" in a cursory way.[42] "Young girls watch my films," she has said, "and this was not the depiction of an African-American character I would want to show them."[43] Ultimately, then, we are left wondering if the eschewed question of race in *The Beguiled* was too big, too delicate, too foreign or just irrelevant, with respect the real-life experiences that undergird and inspire much of Coppola's work. Nevertheless, the conscious decision to eliminate this character, and sociohistorical reality she represents, carry artistic and political weight. Therefore, if, here or elsewhere, Coppola exercises poetic freedom, telling a story as she conceives it, or if she turns a public, national, historical truth into a subjective treatment of female desires and complicities, of female psyches and personalities, and of female perspectives, empowerment, and self-discoveries, then she will also bear the widespread critique of elitism in her work.

Arguably, much like the decision to leave political discourse out of *Marie Antoinette* (2006), or to subtract the real-life Latina leader from the *Bling Ring* gang (2013), the choice to remove the black slave woman from *The Beguiled* exposes Coppola to allegations of evasion or dismissal, even intellectual short-sightedness and suppression of complex sociocultural situations. As critic Kaleem Afteb has remarked,

> [Coppola's] are all depictions of people hermetically sealed off, refusing to engage with the world beyond their own narcissistic experience. It's unfortunate then that Coppola seems to be in part guilty of the same myopia. She is a member of the entitled, who can pick or choose how she engages with the experience of others. She is part of the very problem that her films purport to criticize. [44]

Is it myopia or, simply, honesty? For Antonio Gramsci, whether she was a traditional or organic intellectual, Coppola would have an obligation to portray historical truths and/or to position herself ideologically concerning all questions of social identity and justice. But in an age where auteurism and subjective, lived experiences prevail, is it not more authentic to show and critique the privileged, protected world in which Coppola's artistic vision incubated and took shape? It seems that if Coppola, despite her world travels, grew up in an ethnically assimilated and essentially "white" universe, that we cannot hold her necessarily accountable for treating subjects with which she has little firsthand experience, does not feel expert, nor in which she has any direct stakes. Guy Lodge expresses an analogous view about *The Beguiled*'s omissions, which he finds "tacitly haunted by suggestions of abuse and oppression." Coppola's deflection of tension-ridden topics could be interpreted, he says,

> as kind of humility, a director acknowledging the specificity of her own world view. It's not the first time Coppola's films, many of which centre on the frustrations of white characters blessed with enviable wealth and or celebrity, have been accused of betraying the social and cultural privileges of her own upbringing. [45]

At the same time, I concede, Afteb makes a more convincing claim vis-à-vis these justifications

> I think of all the auteur directors working in Hollywood today, she should understand race and racial dynamics more than most. After all her father, Francis Ford Coppola, made *The Godfather,* that legendary series of films about immigrants and the attempt by the "other" to make it in an America that is structured to put White Anglo-Saxon Wasps at the top of the pyramid. Meanwhile white privilege is an implicit target throughout her work. [46]

White privilege may indeed be an implicit target, but not in a celebratory or self-aggrandizing sense. If cinema can indeed function as a mirror, the images reflected back on the white privileged viewer are far from serene, healthy, self-loving and well-adjusted.

One could viably make the case, therefore, that the absence of black and other minority, marginal, underprivileged, or underrepresented figures speaks louder than words (or images), precisely because it captures an ongoing reality of segregation. Coppola's everyday world and perspective, that is, do not readily include the firsthand experiences of these types of people. In other words, this third-generation Italian American director may be narrating and depicting white, privileged, female stories to aptly reflect—unfairly, unduly or not—the authentic, lived cultural reality of the fully assimilated and highly successful American Dream as she knows it.

Coppola's female-empowering interpretation of Cullinan's novel combines her elegantly detailed yet hazy-dreamy aesthetic, with alluringly enigmatic tones and play with light (*The Virgin Suicides*), and the at times tryingly slow pace and minimal dialogue (*Somewhere*), affirming that as the emphases and specificities of cultural tensions shift and evolve across time and place, these tensions remain at the heart of our lives and of our storytelling instinct.

CONCLUSION

Feminism, *auteur*ship, and autobiographically star-studded self-branding aside, Coppola holds a central place in a lineage of female filmmakers of Italian descent—a grouping of artists which has yet to be fully conceived, claimed, acknowledged, and assessed. Along with Penny Marshall inside Hollywood, and Nancy Savoca, Marylou Tibaldo Bongiorno, and Helen DeMichel working in the independent industry, Coppola is a primary representative of this ensemble and, as such, a model for current and future generations. As Bona reminds us, the *italianità* we trace in Italian American women's works is not a defense "against being perceived narrowly and injudiciously by the American culture. Rather, it is a strategy of commemoration, recovery, and recreation of their Italian familial cultures."[47]

What is Italian about Sofia Coppola, then, and how does she represent the interrelationship between gender, ethnicity, and class? And "why," to add one of Thomas Ferraro's key questions, "does American Italianness matter in a post-ethnic, gender-liberated, transnational, racially utopian United States?"[48] American Italianness or Italian Americanness matters because the lasting claim to part or all of one's ethnic identity, even if radically transformed through assimilation, is still a way of knowing the world and oneself for many human beings. In other words, ethnicity and migration experiences, even if emotionally removed and filtered through four generations of transformation, remains an irrefutable piece of one's "identity pie," if you will, which we instinctively use to understand our cultural practices and perspectives, to draw analogies with other assimilatory experiences, and through which many artists find their voices or derive their creative visions. [49]

Sofia Coppola deploys Italian signs, subjects, and sensibilities in order to interpret and then recast her personal/female/third-generation/Hollywood grown/Napa vineyard-raised/famous father and *Godfather*-inflected identity. Her cinema of girlhood and whiteness, of the familiar and the foreign, and of inside versus outside of closed communities, critiques the cultural mores, gender relations, and power dynamics inherent in all of these.

NOTES

1. See Fiona Handyside, *Sofia Coppola. A Cinema of Girlhood* (London: I.B. Tauris, 2017), 8.

2. The complete list of her films includes a short, *Lick the Star* (1998), and six features, *The Virgin Suicides* (1999); *Lost in Translation* (2003); *Marie Antoinette* (2006); *Somewhere* (2010); *The Bling Ring* (2013); and *A Very Murray Christmas* (Netflix, 2015).

3. For further reading, see: https://www.vulture.com/2019/01/bill-murray-movie-on-the-rocks-sofia-coppola.html.

4. For a compelling, gender-rich discussion of Sofia Coppola's cinematic origins at the service of her father's renowned trilogy, as well as her cinema at large, see Handyside, 6–8. A second essential feminist reading of Coppola's aesthetic vision and cinematic productions is to be found in Anna Backman Rogers, *Sofia Coppola: The Politics of Visual Pleasure* (New York: Berghahn, 2019).

5. Giovanna Grassi, "Tra Hollywood e l'Italia la storia di un attore in crisi: In viaggio con papà 'Nella pellicola c'è il ricordo di un viaggio italiano con papà Francis quando avevo undici anni,'" *Corriere della sera* August 26, 2009, 41.

6. Edvige Giunta, *Writing with an Accent. Italian American Women Authors* (New York: Palgrave, 2002), 1–2. "One must recognize that, as is the case for other ethnic groups, the term "Italian American" may turn out to be, specifically in the contemporary context—rather "empty," up for grabs for anyone interested in ascribing certain political beliefs and agendas to ethnic identity. . . . Ultimately, what interests me is not IA identity per se, but what forces are at work in this literature and how the label Italian American and its concomitant historical ramifications—have led to the reliance on certain literary and political strategies by these authors.

See also Mary Jo Bona, *Claiming a Tradition. Italian American Women Writers* (Southern Illinois University Press, 1999) and Helen Barolini, *The Dream Book: An Anthology of Writing by Italian American Women* (Syracuse, NY: Syracuse University Press, 2000).

7. In her touchstone volume, *Claiming a Tradition: Italian American Women Writers*, Mary Jo Bona states up front the importance of gender in artistic self-expression: "For Italian American women who write, the category of gender functions as an equally necessary lens through which to interpret their negotiation between the Italian familial culture and the American milieu. (6) She later quotes Barolini to underscore the importance of identifying founding figures or ratifying models for this tradition "Models are important in as much as they connect the present writer [artist] to her past, providing continuity that makes a shared culture of valuable resource, one's own culture is important to the spirit of the writer and to the writing itself" (*The Dream Book*, 33).

8. Eleanor Coppola was born Eleanor Jessie Neil, on May 4, 1936, in Los Angeles, California. Her father, a political cartoonist for the Los Angeles *Examiner*, died when she was ten years old. She was raised by her mother, Delphine Neil (nèe Loughton) in Sunset Beach. Eleanor graduated from UCLA with a degree in applied design and was a member of the Alpha Chi Omega. To read more, see *Eleanor Coppola: Notes on a Life* (Applause Theater and Cinema Books, 2010).

9. A cursory view at the Coppola Winery website reveals the breadth of the family brand and suggests how difficult is to demarcate where family influence begins and ends. See *Cinema, Wine, Food, Hideaways, Adventures* at https://www.francisfordcoppolawinery.com.

10. Robert Casillo, "Moments in Italian-American Cinema: From Little Caesar to Coppola and Scorsese," in *From the Margin: Writings in Italian Americana.* Anthony Julian Tamburri, Paolo Giordano, Fred L. Gardaphé, eds. (West Lafayette, IN: Purdue University Press 1991, 2000), 394–416.

11. See Vito Zagarrio, "F.C.-F.C. Ovvero: Italian-American Dream dal film muto alla televisione," *Cinema & Cinema* 38 (January–March 1984) 37–38.

12. Casillo, "Moments," 394. Casillo cites Raymond Carney, *The Films of Frank Capra* (London: Cambridge University Press, 1986), 36–39.

13. According to Casillo, Italian American cinema, at least "in its highest form," has been made by only two directors—Francis Coppola and Martin Scorsese—and only "through a handful of brilliant films." See: Casillo, "Moments," 397. Furthermore, acknowledging the "twilight of ethnicity" theorized by Alba in the eighties, Casillo predicted that Italian American cinema would be a short-lived and largely nostalgic phenomenon—a "recollection of what is passing or long past, of what was once experienced spontaneously, immediately, without self-reflection"—and one almost certain to wane with the passing of time. (414) See, also, "Introduction" in Robert Casillo, *The Gangster Priest: The Italian American Cinema of Martin Scorsese* (University of Toronto Press, 2007).

14. Richard Alba, "The Twilight of Ethnicity: What Relevance for Today? *Ethnic and Racial Studies* 37, no. 5 (2014): 78. See also Richard Alba, *Italian Americans: Into the Twilight of Ethnicity* (Englewood Cliffs, NJ: Prentice Hall 1985); and Casillo, "Moments," 414.

15. Rudolph Vecoli, Jr., "Are Italian Americans Just White Folk? *Italian Americana* 13, no. 2 (Summer 1995): 154. See also Vecoli, "Searching for an Italian American Identity: Continuity and Change," in *Italian Americans: New Perspectives in Italian Immigration and Ethnicity,* Lydio Tomasi, ed. (New York: Center for Migration Studies, 1985), 88–112.

16. Thomas J. Ferraro, *Feeling Italian: The Art of Ethnicity in America* (New York: New York University Press, 2005), 2.

17. Ibid., 3.

18. There is a sizable bibliography on Coppola and her six feature length films. After her debut with a *nouvelle vague*-style short called *Lick the Star* (1998), Coppola adapted, co-wrote and directed *The Virgin Suicides* (1999), the Oscar-winning *Lost in Translation* (2003), *Marie Antoinette* (2006), the Venice Lion-winning *Somewhere* (2010), *The Bling Ring* (2013); and, most recently, the *Beguiled* (2017). While some of the shorter works are thematic treatments, the majority of critical interventions focus on Coppola as a feminist director, demonstrating her unique filmic signature, considering her an auteur worthy of critical attention and/or critiquing her perception and reception as a spoiled and cosmopolitan fashionista. See, for example, this mere smattering of shorter works: Homay King, "Lost in Translation," *Film Quarterly* 59, no. 1 (Fall 2005): 45–48; Debra Shostak, "Impossible Narrative Voices: Sofia Coppola's Adaptation of Jeffrey Eugenides's 'The Virgin Suicides,'" *Interdisciplinary Literary Studies* 15, no. 2 (2013): 180–202; Belinda Smaill, "Sofia Coppola," *Feminist Media Studies* 13, no. 1 (2013): 148–162; Suzanne Ferriss and Mallory Young, "Marie Antoinette: Fashion, Third-Wave Feminism, and Chick Culture," *Literature/Film Quarterly* 38, no. 2 (2010): 98–116; Todd Kennedy, "On the Road to 'Some' Place: Sofia Coppola's Dissident Modernism against a Postmodern Landscape," *Miscellanea: A Journal of English and American Studies* 52 (2015): 55–67; and Sara Pesce, "Ripping off Hollywood Celebrities: Sofia Coppola's *The Bling Ring*, Luxury Fashion and Self-Branding," *California, Film, Fashion & Consumption* 4, no. 1 (2015): 5–24.

19. Handyside, 13. On the one hand Coppola's films participate in postfeminist cultural norms (interested in femininity, questions of female agency and power, and showcasing friendships, girliness, fashionable clothes and beautiful homes) On the other hand, they also draw on a significant feminist critical inheritance, showing her films as literally postfeminist (as in being able to learn from these interventions of feminist filmmakers from the 1970s, rather than disavowing them) and thus display a particular interest in questions of form that tend to be unusual in most female-focused films.

20. Ibid., 2.

21. Ibid., 6.
22. Ibid., 7.
23. Ibid., 11–12.
24. Ibid., 12.
25. Takeyuki Tsuda, "Recovering Heritage and Homeland: Ethnic Revival Among Fourth-Generation Japanese Americans," *Sociological Inquiry* 85, no. 4 (November 2015): 621.
26. Ibid., 621.
27. Jonathan Cavallero, *Hollywood's Italian American Filmmakers: Capra, Scorsese, Savoca, Coppola, and Tarantino* (Champaign, IL: University of Illinois Press, 2011), 158.
28. In *Somewhere* (2010), for instance, Italian signs range from material objects like a car, to family values to such as extreme loyalty or chastity, to geographical locations such as Italy.
29. See Theresa Carilli, "Locating Italianità in *True Love* and *Riding in Cars with Boys*" in *Women and the Media. Diverse Perspectives*. Theresa Carilli and Jane Campbell, eds. (University Press of America, 2005), 79–91. In particular, Carilli cites Gloria Nardini, *Che Bella Figura! The Power of Performance in an Italian Ladies' Club in Chicago* (Albany, NY: SUNY Press, 2001) as well as Fred Gardaphé, *Italian Signs, American Streets: The Evolution of Italian American Narrative* (Durham, NC: Duke University Press, 1996). See also Anthony Tamburri, *Re-viewing Italian Americana: Generalities and Specificities on Cinema* (New York: Bordighera, 2011); and Ben Lawton, "What Is Italian American Cinema?" *Voices in Italian Americana* 6, no. 1 (1995): 27–51.
30. Bona, 10–13.
31. In the original novel Dominic Palazzolo is an immigrant Latino boy from New Mexico. He has dark hair, dark skin, wears sunglasses, and speaks only a few words of English. He's in love with the wealthy Diana Porter. When Diana leaves for a vacation in Europe, a desperate Dominic jumps off the roof of his house, but he is not injured.

In the movie, Dominic is an Italian immigrant staying with relatives in the neighborhood. Cecilia has a crush and watches Dominic has he pines for Diana, instead, and leaps, supposedly to his death, foreshadowing of course Cecilia's similar, but lethal, act.
32. Jeffrey Eugenides's novel recounts that his father takes him on an exotic vacation as a teen, where he is deflowered by an older woman, closes an eye to his father's homosexual activities, and begins dealing drugs. See https://www.sparknotes.com/lit/virginsuicides/character/trip-fontaine/.

"More generally, Trip's drugs, alcohol, hairspray, and hot rod are symbols of new American suburban masculinity. His burgeoning drug trade suggests that Trip is a self-made man, and this endeavor frees him from the restraints of high school. His epicurean love of women suggests the refined taste and conspicuous consumption of the affluent American playboy, while his discretion marks him as a gentleman."
33. J. M. Tyree, "Searching for Somewhere," *Film Quarterly* 64, no. 4 (2011): 12.
34. Jacqueline Reich, *Beyond the Latin Lover: Marcello Mastroianni, Masculinity, and Italian Cinema* (Bloomington, IN: Indiana University Press, 2004), 9–10.
35. See https://friends.fandom.com/wiki/Joey_Tribbiani. Joseph Francis "Joey" Tribbiani Jr. is a fictional character on the American sitcom *Friends* (1994–2004), and the title character in the spin-off, *Joey*, 2004–2006, played by Matt Le Blanc. Joey comes from an Italian American family of eight children, of which he is the only male. For a full analysis of this character and program, see Ryan Calabretta-Sajder in this volume.
36. The *Telegatto* is a cat statue award offered since 1971 by the *Sorrisi and Canzoni* television magazine. It could be compared to People's Choice or TV Guide awards in the United States. The television show during which Johnny receives the award hosts scantily clad dancing girls who prance around and mesmerize him. This scene recalls via contrast his numb, inept, passive state in front of the sexually spectacular pole dance scenes in his bedroom.
37. Grassi, 41.
38. For parallels with Antonioni, see, for example, Debra Shostak, "Impossible Narrative Voices": Sofia Coppola's adaptation of Jeffrey Eugenides's 'The Virgin Suicides,'" and, especially, J. M. Tyree, "Searching for Somewhere," 12–16.
39. Interestingly both of these are long scenes, ranging between 3:30 and 4:00 minutes in length.

40. Guy Lodge, "Sofia Coppola: I never felt I had to fit into the majority view." *The Guardian*, July 2, 2017. https://www.theguardian.com/film/2017/jul/02/sofia-coppola-beguiled-i-never-felt-i-had-to-fit-into-the-majority-view-interview.

41. See Stephanie Zacharek, "Sofia Coppola Returns with *The Beguiled*, Which Builds on 18 Years of Considered Work," *TIME*, 2018. http://time.com/sofia-coppola-best-director/

42. See https://slate.com/culture/2017/06/sofia-coppolas-whitewashed-new-movie-the-beguiled. "While the way that Marie Antoinette mostly omitted class struggle from a story about the French Revolution was arguably an appropriate reflection of its protagonist's worldview, the excuse wears thin across her career, especially as it pertains to the erasure of people of color. In *The Bling Ring*, also based on a true story and itself a sort of tale of class struggle, Coppola fictionalized the gang of teenage celebrity robbers, making them mostly white, and cutting out one member of the real-life bling ring, a young undocumented immigrant from Mexico named Diana Tamayo. In *The Beguiled*, Coppola cuts out the enslaved housemaid Mattie (called Hallie in the 1971 film), and she also turns the character Edwina, who was a free mixed-race teenager in the novel, into a white teacher played by Kirsten Dunst." For an alternate perspective, see https://www.washingtonpost.com/news/act-four/wp/2017/07/06/of-course-sofia-coppolas-the-beguiled-differs-from-the-original-thats-what-makes-it great/?noredirect=on&utm_term=.1cd038511262

43. See Alanna Bennett, "Sofia Coppola Says 'The Beguiled' Is About the Gender Dynamics of the Confederacy, Not the Racial Ones," *BuzzFeed*, posted on June 16, 2017. See also https://www.washingtonpost.com/news/act-four/wp/2017/07/06/of-course-sofia-coppolas-the-beguiled-differs-from-the-original-thats-what-makes-it great/?noredirect=on&utm_term=.1cd038511262.

44. Kaleem Aftab, "Sofia Coppola has a race problem—and there's no excuse for it," *Telegraph*, July 14, 2017.

45. Guy Lodge, "Sofia Coppola: 'I never felt I had to fit into the majority view.'" *The Guardian*, July 2, 2017. https://www.theguardian.com/film/2017/jul/02/sofia-coppola-beguiled-i-never-felt-i-had-to-fit-into-the-majority-view-interview.

46. Ibid.

47. Bona, 10.

48. Ferraro, 2.

49. The author uses this term as a metaphor for the "whole" of each self or person. The pie concept aims to capture the x number of segments or parts representing different aspects of one's self- (or externally) perceived identity. These slices or segments can, of course, change in content and proportion over time.

BIBLIOGRAPHY

Alba, Richard. "The Twilight of Ethnicity: What Relevance for Today? *Ethnic and Racial Studies* 37, no. 5 (2014): 781–785.

———. *Italian Americans: Into the Twilight of Ethnicity*. Englewood Cliffs, NJ: Prentice Hall, 1985.

Aftab, Kaleem. "Sofia Coppola Has Race Problems." *The Telegraph* July 14, 2017, https://www.telegraph.co.uk/films/2017/07/14/sofia-coppola-has-race-problem-no-excuse/.

Ankeny, Jason. "Michelangelo Antonioni." AllMovie. https://www.allmovie.com/artist/michelangelo-antonioni-p79780 .

Atad, Corey. "Lost in Adaptation: Sofia Coppola's *The Beguiled* cuts the book's black characters, whitewashing its tale of the Civil War-era South. At this point, that's hardly a surprise." https://slate.com/culture/2017/06/sofia-coppolas-whitewashed-new-movie-the-beguiled.html.

Backman Rogers, Anna. *Sofia Coppola: The Politics of Visual Pleasure*. New York: Berghahn Books, 2019.

Barolini, Helen. *The Dream Book: An Anthology of Writing by Italian American Women*. Syracuse, NY: Syracuse University Press, 2000.

Bona, Mary Jo. *Claiming a Tradition: Italian American Women Writers.* Carbondale, IL: Southern Illinois University Press, 1999.

Bunch, Sonny. "Of Course, Sofia Coppola's *The Beguiled* differs from the original. That's what makes it great, July 6, 2017, https://www.washingtonpost.com/news/act-four/wp/2017/07/06/of-course-sofia-coppolas-the-beguiled-differs-from-the-original-thats-what-makes-it-great/?noredirect=on&utm_term=.8d438939574.

Casillo, Robert. "Moments in Italian-American Cinema: From *Little Caesar* to Coppola and Scorsese." In *From the Margin: Writings in Italian Americana.* Rev. ed. Edited by Anthony Julian Tamburri, Paolo A. Giordano, and Fred L. Gardaphé, 394–416. West Lafayette, IN: Purdue University Press, 2000.

———. *The Gangster Priest: The Italian American Cinema of Martin Scorsese.* Toronto: University of Toronto Press, 2007.

Cavallero, Jonathan J. *Hollywood's Italian American Filmmakers: Capra, Scorsese, Savoca, Coppola, and Tarantino.* Champaign, IL: University of Illinois Press, 2011.

Coppola, Sofia. *Lick the Star*, Sofia Coppola, 1998.

———. *The Virgin Suicides*, American Zoetrope, Muse Productions and Eternity Pictures, 1999.

———. *Lost in Translation*, American Zoetrope, Elemental Films, Tohokushinsha Film Corporation, Focus Features, 2003.

———. *Marie Antoinette*, American Zoetrope, Pricel, Tohokushinsha Film Corporation, and Pathé, 2006.

———. *Somewhere,* American Zoetrope, Medusa, Tohokushinsha Film Corporation, and Pathé, 2010.

———. *The Bling Ring*, American Zoetrope, StudioCanal, NALA Films, Tobis Film, Tohokushinsha Film Corporation, 2013.

———. *The Beguiled*, American Zoetrope and FR Productions, 2017.

Ferraro, Thomas J. *Feeling Italian: The Art of Ethnicity in America.* New York: New York University Press, 2005.

Ferriss, Suzanne and Mallory Young. "Marie Antoinette: Fashion, Third-Wave Feminism, and Chick Culture." *Literature/Film Quarterly* 38, no. 2 (2010): 98–116.

Gardaphé Fred. *Italian Signs, American Streets: The Evolution of Italian American Narrative.* Durham, NC: Duke University Press, 1996.

Giunta, Edvige. *Writing with an Accent: Contemporary Italian American Women Authors* New York: Palgrave, 2002.

Grassi, Giovanna. "Tra Hollywood e l'Italia la storia di un attore in crisi: In viaggio con papà 'Nella pellicola c'è il ricordo di un viaggio italiano con papà Francis quando avevo undici anni.'" *Corriere della sera*, August 26, 2009, 41.

Handyside, Fiona. *Sofia Coppola: A Cinema of Girlhood.* London: Tauris, 2017.

Kennedy, Todd. "On the Road to 'Some' Place: Sofia Coppola's Dissident Modernism against a Postmodern Landscape." M*iscellanea: A Journal of English and American Studies* 52 (2015): 55–67.

King, Homay. "Lost in Translation." *Film Quarterly* 59, no. 1 (Fall 2005): 45–48.

Lawton, Ben. "What Is Italian American Cinema?" *Voices in Italian Americana 6, no. 1* (1995): 27–51.

Lodge, Guy. "Sofia Coppola: 'I Never Felt I Had to Fit into the Majority View.'" *The Guardian*, Sunday 2 July 2017. https://www.theguardian.com/film/2017/jul/02/sofia-coppola-beguiled-i-never-felt-i-had-to-fit-into-the-majority-view-interview.

Pesce, Sara. "Ripping off Hollywood Celebrities: Sofia Coppola's *The Bling Ring*, Luxury Fashion and Self-Branding." *California, Film, Fashion & Consumption* 4, no. 1 (2015): 5–24.

Ramos, Dino Ray. "Sofia Coppola's *The Beguiled* Divides Critics at Cannes, 'Feminizes' the 1971 Film Starring Clint Eastwood." May 25, 2017. http://www.tracking-board.com/sophia-coppolas-the-beguiled-divides-critics-at-cannes-feminizes-the-1971-film-starring-clint-eastwood/.

Reich, Jacqueline. *Beyond the Latin Lover: Marcello Mastroianni, Masculinity, and Italian Cinema.* Bloomington, IN: Indiana University Press, 2004, 9–10.

Tamburri, Anthony Julian. *Re-viewing Italian Americana: Generalities and Specificities on Cinema* (New York: Bordighera, 2011).

Tsuda, Takeyuki. "Recovering Heritage and Homeland: Ethnic Revival Among Fourth-Generation Japanese Americans." *Sociological Inquiry* 85, no. 4 (November 2015): 600–627.

Tyree, J. M. "Searching for Somewhere." *Film Quarterly* 64, no. 4 (Summer 2011): 12–16.

Vecoli, Rudolph. "The Search for an Italian American Identity: Continuity and Change." In Tomasi, Lydio F. (ed). *Italian Americans: New Perspectives in Italian Immigration and Ethnicity*, 88–112. New York: Center for Migration Studies, 1985.

———. "Are Italian Americans Just White Folk?" *Italian Americana* 13, no. 2 (Summer 1995): 149–161.

Zacharek, Stephanie. "Sofia Coppola Returns with *The Beguiled*, Which Builds on 18 Years of Considered Work," *TIME*, 2018. http://time.com/sofia-coppola-best-director/

Chapter Two

Edible Ethnicity

Italian American Representations, Cinematic Style, and Ethnic Commodification in Stanley Tucci's and Campbell Scott's Big Night

Jonathan J. Cavallero

In the mid-1990s, Stanley Tucci was frustrated. He was a respected character actor who had established himself with a series of recognizable performances. After his debut as a mafia soldier in John Huston's 1985 film *Prizzi's Honor*, Tucci had worked on the wildly popular 1980s television series *Miami Vice* (NBC, 1984–1990), playing two different characters—Steven Demarco and Frank Mosco. He played Rick Pinzolo in five episodes of the Stephen J. Cannell and Frank Lupo show *Wiseguy* (CBS, 1987–1990). He played Lucky Luciano in Robert Benton's *Billy Bathgate* (1991), and Khaled, a Middle Eastern assassin, in Alan J. Pakula's cinematic adaptation of John Grisham's *The Pelican Brief* (1993). Tucci was a successful working actor, collaborating with some of the most respected directors in the business and performing in as many as five films in a single year, as he did in both 1992 and 1995. Yet something was missing. In a 1996 interview with *The New York Times Magazine*, Tucci lamented being cast consistently as "the heavy—if not a goombah then some other kind of ethnic thug."[1] The actor, having longed for a different character type/type of role and not being offered it, decided to write it himself. "If I'd been cast in enough good roles," he told Eric Konigsberg, "I don't think I'd have gotten around to making [*Big Night*]."[2]

Scholars, critics, and the film's creators have suggested that the absence of gangsters in *Big Night* renders a "positive" representation of Italian Americans.[3] This view is enriched by co-directors Stanley Tucci's and

Campbell Scott's decision to incorporate formal techniques inspired by Italian neorealism, Italian filmmakers like Federico Fellini, and Italian American filmmakers like Martin Scorsese. These aesthetic choices treat Italian American subjects with recognizably Italian and Italian American cinematic styles thus expanding the representational possibilities available to Italian Americans. Indeed, *Big Night* makes progressive contributions to the ways Italian Americans are represented in Hollywood and American independent cinema by challenging the stereotypes through which the group is usually represented. However, a simple lack of gangsters does not guarantee a lack of representational issues. In fact, the film's representations break with some conventions of American narrative cinema, particularly in the way the film encourages viewers to identify with Italian American characters and admire their passions, while conforming to others, including, at times, those of the gangster. These contradictory impulses resist attempts to categorize *Big Night*'s representations as "positive" and demonstrate the complexity of the film's characters, narrative, and visual style. Ultimately, *Big Night*'s representations and the ancillary products that emerged after its success contributed to larger cultural trends in the 1990s that commodified ethnicity, disconnected it from genetic and familial histories, and recast identity as performative and purchasable.[4]

REPRESENTING ITALIAN AMERICANS IN BIG NIGHT

Big Night tells the tale of two Italian brothers—Primo (Tony Shalhoub) and Secondo (Stanley Tucci)—who have immigrated to the United States in the 1950s. They settle in a town on the New Jersey shore where they open the Paradise, an Italian restaurant featuring "authentic" cuisine from the motherland.[5] When the film opens, they have been in business two years and they are on the brink of bankruptcy.[6] Primo is a culinary artist whose pursuit of perfection will not be swayed by the uneducated palettes of the Paradise's few customers. Secondo is less interested in artistry and more driven by the pursuit of financial success and material wealth. The divide between the two brothers is accentuated by the fact that in an effort to protect his older brother, Secondo has hidden the financial obstacles the Paradise faces from Primo (although it would be difficult for Primo to miss the fact that the restaurant is mostly empty and often closes early due to a lack of customers). Secondo is seduced by new Cadillacs and the popularity of Pascal's, an Italian-ish restaurant on the same block and just across the street from the brothers' Paradise. Run by Pascal (Ian Holm), a Corsican whose arrogance is evident in his willingness to name a supposedly Italian restaurant after himself, the business is always packed with patrons streaming in and out of the front door night after night.[7] The customers seem to be there at least as much for the presentation as for the food. The ebullient Pascal flambés dishes, uncorks wine bottles, and generally puts on a show. Early on, the film reveals that the bank is about to foreclose on the Paradise, and Secondo goes to his friend Pascal for help. Pascal refuses to lend Secondo the money he needs but says that he will have his friend, the popular jazz musician Louis Prima, bring his band by the Paradise in an effort to drum up publicity for the brothers' business. The film follows the brothers as they prepare for the big night and culminates in a meticulously prepared feast that is exquisitely and lovingly photographed by Tucci, Scott, and cinematographer, Ken Kelsch.

Big Night, which Tucci co-wrote with his cousin Joseph Tropiano and co-directed with Scott, his long-time friend, was an indie darling in 1996. The film premiered at the Sundance Film Festival where it won the Waldo Salt Screenwriting Award. It won Best First Film from the New York Film Critics Circle, was recognized for excellence in filmmaking by the National Board of Review, earned a special jury prize at the Deauville Film Festival, and won the Independent Spirit Award for Best First Screenplay. When it played in the annual "New Directors, New Films" series at the Museum of Modern Art, *New York Times* film critic Janet Maslin called it "the sweetest of all" of the selections and advised attendees to "eat before you go."[8] It has become one of the most iconic of food films, often mentioned alongside classics like *Babette's Feast* (Gabriel Axel, 1987), and today, on the highly oversimplified and nonetheless excessively popular website Rotten Tomatoes, *Big Night* is "certified fresh" with 96 percent of critics and 84 percent of audiences liking it.[9]

The film was hailed not just for the performances of its actors and the subtlety of its script, it was also seen as offering a unique representation of Italian Americans. Sarah Iammarino went so far as to say, "While [Francis Ford] Coppola and [Martin] Scorsese have a love-hate relationship with their own ethnic background, Tucci has a refreshingly positive view of his ancestry."[10] Anna Camaiti Hostert wrote, "[*Big Night*] rather subtly and unpretentiously takes food as its starting point, a theme very dear to Italians, in order to dismantle a series of stereotypes that mask the richness and diversity of Italian culture."[11] Tucci himself has emphasized his desire to offer an alternative representation of Italian Americans. "I hoped to offer not only a positive view of Italians (i.e., no gangsters) but a more humanistic view, one that would show the complexity of this extraordinary people," Tucci offered in a cookbook that was published after the film's success.[12] Tropiano echoed these sentiments in the introduction to the novel that was based on the film. "*Big Night* was born first of a desire on the part of my cousin Stanley Tucci and myself to create a movie in which Italians are portrayed not as clichéd, spaghetti-serving sentimentalists, nor as murderous, back-stabbing Mafiosi," Tropiano asserted, "but as the complex, difficult, funny, stubborn, wonderful people they are."[13]

The idea that *Big Night* avoids the gangster stereotype entirely is questionable at best. While there are no characters in the film who orchestrate murders or hold the position of a mafia chieftain, Pascal does share a number of characteristics with the figure. He is "the boss" of his restaurant. He presides over Pascal's, making sure that others recognize his prominence and power within the space. He takes meetings in the backroom office of his restaurant where he doles out favors as he sits behind a desk that looms over his supplicants. And he even seems to light a worker from his restaurant on fire for unknown reasons, an act of violence that leaves Secondo stunned as he drives by in his car. While Pascal may not be a mafia don per se, he clearly plays into the tropes that have come to be associated with the character type.

While the Italian American gangster is the most consistent and prominent representation of Italian Americans in American cinema, it is far from the only stereotypical representation of Italian American ethnicity. As Fred Gardaphé has argued, "Of the many ways in which Italians have been stereotyped the two most prominent, besides the gangster, are as lovers of food and sex."[14] Neglecting these other Italian American stereotypes creates a narrow understanding of Italian American representations that can lead to comical assertions. In the introduction to the *Big Night* novel, for example, Tropiano points out, "Certainly there have been American films that have portrayed Italians and Italian-Americans humanely, decently, and realistically (*Moonstruck* comes to mind)."[15] The comic appearances of *Moonstruck*'s (Norman Jewison, 1988) female characters may belie their narrative importance, as Mary Ann McDonald Carolan has noted.[16] However, it is difficult to see the opera-loving, overly emotional Ronny Cammareri (Nicolas Cage) as "realistic." Moreover, the film's deceptive, cheating Italians—Loretta Castorini (Cher) and her father Cosmo (Vincent Gardenia)—draw on a long history of stereotypes that hardly makes this film the progressive poster child of Italian American representations that Tropiano suggests.

At their core, many stereotypes of Italian Americans—whether they be gangsters or not—are based on the inability of an ethnic character to resist excess. Volatile gangsters who cannot control their tempers and act out violently and impulsively have been a mainstay of American media for decades. However, non-gangster Italian American characters are not far removed from the impulses that define organized criminals. For instance, Romeo characters like Tony Manero (John Travolta) from *Saturday Night Fever* (John Badham, 1977) cannot control their sexual urges.[17] In *Moonstruck*, Ronny Cammareri impulsively kisses his brother's fiancé when she confronts him about how he lost his hand. In addition, in *Don Jon* (Joseph Gordon-Levitt, 2013), the titular Italian American character (Joseph Gordon-Levitt) has trouble resisting the urge to watch pornography online. Mama Leone characters like Marie Barone (Doris Roberts) on *Everybody Loves Raymond* (CBS,

1996–2005) are overprotective and too close with their sons. An inability to control emotions unites all of these characters, and it is a shared trait that is apparent in any number of Italian American stereotypes. These figures operate on the margins of the mainstream—seemingly American, but somehow not quite American enough. By indulging their excessive appetites, they challenge cultural conventions and brazenly refuse to conform to accepted social norms. The Italian American, especially the Italian American male, in American popular culture is a figure who is simultaneously admired and feared. They engage in too many criminal activities, have too many sex partners, are too aggressive, eat too much, party too hard, dance like everyone's watching (and they usually are), win people over despite their inferior intelligence, and rarely, if ever, apologize for any of it. Their hyper-masculine daring may attract fans, but viewers are encouraged to question what the culture would look like if we were all so selfish and irresponsible. Indeed, the representation of the Italian American male indulges fantasies of total freedom while providing a cautionary tale that endorses social conformity.

It is important to emphasize that *Big Night* conforms to a number of Italian stereotypes. Secondo has multiple lovers. Primo cannot control his passionate, stubborn pursuit of culinary artistry and perfection. The brothers provide an abundant, excessive meal, and they lose their tempers and fight fervidly with one another. Even a minor character like Gabriella (Isabella Rossellini) conforms to archetypes by serving as the sexy, unfaithful Italian temptress. These traits make the characters more complex. They are not perfect individuals. They disappoint at times, and the film castigates them for some of their excesses, particularly Secondo who applies a Madonna-whore paradigm to his girlfriend Phyllis (Minnie Driver) and then cheats on her with Gabriella. The uniqueness of *Big Night*'s Italian American representations is reliant not so much on the absence of archetypal Italian American representations or the fact that it does not feature gangsters, but rather on the way the film humanizes its Italian characters and encourages viewers to identify with and even admire them—particularly the brothers—for their unmitigated passions while pitying those non-Italian characters who have never really learned to appreciate art, value family and friendship, or otherwise live.

Following the film's extravagant meal, the camera tracks along a table of engorged guests. A woman cries, her head resting on her hand. A man leans over her, and asks, "What's the matter?" "My mother was such a terrible cook," the woman responds through her sobs (1:22:43–1:22:50). The camera continues its track, and finds a middle-aged woman lying on the top of the table. She lounges on her side, smoking a cigarette; her head tilted back looking at the ceiling. The food has left her totally satisfied, apparently the best sex she ever had. These moments are played for comedy, but the implication is clear. This night of culinary ecstasy has forced these apparently assimilated, non-ethnic Americans to reevaluate the lack of passion and perhaps art in their lives. The slow track of the camera allows the dinner guests to scroll across the screen and prevents the need to cut to each character individually. This creates a smooth visual style that mimics the mood of the moment—one of subdued contentment. Even when characters are exhibiting strong emotions, they are comfortable in their relaxed poses. Primo and Secondo do not eat with their guests. Instead, they watch over the meal's consumption, proud of what they have accomplished but not surprised by the response.

There are other moments in the film when characters experience moments of ecstasy after consuming Primo's food. In the kitchen, before the meal, Primo prepares a *Fiorentina* sauce for his love interest, the widower and flower shop owner Ann (Allison Janney). Tucci and Scott shoot Primo's preparation of the sauce mostly from a medium two-shot that includes both characters. But when Primo feeds Ann a taste of the sauce, they cut to a close-up of her face, which brings the camera nearer to the character and mimics the intimacy of the moment. Ann's face melts into total bliss. "Oh my God," she moans, "Oh my God" (1:11:12–1:11:16). The film cuts to a reverse shot of Primo that frames him over Ann's left shoulder. The chef looks down at his frying pan and back up at Ann, almost embarrassed. A smile crosses his lips as he responds, "'Oh my God' is right, see? Now you know. To eat good food is to be close to God" (1:11:19–1:11:26). Again, the earnestness with which Primo speaks makes the moment comedic, but Ann's expression as she reaches a kind of culinary epiphany, one which Primo has obviously experienced and created before, speaks to the value of his excesses. His passionate pursuit of art and his embrace of gustatory delight have not limited his life. In fact, they have given him access to a world of pleasure that non-ethnic Americans can only enter with his help.

The film works to establish a sympathetic relationship with Primo and Secondo as early as the first sequence. After a brief exterior scene, the film cuts to the kitchen where Primo and Secondo converse in Italian. Tucci and Scott withhold subtitles from the scene, establishing a degree of distance from the characters (at least for viewers who do not speak Italian). Despite the distance, however, it is clear that these characters care about their work, and they approach it with determination and meticulousness. The next scene follows Secondo as he prepares the dining room for the restaurant's opening. He checks the tables to make sure they are level and secure, placing a matchbook under a table leg that is slightly unstable. He inspects the exterior of the restaurant, turning a potted plant ever so slightly to make the presentation more appealing. It may be true that Secondo does this "without achieving the slightest improvement," as John Simon suggests,[18] but improving the presentation is not really the point. Instead, this small piece of business, like others in the sequence, establishes that Secondo pays attention to the tiniest details in order to create something that is appealing.[19] As the film opens, Secondo fully buys into the idea of the American Dream, believing that he will succeed by working harder and being more meticulous than his competitors. As the film progresses and none of these efforts lead to the kind of results that Secondo desires, he becomes increasingly seduced by the idea that luck, chance encounters with celebrities, and cost outlays will pave the way to financial success.

The next scene further works to establish a sympathetic view of Primo and Secondo. Secondo waits in the kitchen as Primo adds just a little more greenery to a meal. Secondo rolls his eyes at Primo's perfectionism and then exits the kitchen to a mostly empty dining room. As he approaches a table, the camera introduces a non-Italian couple. The filmmakers develop the two unnamed characters (played by Caroline Aaron and Larry Block) as ignorant, ugly Americans even before they begin their conversation with Secondo. A cigarette hangs from the woman's lips, and she refuses to extinguish it before the food arrives. She complains about the time it took for the food to be prepared. She calls Secondo "Monsieur" (00:05:17), apparently believing either that she is in a French restaurant or that "Monsieur" is an Italian word. She expresses dismay at the presentation of her seafood *risotto*, saying that she does not "see anything that looks like a shrimp or a scallop" (00:05:53–00:05:56). Meanwhile, her partner has taken Secondo up on his offer of fresh cheese. Secondo dutifully grates cheese over his dish, and when he tries to stop, the man grabs Secondo's hand and gestures for more cheese, repeatedly. The woman asks, "But I get a side order of spaghetti with this, right?" (00:06:0–00:06:03) To which, Secondo, his veneer cracking, responds in exasperation, "Why?" (00:06:03) He tries to explain that *risotto* and pasta are both starches and therefore do not complement one another, but the couple is undeterred. Then the couple orders a side of spaghetti assuming it will come with meatballs. When Secondo tries to discuss the intricacies of Italian cuisine, they are unreceptive and simply order a side of meatballs. Secondo's assistant waiter, Cristiano (Marc Anthony), looks on, increasingly nervous, knowing that Primo's reaction will be less than accommodating. The scene plays comically, but the object of derision here is the American couple, not the Italian restauranteurs. The Americans are too simpleminded to appreciate the experience they have been offered and too pigheaded to recognize the opportunity they have to learn and appreciate the beauty of Italian culture and cuisine. Instead, they use their financial power as consumers to demand assimilation and conformity in the food they consume. As Margaret Coyle writes,

> The food sense of Americans is seen as more than just "different" from that of Italians; rather, it appears as the defining rupture between the two nationalities. Food nourishes Italians and Americans alike, but only Italians see it as an

artistic and implicit expression of themselves and their national/personal identity. Americans are far more likely to define food as necessary to sustain life,
but not as self. [20]

Indeed, the American consumers end up getting the meal they want, but the
film demonstrates that they lose so much in the process.

This same scene also establishes the film's 1950s setting. In fact, Tucci
and Tropiano's decision to set the movie in the postwar heyday was an
important one. As Peter Matthews notes, the 1950s was a time "when
American materialism still retained its utopian aspect"[21] and according to
Terrence Rafferty, a time "when the popular image of Italian culture was
pretty much exactly represented by a heaping plate of spaghetti and meatballs."[22] In this cultural setting, the brothers face a daunting reality. They can
either remain true to their art (and cultural identity) and be financial failures
or they can compromise their art in the hopes of financial success.

Over the next few scenes, *Big Night* develops the immediate relevance of
this tension. First, Secondo goes to the bank for a meeting with an executive
about the money he owes. The loan officer (Peter McRobbie) looks over and
tells him that extending the payment schedule is impossible. Secondo says he
understands but he is obviously disappointed and lost. Narratively, the scene
encourages a degree of sympathy toward Secondo. He has been established
as a hard worker who runs an artful restaurant that is not appreciated by its
customers, and now, he and his brother are on the cusp of failure. Tucci's and
Scott's formal choices complement the narrative. When the banker tells Secondo that he cannot give the restauranteur any more time to pay back the
loan, the film cuts to a close-up of Secondo. This is the closest the camera
gets to either of the characters in the scene, and it is not matched by a similar
shot of the banker. The camera then holds on Secondo for an extended period
of time, while the off-screen banker continues to talk. This brings the viewer
nearer to Secondo, and emphasizes the mix of confusion and pain on his face
in an effort to solidify identification with the character.

Soon after this scene, Secondo goes to meet with Pascal at his restaurant.
The two retire to Pascal's office and Secondo reveals his financial troubles to
his friend/competitor. Pascal listens, turns down Secondo's request, and then
introduces the idea of having Prima come to the Paradise. Tucci's and Tropiano's choice of Prima, like their choice to set the film in the 1950s, was
deliberate and effective. "The stage persona of the man [the brothers are]
trying to impress, Louis Prima, trades on cliché images of Italians as swarthy,
bouncy, bellowing exhibitionists," Rafferty writes, "Prima—described by
one character, charitably, as 'boisterous'—is Italian in all the ways that Primo and Secondo, to their financial misfortune, are not."[23] Matthews adds that
musically speaking Prima "was about as authentic as frozen pizza pie."[24]
Anthony Julian Tamburri disagrees, writing, "With his music, [Prima] suc-

ceeded in being both American, with Jazz, and Italian, with his folkloric and popular Italian and Italianate songs . . . he is that synthesis of bi-cultural co-existence that the brothers . . . cannot achieve."[25] Nevertheless, Prima's supposed connection to Pascal suggests that the two share a similar perspective on ethnic/cultural identity.

Tucci and Scott seem to have been just as purposeful about their stylistic choices in this scene. The blocking, for example, has Secondo sinking into a leather sofa that is close to the floor, while Pascal (who is small in stature) sits elevated in his chair behind his desk. It is almost as if he is on a throne. Annoyingly, a desk lamp blocks the view between Secondo and Pascal, creating the comical look of an oversized, electrified moustache on Pascal's face. While the two converse the camera remains at Secondo's level not Pascal's. After Pascal slams the light down, the pattern changes somewhat, but the relationship between the camera and Secondo has been established. Viewers experience the world from a perspective that mimics Secondo's, and that encourages a connection between the character and the viewer as well.

The film works to lionize the brothers on a narrative level by endorsing their passion for food and family and on a visual level by representing the world either from the brothers' points-of-view or perspectives that approximate them. These choices are complemented by *Big Night*'s pity or disdain for characters who have never experienced the pleasure of good food, or those that take advantage of the brothers' naivete. A character lamenting her mother's inability to cook tasty food endorses the brothers' way of life. However, a character like Pascal, who never contacts Prima and dooms the Paradise as a result, shows how embracing American capitalism can corrupt an individual. Unlike the starch-loving customers who appear near the start of the film, Pascal recognizes the culinary brilliance of Primo, but his instinct is to possess and corrupt that artistry by essentially giving the brothers no other choice but to work for him. Ownership and profits come first for Pascal. He even describes Primo as "a great investment" (01:38:59–1:39:01). Friendship and art come second. Secondo wants to believe that he can be like Pascal. His affair with Gabriella, Pascal's girlfriend, suggests that he values his friendship with Pascal about as much as Pascal values his friendship with Secondo. But ultimately, Pascal represents what Rafferty calls, "the then current stereotype, of exuberant, excessive, mamma-mia Italianness."[26] Like Louis Prima, Pascal's version of Italianness is much different from that of the brothers.

When Secondo confronts Pascal about his betrayal, the successful restauranteur admits that he lied and that he did so to ruin the brothers financially. Secondo moves toward him, and Pascal stands expecting to be physically assaulted. But Secondo rejects the script that Pascal (and any number of Hollywood films) would have him follow. Instead, he shows restraint, bucking the trend of Italian American stereotypes. The camera cuts to an over-the-shoulder close-up of Secondo, with Pascal, his back to the camera and out-of-focus, in the foreground. Secondo looks directly at Pascal and simply tells him that he will never "have" Primo, that Primo "lives in a world above [him]" (01:39:09–01:39:15). The fact that Secondo does not resort to violence in this situation underlines the ways that the film rejects some Hollywood narratives of masculinity. It also rejects many of the narratives that have been attached to Italian American ethnicity over the years.[27] But it does not reject all of them. In the scene before this, Primo and Secondo engage in a loud screaming match, punctuated with dramatic hand gestures, that eventually descends into the two wrestling on the beach and throwing sand at one another.

ITALIAN AND ITALIAN AMERICAN
AESTHETICS IN *BIG NIGHT*

Big Night's representation of Italian American ethnicity pays homage to many important and prominent Italian and Italian American filmmakers. This allows the film to create a carefully constructed, loving portrait of Italian and Italian American cinematic traditions. Most prominent among these filmmakers are the works of Italian American filmmaker Martin Scorsese, Italian filmmaker Federico Fellini, and Italian neorealist filmmakers such as Roberto Rossellini, Vittorio De Sica, Luchino Visconti, and Giuseppe De Santis. The film's most talked about scene is also its last. The morning after the big night, Secondo, still wearing his tuxedo pants and shirt, enters the kitchen of the Paradise and finds Cristiano sleeping. Cristiano awakes and sits up as Secondo moves toward the stove. Secondo motions to Cristiano to relax, and then he begins preparing an omelet. When the omelet is completed, Secondo serves a portion along with some bread to Cristiano, and then prepares a plate for himself. As the two eat, Primo enters the kitchen still wearing his chef's uniform, which is now disheveled. Secondo returns to the stove, prepares a plate for his brother, and places it on the table next to his own plate. Secondo sits down; Cristiano exits the frame, and then Primo sits next to his brother. The two eat their meal, without speaking, put their arms around each other's back, then sit next to each other their arms at their sides; the film cuts to black. The entire scene takes place in a single long take. Upon the film's release, this scene was hailed by critics. Matthews wrote, "On its slender scale, it's perhaps the most exquisitely touching ending in recent film history,"[28] and Richard Schickel called it "spectacularly confident filmmaking, honoring our ability to draw our own conclusions about what we've seen and the medium's rarely employed ability to convey major emotions through minimal means."[29] The scene is exceedingly well conceived not just for the reasons mentioned but also because the form matches the theme. At this point, Pascal has betrayed the brothers; their restaurant, it seems, will now fail, and Secondo's romantic relationships have ended, but the brothers still have each other.[30] Shooting the scene with a series of cuts would fragment the space, placing the brothers in different shots and separating them visually.[31] Using a single take, especially one where the characters do not speak but still move with almost dance-like precision, provides a degree of cohesion that emphasizes familial unity.

What has been lost in the discussion of the last scene is that there are a number of long takes throughout the film.[32] In fact, the first scene in the kitchen and the first in the dining room are long takes. Additionally, the directors show many of the scenes where characters converse with one another in long takes, forsaking the more typical shot/reverse shot editing pattern of traditional narrative cinema. This choice helps to create a slow, deliberate pace that represents the kind of "confident filmmaking" that Schickel previously noted. Rather than including cuts to quicken the pace, Scott and Tucci trust the script and their vision, believing that the audience will not look away or become bored. The style is also reminiscent of Italian neorealist films from the 1940s and early 1950s, a fact that Tucci, Scott, and Tropiano have acknowledged.[33]

Italian neorealist films such as *Rome: Open City* (Roberto Rossellini, 1945), *Paisan* (Roberto Rossellini, 1946), *Shoeshine* (Vittorio De Sica, 1946), *Bicycle Thieves* (Vittorio De Sica, 1948), *La terra trema* (Luchino Visconti, 1948), *Bitter Rice* (Giuseppe De Santis, 1949), and *Umberto D.* (Vittorio De Sica, 1952) tended to forsake expressive camera movements in favor of an unobtrusive visual style characterized by natural lighting, long shots, and few cuts. As Sidney Gottlieb has shown, the actual visual styles of these films tended to be much more complicated than this framing suggests.[34] At times, both *Rome: Open City* and *Bicycle Thieves* for example, feature highly expressive camera movements. Nevertheless, the use of supposedly more "objective" techniques is present throughout these films and others of this period, and Tucci's and Scott's decision to shoot much of *Big Night* in a similar style pays homage to these earlier Italian filmmakers.

Throughout *Big Night*, the directors block any number of dialogue scenes with the two characters sitting next to each other and facing the camera. Phyllis and Secondo sit on opposite sides of a car, separated by a split windshield but in the same shot. Ann and Primo walk through her flower shop and converse in a single shot, even as Primo climbs into her display case. Secondo and Pascal end up seated next to each other on the sofa in Pascal's office, both characters facing forward. Primo and Alberto (Pasquale Cajano) and Primo and Secondo have conversations that are filmed in long takes. The choice is an interesting one because it is rare for two characters who are talking to one another to not be facing each other. Delbert Mann had used a similar technique in *Marty*, a classic TV show from 1953, and then repeated the same technique in the feature film with the same title in 1955.[35] *Marty* focuses on an Italian American butcher in the Bronx, and Mann openly acknowledged his debt to the neorealists.[36] From a filmmaking perspective, this blocking allows the audience to watch the faces of both characters at the same time and choose the one on which they will focus. However, Tucci's and Scott's use of the technique (as well as Mann's) takes on an added layer of meaning because of the ethnicity of the characters and the historical roots of the style. Here, a visual style works in concert with a loving ethnic representation to more completely embrace Italian and Italian American culture.

At times, Tucci and Scott married this "realistic" style with a more expressive technique inspired by the work of Scorsese. When Secondo goes to Pascal's to speak to his friend about his money troubles, the directors shoot the scene in a long take, yet this long take is much different from the scene that concludes the film or the others previously mentioned. The camera begins by facing Secondo, but as he moves further into the restaurant, it pans away from him. Suddenly, characters begin speaking directly to the camera, breaking the fourth wall and offering Secondo's point-of-view. The camera is almost boozy, panning and tracking as Secondo passes tables filled with guests, a lounge singer, and waiters carrying trays of food (including the Americanized dish of spaghetti and meatballs) that hover in the frame.[37] Tamburri notes that the singer in the scene performs an Americanized version of a classic Italian song.[38] The restaurant is bathed in red light as if it were hell.[39] The camera then pans back to find Secondo again, this time walking toward the camera, which retreats as he advances, before panning away from him again, this time completing a full 360-degree survey of the dining room and then finding Secondo perched at the espresso bar. He has a brief conversation with Gabriella before moving into another part of the restaurant. The camera, still in the same shot, follows behind him as he approaches the bar and Charlie the bartender (Gene Canfield). The camera pans away from Secondo again, this time into an attached room, following his gaze. It tracks quickly toward a table as a drum roll is heard and settles on Pascal as he flambés a dish, ending on a close-up of the restauranteur holding a flaming pan at the bottom of the frame. The camera cuts to a reverse shot to reveal Secondo, pointing and smiling at his friend. The visual style is incredibly complex and demonstrates both careful planning and tremendous skill. But the directors are not just showing off. Thematically, the sequence emphasizes the fact that Secondo is intoxicated and seduced by Pascal's—a restaurant that represents a clear corruption of the culinary art that Primo holds so dear but also a form of corruption that is obviously lucrative and seemingly highly enjoyable. The scene combines neorealism's hesitance to cut with recognizable aspects of some of Scorsese's most famous films. The red lighting and the boozy camera echo the bar scenes in *Mean Streets*, where a drunk Charlie (Harvey Keitel) is bathed in red light as a tracking shot, relatively tight on Charlie, follows him through the establishment and eventually falls to the ground with him. The portions of the scene where characters directly address the camera resemble the scene in *GoodFellas* where Henry Hill's (Ray Liotta) voiceover introduces viewers to the guys in the bar. Similarly, the famous Copacabana long take in *GoodFellas* is an inspiration here, with the camera following Secondo as he works his way into the heart of the restaurant, much like Hill and his date Karen (Lorraine Bracco) did in Scorsese's film.

Finally, Fellini's influence is evident throughout *Big Night*. Critic David Denby wrote of the film, "At times, I thought I was looking at the American equivalent of an early Fellini movie. *Big Night* has a comparable sense of sweet forlornness, of dignity struggling for vindication."[40] Perhaps the most direct reference is to *La Strada* (1954), a film that famously ends with Zampanò (Anthony Quinn) kneeling on a beach, clenching sand in his fists. Having tried to control everything (including those that love him), the character is reduced to a metaphor. The tighter his hands grip the sand, the more it falls through his fingers. At the end of *Big Night*, the brothers fight on the beach, and eventually Primo ends up on his knees pounding the sand with his hands in frustration. Simon has described the moment as "pure Fellini,"[41] but once again, the use of a style inspired by an Italian filmmaker carries increased significance because of the ethnic identity of the film's main characters and its setting. It represents a kind of ethnically-inflected visual style.

EDIBLE ETHNICITY: *BIG NIGHT* AS FOOD FILM

In their seminal work *Unthinking Eurocentrism: Multiculturalism and the Media*, Ella Shohat and Robert Stam suggest that stereotype studies that resort to the positive/negative dichotomy are dependent upon the prejudices of the critic and rely on an equally damaging and limiting "positive stereotype" as the barometer of accuracy. Instead, Shohat and Stam propose that critics shift their focus to what the representation tells us about the cultures that produced and consumed the representation.[42] When it comes to Italian American representations like the gangster, what might be most irritating is the fact that the representation has evolved very little, if at all, over the years. Certainly, some gangster characters have been more complex than others. *The Godfather* trilogy (Coppola, 1972, 1974, and 1990), *Mean Streets* (Scorsese, 1973), *GoodFellas* (Scorsese, 1990), and *The Sopranos* (HBO, 1999–2007) spring to mind immediately. However, the general trend is to have characters who are so obsessed with their public image and material wealth that they will resort to violence, extortion, betrayal, and murder to achieve them. While the representations have remained fairly consistent, the sociocultural standing of Italian Americans has changed significantly. In the second half of the 19th century and the first half of the 20th century, Italian Americans were a marginalized group of largely working-class new Americans, who were the targets of occasional lynchings, bombastic political speech (that sought to deport them as a way to solve the country's economic woes), travel and curfew restrictions during World War II, and in over 250 cases internment.[43] Today, Italian Americans are largely assimilated, hold powerful positions in almost all industries, and are almost universally identified as "white." Following Shohat and Stam, this shifting set of sociocultural factors dramatically recontextualizes the meaning of Italian American stereotypes even if the actual representations have changed very little. Put simply, the Italian American gangster (or other Italian American stereotypes) no longer possess the power to marginalize the group and its members. As Michael Imperioli, who won an Emmy Award for playing Christopher Moltisanti on *The Sopranos*, said when asked about the criticisms that some Italian American groups had leveled at the show, "*The Sopranos* is not going to keep some kid who's Italian American from getting into a good college because the dean thinks his father is a mobster because he happens to be Italian. I mean we're past that."[44]

When it comes to *Big Night*, specifically, it is worth investigating how the representation of Italian American ethnicity played into larger cultural trends in the 1990s. Labeled "one of the first food films produced in the United States"[45] and "the first major U.S. food film,"[46] *Big Night* mobilizes many of the stylistic and narrative elements of this subgenre. In discussing *The Lunchbox* (Ritesh Batra, 2013), a BAFTA-nominated Indian film, Sarinah Masukor includes the following in her list of generic characteristics: "lingering shots of exquisitely prepared food and in-kitchen action sequences that present cooking as a high-speed sport driven by adrenaline."[47] *Big Night* conforms to both. Despite the film's more deliberate pace, the montage sequence during the feast, which features shots from both the dining room and the kitchen, creates the frantic, sport-like feel that Masukor sees as key to the genre.

While these films turn ethnic foods into movie stars, Laura Lindenfeld worries that they also create a "touristic experience" on the part of viewers. Food becomes a way to depoliticize ethnicity and race creating "the illusion of experiencing ethnicity without ever coming into contact with actual, potentially fear-invoking racialized bodies."[48] The use of food in *Big Night*, which focuses on a largely assimilated white ethnic group[49] whose foodways have become a prominent part of the American cultural landscape, may serve a different function than films that feature "potentially fear-invoking racialized" others like *Tortilla Soup* (Maria Ripoll, 2001), *The Hundred-Foot Journey* (Lasse Hallström, 2014), and *Soul Food* (George Tillman, Jr., 1997).[50] Nevertheless, Lindenfeld's critique points to one of the limitations of cinema. No film, whether it concentrates on food or not, will ever bring viewers into "actual" contact with "bodies." In this way, movies are always an "illusion." The hope may be that these films inspire viewers to have contact with ethnic others after seeing the movie. *Big Night* motivated this kind of contact. As Joan Tropiano Tucci, Tucci's mother and Tropiano's aunt, wrote in the cookbook that followed the film's release, "At first we shared these recipes with just our children, but after *Big Night*, we received requests for recipes from far and wide."[51] Additionally, several restaurants began offering *Big Night* dinners.[52] As Diane Negra notes, "Diners who then paid (substantially) to attend a re-creation of Primo Pilaggi's elaborate meal could enjoy cuisine that was doubly certified as authentic while also differentiating themselves from the unadventurous, bland-palleted Americans threatened by Primo's cuisine in the film."[53]

Ethnic engagement like the kind described above carries progressive potential and troubling consequences. For one, *Big Night* may celebrate Italian food, but it also works to fossilize a certain kind of Italian fare. "[The film] implicitly fails to acknowledge Italian-American cuisine as a living and rich tradition with a complex history rooted in the migrant experience and limits true authenticity to the Old World, which looms as a space of nostalgia and emotional longing throughout the narrative, as it does in so many representations of Italian foodways in the United States," argue Lindenfeld and Parasecoli.[54] Additionally, the film levels a decided critique against consumerism,[55] but individual fans sought to recreate the experience that they had watching a commercial movie by purchasing an experience at a commercial restaurant.[56] It may be that the restaurants in question had long been serving the artistic food that *Big Night* advocates or perhaps the restauranteurs changed their methods in response to the film's message. But ultimately, the film and its associated products worked to commodify ethnic culture (even as they celebrated it), which played into a larger cultural trend in the 1990s United States and one that according to Donna Gabaccia had been apparent among ethnic Americans since at least the 1970s. "Being consumers to their American core," Gabaccia wrote about 1970s "new ethnics," "they tried to recreate the past by buying it."[57]

The impulse to commodify ethnicity extended beyond *Big Night* to such pedestrian restaurants as the Olive Garden. The chain's "When You're Here, You're Family" ads, featured "exuberant Italian American families pass[ing] babies around while eating their meal."[58] Diane Negra contends that ads like these were part of a larger cultural effort that also helped to drive the success of food films like *Big Night*. "While Americans in the 1990s were less likely to be members of large, geographically unified extended families, had fewer shared mealtimes, consumed more take-home prepared food, ate more frequently in restaurants, and did less eating in their dining rooms, the films correct all of these features," she explains, "They consistently emphasize shared meals that are home-prepared, laboriously put together according to traditional recipes, and consumed by large groups."[59] In other words, Americans' nostalgic longing for a more cohesive family unit and a more meaningful connection to ethnic roots, drove box office for films like *Big Night* and profits for restaurants like the Olive Garden.

What is troubling about this understanding (or mobilization) of ethnicity is the way it disconnects ethnic identity from lived experience, allowing it to be attained through consumption (of food, popular culture, fashion, or something else) and/or performance. In *Feeling Italian: The Art of Ethnicity in America*, Thomas J. Ferraro examines ethnic identity in the post-modern era and suggests that one no longer needs to be able to claim an ethnic past in order to "feel" ethnic. He posits, "Italian American self-understanding and the portrayal of Italians in American culture at large, then, moved closer together, to the point where the feelings Italian Americans have for themselves, the feeling non-Italians have for Italian Americans, and the feeling they both have for the role of Italianness in America intertwine and interpenetrate: almost—but not quite!—one."[60] This understanding of ethnicity can de-historicize ethnic experiences, erasing the very real prejudice that white ethnic groups once experienced. The kinds of lessons this type of identity construction holds for still marginalized groups today is even more problematic. If it is so easy to "feel Italian," would it be equally easy to "feel Arab," "feel Black," or "feel Mexican?" If inhabiting and shedding those identities is so simple do the prejudices and policies that lead to police shootings, border walls, hate crimes, and the like seem less significant? Does the impetus for change suddenly shift to the targeted minorities who have chosen to maintain identities that seem to be so easy to discard? Indeed, the problem is not that food films like *Big Night* create "the illusion of *experiencing* ethnicity without ever coming into contact with actual, potentially fear-invoking racialized bodies" as Lindenfeld worries [italics added].[61] Rather, it is that food films like *Big Night* might offer the illusion of *being* ethnic.

CONCLUSION

Big Night is a more complex film than many have acknowledged. In some ways, it challenges and breaks with several major stereotypes that have defined Italian American ethnicity in American cinema. In other ways, it mobilizes those same representations by featuring characters that resemble gangsters, have excessive sexual appetites, are prone to the Madonna/whore complex, produce and consume too much food, and have volatile arguments. Nevertheless, the film often embraces the excesses of its Italian American characters, demonstrating that their approach to life allows for passion, enjoyment, and ecstasy. Avoiding excesses may mimic assimilative impulses,

Big Night argues, but it ultimately robs individuals of the fullness of life. As Coyle writes, "One wonders who is marginalized in this view of the world: Americans or Italians."[62] Despite the assertions of some critics and the film's creators, this is the film's major innovation in regards to Italian American representations, not that it avoids stereotypes altogether.

Moreover, the film recycles Italian and Italian American cinematic styles (including some that were originated in crime films) to create a representation of Italian American ethnicity that embraces Italian and Italian American culture. Robert Casillo has famously defined "Italian-American Cinema" as "works by Italian-American directors who treat Italian-American subjects."[63] *Big Night* represents an interesting case study for Casillo's definition since under Casillo's model Campbell Scott's co-direction of the film may threaten its Italian American status. It may be that discussing "Italian-American cinema" is an imperfect approach. After all, Italian Americans were never systematically excluded from Hollywood cinema. They have always been a part of the hegemonic system (unlike African Americans, for example, who had to create their own alternative industry). The investigation of "Italian Americans *and* cinema" or "Italian Americans *in* cinema" are still valuable areas of study, and while the claims such an approach might generate may seem less grand initially, it opens up some possible areas of study that might not exist under Casillo's approach.

For example, *Big Night*'s use of Italian and Italian American cinematic styles to tell a story about Italian and Italian American culture expands Casillo's method by making possible another way to study "Italian Americans and cinema." With this perspective, a style associated with an Italian American filmmaker that may or may not treat an Italian American subject can work to mark a film ethnically (even if the director—or in this case one of the co-directors—of the new film cannot or does not claim Italian heritage). In *Big Night*, then, Tucci's and Scott's decision to incorporate the styles of Italian and Italian American filmmakers works to make the representations more Italian, even if the film does not conform to Casillo's understanding of "Italian-American cinema."

Finally, *Big Night* is very much a product of the time period in which it was produced, not the time period it represents. In the 1990s, commodifying ethnicity continued to be a lucrative enterprise, and the film's embrace of Italian cuisine (perhaps unwittingly) played into this larger cultural trend. The implications for *Big Night*'s importance to American film history and the representation of race and ethnicity generally are myriad. In some ways, the film carries progressive potential; in others it works to make ethnicity accessible for individuals with no lived experience as members of the represented ethnic group. This can be troubling, particularly when it comes to the representation of racialized others who continue to endure institutionalized, systemic prejudice that threatens their very existence. Simply put, watching a movie can in no way stand in for a lifetime of discrimination and prejudice. However, a movie might introduce a previously sheltered or entrenched viewer to experiences of prejudice, and through the viewer's identification, sympathy, or empathy toward ethnic or racial characters, they might come to see the world differently. In this way, a film like *Big Night*, despite its limitations, might help to make the world a more just place.

NOTES

1. Eric Konigsberg, "How to Make Roles? Make Movies." *The New York Times Magazine.* 8 Sept. 1996.

2. Konigsberg, "How."

3. See Sarah Iammarino, "A Celebration of the Italian Culture: Stanley Tucci and Campbell Scott's *Big Night*," *VIA: Voices in Italian Americana* 8, no. 1 (1997): 183–188; Anna Camaiti Hostert, "Big Night, Small Days," in *Screening Ethnicity: Cinematographic Representations of Italian Americans in the United States*, ed. Anna Camaiti Hostert and Anthony Julian Tamburri (Boca Raton: Bordighera Press, 2002), 249–258; Joseph Tropiano, *Big Night* (New York: St. Martin's Griffin, 1996); and Stanley Tucci with Joan and Stan Tucci, Gianni Scappin, and Mimi Taft, *The Tucci Cookbook* (New York: Gallery Books, 1999, 2012).

4. See Diane Negra, "Ethnic Food Fetishism, Whiteness, and Nostalgia in Recent Film and Television," *Velvet Light Trap* 50 (Fall 2002): 62–76.

5. Tamburri suggests that the placement of *risotto* on the menu "underscores the so-called genuine Italian establishment that the brothers' restaurant Paradiso is." See Anthony Julian Tamburri, "Viewing *Big Night* As Easy as One, Two, Three: A Peircean Notion on Italian/American Identity." *Rivista Luci E Ombre* 3, no. 1 (2015): 111.

6. James R. Keller sees the geographic setting of the film as particularly significant. "The placement of the brothers' restaurant on the Jersey shore suggests their tenuous grip on the continent," Keller points out, "They could return to Europe or, figuratively, be swept out to sea at any time." See James R. Keller, *Food, Film and Culture: A Genre Study* (Jefferson, NC: McFarland and Company, 2006), 133.

7. Among other journalists and critics, *Entertainment Weekly*'s Steve Daly identified Pascal as a "Corsican" in a popular press article that appeared at the time of the film's release. See Steve Daly, "Tucci Dines Out: With *Big Night*, Tucci Refused to Let MGM/UA's Cooks Spoil the Story of an Uncompromising Culinary Artist," *Entertainment Weekly*, September 20, 1996, 20.

8. Janet Maslin, "Brothers' Last Chance to Save Their Paradise," *New York Times*, March 29, 1996, C8.

9. See Laura Lindenfeld and Fabio Parasecoli, *Feasting Our Eyes: Food Films and Culinary Identity in the United States* (New York: Columbia University Press, 2016); and Camaiti Hostert, "Big," 250.

10. Iammarino, "A Celebration," 183.

11. Camaiti Hostert, "Big," 251–252.

12. Tucci, et al., *Cookbook*, xii.

13. Tropiano, *Big Night*, vii.

14. Fred L. Gardaphé, *Leaving Little Italy: Essaying Italian American Culture* (Albany: State University of New York Press, 2004), 140.

15. Tropiano, *Big Night*, ix.

16. Mary Ann McDonald Carolan, "Italian American Women as Comic Foils: Exploding the Stereotype in *My Cousin Vinny*, *Moonstruck*, and *Married to the Mob*," *Lit: Literature Interpretation Theory* 13, no. 2 (2002): 155–166.

17. For a further discussion of the Romeo character, see Peter Bondanella, *Hollywood Italians: Dagos, Palookas, Romeos, Wise Guys, and Sopranos* (New York: Continuum, 2004), 132–171.

18. John Simon, "Appetizing and Otherwise," *National Review*, December 9, 1996, 66.

19. The scene was so important to the filmmakers that they rejected an offer to have *Big Night* more widely distributed by MGM/UA when the large studio requested that this scene be shortened. Tucci and his fellow filmmakers opted to work with Samuel Goldwyn, a much smaller distributor, instead. See Daly, "Tucci," 20.

20. Margaret Coyle, "*Il Timpano*—'To Eat Good Food Is to Be Close to God': The Italian-American Reconciliation of Stanley Tucci and Campbell Scott's *Big Night*," in *Reel Food: Essays on Food and Film*, ed. Anne L. Bower, 41–59 (New York: Routledge, 2004), 43.

21. Peter Matthews, "Big Night," *Sight and Sound* 7, no. 6 (June 1997): 48.

22. Terrence Rafferty, "Feast and Famine: A Culinary Comedy and a Remake of 'Yojimbo,'" *The New Yorker*, September 23, 1996, 100.

23. Rafferty, "Feast," 101.

24. Matthews, "Big," 48.

25. Tamburri, "Viewing," 123.

26. Rafferty, "Feast," 100.

27. In the film, Secondo is unfaithful to Phyllis. Pascal seems to engage in criminal activities, and many of the characters (including non-Italians) eat too much.

28. Matthews, "Big," 48.

29. Richard Schickel, "A Movie to Dine For," *Time*, September 23, 1996, 72.

30. Anna Camaiti Hostert says of the scene, "The film ends with an obviously very Italian overture to the importance of familial bonds. Secondo puts his arm around his brother, indicating a tie that cannot be broken by differences of opinion or economic ruin." See Camaiti Hostert, "Big," 255.

31. As previously noted, MGM/UA had requested that the scene where Secondo prepares the restaurant be shortened. They also asked that "a 'more upbeat' voiceover" be added to the ending. Both requests were rejected and *Big Night* ended up being distributed by Samuel Goldwyn. See Daly, "Tucci," 20.

32. Zimmerman notes, "*Big Night* did not escape the scrupulous eye of professional chefs who were critical of its culinary inaccuracies. The kitchen itself is set up oddly. Usually, a table directly behind the cook is necessary for plating food." Zimmerman continues, outlining multiple ways that the mise-en-scene of this fictional film does not conform to the layout of actual restaurant kitchens. Holding a fictional film to a historical reality seems to miss the point of the film and unduly ties the hands of the filmmakers. See Steve Zimmerman, "Food in Films: A Star is Born," *Gastronomica* 9, no. 2 (2009): 30.

33. Lindenfeld and Parasecoli, *Feasting*, 41.

34. Sidney Gottlieb, "Rossellini, *Open City*, and Neorealism," in *Roberto Rossellini's Rome Open City*, ed. Sidney Gottlieb. Cambridge Film Handbooks (New York: Cambridge University Press, 2004), 31–42.

35. See Jonathan J. Cavallero, "Written Out of the Story: Issues of Television Authorship, Reception, and Ethnicity in NBC's 'Marty,'" *Cinema Journal* 56, no. 3 (Spring 2017): 47–73.

36. Gorham Kindem, *The Live Television Generation of Hollywood Film Directors: Interviews with Seven Directors* (Jefferson, NC: McFarland, 1994).

37. Tamburri notes "both in the dishes of the second table and on the trays of the two waiters are abundantly filled plates of spaghetti and meatballs: that heretical dish that Primo refuses to serve in his restaurant." See Tamburri, "Viewing," 117.

38. Tamburri, "Viewing," 117.

39. Both Tamburri and Keller comment on the use of red in this scene. See Tamburri, "Viewing," 117; and Keller, *Food*, 130.

40. David Denby, "A Violent Birth," *New York*, October 28, 1996, 124.

41. Simon, "Appetizing," 66.

42. Ella Shohat and Robert Stam, *Unthinking Eurocentrism: Multiculturalism and the Media* (New York: Routledge, 1994), 178–219.

43. For a discussion of Italian American lynchings, see Richard Gambino, *Vendetta: The True Story of the Largest Lynching in U.S. History*. Picas Series. (Montreal: Guernica, 1977; 2000). For a discussion of efforts to deport Italians during the Great Depression, see "Drive for Law to Deport 6,000,000 Aliens Will Be Organized All over the Country," *New York Times*,

June 23, 1935, sec. 1, pg. 1. For a discussion of World War II-era travel/curfew restrictions and internment, see Lawrence Di Stasi, ed., *Una Storia Segreta: The Secret History of Italian American Evacuation and Internment during World War II* (Berkeley: HeyDay Books, 2001). For a general discussion of the prejudice Italian Americans have experienced, see Salvatore LaGumina, *Wop!: A Documentary History of Anti-Italian Discrimination in the United States.* 1973 (Buffalo: Guernica, 1999).

44. *CBS Sunday Morning,* "Michael Imperioli's Mob Scene: Emmy-Winning Actor Talks to Russ Mitchell about 'The Sopranos,'" Television, CBS, September 26, 2004.

45. Lindenfeld and Parasecoli, *Feasting,* 35.

46. Lindenfeld and Parasecoli, *Feasting,* 38.

47. Sarinah Masukor, "Old Recipe, New Flavour: Ritesh Batra's *The Lunchbox.*" *Metro Magazine* 183 (2015): 72.

48. Laura Lindenfeld, "Visiting the Mexican American Family: *Tortilla Soup* as Culinary Tourism," *Communication and Critical/Cultural Studies* 4, no. 3 (September 2007): 305.

49. Among the dinner guests is a single African American woman name Lenore (Alvaleta Guess). She is not offered a storyline, but given the film's setting in the 1950s, the character's presence carries some significance. In an otherwise segregated world, Lenore is welcomed to the Paradise indicating a degree of progressiveness on the part of the brothers.

50. This is complicated by the fact that many food films are authored by members of the ethnic groups that are represented. For example, *Soul Food* was written and directed by African American filmmaker George Tillman, Jr.

51. Tucci, et al., *Cookbook,* xvii.

52. Lindenfeld and Parsecoli, *Feasting,* 45.

53. Negra, "Ethnic," 72.

54. Lindenfeld and Parasecoli, *Feasting,* 37. For a longer discussion of the conflict between Old World and New World in the film, see Tamburri, "Viewing."

55. Matthews writes, "The generally thoughtful script—by Tucci again and Joseph Tropiano—distributes sympathy just about evenly between the two brothers. It never picks a clear winner in the battle between Old World tradition and rampant, commercialised modernity." See Matthews, "Big," 48. While the film recognizes the pull that both brothers feel, it clearly castigates Pascal's unmitigated pursuit of commercial success, regardless of the artistic consequences. As Keller notes, "The film suggests that the environment most conducive to the exchange and appreciation of genuine art is one in which money is not central. Money is corruptive of art." See Keller, *Food,* 127.

56. Lindenfeld and Parasecoli write, "Featuring a menu of tricolored risotto, *timpano,* and roasted young pig, the film was transformed into a spectacular, supposedly authentic, eating experience, despite the narrative's efforts to critique this very relationship between consumers and food." See Lindenfeld and Parasecoli, *Feasting,* 45.

57. Donna R. Gabaccia, *We Are What We Eat: Ethnic Food and the Making of Americans* (Cambridge: Harvard University Press, 1998), 180.

58. Negra, "Ethnic," 62.

59. Negra, "Ethnic," 65. These efforts also work to justify the cuisine offered at so-called "ethnic" restaurants like the Olive Garden. Negra writes, "The functions of ethnic thematics in the casual dining category are multiple, but in most cases the invocation of heritage rationalizes the consumption of high-fat, unhealthy cuisine." See Negra, "Ethnic," 68.

60. Thomas J. Ferraro, *Feeling Italian: The Art of Ethnicity in America* (New York: New York University Press, 2005), 4.

61. Lindenfeld, "Visiting," 305.

62. Coyle, "*Timpano,*"44.

63. Robert Casillo, "Moments in Italian-American Cinema: From *Little Caesar* to Coppola and Scorsese," in *From the Margin: Writings in Italian Americana,* Revised Edition, ed. Anthony Julian Tamburri, Paolo A. Giordano, and Fred L. Gardaphé (West Lafayette: Purdue University Press, 2000), 394.

BIBLIOGRAPHY

Bondanella, Peter. *Hollywood Italians: Dagos, Palookas, Romeos, Wise Guys, and Sopranos*. New York: Continuum, 2004.

Camaiti Hostert, Anna. "Big Night, Small Days." In *Screening Ethnicity: Cinematographic Representations of Italian Americans in the United States*, edited by Anna Camaiti Hostert and Anthony Julian Tamburri, 249–258. Boca Raton: Bordighera Press, 2002.

Carolan, Mary Ann McDonald. "Italian American Women as Comic Foils: Exploding the Stereotype in *My Cousin Vinny*, *Moonstruck*, and *Married to the Mob*." *Lit: Literature Interpretation Theory* 13, no. 2 (2002): 155–66.

Casillo, Robert. "Moments in Italian-American Cinema: From *Little Caesar* to Coppola and Scorsese." In *From the Margin: Writings in Italian Americana*, Revised Edition, edited by Anthony Julian Tamburri, Paolo A. Giordano, and Fred L. Gardaphé, 394–416. West Lafayette: Purdue University Press, 2000.

Cavallero, Jonathan J. "Written Out of the Story: Issues of Television Authorship, Reception, and Ethnicity in NBC's 'Marty.'" *Cinema Journal* 56, no. 3 (Spring 2017): 47–73.

CBS Sunday Morning. "Michael Imperioli's Mob Scene: Emmy-Winning Actor Talks to Russ Mitchell about 'The Sopranos.'" Television. CBS, September 26, 2004.

Coyle, Margaret. "*Il Timpano*—'To Eat Good Food Is to Be Close to God': The Italian-American Reconciliation of Stanley Tucci and Campbell Scott's *Big Night*." In *Reel Food: Essays on Food and Film*, edited by Anne L. Bower, 41–59. New York: Routledge, 2004.

Daly, Steve. "Tucci Dines Out: With *Big Night*, Tucci Refused to Let MGM/UA's Cooks Spoil the Story of an Uncompromising Culinary Artist." *Entertainment Weekly*, September 20, 1996: 20.

Denby, David. "A Violent Birth." *New York*, October 28, 1996: 122, 124.

Di Stasi, Lawrence, ed. *Una Storia Segreta: The Secret History of Italian American Evacuation and Internment during World War II*. Berkeley: HeyDay Books, 2001.

"Drive for Law to Deport 6,000,000 Aliens Will Be Organized All over the Country." *New York Times*, June 23, 1935: sec. 1, pg. 1.

Ferraro, Thomas J. *Feeling Italian: The Art of Ethnicity in America*. New York: New York University Press, 2005.

Gabaccia, Donna R. *We Are What We Eat: Ethnic Food and the Making of Americans*. Cambridge: Harvard University Press, 1998.

Gambino, Richard. *Vendetta: The True Story of the Largest Lynching in U.S. History*. Picas Series. Montreal: Guernica, 1977; 2000.

Gardaphé, Fred L. *Leaving Little Italy: Essaying Italian American Culture*. Albany: State University of New York Press, 2004.

Gottlieb, Sidney. "Rossellini, *Open City*, and Neorealism." In *Roberto Rossellini's Rome Open City*, edited by Sidney Gottlieb. 31–42. Cambridge Film Handbooks. New York: Cambridge University Press, 2004.

Iammarino, Sarah. "A Celebration of the Italian Culture: Stanley Tucci and Campbell Scott's *Big Night*." *VIA: Voices in Italian Americana* 8, no. 1 (1997): 183–188.

Keller, James R. *Food, Film and Culture: A Genre Study*. Jefferson, NC: McFarland and Company, 2006.

Kindem, Gorham. *The Live Television Generation of Hollywood Film Directors: Interviews with Seven Directors*. Jefferson, NC: McFarland, 1994.

Konigsberg, Eric. "How to Make Roles? Make Movies." *The New York Times Magazine*, September 8, 1996.

LaGumina, Salvatore. *Wop!: A Documentary History of Anti-Italian Discrimination in the United States*. 1973. Buffalo: Guernica, 1999.

Lindenfeld, Laura. "Visiting the Mexican American Family: *Tortilla Soup* as Culinary Tourism." *Communication and Critical/Cultural Studies* 4, no. 3 (September 2007): 303–320.

Lindenfeld, Laura, and Fabio Parasecoli. *Feasting Our Eyes: Food Films and Culinary Identity in the United States*. New York: Columbia University Press, 2016.

Maslin, Janet. "Brothers' Last Chance to Save Their Paradise." *New York Times*, March 29, 1996: C8.

Masukor, Sarinah. "Old Recipe, New Flavour: Ritesh Batra's *The Lunchbox.*" *Metro Magazine* 183 (2015): 70–73.

Matthews, Peter. "Big Night." *Sight and Sound* 7, no. 6 (June 1997): 47–48.

Negra, Diane. "Ethnic Food Fetishism, Whiteness, and Nostalgia in Recent Film and Television." *Velvet Light Trap* 50 (Fall 2002): 62–76.

Rafferty, Terrence. "Feast and Famine: A Culinary Comedy and a Remake of 'Yojimbo.'" *The New Yorker*, September 23, 1996: 100–102.

Rotten Tomatoes. *Big Night*. Accessed June 18, 2019. https://www.rottentomatoes.com/m/big_night/

Schickel, Richard. "A Movie to Dine For." *Time*, September 23, 1996: 72.

Shohat, Ella and Robert Stam. *Unthinking Eurocentrism: Multiculturalism and the Media*. New York: Routledge, 1994.

Simon, John. "Appetizing and Otherwise." *National Review*, December 9, 1996: 65–66.

Tamburri, Anthony Julian. "Viewing *Big Night* As Easy as One, Two, Three: A Peircean Notion an Italian/American Identity." *Rivista Luci E Ombre* 3, no. 1 (2015): 100–123.

Tropiano, Joseph. *Big Night*. New York: St. Martin's Griffin, 1996.

Tucci, Stanley with Joan and Stan Tucci, Gianni Scappin, and Mimi Taft. *The Tucci Cookbook*. New York: Gallery Books, 1999, 2012.

Zimmerman, Steve. "Food in Films: A Star Is Born." *Gastronomica* 9, no. 2 (2009): 25–34.

Chapter Three

Questioning the Italian American Palooka

Race and Disability in the Rocky *and the* Creed *Series*

Alan J. Gravano

The question of what is Italian American cinema has been widely debated in Italian American studies, with scholars such as Robert Casillo proposing the encompassing definition of "works by Italian-American directors who treat Italian-American subjects."[1] Casillo does not address the role of producer or writer, even though Sylvester Stallone wrote the screenplay for *Rocky* and co-wrote the one for *Creed II*. In addition, the *Creed* series lists him as one of several producers. This paper addresses the lack of scholarship on the portrayal of Italian Americans by examining non-Italian American filmmakers and films such as John G. Avildsen's *Rocky* (1976), Ryan Coogler's *Creed* (2015), and Steven Caple, Jr's *Creed II* (2018). Avildsen introduces audiences to the most iconic Italian American character that has now appeared in seven sequels: *Rocky II* (1979), *Rocky III* (1982), *Rocky IV* (1985), *Rocky V* (1990), *Rocky Balboa* (2006), *Creed*, and *Creed II*. This project explores the conflicts and collaborations among the fictional characters of Balboa, Apollo, and Adonis (Donnie) Creed as representations of outsiders, and provides evidence that non-Italian American filmmakers can add to the body of work started by their Italian American counterparts on Italian American topics and themes.

ROCKY SCHOLARSHIP AND NOW *CREED*

Substantial scholarship on the *Rocky* series is available. For instance, analyzing the films *Rocky* and *Rocky Balboa*, Jacqueline Reich points out that "the boxing films that feature Italian Americans are especially complicit in the articulation of a white racial identity at the expense of the African American other,"[2] while Lawrence Webb focuses on "the urban realist tendencies that characterized certain strands of early 1970s cinema and an individualist, rise-to-success plot that would become commonplace in 1980s Hollywood."[3] In his conclusion, Brett Conway stresses, "that only by smashing the Other can" the white-male-as-victim ethos "be overcome."[4] Joel W. Martin's argument connects with this idea of "smashing the Other" when analyzing the bicentennial match between Rocky and Apollo: "The placard's slogan [Creed is King] . . . urges us to equate Creed with yet another 'king': Martin Luther King Jr."[5] In 2017, the journal *Italian Americana* published three articles concentrating on *Creed*. Only one other article published in 2016 analyzes *Creed*; however, Amelie Hastie uses the film to interweave her own narrative of surviving a nonmalignant brain tumor with that of Rocky's battle with cancer. Jim Cocola argues that "[Stallone] made *Creed* precisely by not making it, granting writer and director Ryan Coogler a shot at the title in the same way that Creed had granted Rocky a shot at the title forty years earlier."[6] Cocola's argument perpetuates the idea of Stallone as an actor, director, producer, and writer as a white savior. In reality, Coogler approached Stallone with the pitch for the reboot. In an interview with Kristopher Tapley, Coogler admits that it was his relationship with his father "that inspired [him] to write this story and to pitch it to Sly and pitch it to MGM."[7] Meanwhile, two other articles published in the same journal, Stephen Hock's "Negotiating Whiteness" and Jessica Maucione's "White Ethnic Racial Backlash and Black Millennial Counter-narrative Intersections of Race and Masculinity," apply White Studies to the *Rocky* and the *Creed* series. Although the critical lens of whiteness and the white messiah add to the existing scholarship, no one has explored the concepts of disability and abledness in these films or Italian American cinema in general. This paper's dual purpose is to examine the Italian American character Rocky as portrayed by non-Italian American filmmakers.

CREED SERIES AS LENS FOR DISABILITY AND ABLEDNESS

For a younger generation of viewers, Coogler's depiction of Rocky "The Italian Stallion" Balboa (Sylvester Stallone) shows how the dynamics between Adonis/Donnie Creed/Johnson (Michael B. Jordan) and Balboa acknowledges a past of strife and racism, while, at the same time, reinforces the importance of the nationwide movement Black Lives Matter. Coogler highlights the precarious nature of Italian Americans now seen as white and/or part of the dominant group, while recognizing the historical truth that they were not always white (Other and/or on the periphery).[8] Caple's sequel does not match the social criticism in *Creed*; however, he adds more complexity to the character of Bianca (Tessa Thompson), her relationship with Donnie, and their bond with their daughter, Amara. In an interview, Caple points out,

> With *Creed*, you have people like Ryan Coogler, Mike, Tessa, people of color, who are making a project together, collaborating. That's important. That's why this project particularly was important for me to do. It wasn't a platform for my career but about saying something on-screen and off-screen. That's more important to me than trying to do a bigger project.[9]

Caple acknowledges the first *Rocky* is a true underdog story, and it is his favorite one.[10] In addition to Bianca and Amara's deafness, Rocky battles cancer (*Creed*) and becomes a survivor; "he's taking his medication; he's in remission."[11] In *Contours of Ableism: The Production of Disability and Abledness*, Fiona Kumari Campbell argues, "central to regimes of ableism are two core elements. . . namely *the notion of the* normative (and normate individual) and the enforcement of a *constitutional divide* between perfected naturalized humanity and the aberrant, the unthinkable, quasi-human hybrid and therefore non-human."[12] Considering Campbell's binary, in the 1976 film, the Italian Stallion represents the "non-human" and Apollo the "normate individual." While in *Creed*, Tony "Little Duke" Burton (Wood Harris) finds training Donnie "unthinkable" compared to the other young black men at the Adelphi gym in Los Angeles, Coogler conveys the lives of African American young adults as precarious in US society. The Adelphi affords these black adolescents an opportunity. Like *Rocky IV*, in *Creed II* Caple Jr. encourages audiences to view Viktor Drago (Florian Munteanu) as they did his father, Ivan Drago (Dolph Lundgren), before him as "aberrant." They represent the other, the ones on the periphery of even Russian society; they live in drab housing somewhere in Kyiv, Ukraine. If characters with disabilities such as Bianca signify the other, then this motif connects Russians (Ivan and Viktor), African Americans (Apollo and Adonis), and Italian Americans (Rocky) as subordinate groups in the United States.

The hyphenated identity of these characters makes them interesting and complex because they oscillate between two cultures and for Bianca even more. She is a deaf person; she is African American, and she is a woman. Schwalbe et al. (2000) identify *othering* as "the process whereby a dominant group defines into existence an inferior group."[13] Othering "treats a male body and Caucasian features as signs of competence peremptorily discredits those with female bodies and African features."[14] Thus, African Americans (blacks), the deaf community, and Italian Americans embody the other, those who live on the fringes of US society. The first *Rocky* attempts to recoup working-class Italian Americans within a more generalized whiteness; however, Stallone's character embodies aspects of the non-dominant group because of his Italianness, and in the *Creed* series, Rocky's cancer produces a disability in the character. He undergoes treatment, while Donnie trains in the confines of the hospital. He runs up and down the staircase; he even shadowboxes and performs pushups in Rocky's room. Matthew Frye Jacobson argues that "if the Italian Stallion is indeed white, the film [*Rocky*] suggests, he is not *that* white."[15] Jacobson's point reinforces the idea that the character of the Italian Stallion in the original movie is not part of the dominant group. In both series, the spaces such as the ring, gym, and neighborhoods with economically and ethnically diverse members highlight the peripheral status and implicitly "non-whiteness" of Rocky and Donnie.

In addition, "preserving inequality requires maintaining boundaries between dominant and subordinate groups. These boundaries can be symbolic, interactional, spatial, or all of these."[16] The *Creed* series frustrates "these boundaries" by developing a black love story between Donnie and Bianca and a disruptive, multiracial definition of family with Balboa as a surrogate father figure to Adonis Creed. As screenwriter, Stallone did not develop the character's back-story; the audience assumes that Rocky's mother and father are dead in the original movie, which strengthens the similarity between Balboa and Donnie. Although Jaime Schultz argues that "white saviors, as the term suggests, are those characters who rescue people of color from dire circumstances because, for whatever reason, they cannot seem to do it of their own accord."[17] However, the Italian Stallion does not represent the white dominant group or white savior. Instead, Rocky Balboa in the *Creed* series (directed by African American directors) epitomizes a hybrid identity. In an interview for *ScreenCrush*, Matt Singer asked Steven Caple how Stallone had this script, but also how he felt that it needed some work; it required a younger generation's voice. For Caple, Black people represented that missing voice.[18] Indeed, some or possibly most moviegoers see Balboa as white; however, some Italian Americans know the immigration history of Italians. Donna R. Gabaccia writes that "northern Italians increasingly disparaged southerners in the language of scientific racism."[19] These prejudices moved across the Atlantic and pervaded American society. Thus, stereotypes of southern Italians continue into the present with constant references to Coppola's *The Godfather* and Italian Americans (especially Sicilians) as always associated with the Mafia and criminal activity. Indeed, the Italian Stallion embraces his palooka nature in *Rocky* and *Rocky II*; however, in *Rocky Balboa* and the *Creed* series, Balboa owns a restaurant and makes pasta, which audiences never witnessed in the previous installments. Perhaps, Stallone as screenwriter borrowed from either Martin Scorsese's *Raging Bull* or Jake LaMotta's memoir, *Raging Bull: My Story*, in order to present the aging Italian Stallion mingling with customers about his accomplishments as a fighter.

In the *Creed* series, Rocky's connection with the hospitality industry plays into stereotypes of Italian Americans; however, Coogler includes moments that differentiate Rocky's food from Donnie and Bianca's ethnic cooking. In "What is 'Italian American' Cinema?" Ben Lawton argues that "many Italian Americans, like many other ethnics, feel that they are on the margins, that they are not at the center of either culture, Italian or American."[20] For example, Rocky earns money working as a collector for "a second-rate loan shark," and his behavior is "constrained and determined" by his existence in a blue-collar Philadelphia neighborhood. In Stallone's screenplay, Balboa lives in an apartment in the most deprived section of South Philly. "The one-room apartment is drab" with a mattress "nailed against the far wall . . . used as a punching bag. Stuffing spills out of the center."[21] These details reveal Rocky as empowered but on the fringe of Philadelphian society. In a similar manner, Apollo remains marginalized from the African American community even though he is heavyweight champion of the world. Although probably impossible for audiences in the 1970s to imagine an African American president, Apollo epitomizes the American dream, which is to break through the barriers of one's humble social station. Avildsen depicts him as a perceptive businessperson; Creed even parades into the ring as George Washington and imitates Uncle Sam.

In *Creed*'s plot, Adonis Johnson's birth mother had an extramarital affair with Apollo Creed (Carl Weathers). Donnie grows up in foster care until Apollo's wife, Mary Anne Creed (Phylicia Rashad), raises him as her own son. Coogler's casting of the most famous black television mother, Claire Huxtable, from the sitcom *The Cosby Show* highlights the significance of an 80s show that had a married black couple who were both successful professionals: Cliff Huxtable, an obstetrician and Claire Huxtable, an attorney. In *Creed II*, Bianca and Donnie continue this positive portrayal of successful, married African Americans; both characters epitomize independent professionals: a singer and a boxer. Coogler's decision to include positive representations demonstrates the importance of the Black Lives Matter movement both to him and to Caple. As the widow of Apollo Creed, Mary Anne lives in a gated mansion that contrasts with Rocky's skid row-like apartment and Donnie's youth in and out of juvenile detention centers and foster homes. In *Yearning: Race, Gender and Cultural Politics*, bell hooks posits that the margin is "more than a site of deprivation . . . it is also the site of radical possibility, a space of resistance."[22] Coogler's *Creed* and Caple's *Creed II* become "the site of radical possibility" and "resistance." Donnie exemplifies the Black Lives Matter movement because of his experiences as a young black man with no father and no mother who spends significant time behind bars in juvenile detention; however, in this fictional story, he grows up to beat the odds. Coogler underscores outward signs of race, as Donnie arrives in Philadelphia in a taxi advertising Hershey Chocolate on its roof, perhaps reminiscent of New Orleans Mayor Ray Nagin who called New Orleans a chocolate city on national television during the 2005 news coverage of Hurricane Katrina and its aftermath. According to the 2017 United States Census, Philadelphia County is 44.8 percent White and 43.9 percent Black or African American. North Philly is 49.8 percent Non-Hispanic Black, and South Philly is 51.8 percent Non-Hispanic White.[23] These statistics demonstrate the makeup of Philadelphia as roughly half white and half black. Thus, Italian Americans contributed to South Philly demographics of the 1970s and to a certain extent today, while African Americans represent a significant number in North Philly, which is why the spatial movement from Mighty Mick's to Front Street gym has so much importance. In addition, North Philly, where Rocky trains Donnie, is mostly black, while South Philly where Rocky lived and trained in the original film is mostly white. In *Creed II*, Donnie and Bianca relocate to Los Angeles to be closer to Donnie's mother and to take Bianca's musical career to the next level. Donnie purchases an apartment large enough to include a music studio for Bianca. Although 2017 represented the twenty-fifth anniversary of the Los Angeles riots, the scenes with Donnie and Bianca demonstrate an upward mobility. The Rodney King verdict triggered riots, which the black community saw as an act of injustice. The jury acquitted four white police officers for usage of excessive force in the arrest and beating of the African American motorist Rodney King. George Holliday filmed the incident from his nearby balcony and sent the footage to a local news station. Similarly to *The Cosby Show*, the *Creed* series emphasizes positive images of African Americans. Perhaps, more importantly, Ryan Coogler and Steven Caple Jr. represent the next generation of African American filmmakers who depict positive portrayals of African Americans. In addition, Coogler, who went on to direct *Black Panther* (2018), hired the best women for positions behind the scenes such as Rachel Morrison who is the first woman nominated for an Oscar in cinematography.[24]

HISTORY: OTHERING ITALIANS

In order to see Rocky Balboa as something other than white, one needs to understand how the dominant group in the United States viewed Italians and/or Sicilians. In "'No Color Barrier': Italians, Race, and Power in the United States," Thomas A. Guglielmo cites two historical examples of Italians as blacks:

one newspaper wrote, "When we speak of white man's government, they [Italians] are as black as the blackest Negro in existence." In the sugarcane fields of Louisiana, one Sicilian American recalled, "The boss used to call us niggers" and "told us that we weren't white men."[25]

Although *Rocky* develops problematic depictions of Italian Americans and African Americans, Coogler and Caple Jr. position Balboa and his Italianness in stark contrast to the *Rocky* series. Audiences must contend with the question: Is Rocky Balboa white? Guglielmo's examples problematize not only the color line regarding Italians, Italian Americans, and/or Sicilian Americans but also their marginalization as "other." Although in the 21st century a number of Italian Americans identify with the Anglo-Saxon dominant group, in films such as *Rocky* and the *Creed* series, the Italian American Balboa finds himself part of the subordinate group. In "Invisible People: Shadows and Light in Italian American Culture," Fred Gardaphé argues,

> Italian Americans are invisible people. Not because people refuse to see them, but because, for the most part, they refuse to be seen. Italian Americans became invisible the moment they could pass themselves off as being white. And since then they have gone to great extremes to avoid being identified as anything but white, they have even hidden the history of being people of color.[26]

In *Rocky*, Apollo typifies aspects of the dominant culture. He is the heavyweight champion, is educated, and demonstrates business prowess. On the other hand, Rocky represents the opposite; he is a "ham and egger," uneducated, and has no business acumen. The connotations of the phrase "ham and egger" range from ordinary to loser. Like his father, Donnie is educated. He works in a corner office with a view; however, he chooses boxing over a desk job. The containment of "normative" versus "non-human" and center versus margin erodes. Coogler repositions Rocky from the star in six films to the supporting role; however, the Italian Stallion transforms into something more. For instance, when Donnie decides to move in with Rocky, Bianca yells down from her window, "your uncle, he's white?" referring to Balboa, and he responds, "yea, long time now." This crucial moment concentrates on ethnic and racial positioning. The dominant culture sees Rocky "the Italian Stallion" Balboa as white, perhaps unaware of the "hidden. . . history of being people of color." In the original *Rocky*, Stallone's character represents the other even more than Apollo Creed does, who is heavyweight champion of the world. Rocky's working-class background, his job as a leg breaker for a small-time mob figure, and his Italian heritage reinforce his inclusion in the subordinate group. Several plotlines reinforce Balboa's peripheral status: collecting for the local loan shark, Gazzo (Joe Spinell), and boxing at neighborhood club bouts. Even his Italian American heritage as "the Italian Stallion" highlights Rocky as other. In many respects, Apollo—a character, based partially on Muhammad Ali—displays features of the dominant group in terms of his stature, wealth, and physical prowess, even though he is African American. Film scholars have criticized the *Rocky* series for the construct of Balboa as the great white hope that goes the distance and breaks Apollo's ribs; however, Creed inhabits both the dominant and the subordinate groups simultaneously. In the original film, the African American Apollo receives the most complex treatment as a character.

Even before the *Creed* series reboot, Mighty Mick's gym encloses the characters; the locations of Philadelphia and Los Angeles perform the same function. Lawrence Webb argues that the film *Rocky* "develops a strong sense of containment within the Italian neighborhood through a series of distinctive locations: the boxing gym and the pet shop, the docks and peripheral industrial spaces, the characteristic Philadelphia row houses and street corners."[27] In both series, the boxing gym represents a mixed space of black, brown, and white fighters. In the original screenplay, Stallone describes Mighty Mick's as "fifty percent Black—thirty-five percent Latin—ten percent white—five percent other."[28] For the climactic battle between the two fighters, Apollo inhabits George Washington in his theatrical entrance to fight, and once inside the ring, becomes Uncle Sam, pointing at Rocky and shouting: "I want you." Even Apollo Creed's iconic red, white, and blue boxer trunks transform throughout the three films. In *Rocky*, Apollo wears the iconic American flag version. In *Creed*, Mary Anne presents Donnie with a gift: the red, white, and blue trunks with Creed on the front and Johnson on the back. Donnie dons them in his fight against Ricky Conlen (Tony Bellew), while in *Creed II*, the trunks start the same, but for the second fight against Viktor Drago, they are shaded black. Similar to Colin Kaepernick, the NFL player taking a knee during the sounding of the national anthem to draw attention to the police shootings of unarmed black men, the black boxing trunks come to symbolize the importance of African Americans as role models. In *Creed II*, Donnie transcends his parentless condition to become world champion as his father Apollo did, and, at the same time, falls in love with a strong independent woman with progressive hearing loss.

In addition to the boxing trunks, several other similarities materialize in the original of each series. For *Rocky*'s title sequence, the word ROCKY appears in all white as it enters on the right and exits the screen on the left. The conditioned spectator expects a white hero. During the opening sequence, the first image to appear after the title is that of a white Christ holding the communion wafer and chalice. Then the camera pans down toward the ring to Rocky, and the audience can make out the sign below Christ: Resurrection AD. As has been discussed by other critics, Rocky appears to be a Christ-like figure. Hernán Vera and Andrew M. Gordon interpret Rocky's character as a "white messiah . . . who triumphs despite impossible odds."[29] Although a legitimate critique, especially of the other films in the franchise, the new reboot boasts two African American writers and directors who include storylines imperative to their community, while, at the same time, recognizing the importance of Balboa. Donnie encourages Rocky to fight cancer, and in the sequel, Rocky takes medication as maintenance therapy. In a sense, Donnie represents Balboa's "black" messiah.

In *Creed*, Coogler films several scenes in the detention center. Mary Anne, Apollo Creed's wife, informs the younger Adonis that he had a father. The boy asks what his name was. Then the opening sequence emerges from a black background, moves to the forefront of the screen, looks degraded, and faded to almost black and white. The title sequences, reminiscent of the *Rocky* series, signal the movement from the binary of white and black to the more complex racial makeup of the *Creed* series. Coogler creates parallels between Rocky and Donnie, and even the patrons watching Rocky and Donnie's opening fights represent mixed audiences. In *Rocky*, the Italian Stallion first brawls Spider Rico, a Puerto Rican, played by a former Argentine heavyweight boxer, Pedro Lovell. The *Rocky* screenplay describes the club as "a large unemptied trash-can" and the spectators "resemble specters."[30] The script's descriptions strengthen the idea of the ring as a receptacle and that these boxers survive on the periphery in a non-human-like state. After Balboa wins the match, a woman from the audience calls him a "bum." Later, Mickey (Burgess Meredith), owner of the gym and eventually Rocky's trainer, reinforces the sentiment when he comments on Rocky's win against Spider Rico: "he's a bum." Rocky responds, "you think everyone I fight is a bum." Mick remarks, "well, ain't they?" Balboa's working-class background as a thug for a neighborhood loan shark heightens his isolation and peripheral status. Although a bum does not represent a "non-human," the othering putdown discredits Balboa and his male body and Caucasian features.

Although not an intimidating enforcer like Rocky, Donnie—the product of Apollo's infidelity—presents himself as an outsider, too; he likes to fight both as a child and as an adult. Just as in Rocky's opening match, Donnie prepares for a fight against a Mexican boxer in Tijuana, Mexico. Coogler's screenplay describes "a mural of Jesus Christ,"[31] which might remind some audience members of Balboa's bout with Spider Rico. In that scene, there is an image of Christ holding a chalice and Eucharist; however, for whatever reason, the mural does not appear in *Creed*. The camera pans down to reveal dank surroundings where disinterested patrons watch a brutal bout that underscores how insignificant life is in this impoverished city. These types of matches emphasize their status as outsiders to the mainstream boxing world represented by Mickey and Mighty Mick's Boxing as well as Duke (Tony Burton) and his son, Tony "Little Duke," and the Delphi Boxing Academy Home of Apollo Creed. In *Rocky* and *Rocky II*, the credits list Duke as Apollo's trainer; only in *Rocky III* and the other sequels does he have a name listed. The actor and character become increasingly more important with each new installment, and for the *Creed* series, Coogler writes a script with "Little Duke" as the son of "Apollo's trainer." The act of naming brings more humanity to the characters; they are not two-dimensional cutouts. Audiences do not learn Bianca's last name, Taylor, until *Creed II* when Donnie proposes to her in Las Vegas.

Other examples of containment include Donnie's office, Mary Anne's mansion, Rocky's restaurant, Adrian's, with the dining room and basement kitchen, and Rocky's, Donnie's, and Bianca's apartments. Donnie relocates to Philadelphia because Tony will not train him. Rocky oversees Donnie not at Mighty Mick's in South Philly, but at the Front Street Gym in North Philly. Each neighborhood becomes a repository: South Philly of the 70s as Italian American and North Philly as African American in 2015. In *Creed II*, once Bianca and Donnie return from his victory over Wheeler, Bianca confronts Donnie about returning to Los Angeles. She cites several reasons, such as his mother and more opportunities to get Bianca's music out. Donnie shows reluctance because he worries about Rocky. However, Rocky refuses to train Donnie, so Donnie seeks "Little Duke" instead, in order to prepare for his bout against Viktor Drago, which bolsters the couple's decision to relocate to LA. Before the climax, the containment switches from gyms with four walls to a desert sequence where Tony and Rocky prepare Donnie for his rematch. Donnie not only endures sledgehammer workouts, but must also adapt to extreme heat and cold in the desert.

As an adult, Donnie lives with his mother, Mary Anne. He watches his father's first fight against Rocky projected against the wall. He then surprises the audience by shadow boxing as the Italian Stallion and not his father, Apollo. Donnie fights Apollo too, angry about his father's infidelity and accidental death (in *Rocky III* where Ivan Drago kills Apollo in an exhibition match) that left him an orphan. This scene foreshadows the new family dynamics in *Creed* and *Creed II*. The father-son dynamic begins with Rocky and Donnie, and Caple develops it even further with multiple ones: Rocky and Donnie, Ivan and Viktor, Rocky and Robert, and Apollo and Donnie. Balboa, as a proxy for Apollo, incorporates a multiracial dynamic. He coaches Donnie not just in the ring but also in life. He plays as intermediary, and facilitates Donnie's relationship with Bianca. Thus, Mary Anne and Rocky become Donnie's adoptive parents. Even the addition of Ivan and Viktor Drago brings a motif of the outsider because of their status as Russians, "aberrant" and "hybrid human" to the boxing audiences in the United States. Caple's *Creed II* develops several father/son pairings. Although Stallone's direction and screenplay for *Rocky IV* depicted Ivan Drago as a malevolent, Soviet symbol, Caple's direction presents the Soviets as humans, too. Although US audiences cheer for Donnie's victory over the Russian, the scene between Viktor's scenes with his estranged mother reveal a more complex character, in comparison to his father's one-dimensionality in *Rocky IV*.

Ivan pressures Viktor to reclaim his missed opportunity to beat an American heavyweight champion.

Like the friendship that develops between Balboa and Apollo Creed over the course of three sequels, a sort of intimacy flourishes between Rocky and Donnie. He moves in with Rocky and bunks in Paulie's (Burt Young) room. Coogler shows us his familiarity with cinematic history and films the pair walking down the street; Donnie puts his arm around Rocky and imitates Marlon Brando's Don Corleone by saying, "Let me make him an offer he can't refuse." The term, "Unc," and the embrace strengthen and develop the bond between the two, which continues to blossom in the sequel. Although both Rocky and Creed sexualize the male body, the love interests (Adrian in *Rocky* and Bianca in *Creed*) stabilize the triangle dynamics. Aaron Baker and Juliann Vitullo point out, "Central to these urban communities are conservative characterizations of Italian-American women devoted to home and family, revered and protected for their support and self-sacrifice. . . . Talia Shire established her career playing this kind of woman in *The Godfather* and *Rocky* films."[32] In the original screenplay, Adrian's last name is Klein,[33] a common Jewish surname; however, Father Carmine (Paul Micale) uses Adrian's maiden name, Pennino, for the first and only time in *Rocky II* during the marriage ceremony in the Catholic Church. A failure to provide last names for characters such as Tony and Adrian demonstrates one problematic thread in the Rocky series. Supporting characters such as Apollo's black trainer and Rocky's love interest do not require more development; each one's identity connects with the more powerful, more important protagonist/antagonist. Although in *Rocky Balboa* and the *Creed* series, the Italian Stallion visits the grave of Paulie and Adrian, their last name is only mentioned once in the previous five films.

In the 1976 film, Rocky's character allows Apollo to transform from the epitome of the capitalist entrepreneur—a fighter wrapped up in the business of boxing—to the top athlete he exemplified earlier in his career. For example, musing over the match-up, Apollo laughs, "Apollo Creed versus the Italian Stallion . . . sounds like a damn monster movie." Apollo develops the historical rhetoric of his heavyweight title fight when he discovers Rocky, or rather Balboa's name, "the Italian Stallion." The fight's significance changes from one of patriotic rhetoric to that of racial melodrama when Apollo reflects, "who discovered America? An Italian, right? What would be better than to get it on with one of his descendants?" In "The Religious Boundaries of Inbetween People: Street Feste and the Problem of the Dark-Skinned Other in Italian Harlem: 1920–1990," Robert Orsi explains, "that Italian-American history began in racially inflected circumstances everywhere in the United States . . . and who were described as lazy, criminal, sexually irresponsible, and emotionally volatile."[34] Indeed, Rocky personifies some of these traits such as his work for Gazzo, a street-level "criminal," and his outbursts with Mickey in his apartment and with Paulie at the meatpacking plant, both "emotionally volatile." In an interview, Coogler remembers his favorite iconic moments from the original *Rocky*: "the scene where Mickey comes back to his apartment and tries to convince Rocky to [accept the challenge from Apollo Creed], and then Rocky has that breakdown where" the audience "see[s] his anger" and "realize[s] how broken he is."[35] The reconciliation between Rocky and Mickey occurs in the streets of Philadelphia and not in Balboa's row house.

Coogler's *Creed* breaks down the containment and transforms it. Indeed, Coogler and Caple concentrate on developing Bianca, Donnie's girlfriend and future wife, who represents a change agent more so than Adrian does. After his first meeting with Rocky, Donnie calls him "Unc" throughout the rest of the series. The term of endearment relies on the construction of Rocky and Donnie as family, and both directors fully integrate Bianca into the dynamic. In *Creed*, Bianca and Donnie cook for Rocky after his cancer treatment and hospitalization. He comments on the meal they prepared and on how his food always has some type of sauce. He brings Bianca to view Donnie's match in Liverpool, England, as a surprise. This moment illustrates how Rocky acts as a loving father to Donnie, who feels despondent after a recent argument with Bianca before his title bout against Ricky Conlen. Interestingly, Donnie's and Bianca's love story parallels Rocky's and Adrian's; however, Bianca represents a strong, independent woman, unlike Adrian in the *Rocky* series. She enters various spaces such as the dressing room and the ring itself for both the Leo "The Lion" Sporino (Gabe Rosado) and "Pretty" Ricky Conlan fights (*Creed*) as well as the Danny "Stuntman" Wheeler (Andre Ward) and Viktor Drago matches (*Creed II*). She watches all fights ringside, cooks and sleeps in Rocky's house, and sings to the packed stadium during Donnie's remarkable entrance to fight Viktor in Russia. In an interview, Coogler states,

> Bianca represented Philadelphia today. She also represented the millennial generation. . . . Women are very career-oriented. We're dealing with the lean-in generation, especially in the African American community. Women know what they want to do. They know what they want out of relationships. They know what they want professionally. [36]

A unique treatment of Bianca is the history of her progressive hearing loss, which Coogler created and Caple Jr. further develops. In addition, as Donnie's relationship with Bianca blossoms, so does his bond with Rocky. For instance, Donnie demands that the Italian Stallion fight his disease, and Donnie and Bianca care for him during and after his treatments.

An important dimension of the *Creed* series involves Bianca's hearing loss or deafness. Although not specified in either film, Bianca most likely suffers from sensorineural hearing loss. Interestingly, Donnie embraces Bianca and her flaws. Only after the film's release in a series of interviews do audiences learn of details regarding the script. For example, Coogler reveals, "it was very interesting with progressive hearing loss. My fiancée is a sign language interpreter and her mother has hearing loss. Her younger sister has hearing loss. So it was great to kind of bring awareness to those folks."[37] In *Creed*, Bianca pursues her musical career playing at Johnny Brendas and the Electric Factory.[38] Bianca concentrates on her music while she still can hear. During their first meeting, Donnie cannot sleep because of loud music coming from a downstairs apartment. He first knocks with his hand, then uses his foot to pound even louder. When the door opens, Bianca appears, and his anger morphs into interest. Later, on their first date, he confronts Bianca about her hearing aids while eating at Max's Cheesesteaks. Donnie does not utter the question, but rather points to his right ear. Bianca replies that she has progressive hearing loss and only recently started wearing the hearing aids. Looking down, Donnie starts but does not finish his sentence. Instead, the audience witnesses language broken down with silent pauses mimicking the eventual complete loss of hearing that Bianca acknowledges. Neither character mentions the word deaf. Campbell asserts, "the disabled body induces a fear as being a body out of control because of its appearance of uncontainability."[39] Donnie, however, never fears Bianca's independence or progressive hearing loss; instead, he embraces both. He supports her independent musical pursuit both in Philadelphia and later in Los Angeles. Coogler acknowledges, "Philadelphia is a city that's known for its sports and its known for its music . . . that's how Bianca's character evolved into this musician, and a musician who makes her own music. She produces her own stuff. She leads the band, and that's very much a part of the now, how music is made now with technology. It's DIY."[40]

In *Creed II*, Bianca adjusts her hearing aids as she listens to the roar of the crowd in anticipation of Donnie's heavyweight championship bout against Danny 'Stuntman' Wheeler. In the dressing room, she signs to Donnie: "did you take a shit yet?" The moment, of course, provides comic relief referencing a similar moment in the first film, but also demonstrates that Donnie and Bianca communicate using sign language as well as spoken language. In this scene, Caple acknowledges Coogler and the original movie, and proves to audiences that Donnie loves Bianca; he learns sign language between the beginnings of their relationship to this moment. Throughout *Creed*, audiences witness several scenes where Donnie and Bianca share headphones and listen to her music. Sound becomes a character that continues in *Creed II*. Although an element of "uncontainability" connects with Bianca's progressive hearing loss, Donnie enters the silence and learns sign language.

When Donnie and Bianca relocate to Los Angeles in *Creed II*, audiences become aware that Bianca is pregnant. First, she claims that the flight made her sick. Then Mary Anne observes Bianca at the dinner table and asks, "how far along are you?" Later that night in their bedroom, Bianca confides in Donnie: "what if the baby can't, D? Can't hear? You know it can be hereditary, right?" Campbell posits, "from the moment a child is born, he/she emerges into a world where he/she receives messages that to be disabled is to be *less than*, a world where disability is *tolerated*, but in the *final instance*, is *inherently negative*."[41] The *Creed* series concentrates on the importance of strong female characters. In stark contrast to *Rocky II*, where Rocky and Adrian have a boy, in *Creed II*, Donnie and Bianca have a girl. Rather than stressing the importance of a firstborn son to carry on the family name, Caple updates and adds to the importance of women and their equal roles with, rather than support for, husbands and their endeavors. Adrian worked in a pet store, while Bianca makes music. Coogler and Caple deserve credit for writing, casting, and developing a fierce, liberated character. Unlike Adrian, who waits in the dressing room for Rocky, Bianca navigates male spaces with ease. In *Creed II*, she leads Donnie and his entourage to the ring; she refuses docility. In addition, Donnie and Bianca grapple with her pregnancy in the bathroom as they ascertain the results of the over-the-counter pregnancy test. Although they both struggle with several concerns such as the timing, the main apprehension relates to whether or not the child will inherent Bianca's disability. Campbell asserts, "the aim of CIs [Cochlear Implants] is to simulate (fabricate) 'hearing' in order to facilitate the assimilation of deaf individuals into the dominant hearing world, thereby ensuring the deaf become productive citizens."[42] Like Rocky as Italian American and Apollo and Donnie as African Americans, a deaf child functions as another example of how the dominant group positions the other as "*less than*." While still in the hospital, Amara has a hearing screen. The medical technician tells the couple that "we are not seeing any waves or spikes." One can deduce the staff administered an Otoacoustic Emmisions (OAE) test, which measures sound waves produced in the inner ear. Donnie and Bianca communicating through sign at the Wheeler fight and the family's visit to Apollo's grave at the end frame the narrative importance of ableism. If the African American represents the other, and the other has progressive hearing loss, then that character turns into a kind of other-other.

In the final scene of *Creed II*, Donnie and Bianca bring Amara to Apollo's grave. In plain view, Amara wears hearing aids. Campbell continues, "like other forms of different bodies considered impaired, the life of Deaf people (because of deafness) has been considered one that is inherently negative—silent and pitiful."[43] The *Creed* series challenges the dominant white culture and the notion that Italianness, blackness, and/or deafness are "inherently negative—silent and pitiful." On the contrary, the audience does not find Amara and especially Bianca pitiful. Bianca acts as a strong, autonomous woman who pursues her career, and, at the same time, supports Donnie's violent life as a boxer. Although Stallone, as Balboa in the *Rocky* series, epitomized the palooka, Rocky as a thoughtful trainer and father figure to Donnie transcends that role, and Coogler and Caple Jr. ensure that Michael B. Jordan's Adonis Creed exemplifies an articulate, educated African American boxer who embraces his wife's progressive hearing, and is ready to accept their deaf daughter. Furthermore, Edward Dolnick argues that the deaf community is "simply a linguistic minority (speaking American Sign Language) and [is] no more in need of a cure than are Haitians or Hispanics."[44] Important to this discourse on disability studies, Donnie turns to Bianca in his rematch against Viktor Drago, and she signs to him: "you got this." Donnie nods his head in understanding. This powerful moment reinforces Dolnick's argument about deafness as "a linguistic minority." Between *Creed* and *Creed II*, Donnie learns how to sign. Thus, he becomes an accepted member of the community; however, Bianca's and Amara's "non-abledness" makes them outsiders, the other-other. Donnie negotiates both the hearing and deaf world.

The African American couple, Donnie and Bianca, negotiate an American society where being black and deaf means one is less than the dominant group. "Oppressed people," Bonnie Burstow explains, "are routinely worn down by the insidious trauma involved in living day after day in a sexist, racist, classist, homophobic, and ableist society."[45] Apollo, Rocky, Donnie, and Bianca all fit this image. Nevertheless, in the *Creed* series, each finds a way to overcome the barriers placed before them by American society. The love story between Donnie and Bianca thrives over the course of the two films. The subplot involving Bianca's progressive hearing loss heightens the dichotomies of "normate" (regular) versus "aberrant," center versus periphery, and dominant versus subordinate. The inclusion of signing and passing a hereditary trait to one's child intensifies the conversations Coogler and Caple Jr. explore regarding ableism, classism, homophobia, racism, and sexism.

In the twelfth round against "Pretty" Ricky Conlan, Donnie admits to Rocky that he still has to prove that he was not a mistake. The audience realizes that his rage and obsessive fighting stems from the fact that he was the result of an extramarital affair. Donnie feels responsible for his own existence despite his innocence; however, he struggles throughout to accept himself as a valuable "normate" individual. Thus, Donnie's ability to go the distance with Conlan, like Balboa's ability to do the same with Apollo, illustrates the dominant group's power of the other. Donnie grows up without a mother and a father. However, in the *Rocky* series, Mary Anne (Lavelle Roby in *Rocky*; Sylvia Meals in *Rocky II* and *Rocky IV*) and Apollo represent a married African American couple, which predates *The Cosby Show*. Although Lavelle Roby as Mary Anne did not receive an on-screen credit in the main or end titles, Sylvia Meals, who plays Mary Anne in two of the sequels, did. Once again, the importance of naming comes in later sequels or, in the case of Adrian and Bianca, during the marriage and proposal scenes. Supporting characters such as characters of color or women deserve the recognition of naming. The failure to name connects with the binary of dominant versus the subordinate, able versus disabled.

Creed II ends at Apollo's grave, where Donnie reenacts the ritual that audiences witnessed in *Rocky Balboa* and the *Creed* series with Rocky visiting Paulie and Adrian's two plots. Rocky reconnects with his son, Robert, and his grandson, Logan. The Italian Stallion travels to and from Los Angeles, and perhaps that movement and his inclusion in Donnie and Bianca's life allow him to seek out his independent son. Rocky attempts to call Robert, while at the hospital when Bianca gives birth to Amara; however, he hangs up the receiver. The dynamics of this new family demonstrates to him the importance of his own. Balboa's relationship with Donnie over the course of two movies teaches him about the importance of family again. Rocky winds up with two, and realizes that both families make life worth living. Donnie exemplifies the agency that animates the Italian Stallion to seek treatment for his cancer and finally to reconnect with his estranged son. Even Ivan and Viktor appear in a final scene running together. Meanwhile, Donnie introduces Apollo to his granddaughter, Amara, who has binaural hearing aids. Caple Jr. highlights the circle of life with two generations of Creeds present. In addition, Donnie and Bianca overcome the sexist, racist, and ableist environment by concentrating on their careers and their relationship. Thus, *Creed II* returns audiences to *Rocky IV* and Rocky's bereavement of Apollo; however, Amara's addition signifies rebirth and hope.

Avildsen, Coogler, and Caple Jr. all represent non-Italian filmmakers whose movies deserve critical attention alongside those of Coppola and Scorsese. Rocky—as an Italian American—and Donnie—as an African American—wrestle against the dominant group because as outsiders they inhabit the periphery. Identifying the characters as hyphenated identities places them in the subordinate group. Although Rocky, because the color of his skin, may be identified as white or part of the dominant group, enough markers in all three films prevent the audience from making that determination, or, at the very least, from viewing him as 100 percent white. In order to develop Italian American Studies, scholars need to expand their scope or, in this case, definition, of "works by Italian-American directors who treat Italian-American subjects." The *Rocky* and *Creed* series intersect and deliver opportunities for the exploration of African American and Italian American topics and the themes of agency. Most interesting, the *Creed* series introduces audiences to a 21st century black, female lead, Bianca, who has progressive hearing loss. She both inhabits and transcends her traditional role as the Adrian figure: girlfriend, wife, and mother. She refuses the status of other and demonstrates self-determination and fearlessness. In terms of space, she moves in and out of the male spheres such as the boxing ring. The *Rocky*, but, more importantly, the *Creed* series offers young black men and women role models, especially when faced with adversities such as hearing loss, pregnancy, and dual careers, as well as a deaf child and living on the fringes of society. Three types of marginalization, ethnic, racial, and sensory disability occur in these films. Italian American identity adds to the discourses of access and privilege around African American and disabled bodies.

NOTES

1. Robert Casillo, "Moments in Italian-American Cinema: From Little Caesar to Coppola and Scorsese," in *From the Margins: Writing in Italian Americana*, ed. Anthony Julian Tamburri, Paolo Giordano, and Fred L. Gardaphé (West Lafayett, IN: Purdue University Press, 2000), 394.

2. Jacqueline Reich, "'Ain't Nothing Over 'til It's Over': The Boxing Film, Race, and the *Rocky* Series," in *Mediated Ethnicity: New Italian-American Cinema*, ed. Giuliana Muscio, Joseph Sciora, Giovanni Spagnoletti, and Anthony Julian Tamburri (New York: John D. Calandra Italian American Institute, 2010), 182.

3. Lawrence Webb, "New Hollywood in the Rust Belt: Urban Decline and Downtown Renaissance in *The King of Marvin Gardens* and *Rocky*," *Cinema Journal* 54, no. 4 (2015): 118.

4. Brett Conway, "To Roll Back the Rock(y): White Male-Absence in the *Rocky* Series," *Aethlon: The Journal of Sport Literature* 22, no. 1 (2004): 77.

5. Joel W. Martin, "Redeeming America: *Rocky* as Ritual Racial Drama," in *Screening the Sacred: Religion, Myth, and Ideology in Popular American Film*, ed. Joel W. Martin and Conrad E. Ostwalt Jr. (Boulder, CO: Westview Press): 132.

6. Jim Cocola, "Stallone's *Creed*," *Italian Americana* 35, no. 2 (2017): 121.

7. Kristopher Tapley, "Ryan Coogler on *Creed*, Filmmaking as Journalism and the Need for Female Voices (Q&A)," *Variety*, January 5, 2016, http://variety.com/2016/film/in-contention/creed-director-ryan-coogler-on-filmmaking-as-journalism-andthe-importance-of-female-voices-1201670613/.

8. See Guglielmo and Salerno.

9. Zack Sharf, "*Creed II* Director Steven Caple Jr. on Ryan Coogler's Advice and Directing a Rocky Film after a Low-Budget Indie—Exclusive," September 28, 2018, https://www.indiewire.com/2018/09/creed-2-steven-caple-jr-interview-replacing-ryan-coogler-1202007531/.

10. Ibid.

11. Ibid.

12. Fiona Kumari Campbell, *Contours of Ableism: The Production of Disability and Abledness* (New York: Palgrave Macmillan, 2006): 6.

13. Michael Schwable et al., "Generic Processes in the Reproduction of Inequality: An Interactionist Analysis," *Social Forces* 79, no. 2 (2000): 422.

14. Schwable, 424.

15. Matthew Frye Jacobs, *Roots Too: White Ethnic Revival in Post-Civil Rights America* (Cambridge: Harvard University Press, 2006): 101 [emphasis in original].

16. Schwable, 430.

17. Jamie Schultz, "*Glory Road* and the White Savior Historical Sport Film," *Journal of Popular Film and Television* 42, no. 4 (2014): 206.

18. Matt Singer, "Director Steven Caple Jr. on Directing *Creed II* and Ranking *Rocky*s," *ScreenCrush*, November 21, 2018, https://screencrush.com/steven-caple-jr-creed-2-interview/.

19. Donna R. Gabaccia, *Italy's Many Diasporas* (Seattle: University of Washington Press, 2000), 73.

20. Ben Lawton, "What Is 'Italian American' Cinema?" *Voices in Italian Americana: VIA* 6, no. 1 (1995): 40.

21. Ibid., 5.

22. bell hooks, *Yearning: Race, Gender and Cultural Politics* (Boston: South End Press, 1990): 149.

23. QuickFacts: Philadelphia County, Pennsylvania. United States Census, July 1, 2017, https:www.census.gov/quickfacts/philadelphiacountypennsylvania.

24. Esme Douglas, "Director Ryan Coogler Wants to Celebrate the Women behind the Production of '*Black Panther*,'" *HelloGiggles*, February 5, 2018, https://hellogiggles.com/news/ryan-coogler-black-panther-women-behind-scenes/.

25. Thomas A. Guglielmo, "'No Color Barrier': Italians, Race, and Power in the United States," in *Are Italians White? How Race Is Made in America*, ed. Jennifer Guglielmo and Salvatore Salerno (New York: Routledge, 2003): 36.

26. Fred Gardaphé, "Invisible People: Shadows and Light in Italian American Culture," in *Anti-Italianism: Essays on a Prejudice*, ed. William J. Connell and Fred Gardaphé (New York: Palgrave Macmillan, 2011): 1.

27. Webb, 119.

28. Stallone, 15.

29. Hernán Vera and Andrew M. Gordon, "The Beautiful American: Sincere Fictions of the White Messiah in Hollywood Movies," in *White Out: The Continuing Significance of Racism*, ed. Ashley W. Doane and Eduardo Bonilla-Silva (New York: Routledge, 2003): 119.

30. Stallone, 2.

31. Ryan Coogler, "Creed," Film script, 2015, 2.

32. Aaron Baker and Juliann Vitullo, "Screening the Italian-American Male," in *Masculinity: Bodies, Movies, Culture*, ed. Peter Lehman (New York: Routledge, 2001): 214.

33. Stallone, 9.

34. Robert Orsi, "The Religious Boundaries of Inbetween People: Street Feste and the Problem of the Dark-Skinned Other in Italian Harlem: 1920–1990," *American Quarterly* 44, no. 3 (1992): 314–15.

35. Mike Fleming Jr., "How Director Ryan Coogler's Own Father-Son Saga Fueled *Rocky* Revival *Creed*," Deadline, November 19, 2015, https://deadline.com/2015/11/ryan-coogler-creed-rocky-balboa-sylvester-stallone-michael-b-jordan-1201629948/.

36. Tapley.

37. Tapley.

38. The Electric Factory is a music venue where The Roots and John Legend got their start.

39. Campbell, 8.

40. Tapley.

41. Campbell, 17.

42. Campbell, 90.

43. Campbell, 92.

44. Edward Dolnick, "Deafness as Culture," *The Atlantic* 272, no. 3 (1993): 37.

45. Bonnie Burstow, "Toward a Radical Understanding of Trauma and Trauma Work," *Violence Against Women* 9, no. 11 (2003): 1296.

BIBLIOGRAPHY

Baker, Aaron, and Juliann Vitullo. "Screening the Italian-American Male." In *Masculinity: Bodies, Movies, Culture*, edited by Peter Lehman, 293–317. New York: Routledge, 2001.

Bujalski, Andrew. "A Unified Theory of the *Rocky* Movies." *The New Yorker*, November 10, 2015, https://www.newyorker.com/culture/cultural-comment/a-unified-theory-of-the-rocky-movies. Accessed 14 December 2018.

Burstow, Bonnie. "Toward a Radical Understanding of Trauma and Trauma Work." *Violence Against Woman* 9, no. 11 (2003): 1293–1317.

Campbell, Fiona Kumari. *Contours of Ableism: The Production of Disability and Ableness*. New York: Palgrave Macmillan, 2006.

Casillo, Robert. "Moments in Italian-American Cinema: From *Little Caesar* to Coppola and Scorsese." In *From the Margins: Writing in Italian Americana*, edited by Anthony Julian

Tamburri, Paolo Giordano, and Fred L. Gardaphé, 394–416. West Lafayette, IN: Purdue University Press, 2000.

Cocola, Jim. "Stallone's *Creed*." *Italian Americana* 35, no. 2 (2017): 121–144.

Conti, Bill. Interview with Carla Simonini. *Italian Americana* 35, no. 2 (2017): 185–197.

Conway, Brett. "To Roll Back the Rock(y): White Male-Absence in the *Rocky* Series." *Aethlon: The Journal of Sport Literature* 22, no. 1 (2004): 63–79.

Coogler, Ryan. "Creed." Film script, 2015.

Creed. Directed by Ryan Coogler, performances by Michael B. Jordan, Sylvester Stallone, Tessa Thompson, and Phylicia Rashad, Metro-Goldwyn-Mayer (MGM), Warner Brothers, New Line Cinema, Chartoff-Winkler Productions, 2015.

Creed II. Directed by Steven Caple Jr., performances by Michael B. Jordan, Sylvester Stallone, Tessa Thompson, Phylicia Rashad, and Dolph Lundgren, Metro-Goldwyn-Mayer (MGM), Warner Brothers, New Line Cinema, Chartoff-Winkler Productions, 2018.

Dolnick, Edward. "Deafness as Culture." *The Atlantic* 272, no. 3 (1993): 37–53.

Douglas, Esme. "Director Ryan Coogler Wants to Celebrate the Women behind the Production of *Black Panther*." *HelloGiggles*. February 05, 2018. Accessed March 28, 2019. https://hellogiggles.com/news/ryan-coogler-black-panther-women-behind-scenes/.

Elmwood, Victoria A. "'Just Some Bum from the Neighborhood': The Resolution of Post-Civil Rights Tension and Heavyweight Public Sphere Discourse in Rocky." *Film & History* 35, no. 2 (2005): 49–59.

Fleming, Mike Jr. "How Director Ryan Coogler's Own Father-Son Saga Fueled *Rocky* Revival *Creed*." Deadline, November 19, 2015, https://deadline.com/2015/11/ryan-coogler-creed-rocky-balboa-sylvester-stallone-michael-b-jordan-1201629948/. Accessed 14 December 2018.

Gabaccia, Donna R. "Race, Nation, Hyphen: Italian-Americans and American Multiculturalism in Comparative Perspective." In *Are Italians White? How Race Is Made in America*, edited by Jennifer Guglielmo and Salvatore Salerno, 44–59. Routledge, 2003.

Gallantz, Michael. "*Rocky*'s Racism." *Jump Cut: A Review of Contemporary Media*, no. 18 (1978): 33–34.

Galuppo, Mia. "How *Creed II* Director Crafted His *Rocky IV* Successor." *The Hollywood Reporter*. November 21, 2018. Accessed January 31, 2019. https://www.hollywoodreporter.com/heat-vision/creed-ii-director-steven-caple-jr-interview-his-sequel-1163109.

Gardaphé, Fred. "Invisible People: Shadows and Light in Italian American Culture." In *Anti-Italianism: Essays on a Prejudice*, edited by William J. Connell and Fred Gardaphé, 1–10. New York: Palgrave Macmillan, 2011.

Guglielmo, Jennifer, and Salvatore Salerno. *Are Italians White?: How Race Is Made in America*. New York: Routledge, 2003.

Hastie, Amelie. "Ryan Coogler's *Creed*: Showing the Love." *Film Quarterly* 69, no. 4 (2016): 72–77.

Hock, Stephen. "'That's Your Uncle? He's White!' 'Yeah, A Long Time': Negotiating Whiteness in the *Rocky*/*Creed* Series." *Italian Americana* 35, no. 2 (2017): 145–168.

Hooks, Bell. *Yearning: Race, Gender and Cultural Politics*. Boston: South End Press, 1990.

Jacobs, Matthew Frye. *Roots Too: White Ethnic Revival in Post-Civil Rights America*. Cambridge: Harvard University Press, 2006.

Keller, Alexandra, and Frazer Ward. "The *Rocky* Effect: Sylvester Stallone as Sport Hero." In *The Ultimate Stallone Reader: Sylvester Stallone as Star, Icon, Auteur*, edited by Chris Holmlund, 171–96. New York: Columbia University Press, 2014.

Lawton, Ben. "What Is 'Italian American' Cinema?" *Voices in Italian Americana: VIA* 6, no. 1 (1995): 27–51.

Mari, Christopher. "Ryan Coogler." *Current Biography Yearbook* 77, no. 5 (2016): 17–21.

Martin, Joel W. "Redeeming America: *Rocky* as Ritual Racial Drama." In *Screening the Sacred: Religion, Myth, and Ideology in Popular American Film*, edited by Joel W. Martin and Conrad E. Ostwalt Jr., 125–33. Boulder, CO: Westview Press, 1995.

Maucione, Jessica. "White Ethnic Racial Backlash and Black Millennial Counter-narrative: Intersections of Race and Masculinity in Sylvester Stallone's *Rocky* Series and Ryan Kyle Coogler's *Creed*." *Italian Americana* 35, no. 2 (2017): 169–182.

Motley, Clay. "Fighting for Manhood: *Rocky* and Turn-of-the-Century Antimodernism." *Film & History* 35, no. 2 (2005): 60–66.

Orsi, Robert. "The Religious Boundaries of Inbetween People: Street Feste and the Problem of the Dark-Skinned Other in Italian Harlem: 1920–1990." *American Quarterly* 44, no. 3 (1992): 313–47.

QuickFacts: Philadelphia County, Pennsylvania. United States Census. July 1, 2017. https://www.census.gov/quickfacts/philadelphiacountypennsylvania Accessed 18 December 2018.

Reich, Jacqueline. "'Ain't Nothing Over 'til It's Over': The Boxing Film, Race, and the *Rocky* Series." In *Mediated Ethnicity: New Italian-American Cinema*, edited by Giuliana Muscio, Joseph Sciora, Giovanni Spagnoletti, and Anthony Julian Tamburri, 181–88. New York: John D. Calandra Italian American Institute, 2010.

Rocky. Directed by John G. Avildsen, performances by Sylvester Stallone, Talia Shire, Burt Young, Carl Weathers, and Burgess Meredith, Chartoff-Winkler Productions, 1976.

Schultz, Jaime. "*Glory Road* and the White Savior Historical Sport Film." *Journal of Popular Film and Television* 42, no. 4 (2014): 205–13.

Schwable, Michael et al. "Generic Processes in the Reproduction of Inequality: An Interactionist Analysis." *Social Forces* 79, no. 2 (2000): 419–52.

Sharf, Zack. "*Creed II* Director Steven Caple Jr. on Ryan Coogler's Advice and Directing a *Rocky* Film after a Low-Budget Indie—Exclusive." *IndieWire*. September 28, 2018. Accessed January 31, 2019. https://www.indiewire.com/2018/09/creed-2-steven-caple-jr-interview-replacing-ryan-coogler-1202007531/.

Shor, Ira. "*Rocky*: Two Faces of the American Dream." *Jump Cut: A Review of Contemporary Media* no. 14 (1977): 1.

Singer, Matt. "Director Steven Caple Jr. on Directing *Creed II* and Ranking *Rockys*." *ScreenCrush*. November 21, 2018. Accessed January 31, 2019. https://screencrush.com/steven-caple-jr-creed-2-interview/.

Stallone, Sylvester. "Rocky." Film script, 1976.

Tapley, Kristopher. "Ryan Coogler on *Creed*, Filmmaking as Journalism and the Need for Female Voices (Q&A)." *Variety*, January 5, 2016, http://variety.com/2016/film/in-contention/creed-director-ryan-coogler-on-filmmaking-as-journalism-andthe-importance-of-female-voices-1201670613/. Accessed 14 December 2018.

Vera, Hernán, and Andrew M. Gordon. "The Beautiful American: Sincere Fictions of the White Messiah in Hollywood Movies." In *White Out: The Continuing Significance of Racism*, edited by Ashley W. Doane and Eduardo Bonilla-Silva. New York: Routledge, 2003.

Webb, Lawrence. "New Hollywood in the Rust Belt: Urban Decline and Downtown Renaissance in *The King of Marvin Gardens* and *Rocky*." *Cinema Journal* 54, no. 4 (2015): 100–125.

Part II

Blurring the Lines
between Italian and
American on Screen

Chapter Four

The Italian Pursuit of Hollywood

Pursuit of Happyness *(Muccino, 2006)*

Mary Ann McDonald Carolan

The exchange between Italian and American filmmakers has been both long-standing and widespread. Screenwriters, producers, and directors from Italy and the United States have engaged in a transatlantic dialogue since the early days of cinema. Italian filmmakers exerted a profound and sustained influence on American cinema; they have in turn been drawn to the professional and economic possibilities that Hollywood offers. In the past decade or so, a number of Italian directors have decided to adapt American texts to the screen.[1] This essay will consider the case of Gabriele Muccino whose direction of *The Pursuit of Happyness* (2006) launched his American filmmaking career.[2] That film hews to the distinctly American narrative of rags to riches as it recounts Chris Gardner's struggle with homelessness as a single parent in San Francisco, which he chronicled in his eponymous memoir.[3] Muccino's film traces the trajectory of an African American underdog from the margins to the pinnacle of American society. My analysis of Muccino's adaptation also considers race and genre as factors in the reception abroad of films that tell essentially black stories. Such films cause us to reflect upon cross-cultural exchange as they mirror changes in the art and business of filmmaking in an increasingly global environment.

TRANSATLANTIC CINEMATIC EXCHANGE

The profound and sustained indebtedness of American film to Italian cinema began with the historical epic, a genre perfected by the Italians in the 1910s. We remember the powerful influence that Giovanni Pastrone's *Cabiria*

(1914) exerted on D. W. Griffith, which led him to make *Intolerance* (1916) after traveling from Hollywood to San Francisco to view the Italian historical epic. In *My Voyage to Italy* (1999), Martin Scorsese describes the importance of directors such as Roberto Rossellini, Vittorio De Sica, Luchino Visconti, Federico Fellini, and Michelangelo Antonioni to his development as a filmmaker. Woody Allen readily acknowledges his appreciation of Federico Fellini's oeuvre; his *To Rome with Love* (2012) is a clever homage to *Notti di Cabiria/Nights of Cabiria* (1957), the *maestro*'s dark comedy about photoplays, celebrity and female vulnerability. The neorealist sensibilities of De Sica and Rossellini have continued to influence filmmakers such as Lee Daniels, whose *Precious: Based on the Novel* Push *by Saphhire* (2009) includes a series of clips from De Sica's *La Ciociara/Two Women* (1960).[4] Of course, American filmmaking has had an enormous impact on global cinema, and Hollywood has exerted an irresistible pull for many Italian directors. Roberto Rossellini collaborated with the well-connected Hollywood actress Ingrid Bergman to make *Stromboli, terra di Dio/Stromboli* (1950), an Italian American coproduction that elicited much controversy due to the very public extramarital affair between the Italian director and Hollywood star. Michelangelo Antonioni, after directing his English language debut with the critically acclaimed *Blow-Up* (1966) set in swinging London, traveled to the southwest of the United States to make *Zabriskie Point* (1970).[5] In addition to its American cast and setting, this paean to American counterculture contained a soundtrack featuring Pink Floyd and the Grateful Dead. Sergio Leone's most beloved film project, and his last, was the epic tale of the Jewish-American mafia (a jab at the Hollywood studio moguls perhaps?) in *Once upon a Time in America* (1984). Based on *The Hoods* (1952), the thinly veiled autobiography of the Russian born American businessman and police informer Harry Grey (Herschel Goldberg), this film chronicles the lives, loves, and criminal activities of four buddies involved with the mob in Manhattan in the 1920s and 1930s. More recently, two prominent Italian directors, Paolo Virzì and Luca Guadagnino, have engaged with Hollywood and American texts. Virzì's *Leisure Seeker* (2017), the director's first English language film, is a retelling of American author Michael Zadoorian's eponymous 2009 novel about an elderly couple, played by Donald Sutherland and Helen Mirren, who set off on a road trip from Massachusetts to Florida. Luca Guadagnino achieved international success with *Call Me by Your Name* (2017), a filmic adaptation of the novel by American writer André Aciman, set in northern Italy with mostly English dialogue infused with Italian. In October 2018, Guadagnino announced that he planned to direct the film adaptation of Bob Dylan's "Blood on the Tracks." That film, based on a screenplay by Italian American writer Richard LaGravenese, is inspired by Dylan's seminal album from 1975.

GABRIELE MUCCINO'S *PURSUIT OF HAPPYNESS*

The Pursuit of Happyness, directed by Gabriele Muccino and starring Will Smith, proved to be an enormously successful American-Italian collaboration. This international partnership bridged the racial divide of black (American) film and white (European) audience in its telling of the true story of Chris Gardner (Will Smith) who struggled with homelessness as a single parent but eventually became a successful entrepreneur. Will Smith's decision to engage Muccino, whose work he had admired, was a savvy way to promote this quintessentially American story beyond the borders of the United States.

But how did this improbable collaboration develop? According to critic Emanuel Levy, executive producer Mark Clayman thought that Gardner's story, which was featured on the television program *20/20* in 2003, would be a "home run" for Will Smith from both personal and professional perspectives. Written by Steven Conrad, the script captivated Smith. Along with James Lassiter, his partner in Overbrook Entertainment, Smith lobbied for Gabriele Muccino to direct the film even though the Italian, who was barely conversant in English, had not helmed a film in that language before. Yet Smith was impressed with Muccino's ability to render complex human emotion in both *L'ultimo bacio/The Last Kiss* (2001)[6] and *Ricordati di me/Remember Me, My Love* (2003). Others, including producer Todd Black, were less sanguine about the choice of a foreign director for such a quintessentially American story. But Muccino convinced everyone that Gardner's story was a universal one that demonstrated how grit and determination could overcome serious obstacles as homelessness. It was, as well, the story of Chris's great fatherly love for his young son, also named Chris (Will Smith's son, Jaden). In an interview entitled *The Pursuit of Happyness-Backstage: An Italian Take on the American Dream*, the Italian director emphasized how his foreignness could bring a fresh perspective to this story because the "American dream is not only for Americans."[7]

Throughout his long and successful career, Will Smith has sought to promote black actors and films outside the United States. The African American/Italian collaboration between Smith, as actor and producer, and Muccino, as director, resulted in an enormously successful run in Italy. *The Pursuit of Happyness* grossed $163,566,459 domestically and almost the same amount ($143,510,836) in foreign markets. In Italy alone the film made $21,309,984, more than three times what *12 Years a Slave* (McQueen, 2013) would bring in when it opened there.[8]

AFRICAN AMERICAN STORIES IN ITALY

The box office success in Italy of *The Pursuit of Happyness* appears as somewhat of an anomaly when we consider how films about the African American experience have been received abroad. In 2007, Reginald Hudlin, former president of BET (Black Entertainment Television) whose credits include directing *House Party* (1990) and *The Ladies Man* (2000) and producing Tarantino's *Django Unchained* (2012), drew parallels between international and southern audiences in an article outlining the ways in which *Dreamgirls* (Condon, 2006) sought to improve its foreign appeal: "I always call international the new South. In the old days, they told you black films don't travel down South. Now they say it's not going to travel overseas."[9] In fact, DreamWorks and Paramount Pictures hoped that major awards and a singing appearance at the Oscars by the film's stars Beyoncé Knowles, Jennifer Hudson, and Anika Noni Rose might lessen foreign objections to its musical genre and almost all-black cast. Writing in the *New York Times,* Cieply observed,

> Only recently have movies begun to crack one of Hollywood's most troubling and least openly discussed problems: an international "color line" behind which films relying on black stars often do not perform well. The box office prowess of "Dreamgirls" overseas will help signal whether this newfound success is fleeting or more lasting.

Dreamgirls grossed $103,365,956 domestically, and one half of that amount ($51,571,724) from foreign sales. Yet, it only earned $687,157 in Italy where it had a very short run from January 26–February 4, 2007.[10] We note that *Dreamgirls* opened in Italy a few weeks after the premier in that country of Smith's hugely successful *The Pursuit of Happyness.*

Italian reception to highly acclaimed movies about the African American experience in recent years renders the success there of *The Pursuit of Happyness* even more striking. In 2013, the Tumblr blog "Carefree Black Girl" commented on the Italian publicity materials for director Steve McQueen's *12 Years a Slave,* which showcased Brad Pitt, the movie's producer who plays a minor, but critical role as Bass, a Northerner responsible for the protagonist Solomon Northup's liberation, and Michael Fassbender, the demonic slave master Edwin Epps. In the lower right-hand corner of the Italian posters Chiwetel Ejiofor, the British actor of Nigerian parentage who plays the title character Solomon Northup, appears in a miniature version of the image that was literally and figuratively at the center of the film's American ads. The message was clear: in order to appeal to Italian audiences, white, not black, actors were foregrounded despite—or account of—changing demographics in Europe resulting from the vast migration from sub-Saharan Africa. Deemed racist online and by the press, the posters were recalled, and the distribution company (BiM) apologized for its racial insensitivity.[11] The anti-black bias seems particularly disturbing considering the narrative of *12 Years a Slave*. Based on the eponymous 1853 memoir by Northup, a Northern, free African American man who was kidnapped and forced into slavery on a trip to Washington, D.C., the film was directed by black British director Steve McQueen. *12 Years a Slave* addresses the inhumane and cruel system of slavery from the perspective of its black victim (Northrup) while BiM's materials focus on the positive (Pitt) and negative (Fassbender) white responses to it.

Theses advertisements, and the strategy behind them, confirms Hudlin's issues with the challenges of marketing films with black casts. Yet, ironically, this controversy also renewed interest in the film because it increased media attention as Mendelson points out.[12] While agreeing with critics that using white stars to sell a film about slavery is "disagreeable" on a visceral level, Mendelson argues that since the goal of advertising is to make people buy tickets, showcasing white actors (the famous American, Pitt, and lesser known, German born, Irish actor Fassbender) to Italian audiences in the publicity materials was a means to that end. According to Mendelson, "If the posters worked to get people to see *12 Years a Slave* who otherwise would not have, then they did their job, for better or worse." Acknowledging the unfairness of the American system for black actors, Mendelson describes the reality of Hollywood: "Chiwetel Ejiofor is one of the best actors on the planet, but he is not yet a 'movie star.' He should be. If we lived in a more racially-just Hollywood, he would be. But he's not." *12 Years a Slave,* which won three Academy Awards—for Best Picture, Best Supporting Actress (Lupita Nyong'o) and Best Adapted Screenplay (John Ridley)—grossed $56,671,993 in the United States and $131,061,209 in foreign markets. In Italy, where it was screened initially in over three hundred theaters and played for five months, the film earned $6,617,083.

Italian audiences and journalists reacted in a subdued fashion when Barry Jenkins's Oscar-winning film *Moonlight* launched the 11th Rome Film Festival in November 2016. Based on Tarrell Alvin McCraney's play "In Moonlight Black Boys Look Blue," this movie recounts the story of Chiron[13] (played in three disparate chapters by Alex Hibbert, Ashton Sanders, and Trevante Rhodes), a black, gay boy who grows up in South Florida. Yet despite the director's heavy promotion of the film in Europe—following the example set by Will Smith—the Italian response to this moving film was tepid. Natalia Aspesi, writing in *La Repubblica*, remarked upon the indifference of the Italian audience. In her review of *Moonlight* in that paper which was subtitled "Giudicato un capolavoro dalla critica americana, ma accolto con indifferenza in Italia," ("Deemed a masterpiece by American critics, but received with indifference in Italy") Aspesi suggested that perhaps some collective soul-searching was in order for Italians who preferred the fiction of soap operas to the reality of Jenkins's film:

> Why was a film considered to be a masterpiece by most American critics, surrounded by intense scholarly interest, received with partial enthusiasm and, in some cases, indifference, by most Italian critics when it opened the Rome Film Festival in 2016? *Moonlight* had won the Golden Globe for best drama, and was nominated for 8 Academy Awards (best film, director, supporting actor and actress, screenplay, photography, montage, original score) and has already won all sorts of international prizes. Have we Italians become more skeptical, more wicked, more inclined to cry at benign soap operas than at the painful and dangerous reality that surrounds us but that we would prefer to ignore? [14]

Perhaps the reality in Jenkins's film is too harsh, too foreign for Italian audiences? *Moonlight* opens up a window into a particular time and place, the 1980s and 1990s in Miami's Liberty Square housing project, where the director and the playwright both lived, and where both of their mothers, who gave birth to them as teenagers, fell prey to crack cocaine. [15] Yet in Italy, a country whose writers and directors honored the downtrodden in neorealist film, melodrama now appeals more than the beautifully stark tale of *Moonlight*.

The 2017 Oscar winner for best picture, *Moonlight,* a film that *New York Times* critic A. O. Scott called "an urgent social document, a hard look at American reality and a poem written in light, music and vivid human faces," [16] ultimately was more successful outside the United States, grossing $37,191,755 in foreign markets as compared to $27,854,932 at home. In Italy, the box office receipts reached $1,574,935 after 13 weeks of screening. Still, only 83 theaters screened *Moonlight* when it premiered in Italy in February 2017; that number increased to 149 theaters following the film's receipt of an Academy Award for Best Picture. Meanwhile, total receipts in Italy for Muccino's 2006 film *The Pursuit of Happyness* were approximately 20 times that amount. For the Italian premiere, the film played in 391 theaters; that number increased to 441 the following week.

Perhaps the relative lack of enthusiasm for *Moonlight* correlates with its genre. In many ways, *Moonlight* may be considered the male version of Lee Daniels's *Precious: Based on the Novel Push by Sapphire* (2009), another predominantly black drama, which arrived in Italy a year after its American debut in November 2010. This heartbreaking saga, filled with incest, abuse, and entrenched poverty, was screened in only seventy-six theaters in Italy despite its Academy Awards (Mo'nique for Best Supporting Actress, Geoffrey Fletcher for Best Adapted Screenplay), famous producers (Tyler Perry and Oprah Winfrey), and director Daniels's professed love of European style movies. [17] Both *Moonlight* and *Precious* are dramatic coming-of-age tales that chronicle in excruciating detail the *realtà dolorosa e pericolosa* (to use Aspesi's term) of a life of poverty and marginalization. Set in predominantly or all black environments, *Moonlight* and *Precious* unflinchingly display the reality of African American communities without attempting to sanitize the degraded conditions. In that way both directors adhere to neorealist sensibilities from the postwar period in Italy with authentic portrayals of humble protagonists such as Antonio Ricci (the amateur actor Lamberto Maggiorani) in *Ladri di biciclette/Bicycle Thieves* or the title character in De Sica's compelling description of the plight of elderly pensioners in postwar Italy, *Umberto D.* (1952).

African American director Lee Daniels underscores his connection to neorealist predecessors when, midway through this disturbing tale about Claireece "Precious" Jones (Gabourey Sidibe), a pastiche of clips from De Sica's *La Ciociara/Two Women* (1960) appears on the television screen which mother Mary (Mo'Nique) and daughter watch in their Harlem walk up.[18] Daniels's film inserts scenes from before and after the violent rape of mother and daughter in an abandoned church by French colonial troops known as Goumiers following the final battles of Monte Cassino and the declaration of armistice.[19] In my reading, the inclusion of the Italian film, for which Sophia Loren (1960), like Mo'Nique fifty years later, won an Academy Award, reveals the relevance of the neorealist genre for African American directors such as Lee Daniels in the new millennium.

While watching *Two Women* on television, Precious daydreams, imagining herself, along with her mother, in these scenes. Her complete identification with the daughter in De Sica's film occurs when she sutures herself into that narrative. This fantasy, like others in the film in which the protagonist imagines yearbook photos that speak and herself as a celebrity, represents a sanitized version of events in her life. The imagined scene, which does not occur in De Sica's film, takes place in Italian around a table adjacent to the bombed-out church in which mother and daughter have sought refuge. Here, Mary, as Cesira, uses vulgarities, but in a calm tone, telling her daughter "Metti il culo sulla sedia" ["Sit your ass down on the chair"] or "Mangia, puttana" ["Eat, you whore"]. Their calm discussion of food contrasts with the crude and unappetizing exchange between mother and daughter when Mary insists that Precious eat, and then eat some more, despite her protestations. Food and punishment are connected as Mary tells Precious, who did not prepare collard greens with the pigs' feet: "You fucked it up now you gonna eat it up."

Lee Daniels, who calls himself "a little homo, . . . a little Euro and . . . a little ghetto,"[20] favors on-location shooting, long shots, natural lighting, nonprofessional actors, working-class protagonists, and open-ended narratives that defy quick summaries or facile categorization. Daniels shares with the neorealist directors who came before him a deep concern for individuals who inhabit the margins of society. In this film there are no easy solutions, for in the end, Precious gives birth to her second child only to be diagnosed with AIDS, having contracted the disease from her late father. Like the endings of *Bicycle Thieves* and *Roma città aperta/Rome, Open City* (Rossellini, 1945), in *Precious* a sliver of hope appears when the title character leaves her mother's house, the locus of her physical and emotional abuse, to begin a new life with her children.

The Italian film, within Daniels's film, underscores Precious's marginalized state for she cannot read the film nor grasp the historical events that inform its narrative. Clearly from Precious's distorted perspective, De Sica's film suggests an antidote to her abusive situation. Yet the omission of the original rape scene provides a powerful commentary about the young woman's misguided fantasy in Reagan era America, which is removed spatially and chronologically from war-torn Italy. The two films are linked visually by the image of a hole in the ceiling that appears after rapes—in the church for Rosetta and at home for Precious. These images suggest a false sense of liberation for the young women who stare at them. They also reveal, in my reading, the dialogue between the directors De Sica and Daniels. Yet, due to its limited release in Italy, audiences there could not appreciate *Precious*'s homage to one of the masters of neorealism. Daniels's film earned very little at the box office in Italy—$767,729, a small percentage of the $16 million from international receipts.

For the sake of comparison, let us consider the fortunes of another film with a distinct Italian connection. *Nine,* a musical film based upon the Broadway show of the same name which was a loose adaptation of Fellini's autobiographical film *8½* (1963), opened in January 2010 in 250 theaters in Italy where it eventually grossed $1.6 million (through 01 Distribution, a division of RAI) despite the mostly negative critical reception in the United States where it premiered on December 19, 2009. Scott Foundas, writing in the *Village Voice,* describes this cinematic adaptation of the earlier Tony-award-winning musical as follows: "An assault on the senses from every conceivable direction—smash zooms, the ear-splitting eruption of something like music, the spectacle of a creature called Kate Hudson—*Nine* thrashes about in search of 'cinema' the way a child thrown into the deep end of a pool flails for a flotation device."[21] Other critics were no less harsh. Writing in the *Los Angeles Times,* Betsy Sharkey observed that *Nine* was "one of those films that couldn't look better on paper—so many Oscar, Tony and Grammy winners involved that the production should have literally glittered with all that gold. But in the end, nothing adds up. Perhaps 'Zero' would have been a better name."[22] Although this purported homage to Fellini's Academy Award-winning film was an unmitigated critical disaster, in Italy it still brought in almost $1 million more in ticket sales than did *Precious* later that same year. It appears that Italians are more apt to see a failed musical, a genre which Nanni Moretti's *Aprile/April* (1998) parodies and which has played an inconsequential role in Italian cinema, than a critically acclaimed drama centered on the plight of a disadvantaged young American female of color.

Although *Precious* addresses a particularly American demographic with its predominantly black cast, black director, and Harlem setting, I would argue that this film, like Jenkins's *Moonlight,* sheds light onto the plight of marginalized individuals—and African American youth in particular—just as De Sica's *Bicycle Thieves* examined the breakdown in society and the alienation of the individual in postwar Italy.

THE PURSUIT OF HAPPYNESS FROM
AUTOBIOGRAPHY TO FEATURE FILM

Unlike the fictional tale *Precious*, *The Pursuit of Happyness* omits much of Chris Gardner's disturbing behavior as outlined in his autobiography. The decision on the part of screenwriter Conrad and director Muccino to exclude explicit details in *The Pursuit of Happyness* perhaps was the key to the film's success outside the United States. Whereas Chris Gardner's memoir does not spare the reader any of the sordid or illegal activities that defined his youth and young adulthood, the script tells a much more appealing story. Gardner, who acknowledged suffering from the "No-Daddy Blues," did not meet his biological father until he was already a parent himself. He dedicates the book to his mother, Bettye Jean Gardner Triplett, a spectral presence in his life who tends to disappear periodically due to her involvement in nonviolent crimes for which she is imprisoned. Gardner writes of his hatred for, and indeed his wish to murder, his abusive step-father Freddie Triplett. He re-counts in great detail his assault on the man who raped him after an ill-fated attempt to sell stolen goods. Gardner does not spare the reader intimate particulars of his love life, either. He tells of his hasty decision to marry a respectable young black woman, their elegant wedding in Virginia, and their life together in San Francisco before he cheats on her with Jackie, a dental student who will bear his children but will never become his wife. He re-counts in great detail his unfaithfulness to her, and the resulting violence including the vandalization of his car. The movie, on the other hand, presents a hardworking and docile wife (played by Thandie Newton) in a marriage that dissolves according to a more traditional narrative of financial disap-pointment and the couple's gradual parting of ways. The script ignores the cataclysmic consequences of Gardner's decisions, while the frank autobiog-raphy raises doubts about his responsibility for the calamity that surrounds him. The optimistic film triggers no such difficult questions.

Perhaps herein lies the reason behind the positive Italian reception of Will Smith's film in relation to those that present a more realistic cinematic representation of the black experience in the United States. The American production has opted to be a "happy end" (the Italian term for a film with a happy ending), rather than a realistic portrayal of a difficult and, at times, less than commendable life. The screenplay, expunged of the messy bits of Gardner's life, tells the universal story of man's battle with obstacles such as homelessness, underemployment, and fractured families. This poignant but ultimately uplifting tale appeals to the moviegoer in search of entertainment. It speaks to the spectator who wishes to focus on overcoming hardship instead of confronting the vicissitudes of life in the manner of neorealist directors such as Rossellini, De Sica, and Visconti. Masterpieces of that Italian genre leave viewers to wonder what might happen to the protagonists; they provide no conclusive or heartening messages. *The Pursuit of Happyness,* on the other hand, inspires spectators as Chris and his son survive, indeed thrive, against all odds. This tale of a father who cares for his son in grim circumstances, including a night spent in a BART bathroom that Gardner recounts in his memoir, recalls Guido's (Roberto Benigni) attempt to protect his son Giosué (Giorgio Cantarini) from the realities of the concentration camp by devising an elaborate game in Robert Benigni's *La vita è bella /Life Is Beautiful* (1997).

In Muccino's film, we see Chris Gardner weighed down by the portable X-ray machine he attempts to sell to doctors. Most of the time he is running through the streets of San Francisco, carrying all his belongings, as if he were chasing the American dream. Muccino shoots Gardner as he races to his son's day care center, or to an appointment, or to prevent his car from being impounded. This frenetic movement mirrors Gardner's sense of urgency. The spectator responds viscerally to this attempt at bettering oneself. The dynamism of Muccino's film provides a stark contrast to the deliberately slow pace of father and son, Antonio and Bruno, in *Bicycle Thieves* (De Sica, 1948) that is mirrored in *Precious* and *Moonlight*. At the end of De Sica's film, Antonio steals a bicycle only to be apprehended. His desperate attempt informs our understanding of the film's title as the victim now becomes the aggressor in this hopeless world in which everyone is a potential thief. Slow moving and open-ended narratives such as these force us to consider larger, existential questions. The commercial success of Muccino's film demonstrates that we, Italians and Americans alike, prefer the success story of Chris Gardner, who in the end, realizes the American dream and finds the happiness that the film's title promises.[23]

NOTES

1. For an analysis of literary adaptations in Italian film, see Millicent Marcus, *Filmmaking by the Book: Italian Cinema and Literary Adaptation.* Baltimore: Johns Hopkins University Press, 1992.

2. Muccino entered his American phase following the success of *The Pursuit of Happyness.* After that, he directed *Seven Pounds* (2008), *Playing for Keeps* (2012), *Fathers and Daughters* (2015), and *Summertime* (2016).

3. Christopher Gardner, with Quincy Troupe and Mim Eichler Rivas, *The Pursuit of Happyness.* New York: Amistad, 2006. The "happyness" of the title derives from the misspelled word at the day care center which Gardner's toddler son attended in San Francisco. The author made many unsuccessful attempts to correct this error.

4. In *The Transatlantic Gaze: Italian Cinema, American Film.* Albany, NY: SUNY Press, 2014, I explore the cinematic dialogue in a number of case studies including chapter V, "Neorealism Revisited by African American Directors in the New Millennium: *Precious*: Based on the Novel *Push* by Sapphire (Daniels, 2009) and *Miracle at St. Anna* (Lee, 2008)," 85–108.

5. Paola Randi's recent release of *Tito e gli alieni/Tito and the Aliens* (2018) revisits Antonioni's suggestive setting in *Zabriskie Point* (1970) in the tale of a widowed professor who lives a hermit-like existence in the Nevada desert where he should be working on a top-secret project for the United States but instead spends his days on the couch listening to the sounds of space. The professor's life changes dramatically when his dying brother sends his young children from Naples to live with him. They expect the excitement of Las Vegas, but find instead that they are in the middle of nowhere.

6. Ironically, the American remake of Muccino's film, *The Last Kiss* (2006), directed by Tony Goldwyn and starring co-screenwriter Zach Braff, was a commercial and critical flop.

7. *The Pursuit of Happyness—Backstage: An Italian Take on the American Dream.* https://www.youtube.com/watch?v=a0sv-b4Yhws.

8. All statistics regarding box office receipts can be found on boxofficemojo.com.

9. Michael Cieply, "Films with Black Stars Seek to Break International Barriers," *New York Times,* 28 February 2007. http://www.nytimes.com/2007/02/28/movies/28color.html.

10. Ten years later, another film that focuses on African American women, *Hidden Figures* (Melfi, 2016), which premiered in the United States in December 2016, was screened in Italy for 23 weeks, beginning in March 2017, grossing $3,326,332 up until mid-August. Total foreign sales were $61,162,122; domestic sales were $169,375,247.

11. See, for example, Ethan Sacks, "*12 Years a Slave*'s Italian distributor apologizes for controversial movie posters that focus on Caucasian actors," *Daily News,* 1 January 2014. http://www.nydailynews.com/entertainment/tv-movies/12-years-slave-star-pulls-italian-screening-poster-controversy-swirls-article-1.1559697.

12. Scott Mendelson, "In 'Defense' of the Brad Pitt *12 Years a Slave* Posters," *Forbes,* 31 December 2013. https://www.forbes.com/sites/scottmendelson/2013/12/31/in-defense-of-those-brad-pitt-12-years-a-slave-posters/#19dd668b3200.

13. With the name of the immortal leader of the Centaurs who tutored Hercules and Achilles, Chiron recalls the character who appears in Dante's *Inferno,* canto XII. For an analysis of the intersections between Dante and African American culture, see Dennis Looney. *Freedom Readers: The African American Reception of Dante Alighieri and the Divine Comedy.* North Bend, IN: Notre Dame University Press, 2011.

14. Italian: "Perché un film considerato un capolavoro dalla maggior parte della critica americana, precipitata nella commozione più erudita, è stato accolto con entusiasmo parziale e in certi casi indifferenza, dalla maggior parte della critica italiana, quando è stato presentato in anteprima alla Festa di Roma 2016? *Moonlight* ha vinto il Golden Globe per il miglior film drammatico, ha 8 candidature all'Oscar (film, regista, attore e attrice non protagonista, miglior sceneggiatura, fotografia, montaggio, colonna sonora originale) e ha già accatastato ogni sorta di premi internazionali. Siamo noi italiani diventati più scettici, più cattivi, più portati a lacrimare per le riposanti finzioni delle soap opera che per quella realtà dolorosa e pericolosa che ci circonda e preferiamo scansare?"

15. Nikole Hannah-Jones, "From Bittersweet Childhoods to *Moonlight,*" *New York Times,* 4 January 2017. https://www.nytimes.com/2017/01/04/movies/moonlight-barry-jenkins-tarell-alvin-mccraney-interview.html.

16. https://www.nytimes.com/2016/10/21/movies/moonlight-review.html?referrer=google_kp.

17. In an interview with Scott Foundas for the Directors Guild of America website entitled "The Next Act," Lee stated: "I was always intrigued with European cinema, and hated most American cinema. I didn't like the one, two, three-*boom*! style, with a neat and tidy ending. That was never my scene." https://www.dga.org/Craft/DGAQ/All-Articles/1102-Summer-2011/Indie-Voice-Lee-Daniels.aspx.

18. When queried about this film, Daniels explained this clip in an interview with Gary Kramer in *Chelsea Now* entitled "*Precious* & Queer," on December 11, 2009: "Because I am watching *Two Women* and it's my movie. You're in my world!"

19. See Rick Atkinson, *The Day of Battle: The War in Sicily and Italy, 1943–1944.* New York: Macmillan, 2008, 557–558, for a description of the brutal post-Armistice period and Edward Bimberg, *The Moroccan Goums: Tribal Warriors in a Modern War.* Westport, CT: Greenwood, 1999, for a discussion of the Goumier troops.

20. Lynn Hirschberg, "The Great Audacity of *Precious,*" *New York Times,* 21 October 2009, http://www.nytimes.com/2009/10/25/magazine/25precious-t.html.

21. Scott Foundas, "Fellini Fantasy Meets a Harsh Reality in Rob Marshall's *Nine,*" *The Village Voice,* 15 December 2009. https://www.villagevoice.com/2009/12/15/fellini-fantasy-meets-a-harsh-reality-in-rob-marshalls-nine/.

22. David Ng, "Rob Marshall's *Nine:* What Did the Critics Think?" *Los Angeles Times blog.* 28 December 2009. https://latimesblogs.latimes.com/culturemonster/2009/12/rob-marshalls-nine-what-did-the-critics-think.html

23. In his memoir, Gardner tells of founding his own brokerage firm, and giving back to institutions such as Glide Church, a place where he found refuge in his darkest hour.

BIBLIOGRAPHY

Aspesi, Natalia. "*Moonlight,* vita nel ghetto nero di Miami," *La Repubblica.* 23 febbraio 2017. Web. http://www.repubblica.it/speciali/cinema/oscar/edizione2017/2017/02/23/news/_moonlight_vita_nel_ghetto_nero_di_miami-159021525/.

Atkinson, Rick. *The Day of Battle: The War in Sicily and Italy, 1943–1944.* New York: Macmillan, 2008.

Bimberg, Edward. *The Moroccan Goums: Tribal Warriors in a Modern War.* Westport, CT: Greenwood, 1999.

"Box Office Mojo," https://www.boxofficemojo.com/.

Carolan, Mary Ann McDonald. *The Transatlantic Gaze: Italian Cinema, American Film.* Albany, NY: SUNY Press, 2014.

Cieply, Michael. "Films with Black Stars Seek to Break International Barriers," *New York Times,* February 28, 2007. http://www.nytimes.com/2007/02/28/movies/28color.html.

Foundas, Scott. "Fellini Fantasy Meets a Harsh Reality in Rob Marshall's *Nine,*" *The Village Voice,* 15 December 2009. https://www.villagevoice.com/2009/12/15/fellini-fantasy-meets-a-harsh-reality-in-rob-marshalls-nine/.

Foundas, Scott. "The Next Act," Directors Guild of America, https://www.dga.org/Craft/DGAQ/All-Articles/1102-Summer-2011/Indie-Voice-Lee-Daniels.aspx.

Gardner, Christopher with Quincy Troupe & Mim Eichler Rivas. *The Pursuit of Happyness.* New York: Amistad, 2006.

Hannah-Jones, Nikole. "From Bittersweet Childhoods to *Moonlight,*" *New York Times*, January 4, 2017. https://www.nytimes.com/2017/01/04/movies/moonlight-barry-jenkins-tarell-alvin-mccraney-interview.html

Hirschberg, Lynn. "The Great Audacity of *Precious,*" *New York Times,* October 21, 2009, http://www.nytimes.com/2009/10/25/magazine/25precious-t.html.

Kramer, Gary. "Precious & Queer," *Chelsea Now*, December 11, 2009.

Kroll, Justin. "Bob Dylan's 'Blood on the Tracks' Album Getting Movie Treatment," *Variety*, October 17, 2018. https://variety.com/2018/film/uncategorized/bob-dylan-blood-on-the-tracks-movie-luca-guadagnino-1202983403/

Levy, Emanuel. "*Pursuit of Happyness*' Gabriele Muccino," *Cinema 24/7*. November 18, 2006. http://emanuellevy.com/interviews/pursuit-of-happyness-gabriele-muccino-9/.

Looney, Dennis. *Freedom Readers: The African American Reception of Dante Alighieri and the Divine Comedy*. North Bend, IN: Notre Dame University Press, 2011.

Marcus, Millicent. *Filmmaking by the Book: Italian Cinema and Literary Adaptation*. Baltimore: Johns Hopkins University Press, 1992.

Mendelson, Scott. "In 'Defense' of the Brad Pitt '12 Years a Slave' Posters," *Forbes*, December 31, 2013. https://www.forbes.com/sites/scottmendelson/2013/12/31/in-defense-of-those-brad-pitt-12-years-a-slave-posters/#19dd668b3200

Ng, David. "Rob Marshall's *Nine:* What Did the Critics Think?" *Los Angeles Times blog*. December 28, 2009. https://latimesblogs.latimes.com/culturemonster/2009/12/rob-marshalls-nine-what-did-the-critics-think.html.

Sacks, Ethan. "*12 Years a Slave*'s Italian distributor apologizes for controversial movie posters that focus on Caucasian actors," *Daily News*, January 1, 2014.

Scott, A. O. "Moonlight: Is This the Year's Best Movie?" October 20, 2016. https://www.nytimes.com/2016/10/21/movies/moonlight-review.html?referrer=google_kp.

"The Pursuit of Happyness—Backstage: An Italian Take on the American Dream." https://www.youtube.com/watch?v=a0sv-b4Yhws. http://www.nydailynews.com/entertainment/tv-movies/12-years-slave-star-pulls-italian-screening-poster-controversy-swirls-article-1.1559697.

The Pursuit of Happyness. Dir. Gabriele Muccino, 2006. Sony Pictures.

Chapter Five

Comedies of Identity

*Italian Cinema and Television
Narrating Italian Americans*

Giuseppe Sorrentino

In 1987 the Neapolitan actor and comedian Massimo Troisi, appeared live from New York on an Italian television show[1] and offered a rather unique and provocative perspective on the concept of "Italianness/*italianità*," and on the concept of national identity at large. Sitting in the middle of the street in what was Chinatown, together with two men of Asian somatic traits, he pretended to be in Little Italy and sarcastically told the host of the show, Pippo Baudo, how incredible it was to be there, how he felt like being home, while praising everyone's strong Italian identity in that neighborhood. To all those watching him, however, it would have been clear that he was not in Little Italy but rather in Chinatown as the signs of the stores were in Chinese. In fact, there were no traces of Italian culture anywhere around him. The sketch continued to the extent in which even the two Asian men sitting with him were presented as Italian Americans, with Italian names, Don Salvatore and Pasquale, suggesting they were Neapolitans. When they would speak in their native language (probably Chinese), Troisi would say that their dialect was so old that he was unable to understand them. When he asked the two men to say something to the Italian audience, they came up with two Neapolitan expressions that they had been trained to repeat: "Maradona is better than Pelé" and "San Gennaro, take care of it!"[2]

What was Massimo Troisi really up to in this sketch? What was its aim? Was he making fun of Italian pride, of the rhetoric sometimes connected to Italians abroad? Or was he trying to signal the disappearance of the Little Italies, like the one in New York, which for the most part has been devoured by Chinatown? Even better, was he trying to make fun of Italian Americans by saying that they are no more Italian than the two Chinese men in New York? Maybe he was ultimately trying to say that what we define as identity is a rather weak concept, prone to various interpretations and open to constant reflection and redefinition.

It is difficult to understand his true motives. We can generally agree, however, that Troisi was reminding us about how complicated the relationship is between Italians and Italian Americans, always mediated along a thin border between recognition and refusal, acceptance and criticism, stereotypes and mutual understanding. This chapter attempts to investigate this relationship by exploring how Italian immigrants have been portrayed in Italian films of the 1970s, 1980s, and 1990s, three decades in which Italian society was marked by rapid and crucial cultural and political changes. In particular, the chapter aims to underscore a shift in the perspective Italian filmmakers assumed of Italian immigrants throughout the last three decades of the 20th century; a shift, from empathy to derision that mirrors the many deep cultural/identity transformations that affected Italy in that same period.

TWO ITALIES

Throughout the history of the Italian diaspora, there has been a constant dialogue, at times a clash, between the Italians in the homeland and Italians abroad, between those who stayed and those who left. Both have grown and developed as cultures and societies in parallel ways, creating distinctive sociocultural traits that have ended up caging them in well-defined stereotypes and behaviors. Because the Unification of Italy in 1861 came with the cost of millions of Italians leaving the newly created country, one can say that the history of Italy is also the history of Two Italies: on the one hand, the Italy/country characterized by a dynamic historical process of constant redefinition and yet on the other hand, the Italy/ideal locus of identity, kept alive by the millions of generations of Italians that became citizens of other nations. The case of the Italians in the United States is particularly telling: a story of social transformation that took them from the lowest layers of society, from a class-structure perspective, often considered "non-white" and inferior in the first half of the 20th century, to slowly emerge, after World War II as protagonists of the social and economic transformations of the country, finally becoming "white," occupying crucial roles in American society across sectors.[3] All of this, while still maintaining a strong ethnic identity, defined by social practices and rituals (food, religion, family gatherings), rarely by language, to which they generally cling with pride. Mass media, moreover, played an essential role in building this identity, primarily through the critical emergence of Italian American filmmakers in the 1970s, who contributed in large part to creating the popular image of the Italian American. When, in his seminal work, Robert Casillo reflects on Italian American cinema,[4] he argues that Scorsese and Coppola responded to early stereotypical representations of Italian Americans in Hollywood, from the perspective of white culture, and created an original version of that culture. They created a unique way of being Italian in America from the perspective of Italian Americans. This new approach, however, will end up becoming a new stereotype, with specific attitudes and a lifestyle that will define what it means to be Italian in America. Later in this chapter, we will see how some Italian filmmakers intentionally mock that stereotype.

Emilio Franzina argues that prejudice is but a transposition in the new world of the Northern/Southern Italian dichotomy that informs Italian history since the birth of the nation.[5] Reflecting on the issue of race, which at the beginning of the 20th century strongly framed the debate on immigration to the United States, Franzina recognizes in the "Two Italies" of North and South, the crux of the matter with American popular culture using that difference to stigmatize Southern Italians as dangerous and inferior. That prejudice is, therefore, the prejudice of Northerners against Southerners,[6] which transforms itself throughout the 20th century in the prejudice of Italians toward Italian Americans. To Franzina's analysis, however, one can add that the prejudice takes new shape because of the parallel history of the "Two Italies."

Indeed, while Italian Americans were transforming themselves in Pacinos and De Niros, in Cuomos and Lorens, Italians in Italy went through a similar process of constant redefinition of their own national identity. That process is arguably informed by the role Fascism had in building that identity. The emergence of Fascism in the 1920s was the catalyst for a crucial structuring of an idea of Italy that will be the focal point around which every future political reflection on Italy and Italians will be built. When, after World War II, Italy will go through the most rapid and revolutionary transformation of its whole history, from an agrarian society to an industrial technocratic one (with several traumatic accidents along the way), the Italian fascist past will be continuously challenged, denied, removed in favor of a very liquid, anti-nationalist identity that will look more openly to other cultures as models. Among them of course, the United States' position as the hegemonic culture of the 20th century, will be so strong that Italians will often adopt mainstream/white America as a cultural model. In this context, a significant crack, separation, or gap between Italian and Italian American culture takes place, with Italians in Italy adopting a hegemonic gaze toward minorities and therefore looking at cultural traits of Italian Americans as ridiculous, unrealistic ways of being Italian. The Italian American stereotype becomes, therefore, perceived by Italians as unfavorable, as something from which the Italians want to distance themselves. By distancing themselves from that stereotype,

Italians ended up distancing themselves from the whole experience of immigration. Yet, it was not always the case.

ITALIANS AND ITALIAN IMMIGRANTS

One can trace a cultural history of the encounter between Italians and Italian immigrants and find a multifaceted scenario in which the dynamic between the two experiences is often on the edge between recognition and the impossibility of reconciliation. Examples abound in many fields; however, it is in Italian literature that we find the first essential traces of this dynamic that will then be transposed into cinema. In his famous poem, "The Southern Seas" (*I mari del Sud*),[7] for example, Cesare Pavese reflects on this situation by imagining a walk on a hillside with an immigrant cousin who has left Italy and returned a richer man twenty years later to his hometown. In a meditative text mixing the poet's memory and imagination, with the reality and the desolation of an agrarian world slowly disappearing under the eyes of the two protagonists of the poem, the immigrant cousin emerges as an oxymoronic living ghost, who wanders, driving around the region with not much to do. He is a dramatic figure, one that embodies the tragic experiences of immigration, as an experience of loss and dispossession. "My cousin's face is cut,"[8] writes Pavese, presenting to the reader a split individual, somebody who does not belong anymore, whose stubborn capitalist spirit is in contrast with the agrarian magic world of the Langhe. In Pavese's poem, the immigrant becomes an alien to the eyes of the Italians who stayed, simply because he left, because he was unable to be part of the community. Moreover, the fact that he returned does not mean much because he can never belong again, and he is split between a world that never understood him and another one that was never able to welcome him. The Italian immigrant, in the words of Pavese, is a lonely individual, somebody who is going to live the rest of his life in a sort of identity limbo, never knowing who he was or who he is.

This figure of the lost immigrant, of the individual who is split between two worlds, but who is not firmly holding himself to either of the two and rather wanders like a ghost in the limbo of his own identity, frequently returns in certain Italian filmic comedies of the late 1960s and early 1970s. Some examples include Nino Manfredi in *Bread and Chocolate/Pane e cioccolata* (Franco Brusati, 1974) or Pasquale, a Calabrese emigrant in Germany who goes to Italy to vote for the national election in *White, Red and Verdone/Bianco, Rosso e Verdone* (Carlo Verdone, 1981). These comedies represent a critical step in understanding the perception that Italians had of Italian immigrants. However, before reflecting on that perception, it is crucial to introduce the profound cultural shifts—happening in post–World War II Italy—that will mold it.

The end of World War II marks a pivotal point in Italy's history. After 1945, the country emerges as an entirely different nation: a republic where women can vote, Fascism is declared illegal, and a new modern constitution carries the promise of a new democratic era. Most importantly, in the new Italy, the cultural/political debate does not take place anymore in an incubator of nationalism, but in a nation that prefers to put that nationalism aside and project itself into a globalized world, becoming a protagonist in a geopolitical scenario of new alliances and distinct cultural blocks. In this new reality, the influence of the United States has a significant impact, with economic and cultural contributions that aim to keep Italy (strategically placed in the Mediterranean during the Cold War) within their sphere of influence. The Italians, who were eager to put the experience of Fascism and the War behind them, were particularly prone to follow new cultural modes, to adopt new perspectives on life, to see themselves as a new people. Whereas Fascism, in its nationalist frenzy, had tried its best to keep away any form of foreign influence, the new Italy, liberated by any cultural constriction, was ready to embrace cultural differences. Italians were ready to be colonized, and they were ready to be Americans, to paraphrase Renato Carosone's famous song, *Tu vuo' fa' l'americano*.

What does this Americanization of Italy mean for an analysis on the relationship between Italians and Italian Americans in cinema? It is crucial. In the moment in which Italians start to embrace an American, global, modern lifestyle, and project themselves as different from what they were in the past, then the Italian Americans (especially those who had arrived in the United States before World War II and in the first two decades right after the war), who did not partake of the rapid transformations in Italian culture, were stuck—in the eyes of Italians—in an antiquated idea of Italy, a national idea that for them was now long gone, disappeared in the caesura caused by the war.

However, Italian Americans after World War II experience their journey of transformation, a journey in which generations emerged from the margins of society into white America. After decades of marginalization, racism, and prejudice, Italians (and with them many other historical immigrant groups of the first half of the 20th century), participate in the suburban revolution of the 1950s and, finally, see themselves as fully American. In their case, the journey did not happen without traumatic steps and conflicts, especially among the various generations of fathers and sons, mothers and daughters, and left signs of an erasure of the past that for many years will define the Italian American consciousness and experience. While Italians in Italy joyously embraced a new culture and lifestyle, without sacrificing aspects of their culture, Italians in America, to belong, had to cut their connection with the past or at least hide it in their basement.[9]

It is with these two parallel, different developments of two Italian cultures that a clear picture emerges: Italy, after World War II, was not even one hundred years old as a nation and had already gone through one of most traumatic experiences that a nation can go through. At first, it had gradually lost one-third of its actual population while at the same time, it also had clearly separated and distanced itself from that one-third. While Italians in Italy did whatever was possible to forget their past and move toward their future, Italians in the United States (and in other countries) were forcibly losing part of themselves, sacrificing themselves on the altar of "whiteness."

ITALIAN CINEMA NARRATING
ITALIAN IMMIGRANTS

Understanding this shift is essential if one wants to examine Italian cinema as a privileged area of Italian culture that offers an essential perspective on the separation between Italians and Italian Americans (or Italians abroad at large). When Italian filmmakers decide to narrate the "other" Italians, they do so by adopting a stance that walks a thin line between compassion and derision. It is as if they continue the approach Cesare Pavese had inaugurated in "The Southern Seas" and described the Italian abroad as that distant cousin who had lost his own identity and was unable to reconcile himself with his past. This is the approach that one can recognize in two directors that both have produced two movies about Italian immigrants in the 1970s: Mario Monicelli and Luigi Zampa. Both Monicelli and Zampa are historically identified with the movement of comedy Italian style (*Commedia all'italiana*), and mainly focused on an open social criticism of Italian society and its "tics." It is important to underline this aspect because the experience of the Italian immigrant in Italian cinema takes place in this context, in the context of the social comedy, while most of the American movies on Italian Americans in the 1970s are dramas.

In 1971, Mario Monicelli directed *Lady Liberty/La Mortadella*. The movie tells the story of a new immigrant, Maddalena Ciarrapico (Sophia Loren), arriving in New York to marry her fiancée. Because she decided to bring a big piece of mortadella as a gift to him, she is blocked at US customs, as she refuses to let go of the mortadella. Aside from the comedic effect of the simple and innocent Italian woman who is just trying to bring part of her culture with her in the new country and does not understand how some mortadella can be considered harmful, the movie is noteworthy on two levels. First, it presents the clash of the immigrant with the new culture, the impossibility of mutual understanding. At the same time, it also presents the idea of the cultural exploitation of the immigrant, which can be used for political/journalistic purposes; second and, in a way, more importantly, the encounter between the Italian Maddalena and the Italian American Michael Bruni (Maddalena's fiancée, interpreted by Gianni Proietti) is telling the differences and irreconcilable realities of the old world vs. the new world. [10] Michele has become Michael, and completely renounced his Italian past (interestingly characterized by political commitment in union struggles) in favor of American capitalism and greed. Maddalena, unable to recognize her "new" fiancée, is left alone in a (maybe exaggeratedly) bleak New York City, the protagonist of an almost Kafkian tale, lost in a journey that struggles to begin.

Differently from Maddalena, Amedeo Battipaglia, the protagonist of *A Girl in Australia/Bello Onesto Emigrato Australia sposerebbe Compaesana Illibata* (Luigi Zampa, 1971), is not a new immigrant. He has lived in the Australian outback for roughly twenty-five years. Having lost any contact with Italy, but, at the same time, unable to see himself as an Australian, he is split between the two cultures and, lonely as he is, would like to marry an Italian woman. The story follows Amedeo as he welcomes Carmela (interpreted by Claudia Cardinale), a young mail bride he managed to convince to marry him, to the new land. However, Amedeo is ashamed and unable to reveal himself to Carmela, as he feels he is too old for her. When he started corresponding with the girl, he sent her a picture of his friend Giuseppe in lieu of his own. When he goes to pick her up at the airport, he pretends to be Giuseppe (while he is indeed the real Amedeo), a friend of Amedeo's (who, to the girl, looks like Giuseppe) who is accompanying her to her future husband. At the same time, Carmela hides her true identity; in Italy she was a prostitute and not the chaste Italian girl Amedeo imagined marrying. The entire comedy is built on this misunderstanding between the two protagonists and on their inability to reveal their true identities to each other. However, there is another aspect of the movie that reveals a critical reflection on the immigrant experience.

The journey that Amedeo/Giuseppe takes Carmela on, back to the small town in the outback where he lives, is, in reality, a journey through his life as an immigrant in that country for over two decades. A particular moment of that experience is the period (almost ten years) he and two other friends spent in a forest, building a path through it. A period of extreme solitude and separation from the world that led one of the friends, Bambo, toward complete madness. During the trip to their new home, Amedeo and Carmela stop at the mental institution where Amedeo's friend, Bambo, is a patient. They discover that he is about to be sent back to Italy and that he completely lost the ability to speak. He spends all his days sitting on a bench in the park surrounding the hospital, smoking with an absent look. Amedeo supported him throughout the years, probably out of pity, but also because he cannot but feel empathy for his friend's experience. Bambo's experience becomes the epitome of the immigrant experience, the idea of the loss of oneself, the loss of one's voice, and the inability of belonging, being part of anything. Bambo, in his extreme condition, serves only a mirror for Amedeo, a mirror of what they have become as immigrants—lost and voiceless.

Coincidently being released in the same year, 1971, both Monicelli's and Zampa's films present similar reflections on immigration. They do so by using the lens of comedy Italian style, which traditionally wavers between tragedy and comedy, to explore the experience of immigration as a dramatic loss, a sacrifice of one's identity. The two directors produced their movies in a moment of Italian history when their country had just experienced an economic boom that had brought it directly in the group of the wealthiest and most industrialized nations in the world. At that moment in time, when in a sense Italians were not poor anymore and did not need to emigrate, the immigrant experience is seen as a tragic consequence of the turbulent history of the country, a sad event that marked the separation between many and their own country forever. Moreover, the most tragic aspect of that separation is that it can never be reconciled.

ITALIAN CINEMA MISREPRESENTING ITALIAN AMERICANS

The irreconcilable separation becomes evident in the 1980s, when the gaze of Italian filmmakers on Italian immigrants moves beyond the empathic approach of Monicelli and Zampa, and becomes inexplicably derisive, almost cruel, reading the immigrant experience in a very superficial, offensive way. The movie that best demonstrates this interpretation is *Vacanze in America* (Carlo Vanzina, 1984). Part of the tradition of the *cinepanettoni*,[11] this film is a container of many horrible stereotypes, ridiculing race, homosexuality, diversity, and expression of despicable attitude Italians start developing about themselves, especially in that period. After the economic boom of the 1960s, Italians begin seeing themselves as "superior" to *other* cultures, adopting a form of ethnocentrism that puts them in contrast with the rest of the world. Some characters in *cinepanettoni* and, in particular, in *Vacanze in America*, are perfect embodiments of this attitude. In this case, for example, the vacation has the role of reinforcing the correct moral/cultural standards of Italians as opposed to the "strangeness" of other countries.

Vacanze in America tells the story of a group of Italian high school students, along with some teachers, on a school trip to the United States. The movie is punctuated by various episodes in which the characters react and interact with a different world, a world in which they are in awe. The comedic element is usually given by these reactions and mostly connected to extreme judgments the characters make about American culture or themselves. The first part of the trip is set in New York City, and it is in this section that an encounter with Italian Americans occurs.

Two of the students and an alumnus of the school who is on the trip with them, coincidently find themselves in an adult movie theater in Times Square (the Times Square of the 1980s) and decide to go to a strip club together. In the club, they approach two girls who very quickly recognize them as Italians (they are used to foreigners coming to the club) and soon, as they sit together at a table, reveal themselves as two Italian Americans from Brooklyn. Their grandparents are from Avellino, and the Italian guys, hoping to end up in bed with them, start buying them drinks. The night, however, ends up quite differently from what they had expected. The girls, Marta and Monica, make them pay for a cab to their home in Brooklyn, not to have sex, but to meet their family. It is in this way that the stereotypical working-class Italian American family, popularized by many American movies of those years, enters into Italian cinema.

Carlo Vanzina pans on a picture of Pope John Paul II, followed by a series of religious images, while the Neapolitan singer Aurelio Fierro is singing in the background. One of the kids sits on the couch, drinking a cup of espresso with the grandmother, and an Italian flag hangs behind them. They talk about Italian music: the grandmother says that Aurelio Fierro is her favorite singer, and when the Italian kid asks her if she knows Lucio Dalla (who was very popular in Italy in the 1980s), she says that the only "good" music is Neapolitan music, and she does not care about anything else, which clearly reiterates the old/new world dichotomy. The other two boys end up playing a game of cards with the men in the house, gambling and losing all the money they have, disappointed by the experience. When one of the girls asks: "Are you having fun?" Jerry Calà (the actor interpreting the alumnus, who is a very popular comedian in Italy at that time) says in a northern Italian accent: "Sure! Instead of being in America, it feels like I am in a cockroach motel in Caserta." He addresses one of the men as Rocky (referring to the Sylvester Stallone character, also very popular in Italy at that time) and vulgarly criticizes them for letting the two women (a wife and a sister) work in a strip club (he hints at a possible incestuous environment).

Who are these Italians? Where do they come from? In what way do they arrive, in the middle of the 1980s, and disrupt their relationship with their Italian American cousins. A historical perspective provides answers to these critical questions. The characters in the movie represent a generation of Italians born at the end of the 1960s[12] that will pass through the 1970s immune to the political disruptions of that decade (economic crisis, the political terrorism of the Red Brigades) and will come of age in the hedonistic decade of the 1980s, during which Italy will experience the peak of its capitalistic expansion, and project itself firmly as a "brand" in the world (mostly in the fashion industry and manufacturing). In this historical context, that generation is bound to look at the Italian Americans in *Vacanze in America* as aliens from another planet, non-Italians that are a source of shame to Italian culture at large. However, there is more to it. The scene in the Italian American household in *Vacance in America* presents a microcosm of social anxieties that are at the core of the Italian experience at the end of the 20th century. These anxieties can be traced into three primary categories: class, gender, and the North/South differences.

The three high-schooler protagonists of the episode in Brooklyn are each representative of classes that have little in common with the Italian Americans in Brooklyn. One is the son of an upper-middle-class family who lives in the suburbs of Rome; another one is the descendant of an aristocratic family (he is addressed as the "count"); and the third one, the alumnus, is a product of the modern urban environment of that city that best interpreted the hedonism of the 1980s in Italy: the city of Milan. While they are visiting the Italian American family, everything from their appearance to their attitude serves as a reminder that they are from different classes. Dressed in clean "bourgeoisie" clothes that are in stark contrast to the "wife-beaters" of the two men with whom they are playing a card game, the Italians are boringly engaged in their interaction with their "cousins" and even mock the excitement of the Italian Americans who are winning the game. Their perspective is condescending, to say the least, utterly disrespectful toward the working class, it can be read as an early signal of that gap between the wealthy and the poor that characterizes contemporary capitalistic societies.

The three Italians are three men. They are "white," in the sense that they occupy a privileged place within Italian society, and their attitude toward women is exclusively predatory and objectifying. The alumnus is on a mission to sleep with as many women as possible, and the other two kids are not different. The fact that they meet by chance in an adult movie theater is not only telling of what they want, as the adult movie theater also becomes their shared environment, the place where their common predatory gaze finds expression. They are entirely insensitive to the fact that the strippers they meet at the club identify themselves as "grand-daughters," and, later, as mothers and sisters. To them these "lost" girls are only the perfect symbol, the perfect reminder that those who left, the Italian immigrants who went to the United States did not make it, they are stuck in their rural world, stuck as a working-class, and forced to resort to prostitution to survive in America. Their situation suggests to them, and the Italian spectators who watched the film in the 1980s, that Italy has developed; it is no more the impoverished country from which millions of people had to escape and that those who left it were wrong. The scene reinforces a sense of nationalistic pride for what Italians have accomplished, and Italian Americans cannot participate in all this, as they have isolated themselves in a past that does not exist anymore.

A third important element within the scene is that the interaction between the Italians and the Italian Americans reiterates another essential social conflict, characteristic of the national debate in Italy: the differences between North and South. The alumnus does not hesitate to continually underline that because those Italian Americans are from the South; they are automatically inferior. He does so by sarcastically mocking the two girls when they say that their family is from Avellino and by describing their household as a "cockroach motel" in Caserta. The dichotomy between North and South is therefore transported to the other side of the Atlantic, in ways that are revelatory of its centrality in the debate over Italian identity. It has been statistically proven that a vast majority of the Italian immigrants who came to the United States originated from Southern Italy (or in other poor regions of the country, such as Abbruzzo or Molise). This situation functions, for Italians like those in *Vacanze in America*, as proof that Southern Italians never really belonged to Italy, and that the "annexation" of the South to an ideal country of which they have never really been part of, was never fully accomplished. It is not surprising, then, to the Italian tourists that this is the culture of Italian Americans: they are Southerners, not Italians. They have never really belonged.

One can, therefore, place this encounter at the center of the Italian and Italian American experience as symbolic of that rupture between the two cultures, reaching its maturity precisely in that period. The confidence of the Italian kids, a generation born in the late 1960s, in seeing themselves as superior to their Italian American "cousins" speaks volumes of the condescending way in which Italians were now looking at themselves. The Italians of the 1980s have entirely forgotten their immigrant past and when, in a decade or so, other immigrants coming mostly from North Africa and Eastern Europe, will be knocking at their door reminding them of what it means to be immigrant, most of the country will prefer to be oblivious to that call, placing that immigrant experience in a remote, distant past that does not allow for comparisons. This attitude starts here, in an Italy that wanted to erase part of its history and *laugh* at the Italians that had left the country.

This sense of superiority toward Italian Americans affects Italians across the spectrum of the political palette. Even intellectuals and filmmakers that are usually associated with the left (which is usually prone to a more "empathic" approach to immigration) are not immune to this treatment of Italian Americans. Almost twenty years after *Vacanze in America* in *My Name Is Tanino* (Paolo Virzì, 2001), the director Virzì, tells the story of Tanino, a Sicilian university film student in love with American independent cinema and with a stereotypical American girl (a very young Rachel McAdams), uses a similar (just maybe less vulgar) approach in describing the Italian American family of Tanino's relatives. In a period in which the stereotype had been refreshed by the HBO series *The Sopranos*, Virzì creates a family that is similar to the one in the series, and that, at the same time, is character-ized by ignorance, unrefined ways, loud, and –ultimately—intellectually in-ferior to Tanino, who instead studies in Rome and knows about independent filmmakers. What is worse is that Virzì also falls in the trap of describing them as suspiciously "mafiosi" and has Tanino briefly flirt with the possibil-ity of becoming himself an Italian American like "them." However, at the end of the movie, he escapes, disgusted by the world of Italian Americans. Unlike the previously mentioned protagonists, Tanino is an Italian young adult of the 1990s, open-minded, intellectual, educated, who looks at his Italian American family with a mix of boredom and loathing. There is never a mention of the contribution of Italian Americans in defining American culture in the 20th century. Italian Americans do not have, according to Tanino, anything to do with culture.

It is worth looking in more detail at this section of the movie in which Tanino initiates a relationship with an Italian American girl. The movie is narrated by the voice-over of Tanino who, in a flashback, looks at his experi-ences in the United States, as he writes a letter to his friend, Giuseppe, back in Sicily. Tanino is initially in the United States, in Rhode Island, because he decides to follow an American girl, Sally, he met the summer before while she was visiting Sicily. He and the girl have a brief summer fling, and Tanino takes the liberty of surprising her in her suburban, upper-middle-class world, almost unannounced, even though she had stopped replying to his emails for now months. Tanino is, nonetheless, welcomed by Sally's family and lives with them for a bit, only to discover that not only is Sally not interested in him anymore, but there are also irreconcilable cultural differences between himself and these white Americans who have always perceived with a little bit of suspicion his olive skin.

After his experiences with "white" America, Tanino is forced to stay with his Italian American relatives, and during this stay, his interactions expand from the familial to the larger Italian American community of Providence, Rhode Island. In this context, Paolo Virzì takes the differences between Italian and Italian Americans to a whole new level, quasi-grotesque. Tanino's journey into Italian American culture starts ambiguously, almost as a dream. After leaving Sally's dysfunctional and hypocritical family, Tanino is lost like a stray dog in the streets of Seaport. At a certain point, he is about to be run over by a truck with a blinking yellow cross on its front. Virzì offers us a subjective shot of the cross blurring and then Tanino fainting.

As Tanino wakes up, we hear the Italian language coming from a TV screen in the background. He is confused. Is he back in Italy? He wakes up in a room where, besides an Italian television show on the wall, there are pictures of immigrants and Italian relatives of those immigrants, among them Tanino's father. An older man, an old Italian immigrant, is in the room. A grandfather? He starts enumerating the Italians on the wall, he calls them, in

Sicilian, "beddi picciriddi" (sweet kids) and then starts kissing Tanino's hand. Tanino is annoyed by him, he finds him awkward, slowly realizing that he is at his Italian America relatives' home. He then says, in a voice-over, introducing this new chapter in his story: "My dear friend, have you ever felt like suffocating, when you know that you cannot escape your destiny, because, in the end, it always finds you and puts its dirty hands on you."[13] The Italian protagonist of this story does not want to be there, he wants to escape his *italianità*, as he finds it suffocating, and now he is forced to experience it. As Tanino continues describing his relatives in the background, Virzì uses this moment to create a sort of mini-documentary on Italian Americans. Tanino describes them in this way: "They are the children of the most disgraced and hungry in our country. They worked their asses off, and now they have designer suits, new cars, and wives with big butts."[14] Paolo Virzì essentializes the Italian Americans, caging them in a way of being. While Tanino is talking, we see images of Italian restaurants, "wise guys" talking among them (that scene seems to be directly taken from a *Sopranos* episode) and women yelling: "mangia, mangia!"

The next step in Tanino's journey is a party of the fictional Italian American Friendship Society celebrating the reelection of the successful Italian American mayor, Buddy Ommobono, who is hinted at as being a mafioso, starting with the irony of his name. At the party, Tanino meets a Giuliana De Marco, professor of Italian Studies at Brown University, who functions as a sort of Virgil to Tanino, for a brief moment. She comments on the surroundings with decadent flair, implying a sense of superiority through which she judges and gazes at the Italian immigrants, suggesting that they could be the perfect subject for a satiric movie, a la Robert Altman. Tanino's relatives, seem to be very close to Buddy Ommobono, to the point that they introduce the two men, but more importantly, they introduce Tanino to Buddy's daughter, Angelina, who has an instant crush on the Italian kid. Here, Virzì's cruelty reaches new heights: the Italian American girl is "culona," on the heavy side, and with a great passion for ice cream. Tanino reluctantly agrees to go out with her, and comments:

> What was happening to me, my friend? Was I throwing in the trash all of my ideals? Ideals for which we fought so much. Was I just cynically hunting a good marriage? I was treated like the special one among that group of criminals, and I felt somewhat awkward. As if in my DNA was deeply hidden a mafia soul that had suddenly emerged.[15]

According to Tanino, dating an Italian American such as Angelina means compromising his ideals (never really clearly expressed in the movie) and awakening the mafioso in him. As if you cannot be Italian American, without being mafioso.

Angelina is supposed to represent for the Italians who share Tanino's perspective, all the negative aspects of Italian America, aspects that reinforce the superiority of the "real" Italians over them. Ugly, rich, overweight, and excessive in the way she consumes things, she does not share the cultural "finesse" of Tanino. She also seems to be "troubled" by the gender role assigned to her, as during an intimate moment with Tanino she cries. Tanino's relationship with her is unlikely and surreal, a descent into the corruption and darkness, or at least that is the way Tanino describes the experience to the viewers. For an Italian, entering in contact with Italian Americans is almost like selling their souls to the devil. It is a terrible experience, one from which the only solution is escaping. However, the "troubled" Angelina would not be enough as a character to justify Tanino's disgust toward Italian Americans, and therefore, Virzì has to portray her as meaner, as horrible, as a "mafiosa." During a fight, the two kids end up telling each other what they think of one another: for Tanino, Angelina is just a "mafiosa"; for Angelina, Tanino is just an "italiano morto di fame." The conflict between the two cultures, the two Italies, explodes. There is no reconciliation, only hate and reciprocal disapproval; no shared history, no shared ideals, two worlds colliding.

In *My Name Is Tanino*, Virzì reinforces the divisions between Italian and Italian American culture. His movie, set at the end of the 20th century, seems to be closing any possible connection between the two Italies. It shows how these two cultures grew apart in the course of over one hundred years. They took two different paths. Their historical experiences, in a way, set them apart. On one side, Italian America cherished and developed its role in American society by conquering a place in that society, fighting prejudice and discrimination, and being able to rise to the highest hierarchical places in that same society; on the other side, Italy reimagined and reenvisioned itself after World War II, as always less nationalistic, less "Italian" and more global, as part of large international project, first within the NATO and then in the European Union. One, Italian American society, found strength in a specific Italian identity that would not collide, but rather coexist with their American one; the other, Italian society, trying to escape a narrow nationalistic identity toward one that was more modern, more open to hybridization and complete transformation.

Both *Vacance in America* and *My Name Is Tanino*, expressions of two separate moments in Italian history, use and exploit Italian Americans in order to assert some detachment, a distinction between the two cultures, as if Italy is moving ahead and Italian Americans are stuck in a stereotypical image that they are not able to liberate themselves. Why? Where does this perspective come from? What separated the two Italies in such a way that they have difficulties recognizing each other?

NEGOTIATING ITALIAN IDENTITY

One of the main differences between the two Italies is that they have experienced the history of the 20th century in various ways. In particular, this difference can be outlined in two crucial moments: first, the early 20th century and, second, World War II. Italians in Italy did not have to experience the social hostility of the United States at the beginning of the 20th century, which characterized the social anxieties of American society toward the otherness of immigrants. In that context, Italians had to suffer prejudice and discrimination. Italians in Italy, instead, in that period, experienced a peak of nationalism, with the advent of Fascism. Also, World War II was a watershed moment for Italian Americans. It represented the entry ticket into mainstream/white America; while for Italians in Italy, it represented the forceful rethinking of Italian identity and nation.

There is a significant difference that needs to be taken into consideration when we compare the Italian and the Italian American experience. Italians did not have to go through the problem of identity, of race, while Italian Americans had to experience the sense of inferiority that united many ethnic minorities in the United States in the first half of the 20th century. This difference is crucial in understanding the dynamics in the relationship between Italians and Italian Americans.

It is possible to trace in Italian cinema a shift in the way in which Italians have viewed themselves in relation to Italian Americans. The development parallels the slow creation of an ever-changing Italian identity that moved toward a new understanding of identity as a very "liquid" concept, an identity that is willing to sacrifice history and embrace cultural models that arrive especially from the other side of the Atlantic. In this way, Italians started seeing themselves, recognizing themselves more as members of a hegemonic "white" America, rather than with the Italian Americans who were forced into that category. Italians could do so because they did not have to experience the complex social structure of the United States that put ethnic groups against one another in order to survive and emerge within society.

In doing so, however, Italians did erase part of their history and preferred to see themselves as untouched by the social transformation of the 20th century. This attitude trained them to assume the role of hegemonic culture in relation to those immigrant groups that started arriving in their country in the 1990s and continued changing the face of the nation into the new millennium. Italian cinema offers a unique perspective in this development, as it mirrors the slow change of Italian society. While right after World War II, Italian filmmakers (in particular Pietro Germi and Francesco Rosi) were able to reflect on the immigrant experience from within, because that experience was still part of the Italian experience, in the post-economic boom years however, one can witness a shifting trend. The history of immigration is no more the history of Italy, but of those individuals who lost themselves into the world. While Cesare Pavese in the 1930s could still find a connection with the Italian cousin who came back from abroad, Monicelli and Zampa would view that cousin and his traumatic experience with pity and sadness, but also from a distance that later will evolve into disgust and loathing of the immigrant experience as something that never interested Italians directly, something to be almost ashamed of.

In *The Lies That Bind*, the philosopher Kwame Anthony Appiah builds a comprehensive theory of identity, based on the idea that how we talk about identity nowadays is indicative of inherent epistemological flaws that characterize humans. According to Appiah, we have a natural tendency toward essentialism, driven by our habitus (a term coined by the French sociologist Pierre Bourdieu), our set of disposition to respond to the world spontaneously, and a form of tribalism that is our tendency "to ascribe a great deal of significance to the distinction between those who share our identity and those who don't."[16] These traits are evident in the distinction that Italians started making between themselves and Italian Americans starting from around the early 1970s of the 20th century, as shown in Italian comedies of that era.

However, when speaking about countries and national identities, Appiah finds the concept flawed and recognizes that there is substantial incoherence at the heart of the ideal of national identity connected to sovereignty and political independence. A concept that is central to the idea of Italy today. The flaw of that concept remained evident since the beginning of the history of Italy as a nation. Following Appiah's theory, indeed, one can see how the ideals of the Risorgimento where often in contrast with a fragmentation of Italy that was not only geographical, but rather cultural. The Romantic ideal of a nation united did not take into account the dramatic differences that characterized the peninsula. To the point that once "invented," the Italian nation had to deal with a process of reconciliation; as shown by the representation of Italian Americans by Italian film makers in the late 20th century, that reconciliation was never fully accomplished.

A scene in another more recent movie can be an excellent example of the flawed concept of Italian identities, especially for the early emigrants. In *Golden Door/Nuovomondo* (Emanuale Crialese, 2006), when the prospective immigrant Salvatore Mancuso, in the late 19th century, boards the ship that will take him and his family to New York, comments on the presence of so many like him on the boat, he says: "Who has ever slept with all this *foreigners*!?" Someone tells him: "Foreigners? Where are these 'foreigners?' We are all *Italians.*" Confronted with a fact that he had never previously considered, the fact of being Italian, Salvatore is puzzled and continues: "Italians? What language do you speak?" Another immigrant states, "Why? You don't know that we are Italians?" Salvatore can therefore only accept this reality with skepticism: "Well, if you say so."

The Romantic ideal of a community united by language and culture, Appiah reminds us, is in tension with the "reality of linguistic and cultural variation within a community." This tension is evident in the relationship developed throughout the 20th century between Italians and Italians abroad, especially Italian Americans. The question of what it means to be Italian is, therefore, more pertinent than ever. Massimo D'Azeglio on the eve of Italian unification, in one of his memoirs famously said: "We made Italy, now we have to make Italians/L'Italia è fatta, restano da fare gli italiani,"[17] and that statement is as relevant as ever. Even if Italians have been made, they have been made through rupture, through the contrast of different identities that still struggle in finding common ground. The "questione meridionale" is probably the best symbol of this.

The question of Italian identity becomes, therefore, irremediably the question of this caesura, of this separation of Italy from its history: of a cultural secession, a diasporic identity struggling in reconciling itself with the center, the locus of its origins. It is only in the process of reconciliation between these two parallel histories that one can see the future of Italy. In a sense, from his chair in Chinatown, Massimo Troisi was precisely doing that: telling Italians that only through a profound reflection and rethinking of their identity, going beyond the sterile idea of a nation that was already born incomplete, they could have found themselves. They do not seem to have followed his advice.

NOTES

1. "Massimo Troisi a Little Italy—Intervista di Pippo Baudo," YouTube video, 11:06, "Lucano per caso," January 18, 2014, https://youtu.be/POOty5yweGY

2. "Maradona è meglio 'e Pelé" was a common phrase in the Napoli of the late 1980s, when the Argentinian player Diego Armando Maradona, almost miraculously, was taking the soccer team of the city of Naples to the highest peaks of international soccer; "San Gennaro pensaci tu," instead, is a somewhat proverbial Neapolitan expression that perfectly encompasses the religiosity of Neapolitans, who would trust all their life into the hands of the patron saint. Having two non-Neapolitans saying something so strongly connected to the identity of the South of Italy is undoubtedly funny.

3. See *Are Italians White? How Race Is Made in America.* Jennifer Guglielmo and Salvatore Salerno, eds. New York: Routledge, 2003, as a starting point for this discussion.

4. Robert Casillo, "Moments in Italian-American Cinema: From *Little Caesar* to Coppola and Scorsese." In *From the Margin: Writings in Italian Americana*, ed. Anthony Julian Tamburri, Paolo A. Giordano, and Fred L. Gardaphé (West Lafayette, IN: Purdue University Press, 2000), 394–416.

5. Emilio Franzina, "Italian Prejudice Against Italian Americans." In *Mediated Ethnicity: New Italian American Cinema*, ed. Giuliana Muscio, Joseph Sciorra, Giovanni Spagnoletti, and Anthony Julian Tamburri (New York: John D. Calandra Italian American Institute, 2010), 17–31.

6. In order to make his point, Franzina uses a historically very relevant letter by Bartolomeo Vanzetti to his sister in Italy, in which he criticizes the Southern Italians (Vanzetti was from Piedmont) for their laziness and affiliation with organized crime.

7. Cesare Pavese, *Disaffections: Complete Poems: 1930–1950* (Port Townsend: Copper Canyon Press, 2002), 17–24.

8. *Mio cugino ha una faccia recisa.*

9. For a complete understanding of the process, see David Roediger, *Working Towards Whiteness: How America's Immigrants Became White.*

10. This dichotomy between old and new world, in the context of Italian Cinema, has been beautifully analyzed by Anthony Tamburri in his reading of Emanuele Crielese's *Nuovomondo.* See Anthony Julian Tamburri, *Re-viewing Italian Americana: Generalities and Specificities on Cinema* (New York: Bordighera Press, 2011), 92–128.

11. *Vacanze in America* is included in the canon of "cinepanettoni" by Alan O'Leary in his *Fenomenologia del cinepanettone.* With the term cinepanettone, Italians indicate a specific type of comedy that is distributed traditionally during the Christmas holidays (hence the term "panettone," which is a traditional dessert during Christmas) and that is usually seen as a low-quality product, characterized by too easy laughs and various forms of vulgarity. For more on the term and a profound analysis of this "genre," see Alan O'Leary, *Fenomenologia del cinepanettone* (Soveria Mannelli: Rubbettino, 2013).

12. They are part of a post-1968 Italy. While their older siblings had tried to change the world at the end of the 1960s (the time period in which progressive social movements such as feminism, calls for social justice and anti-war protests arise), they took advantage of those social changes, of a more "liberated" world, without having had to experience directly the conformism and closeness of earlier years. As a consequence, their "progressivism" is only superficial, and their world view is only a reiteration of past oppressive cultural models. An example can be found in another comedy of that time, *Sapore di mare* (Carlo Vanzina, 1983). In a scene in it (set in the 1960s), a foreign woman is sunbathing topless on a beach in Italy. She is arrested. The protagonists of the movie praise her not for her feminist act of defiance, but because they could look at her topless with their predatory and objectifying male gaze.

13. *Caro amico mio, hai presente quel senso di soffocamento, quando capisci che dal tuo destino non ci si può scappare, perché tanto quello sempre ti trova e ti mette le sue manacce addosso.*

14. *Sono i figli dei figli dei più disgraziati e affamati del nostro paese. Si sono fatti un mazzo tanto e adesso hanno tutti la giacca da stilista, la macchina nuova e la moglie culona.*

15. *Che cosa mi stava succedendo, amico mio? Stavo gettando dietro le spalle tutti gli ideali in cui credevo? E in nome dei quali abbiamo tanto lottato? Stavo diventando un cacciatore di dote cinico e spietato? Certamente ero il pupillo di quella specie di malavitosi e devo ammettere che, in fondo, non mi ci sentivo a disagio. Come se nel mio DNA ci fosse nascosto un pochetto di animo mafioso che era improvvisamente venuto su a galla.*

16. Kwame Anthony Appiah, *The Lies That Bind: Rethinking Identity* (New York: Liveright, 2018), 28.

17. We made Italy, now we have to make the Italians.

BIBLIOGRAPHY

Appiah, Kwame Anthony. *The Lies That Bind: Rethinking Identity.* New York: Liveright, 2018.

Bonsignori, Veronica, Silvia Bruti, and Annalisa Sandrelli. 2019. "Paolo Virzì's Glocal Comedy in English Subtitles: An Investigation into Linguistic and Cultural Representation." Perspectives: *Studies in Translation Theory 27* (2): 283–98.

Brusati, Franco, dir. *Pane e Cioccolata.* 1974; Bologna: Cineteca Bologna, 2014. DVD.

Casillo, Robert. "Moments in Italian American Cinema: From *Little Caesar* to Coppola and Scorsese." In *From the Margin: Writings in Italian Americana*, ed. Anthony Julian Tamburri, Paolo A. Giordano, and Fred L. Gardaphé, 394–416. West Lafayette, IN: Purdue University Press, 2000.

Crialese, Emanuele, dir. *Nuovomondo*, 2006; Roma: 01 Distribution, 2007. DVD.

Franzina, Emilio. "Italian Prejudice Against Italian Americans." In *Mediated Ethnicity: New Italian American Cinema*, ed. Giuliana Muscio, Joseph Sciorra, Giovanni Spagnoletti, and

Anthony Julian Tamburri, 17–31. New York: John D. Calandra Italian American Institute, 2010.

Guglielmo, Jennifer, and Salvatore Salerno, eds. *Are Italians White? How Race Is Made in America*. New York: Routledge, 2003.

Heyer-Caput, Margherita. 2013. "For a Cinema of Inbetween-Ness: Emanuele Crialese's *Nuovomondo* (2006)." *Italica 90* (2): 272–85.

Lichtner, Giacomo. 2013. *Fascism in Italian Cinema since 1945: The Politics of Aesthetics of Memory*.

Michaud, Marie-Christine. 2017. "*Nuovomondo*, Ellis Island, and Italian Immigrants: A New Appraisal by Emanuele Crialese." *Quaderni d'Italianistica: Official Journal of the Canadian Society for Italian Studies 38* (1): 37–60.

Monicelli, Mario, dir. *La mortadella*, 1971; Roma: Dear International, 2008. DVD.

O'Leary, Alan. *Fenomenologia del cinepanettone*. Soveria Mannelli: Rubbettino, 2013.

Pavese, Cesare. *Disaffections: Complete Poems: 1930–1950*. Port Townsend: Copper Canyon Press, 2002.

Roediger, David. *Working Towards Whiteness: How America's Immigrants Became White*. New York: Hachette, 2005.

Tamburri, Anthony Julian. *Re-viewing Italian Americana: Generalities and Specificities on Cinema*. New York: Bordighera Press, 2011.

Vanzina, Carlo, dir. Vacanze in America, 1984; Firenze: Cecchi Gori, 2004. DVD.

Verdone, Carlo, dir. *Bianco, rosso e Verdone*, 1981; Milano: Gruppo Mediaset RTI, 2019. DVD.

Virzì, Paolo, dir. *My Name Is Tanino*, 2002; Firenze: Cecchi Gori, 2006. DVD.

Zampa, Luigi, dir. *Bello, onesto, emigrato Australia, sposerebbe compaesana illibata*, 1971; Roma: Warner Bros, 2013. DVD.

Part III

Re-Viewing Italian Americana on Screen: Reception and Reflections

Chapter Six

Who's Laughing at Whom? Masculinity, Humor, and Italian American Lives on Mainstream Television: *Friends*

Ryan Calabretta-Sajder

INTRODUCTION

The NBC hit comedy *Friends*, written by David Crane and Marta Kauffman, aired from September 22, 1994, until May 6, 2004, a run of ten seasons totaling 236 Episodes. With an ensemble cast which grew exceedingly personal as the seasons evolved, *Friends*'s final episode ranks as the fifth most-watched season finale in television history to date, only behind *M*A*S*H*, *Cheers*, *The Fugitive,* and *Seinfeld*, watched by roughly 52.5 million Americans. Besides the plethora of awards the show received over the ten-year run, maybe the greatest testament to *Friends*'s success was the recent threat by Netflix to allow their license to expire, announced via national news. Within two days of the initial announcement, Netflix released a statement, rescinding the previous decision, stating they will continue to air *Friends* due to the huge outcry against their original decision.[1] This movement to support *Friends* is critical to analyze; it demonstrates that *Friends* is not a one-generational television program like most of the previously cited series; it is a sitcom that has gained the international attention of multi-generations willing to cancel their Netflix subscriptions if the company followed through with its cancellation.[2] Kelsey Miller has argued that

> *Friends* has managed to transcend age, nationality, cultural barriers, and even
> its own dated, unrelatable flaws. Because, underneath all that, it is a show
> about something truly universal: friendship. It's a show about the transitional
> period of early adulthood, when you and your peers are untethered from fami-
> ly, unattached to partners, and equal parts excited and uncertain about the
> future. The only sure thing you have is each other.[3]

Miller proposes an interesting observation in her "Introduction" regarding
Friends's agelessness; the sheer number of followers through the generations
warrants a cultural study of the sitcom's relevance. To a seasoned spectator,
however, *Friends* as a cultural representation, provides a much deeper meaning. The fact that so many spectators can indeed relate to the program underscoring the importance of its serious study.[4]

In fact, from both an activist and academic standpoint, the television
series *Friends* is much more than a comedy that traces the unchanging lives
of six friends in a local NYC coffee shop. Instead, the program introduced
contemporary spectators to a society that was very much in flux. Both culturally and politically, it is important to remember that the program ran from
1994–2004, from the Clinton administration to that of George W. Bush,
years of economic prosperity. The program addressed issues of homosexuality, adoption, polyamorous relationships, artificial insemination, and much
more on public television. As a cultural artifact, therefore, *Friends* has remained a critical sign of the changing of American culture, even though the
character of Joey Tribbiani never in fact evolves. Even though we poke fun at
all the friends' quirky behavior, we recall that Joey's character is the only
one remembered with unfavorable implications.

The essay aims to analyze the representation of Italians and Italian
Americans presented in *Friends,* paying particular attention to Joey Tribbiani's character by examining the concept of masculinity as used to define/
stereotype Italian Americans. Although this contribution focuses on Joey, it
will demonstrate how Joey Tribbiani, an uneducated Italian American, is not
a novelty; rather, it stems from earlier tropes already established in mainstream television. Joey's character as seen through work, family, and friendships, perpetuates the negative connotations associated with Italian
Americans: laziness, ignorance/lack of intelligence, and womanizing. Moreover, Joey's character is the only "friend" not granted access to a proper
coupling; as such, Joey can only assume a piece of a triangle according to
Rene Girard's theoretical conceptualization. Thus, the only character cast as
a third-wheel, Joey, perpetuates disavowing perspectives toward Italian
Americans. By the end of the ten-season run, plus another fourteen years of
viewers, the *Friends*'s spectator can only laugh and pity Joey, the only main
Italian American representative of the show.

PREVIOUS RESEARCH

Considering the vast representation of Italian Americans within the realm of cinema and other media, from directors and producers to writers and actors, and from the silent era to the present, little attention has been seriously afforded the role of Italian Americans on and off the big and little screen. To date, few single-authored books exist on the subject. The majority focuses on either one particular director[5] or a small collection of Italian American directors.[6] The most comprehensive monograph on Italian American cinema to date is Peter Bondanella's *Hollywood Italians: Dagos, Palookas, Romeos, Wise Guys, and Sopranos*, which examines the image of Italian Americans both on- and behind the scenes from the days of silent cinema to the launch of *The Sopranos*. Encyclopedic by nature, *Hollywood Italians* provides an introduction to the vastness of Italian Americans mostly in cinema. Outside of *The Sopranos,* however, Bondanella largely ignores the crucial role Italian Americans hold in the media. In fact, a scant amount of research currently exists on any type of representation of Italian Americans on mainstream television although a plethora of material has been written on *The Sopranos* from both within Italian and Italian American Studies and from outside, mainly in film and media studies.[7]

Within the purview of Italian Americans on mainstream television, the research is clearly lacking. Anthony Julian Tamburri has brought some awareness to the field through two pieces, "A Contested Place: Italian Americans in Cinema and Television," which focuses more on cinema than on television, and "Italian Americans and Television." Recently published, the latter serves as a true evolution of the representation of Italian Americans on mainstream television.[8] There exist individual readings of certain characters as far back as Fonzie from *Happy Days* to the much more recent Raymond from the hit sitcom *Everybody Loves Raymond.*[9] Both Tamburri and Massimo Zangari chart an interesting evolution, or more accurately a lack of evolution, of the Italian American portrayed as the Italian "stallion/buffoon" starting as early as Vinnie Barbarino from *Welcome Back Kotter!*, to Tony Micelli in *Who's the Boss*, Joey Tribbiani in *Friends*, and a variety of possibilities including the male characters from *Jersey Shore, Everybody Loves Raymond*, and the numerous characters from *The Sopranos*. Although this piece will focus only on Joey Tribbiani from *Friends*, Italian American scholarship must redirect some of its attention from some of the more saturated fields and seriously analyze the representation of Italian Americans in comedic roles, as it grants the public more than just simply laughs.

JOEY TRIBBIANI: JUST EYE CANDY
OR IS THERE SOMETHING MORE?

When considering the male characters in *Friends*, there are three type-set characters. First and foremost, there is Joey Tribbiani (Matt LeBlanc) who represents the uneducated, sexy Italian Stallion. Then there is Dr. Ross Geller (David Schwimmer), brother to Monica Geller, both nonpracticing Jews.[10] Ross embodies the intellectual, as he is a paleontologist with a PhD from Columbia University who later becomes a professor (he begins as a curator for a museum), who always uses eloquent diction and enjoys highbrow pastimes such as museums and art. Ross reminds the audience of the nerdy, cute, sensible guy. Lastly, there is Chandler Bing, who was Ross's college friend and Joey's roommate until he married Monica. Chandler represents the boy next door type; he is awkward around people, women in particular. He rarely dates throughout the ten-season run; Monica and Chandler wed in "The One with Monica and Chandler's Wedding," Parts 1 and 2 (Season 7, Episode 23/24). Ironically, one of the few girlfriends Chandler does frequently date is Janice, the annoying woman who is in-and-out of a marriage with another man.

Of the three male protagonists, Joey stands out the most visually, for better or worse. There is definite sex appeal, which is associated with his character physically, but also from his personality, as he is charismatic. He is known to be a womanizer and does not treat women with the utmost respect when dating. Overall, he is not long-term relationship minded, and only once does he seem truly interested in a serious relationship when Ross introduces Joey to Charlie Wheeler, another paleontologist who joins Ross's department (although Ross actually helps Joey woo her), but the relationship does not last. By the end of 236 episodes, Joey is the only character on the show who remains single, a rather clear gesture to underscore his "otherness."

The connection between Arthur Fonzarelli (Henry Winkler) in *Happy Days* and Joey Tribbiani (Matt LeBlanc) in *Friends* is an obvious one. Fonzie has been crystalized as the Italian Stallion par excellence for American media. Whenever Fonzie appeared on screen to go out, he almost always dressed in dark, tight blue jeans, a white undershirt, and a black leather jacket.[11] The white undershirt maintains the negative stereotype of the Italian American as not only laborer but also abuser. Even though it was not an actual "A" shirt as previously imagined, the white crew-neck T-shirt still reminds the viewer of the pervading stereotype.

Aside from his dress, Fonzie was known as a womanizer. In fact, when he snapped his fingers, females would swarm around him like animals, just waiting to be acknowledged by him. In one episode, Fonzie is speaking with a woman in a booth at Arnolds and snaps his fingers by mistake. Once he apologizes and sends the women on their way, the lady with whom he is conversing says, "Hey, say, that's a nice trick" to which the Fonz retorts, "Oh, it ain't no trick, it's a gift," cueing the automated audience laughter, signifying acceptance of both this behavior and mentality. A double irony exists in this scene. It is the female character who compliments Fonzie's "trick," yet he retorts, "it's a gift" maintaining masculine control over the female character. Other times Fonzie snaps and a brood of ladies comes running and he acknowledges them one by one, making the girls "wait their turn" for a little dance with Fonzie. On the one hand, one may argue that Fonzie's personality overflows with charism, considered a positive character trait by many, and common for Italians. Yet, when he responds that it is rather a "gift," other connotations ebb, that of an oversexed and egocentric male. To a certain extent, Fonzie represents an even harsher image than Joey Tribbiani evidenced through the egotistical behavior extended through controlling women. His behavior toward women can be defined as one between an animal and its master, especially when considering his actions of "snapping."

Although he is often demonstrating the Casanova type-casted character, unlike Casanova, the Fonz does not exude intelligence. Instead, he has been given, to some extent, strength, namely brawn. First and foremost, the Fonz is distinguished by his ineloquent language and inability to speak in sentence-length discourse. More often than not, Fonzie responds to conversations in lieu of initiating them, and although he does engage in serious discussion, mostly with the Cunningham family, particularly Richie and Joanie, he is remembered for his preverbal "sounds," strange expressions, and ticks. When thinking back to *Happy Days,* for example, we recall Fonzie's "exactamundo" or "correct-amundo," this hybridization of English and Spanish which acts as a double pun—Fonzie is supposed to be Italian American, yet he does not even mix English and Italian, English and dialect, or even Italian and dialect underscoring an absurdity of his character. One of his most repeated lines in the sitcom was "aaaaay," which the character used to communicate various things depending on his tone.[12] Even though the characters and spectators alike find this amusing, it underscores his characterization as illiterate and uneducated, which evidences the Italian Stallion image already crystalized in Italian American cinema.

To conclude this brief snapshot on the Fonz, it is important to consider two more points. Besides his dress, Fonzie was also known for his hair, which was greased and combed back. In fact, most episodes have an ever so brief scene when Fonzie is looking into the mirror and combing his hair, making a gesture and a grunt that denotes it is perfect, as he puts his comb into his back pocket. This recurring ceremony throughout the series demonstrates his own priorities of looks above all else; for him, his hair's perfection and looks represent a sense of *la bella figura*. The Fonz has a mix of *la bella figura* and a greaser complex. Considering his looks are most prevelant for him, there is serious attention drawn not only to looking good but also the process behind it; the spectator consciously watches Fonzie comb it back.

Yet, the semiotic signs associated with Fonzie's dress draw a grim picture of the representation of Italian Americans. The black, slicked back hair denotes him as a "greaser." According to the Urban Dictionary, a greaser is "a person who dresses in a rockabilly fashion and styles his hair in a pompadour or other tall retro hairstyle with a petroleum-based pomade, such as seen in the movies: *Grease, The Outsiders, Westside Story, Rebel Without a Cause,* etc." The movies suggested by the Urban Dictionary alone evidence my point—a greaser is considered to be an undereducated individual who often performs manual labor, or maintains no job, and is considered "trouble" for society. In addition to snapping, Fonzie often responds with the "thumbs up," and when items break, he seems to have the magic touch. This magic touch works on the jukebox at Arnold's as Fonzie never pays to play a song; instead, he taps it, and it plays whatever he wants. Often Mr. Cunningham needs help around the house with things that do not open, like a window or a door, as the camera would capture him struggling and complaining; along comes Fonzie with a "tap" or foot stomp and the item opens immediately. These examples paired with the fact that Fonzie is a mechanic create an image of "brawn" over brains.[13]

Through this perspective, Joey Tribbiani can be analyzed as a direct descendent of the stereotypical Fonzie character, which is established as early as the first episode of *Friends*. Before considering the first episode, however, we remember that Joey is known for his famous pick-up line, similar to Fonzie's, "How YOU doin?" Even though he is memorialized for that expression, he says it only 19 times in the 236 episodes, the first occurring in season 4.[14] Ironically, those numbers are very slim; yet, the audience attributes that expression to his character because we associate him with his uneducated, womanizing nature. In fact, Kevin S. Bright who worked on both *Friends* and later *Joey* (2004–2006) has noted, "On *Friends*, Joey was a womanizer, but we enjoyed his exploits. He was a solid friend, a guy you knew you could count on. Joey was deconstructed to be a guy who couldn't get a job, couldn't ask a girl out. He became a pathetic, mopey character. I felt he was moving in the wrong direction, but I was not heard,[15] concerning the cancellation of the 2004 program.

This sexualized portrayal of Joey begins in the first episode, both filmically and through his characterization. The initial close-up shot of the entire show is that of Joey Tribbiani, dressed in blue jeans with a black T-shirt and leather coat. Joey's hair is dark black and laying over his eyes. He is quickly presented as an Italian greaser before even being formally introduced to the spectator as Italian, which occurs numerous times throughout the ten-season run. Moreover, the camera heavily favors Joey, not only within the opening sequence of the first episode but also throughout that entire episode. In fact, within the first episode, Joey is often in the center of shots when he is within the frame, whether close-ups or medium shots. This blatant use of Joey as a focal point suggests that he has been added as a sex symbol, a means to entice the female viewers of the show.

How exactly does Joey encapsulate the Italian Stallion trope? In *Che Bella Figura!*, Gloria Nardini explores the concept of *"bella figura"* through various interviews, and according to Francesco Nardini, *la bella figura* is more prominent via social class than gender [16] Moreover, Gloria Nardini argues that *figura* could be viewed as either positive or negative: *fare la bella figura* relates to a sense of "honor," while *fare la brutta figura* represents a feeling of shame [17] She continues by discussing the performative aspect of *fare la figura,* claiming that it is not a switch which can be flipped, rather it is "in almost schizophrenic fashion, by the Italian performing it," a concept which recalls Luigi Pirandello and the mask. [18] In this manner the concept of *fare la figura* is doubly noteworthy for Joey's character considering his profession, that of actor. Through his character then, the notion of *fare la bella figura* can in fact be seen on various levels. To further muddle the depth of analysis, as actor, there exists a self-referential aspect of Joey's innate persona which is constantly performative. Jaqueline Reich offers a unique observation concerning *la bella figura:* "Whereas the *flaneur* is the subject of the gaze and the dandy the object, the *bella figura* is at once both spectacle and spectator." [19] Thus, Joey's character is presented as a double-edged sword: he is not only on display but also simultaneously the onlooker. The perspective however complicates even further his representation when we consider his public and private performance because by nature of the camera the spectator is privy to all three levels of the camera (that of the protagonist, the camera itself, and the spectator).

In addition to being characterized as sexy in the first episode, he is presented as less than successful. Throughout the series, Joey more often than not does not have continuous work, and when he does, he becomes a regular on soap operas. Even when he lands a decent role with a soap opera, it eventually ends. In fact in "The One Where Dr. Ramorary Dies," Dr. Ramorary, Joey's character, is actually killed off the program (Season 2, Episode 8). In addition to rarely being employed full-time, a reoccurring theme is Joey missing his auditions for various reasons: often he forgets; sometimes others forget to tell him. Both scenarios underscore a lack of professionalism connected with Joey and his work while reflecting on what Joey's friends think about his acting. Another aspect which contributes to his career issues is his agent, Estelle Leonard (June Gable). It is unclear if Estelle is Italian or Jewish; nevertheless, she is a horrible agent. In fact, when Estelle dies in "The One Where Estelle Dies" (Season 10, Episode 15), both Joey and her only other client, who is even less successful than Joey, offer a brief eulogy. Estelle's role within the series is another one heavily stereotyped. Her ethnic identity is ambiguous but her inability to do her job is clear. In fact, Joey even leaves Estelle and before finding out that she has died, he was ready to rehire her out of guilt. Thus, her death to a certain degree foreshadows Joey's own lack of success, while underscoring his kindness for others and those he holds in high regard.

Another important moment in Joey's career is when he is cast in a small part in *Law & Order* in "The One Where Ross Can't Flirt" (Season 5, Episode 19). Being on *Law & Order* would have been a noteworthy advancement for his career considering it is a primetime show. As such, he gets excited about it and organizes a screening party to which he invites his Italian grandmother (nonnie), who does not speak English. Unfortunately, Joey does not realize until everyone is awaiting his debut that his small role had been cut from the episode; as a quick fix to the situation with nonnie, Joey shoots a brief homemade film in which he pops into the scene, wearing the same clothes in which he enters the apartment earlier in the scene. His grandmother is the only family member supportive of his profession, and this moment is important for their relationship. At the end of Joey's brief moment of fame, the "home video" shows Chandler singing and both Chandler and Joey run to turn the video player off, claiming it is a preview for next week.

From a cultural standpoint, this episode stands out for a few reasons. When nonnie enters, all of the friends ask if this is the nonnie who speaks English or not in a sarcastic tone. This shared statement acknowledges the four, white privileged friends' outlook on Joey and his Italian family—that of ignorant migrants who cannot speak English. Ironically, Phoebe, the other "outsider" of the group, randomly begins speaking to Joey's grandmother in Italian, underscoring a shared experience with Joey. This shared experience will be analyzed in depth later. For now, suffice it to say that the outsiders ironically surprise the viewers with a level of noteworthy culture. This episode also emphasizes the foundational bonds of family. Joey is the only character who openly embraces his family and celebrates their presence; the other characters loathe visiting with family. Simultaneously it demonstrates the importance of the Italian family, as most of the friends do not share positive bonds with their families. In fact, *Friends,* to a certain extent, acts to exhibit how friends can form a family.

Much earlier than Season 5, Joey gets a gig as Al Pacino's butt double in "The One with the Butt" (Season 1, Episode 6). Basically, Joey's role is to serve as Al Pacino's backside replacement in a shower scene. Joey works hard to prepare for this role, as he even asks Monica for moisturizer for his derriere, which he applies in their apartment. When the time comes to perform, Joey tenses up and needs to do a few takes. In the end, he is fired for "over acting" and complains that the moviegoers will know it is not his butt. Upset at his friends' retort, he responds again saying that his mother would know. It becomes rather clear that Joey becomes the "ass" of the joke, first among his own friends, but, more importantly, for the audience. His acting is deemed so bad that he cannot be a stand-in for a shower scene. Moreover, by filling in as Al Pacino's derriere, one can read this act as a complete eraser of Joey, literally stripped down as a sex symbol. Additionally, it assumes another stereotype, that Joey must be a fill in for an Italian American actor. Simultaneously, Joey underscores being the *mammone,* or mommy's boy, having the audience doubly laugh at him, underscoring his ridiculousness. Not only does this joke capture his inability to act, it devotes the entire episode to laughing at him and his status of the *inetto.*

In *Beyond the Latin Lover*, Jacqueline Reich defines the *inetto* as "the particularly Italian incarnation of the schlemiel or anti-hero, . . . this figure is a man in conflict with an unsettled and at times unsettling political and sexual environment."[20] In her chapter "In the Beginning Mastroianni, Masculinity, and Italian Cinema," she discusses its origins in the *commedia dell'arte* as it evolves to contemporary times from Pirandello's character Mattia Pascal of *Il fu Mattia Pascal* and others. In the end, Reich argues that "The Italian male is 'good at being a man' precisely because he masks the *inetto* through the performance of hypermasculinity: protection of honor, procreation, and sexual segregation."[21] Following Reich's characterization of the *inetto,* all the previously mentioned Italian American male television personas can easily be described as *inetti,* starting with the Fonz and ending with Raymond Barone of *Everybody Loves Raymond.* What makes the Joey Tribbiani character particularly unique is the layers of negative stereotypes and the unchanging nature of his persona.

The first episode therefore clearly defines Joey's haphazard career past and foreshadows its future. The show presents him as an Italian Stallion typecast character; his *inetto* personality permeates early in the series. The opening episode features Rachel having fled her wedding still in her white gown. Later in the episode, Joey begins to flirt with Rachel, and she asks about his profession. When he says he is an actor, she inquires if she has seen him in anything, and Monica and Chandler poke fun at him for playing Pinocchio at a local children's theater. Although the *Pinocchio* tale by Carlo Collodi is a historical novel with many levels of meaning, the average American viewer is unaware of the true story. Rather, most Americans are only familiar with the Disney version, and *Pinocchio* is an obvious reference to his *Italianità.* On a basic level, *Pinocchio* is a bildungsroman story of a boy becoming a man, but Monica and Chandler are obviously playing with the image since Joey is performing this role at the children's theater. Therefore, the two seem to suggest that Joey justly belongs at the children's theater, and his hopes of ever becoming a man are unlikely. Moreover, Pinocchio is immature and does not learn his lesson easily; the story, both literally and figuratively, critiques an empirical philosophy to education. In fact, this conversation arises when Joey attempts to flirt with Rachel, representing his "inetto" nature when it comes to adult relationships; remember Rachel just left her fiancée, Barry, at the altar hours before. Like Pinocchio, Joey is often unable to understand social cues and as such is characterized as an outsider or an awkward presence. Finally, like Pinocchio, Joey must always learn through trial and error, which often gets him into trouble. Even at the end of the series, Monica and Chandler make sure to have a special room for Joey in their new house. In the final episode, moreover, Monica prepares Joey's favorite, lasagna, and leaves some in his freezer. In ten years, Joey never grows up (Peter Pan); the final episode demonstrates how Joey still needs someone else taking care of him. If the show is truly adapting to adulthood, like Miller suggests, then Joey is the only character who fails and cannot "become a real boy," to continue the *Pinocchio* metaphor.

In the same episode, Joey and Chandler help Ross rebuild his life away from his lesbian ex-wife, Carol. The guys visit Ross's new apartment and assist in putting together furniture. During their conversation, Joey tries to cheer him up and for the second time in this first episode tells Ross that in order to get over his ex-wife, he needs to engage in sexual activity with other women, or at the very least see some strippers. He creates a metaphor for Ross comparing women to various ice-cream flavors,

> That's like saying there is only one flavor of ice cream Ross, there's lots of flavors out there, there's Rocky Road, and Cookie Dough, and *Bing* Cherry Vanilla. You can get them with jimmies, or nuts, or *whipped cream.* This is the best thing that's ever happened to you . . . grab a spoon.[22]

This discourse highlights Joey's primal nature toward women as sexual objects used to satisfy male appetites. Although a bit exaggerated, Joey's character perpetuates the Italian Stallion stereotype, contradicting his strong familial connections to women. Simultaneously, even if the content is sexist, Joey's metaphor expresses a sense of loyalty and inspiration toward Ross. Even though the metaphor is flawed, Joey's message can still be interpreted as positive, as he attempts to cheer up his good friend and remind him that there are other people out there for him.

Joey's bond with his family is crucial for him and is expressed throughout the ten seasons. Joey shares a close relationship with his Italian grandmother, even though she only appears in one episode. These close familial relationships exist with most of the Tribiani females. In "The One with the Boobies" (Season 1, Episode 13), Joey's dad comes into the city for work and decides to stay with Joey. During a phone conversation in Joey's apartment, Joey grabs the phone from his father to talk to his mother, and he realizes he is talking to his mistress, Ronni. Joey finds Ronni waiting for his father outside his Manhattan apartment. Shocked, he has no idea how to respond. When his father arrives, also surprised to find Ronni in Joey's apartment, he offers to go to a hotel, but Joey blocks them, and the possibility of coitus, as Joey places each in a different bedroom. He tells his father that he needs to make things right with his mother. The next scene reveals Joey's mother paying him a visit with a bunch of groceries, prepared chicken, and a smack across his head for ruining the situation that she knows exists. In the end, Joey has to reverse everything back to the way it originally was.

This episode brings various aspects of Italian American culture into light. First, the audience is presented with another Italian American male who is cheating on his wife, an image that repeats itself throughout the history of Italian American film culture. Moreover, his mother is aware of the cheating and accepts it because it is the best way to deal with his father. She claims that he is calmer at home, more loving with her, and she even senses his guilt in a positive manner toward her. Through his mother's perspective, therefore, the audience views another Italian American stereotype that of "Catholic guilt." Joey's own mother notes that his father has been treating her better because he feels guilty about his own infidelity. The circular nature of destruction is laughable because the Italian American mother is aware, accepting, and even promotes the father's extramarital affair; this theme perpetuates negative views concerning the treatment of women, the sanctity of marriage, and honesty in general. Lastly, Joey's father creates dumb cover stories, while the mother is obviously aware that he is cheating, including, "I'm staying over at my accountant's." Therefore, not only is Joey's father stereotyped as the unfaithful husband to his wife, but he is also characterized as dim-witted, a trait seen also in Joey.

On a side note, this episode shows a soft side to Joey in relation to his mother and women at large. While sleeping on the hideaway bed with Chandler, Joey questions his approach to women and family. Subsequently, the viewer knows this reflection proves fruitless as Joey quickly returns to his "stallion" character throughout the ten-season run; however, early on in the show, he does in fact stop and ponder his current views on relationships. He wants his mother to be the only one for his father. In this regard, Joey's traditionalist persona protrudes; he does not want his mother to be secondary to his father's mistress which is why he tells his father to break things off with Ronni. Joey believes it to be the honorable thing to do and highlights his loyal nature, as characteristic which presents strongly within his character throughout the show. Ironically, it is Joey's mother who accepts this "either/or" type of relationship, portraying once again a patriarchal hierarchy's point of view in Italian American families. It is almost as if to say Italian American men can do whatever they want with other women as long as the mistress(es) is/are kept in the shadows. It alludes to Henry Hills's (Ray Liotta) comment from *Goodfellas* when he states that Friday night is for the mistress and Saturday for the family. Joey's parents' relationship exemplifies this archaic situation of male dominance and control. It is necessary, however, to underscore Joey's intentions: on the one hand, he attempts to honor his mother and correct his father's distasteful actions. On the other hand, he perpetuates the stereotypes of his father. Therefore, even though the spectator would like to cheer for Joey and his honest side, in the end he maintains the status quo as Italian womanizer and the only character to remain single at the end of the series.

Although Joey attempts to save his mother's femininity and wholesome nature, she is in fact not characterized as feminine in the traditional sense, nor are any of the Tribbiani women. Rather, she presents herself as an aggressive, dominant woman and head of the household. We first see this as she slaps Joey's face upon entering his apartment; this image continues as she forces the hideaway bed back into its original, sofa position, a chore Joey could not complete immediately before his mother's arrival. Additionally, her appearance is not overly feminine: she is short and a bit stout, and her diction and voice are both rough. At the end of Joey's conversation with his mother, she begins to propose a question, but Joey interrupts her:

Mrs. Tribbiani: "So tell me, did you see her?"

Joey: "Yeah, you're ten times prettier than she is."

Mrs. Tribbiani: "That's sweet [laughing]. Could I take her?"[23]

This brief dialogue is emblematic of the hierarchy of values in the Italian American community that reflects the stereotypes present in the media: beauty and force. Joey assumes his mother wants to be the prettier one, the more feminine figure, and thus the more desired. His mother, on the other hand, wants to be the domineering one, the smarter woman, the one with power. This perspective can be read as a break from the traditional woman, and although not feminist on the surface, can in fact contain feminist values. It breaks a bit from the theoretical *bella figura* discourse from earlier and calls for power, self-control, and independence over beauty, which is a clear break from the imagined Italian American mothers present on mainstream television.

In this manner, Mrs. Tribbiani invokes gender issues for the show. Considering Joey's predisposition for being a womanizer, his natural reaction seems a bit distorted. The audience can presume Joey would be a bit more empathic to his father; rather, he remains loyal to his mother like a true *mammone.* When his father visits, Joey cooks for him, which is the only time Joey cooks throughout the entire show (in fact, even in the last episode Monica prepares some lasagna for Joey and leaves it in his freezer). It seems as if he is trying to impress his dad by making spaghetti sauce.[24] As Joey begins to hear about his affair, there is a joke launched by his father about him burning the tomatoes. Although there is a bit of male bonding in this episode, he still tries to protect his mother and her honor by demanding his father leave his mistress. This aspect of Joey's character demonstrates his protective nature, which continues throughout *Friends*. Mrs. Tribbiani, however, defies her son's protection and believes to know what is best for herself, in a certain way underscoring another stereotype of the Italian mother, this figure who keeps the family connected and focused: the all-encompassing superwoman. In the final moments of their conversation, Mrs. Tribbiani shows what is more important to her—power over beauty. She is easily defined as *furba* for the Italian or Italian American spectator[25]

Similarly, Joey is protective of his sisters. In "The One Where Chandler Can't Remember Which Sister" (Season 3, Episode 11), the friends throw Joey a birthday party. Chandler is already drunk, evident by the way he feeds the dog statue Jello shots. When Joey's seven sisters arrive to the party screaming his name and happy birthday, they look identical physically: big hair, dressed in black, sharing similar body gestures and speaking loudly. In fact, drunken Chandler asks, "How many of that girl are you seeing?" to which Monica responds that those are all Joey's sisters. When one approaches the drink table and meets Phoebe, they discuss alcoholic beverages. Phoebe says, "I'm drinking a Vodka and cranberry juice." Joey's sister retorts, "No kidding, that's exactly the drink I made myself right after I shot my husband," and Phoebe shockingly states, "Wow, I don't know how to talk to you." This first conversation of the evening echoes the earlier dialogue with Mrs. Tribbiani and how it is more important to be strong and powerful than tame and pretty. The Tribbiani sisters would be considered "rough around the edges" and should have no problem fending for themselves.

The day after the party, Chandler reveals that he had sex with one of Joey's sisters, but he cannot remember which one. As Chandler tries to figure out which sister he slept with, Joey busts into the apartment and says that Mary Angela told him that Chandler said, "he could really fall for her." Joey confronts Chandler and wants to know if he is looking for a rebound fling because of his ex, Janice, or if he is serious about her. When Chandler confirms his interest, Joey becomes excited. Chandler goes to visit Mary Angela, or really to figure out which sister is Mary Angela, and Mary Therese pulls Chandler aside and kisses him before he realizes that she is the wrong sister. Mary Angela enters the scene, catches them, and calls for Joey. The pack of sisters surrounds Chandler and Joey, taunting Joey to punch Chandler. Chandler offers a sincere apology, but this does not suffice. In the end, Joey accepts Chandler's apology but tells him he must apologize to Mary Angela. When Chandler looks around to figure about which one Mary Angela is, still confused partly due to their visual similarities partly due to his drunkenness the night before, he still cannot pick her out of the group. Then Joey gives his sister, Cookie, permission to punch Chandler.

The fact that Joey is not the deliverer of the punch further exemplifies two aspects of my argument. Cookie's physical aggression evidences the combative nature of the Tribbiani women while simultaneously reinforcing the importance of family. As one of the elder sisters, it is her responsibility to watch over and protect the brood. It is clear Joey trusts the power of his sister, as Cookie does in fact deliver a robust punch. At the same time, the spectator understands Joey's loyalty to his friends. Surprisingly, he does not approach the situation with a temper, rather he listens to Chandler and has the sisters deliver punishment. His actions in this episode tend to demonstrate a fair and loyal Joey.

In "The One's with Monica's Boots" (Season 8, Episode 11), Dina Tribbiani wants to get into fashion and meets Rachel for advice. The episode opens with Rachel joking about not sending any more Ralph Lauren clothing to prison, joking about Joey's sister who is in prison. This one-liner reiterates the social status of the Tribbiani family—Italian Americans—as losers and criminals. In this case, the wisecrack is more pointed; it is directed at one of Joey's sisters in prison, emphasizing not only social status but also gender trouble. Dina's real reason for meeting Rachel is because she, like Rachel, is pregnant and she does not know how to tell her family. As soon as she tells Joey and figures out who the father is, Joey goes to find him and brings him back to his apartment. Joey struggles to convince the couple to marry and explains how difficult single motherhood is. Rachel helps Joey understand that Dina can make adult decisions and that she must figure out her own life and not follow what society expects of her. This episode illustrates Joey's traditional conceptualization of Italian American masculinity. On the one hand, he wants the father of his sister's child to "man up" and take responsibility for his actions, as was expected in a previous generation. In fact, once again the Tribbiani family resorts to violence as Joey forcefully brings Bobby from Queens to his Manhattan apartment. This practice also forces two people, who may not love each other, into the bonds of marriage, which almost never ends well. These archaic practices, however, are squashed because of Rachel's influence, probably as a single-mother herself.

This aspect of Joey's character is the last to be examined in this piece. As much as Joey represents all the negative stereotypes associated with Italian Americans, any description of his character would have to include loyalty. However, Joey is the least connected "friend" in *Friends*. In fact, he never had "friendship" status with the other characters originally; he fell into the group as Chandler's roommate by tricking the competition. Joey's honesty is particular. He can never keep a secret, which is evidenced throughout the series, yet all his friends come to him when down or in need of assistance. He is the earnest "go-to" guy when the "going gets tough" and will always make his friends feel better about the situation. He is loyal and will protect his family and friends until the end. He is dedicated to what he holds dear.

To examine the theme further, Joey is not the only Italian negatively stereotyped on *Friends*. In the first season, as Ross is beginning to flirt with Rachel and about to ask her out for the first time, a cat pounces on him and scratches him. Rachel and Phoebe search the apartment building to find its owner and low and behold it is Paolo's, an Italian from Torino. Not only is Paolo sexy but he is also seductive and sweeps Rachel quickly off her feet. The relationship is short-lived because he makes a pass at Phoebe when he goes to the salon where she works as a masseuse. He makes a brief return in Season 2 just to relieve Rachel's jealousy of Ross's relationship with Julie. On a metaphorical level, Paolo and in particular his "pussy cat," cock block Ross, although the viewer can sense they belong together from the first episode and its repetition continues on screen throughout the series. In short, Paolo's attractive looks, although briefly present overall in the show, and sexy accent entice female viewers as does Joey's. As soon as Joey meets Paolo, he becomes extremely self-conscious and worried about "being re-placed" as the Italian friend. Moreover, Paolo's behavior with Phoebe re-minds the viewer of Joey's dad and his extramarital affair. Including Joey, therefore, all Italian men on *Friends* want is sex.

The sense of replacement, however, is an interesting one to ponder. All three male friends feel threatened by Paolo in their own way, Ross being the most direct and overt. Yet, Joey, who at this point in the series is not inter-ested in Rachel, has a different fear, that of eraser. Paolo's presence, in a certain way, threatens Joey's *Italianità*, primarily because he is Italian in-stead of Italian American; he is "more" Italian than Joey and Paolo's accent clearly underscores this aspect. Secondly however, Joey, at least partially, understands his own displacement in the rather "traditionally white" friends group he maintains. In the episodes with Paolo, Joey becomes more con-scious of true relationship with the group at large.

The negative connotations about Italian men and sex extend gender bias on *Friends*. In "The One with the Butt" (Season 1, Episode 6), Chandler asks Aurora, an Italian woman, out at Joey's play entitled "Freud!" Although Chandler believes she is out of his league, Joey convinces him to ask her out; she agrees to a date. On her date with Chandler, she reveals that she is married to a man named Rick, has a boyfriend on the side, Ethan, and wants to pursue Chandler purely for coitus. Although Chandler pretends to be fine with being the third man in Aurora's life, once she adds a fourth, Andrew, he cannot take it anymore. He asks for a monogamous relationship with her; when she refuses, he breaks up with her. Aurora is a very minor character throughout the show, however, once again the view of Italians/Italian Americans is one of sexual beings, incapable of monogamy.[26]

Clearly encouraged with the height of Catholicism in the Western world during the Medieval period, monogamy is a rather new concept in the history of the world. Yet, an honest and open discourse of polygamy is never in fact addressed in *Friends*, even though the character of Aurora identifies as such. Joey encourages Chandler to pursue Aurora, but Chandler cannot accept partaking in a polyamorous relationship, so much so that he attempts to convince her to become monogamous with him. Aurora dismisses the idea before Chandler can formulate the request. It is Joey's Freudian nature, it seems, who would prefer to partake in the relationship with Aurora, or at the very least, an accepted and honest open relationship. Joey encourages Chandler to try it out, but the spectator quickly notes that this type of relationship is not for Chandler, the boy next door.

Therefore, Joey's womanizing nature, Paolo's blatant cheating on Rachel, and Aurora's polyamorous needs all emerge as subversive and negative. Joey's continuous philandering perpetually reminders the spectator of his unfavorable moral compass. The conceptualization of the Latin Lover as Jacqueline Reich has argued maintains the status quo with these characters too. Even though Joey does indeed have a warm, loyal side which his friends not only appreciate but also count on, he remains the sexual pervert of the group.

DICHOTOMY OF *FRIENDS,* OR
GIRARD'S TRIANGLE OF DESIRE

Mainstream Western Civilization has long been built on the conceptualization of dichotomies. Countries and cultures that boast the presence of Christianity also often heavily rely on the importance of dichotomies in the routine of daily life, engrained even in its organization. In American society, married couples receive tax breaks and now homosexual couples can get married. Dichotomies have become part of our daily lives without much thought. It was not until the AIDS epidemic in the late 1980s that Queer theorists and activists actually fought against the dichotomy structure for the LGBTQI-AA+ community.[27] Even today, little substantive change has occurred in adopting a less heteronormative language.

More specifically, throughout the ten seasons of *Friends*, dichotomies are present from the very first episode until the absolute last one. The general make-up of the cast is six characters: three groups of two from the beginning, yet by the end, the organization changes. In fact, Joey is the only "friend" who remains single by the end of season ten, yet in the absolute final shot of the series, Joey and Phoebe, the two outsiders, are naturally "coupled" together. Furthermore, Joey's character partakes in René Girard's conceptualization of the triangle of desire. When discussing triangular desire, Girard argues, "The desire that the subject has for *the object* is nothing else but the desire he has for the prestige that he attributes to the one who possesses the object (or who gets ready to desire the object at the same time as him)".[28]

This use of Girard is appropriate for the triangle between Joey-Ross-Charlie and even Joey-Ross-Rachel but functions less uniformly when dealing with Joey-Chandler-Monica because sexually there is not much there; however, the triangle of desire on a platonic/emotional level is critical for Joey's character. The triangular nature of the Joey-Phoebe relationship works in a different manner.

At this juncture, it is important to remember some aspects relating to our characters. Ross and Monica are brother and sister and are nonpracticing or often called, "half" Jews. According to some bloggers who followed the show, Rachel Green (Jennifer Aniston) is the only "real" Jewish character.[29] Therefore, three of the six characters are Jewish—Ross, Monica, and Rachel—and they all come from upper-class Long Island families. Therefore, even if their religion does not necessarily define them, their social class does, which marks them into another category. Moreover, Chandler is the son of Nora Tyler Bing, a noted erotic/romance novelist, and although he had a rough childhood because his father left the family on Thanksgiving Day with the house-boy, Chandler is the wealthiest of all the friends; not only does it seem as if he comes from an affluent family, he works hard and saves most of his earnings as a mid-level executive in "Statistical analysis and data reconfiguration." This leaves Phoebe and Joey as the dichotomy of the outsiders, first and foremost from a social-class perspective, but also from other aspects. Chandler's religion is not a focus, he is not a follower of any religion; he is a proclaimed Atheist. Phoebe is a follower of the New Age movement and is spiritual rather than religious. Joey mentions early on in the series that he is Catholic. Thus, when we examine the organization from a religious aspect, three characters are Jewish to some degree, Chandler is openly anti-religion, and then Joey and Phoebe practice "minority" religions and are paired together in that manner.

Joey and Phoebe are the only two characters who do not share the main four characters' "childhood." In fact, the four main characters all meet at Thanksgiving, while Ross and Chandler are in college and Monica and Rachel in high school. This event solidifies a major aspect of the show especially when considering it was screened on Thursdays; as such, *Friends* has had noteworthy Thanksgiving episodes and avid fans always looked forward to them. Returning to the moment when all four main characters meet, Chandler rejects Thanksgiving since his father left the family for the houseboy on this holiday, and because when he first meets the Gellers, Mrs. Geller is upset that Chandler will not partake in the typical Thanksgiving Day fare. In this manner, Phoebe and Joey are innocently and indirectly ostracized from the group as they are not childhood friends.

The dichotomy, however, does not completely function within the series. As womanizer, Joey does in fact make sexual attempts with almost every female character on the show, and twice with a man, Ross. In "The One with the Flashback" (Season 3, Episode 6), the show flashbacks to when Joey moves into Chandler's apartment and thus becomes part of the "friends." As Joey attempts to move a box into the apartment, he slips a little and Monica catches his fall; additionally, she does not let go of Joey's back. She invites him into the apartment for some lemonade. He is dressed in a white, V-neck T-shirt, black jeans, and gold *cornicello*, which is visually popping out of his T-shirt; the image screams Italian Stallion, reminding the spectator of Fonzie, minus the jacket. Monica tells him to make himself comfortable as she grabs the lemonade from the fridge. The next thing the spectator sees is Joey getting undressed behind a lamp shade. After the awkward moment of Monica seeing Joey nude, they clarify things and move forward. The next scene shows Joey watching the famous, or infamous, *Baywatch*, which Chandler has never seen before. Once he sees Nicole Eggert (Summer), Chandler joins Joey on the couch and they begin to bond. Years later, of course, we know Joey officiates the wedding of Chandler and Monica. In the final episodes of the series, the audience knows that Monica and Chandler are looking for a home outside of Manhattan since they will be adopting a child. In the final episode, we learn that the adoptee is actually not one child, but twins, and that the happy couple purchased a home in Westchester. Joey is hesitant to see his friends leave as both Chandler and Monica regularly look after him. Joey frequently raids Monica's fridge and in the final episode she has prepared and frozen a few lasagnas for Joey, placing them in his freezer. When Joey finally cracks and visits the house, the final bedroom he sees, he learns, is his. In this regard, Joey becomes part of the triangular relationship of Monica and Chandler, and they will continue to "keep an eye" on him, demonstrating once again how Joey is the only friend never to grow up, reminding the spectator of the reference to Pinocchio in the first episode.

When it comes to Rachel and Joey, the level of desire is much more intense. In Season 8, we learn that Rachel is carrying Ross's child. At first, Rachel lives with Joey, taking Chandler's room, but as Rachel has some pregnancy scares and Joey is caring for her, Ross becomes jealous. Rachel is also depressed because Ross is dating Mona. Joey takes Rachel on a formal date to make her feel better, and he begins to realize he has feelings for Rachel. Rumors are spread about which friend Joey has a crush on; in fact, Phoebe believes that it is her and in that moment the group learns it is really Rachel. In "The One Where Joey Tells Rachel" (Season 8, Episode 16), Rachel breaks Joey's heart even though, as a loyal friend, he respects her decision and maintains their relationship.

The Joey-Rachel story does not end there. Joey once again enters the triangle of desire with Ross, but this time over another character, Charlie, a new colleague of Ross's at the university. After Ross spends the day showing Charlie around, she meets Joey at a party that he secretly organizes every year for his actor friends, and they start kissing (Season 9, Episode 20, "The

One with the Soap Opera Party"). Ross retreats, however, and helps Joey woo Charlie by suggesting intellectual activities for them to do.[30] At the end of "The One in Barbados, Parts 1 & 2" (Season 9, Episodes 23 and 24), Ross gives a keynote address in Barbados at a conference, and the entire gang attends. Joey and Charlie break up, Ross kisses Charlie while Joey watches them secretly, and then Joey kisses Rachel. Season 10 opens with the drama between Ross-Charlie and Joey-Rachel. In "The One After Joey and Rachel Kiss" (Season 10, Episode 1), Ross confesses to Joey that he is seeing Charlie; Joey chickens out and does not tell Ross about Rachel but of course Ross catches them kissing. The issues between Joey and Ross do not come to a head until "The One Where Ross Is Fine" (Season 10, Episode 2), when Ross calls for a double date, which ends horribly but loyal Joey stays the night with Ross to make sure both he and their relationship return to the status quo. By Episode 3, Joey and Rachel agree that they are better as friends after an attempt at sexual relations. This action, of course, allows Ross to woo Rachel in the last episode of the series, concluding the white-privileged fairy tale with which the series opened ten years earlier.

To wrap up this second part of this contribution, we need to return to the character of Phoebe and how Girard's triangle of desire works with her and Joey. Phoebe and Joey are outsider characters from both the development of friendship and social class perspectives. In fact, both characters encounter the four main characters through a situation of housing—they entered the circle through renting rooms in the apartment. On another level, these two entered the world of "friends" out of a basis of need—shelter—according to Maslow's conceptualization. Joey and Phoebe change jobs the most, and Joey in particular is always looking for another role or gig. Phoebe, to some extent, is also an artist as we view her performing with her guitar, usually at the coffee house, Central Perk.

To a certain extent, however, they transform the dichotomy into the triangle. First, Joey and Phoebe made a pact, off screen, to marry each other if they are single at 40. Phoebe however also makes the same pact with Ross. When Rachel tries to get her own pact, it is decided by the end of "The One with the Proposal, Part 2" (Season 6, Episode 25) that Ross and Rachel will have a pact as will Joey and Phoebe. This episode, therefore, solidifies my dichotomy argument, while simultaneously challenging it. Joey has the pleasure of marrying another couple, Phoebe and Mike Hannigan (Paul Rudd) in "The One with Phoebe's Wedding" (Season 10, Episode 12). Even though Mike proposes in Barbados (Season 9, Episode 23/24), he continues to have a minor role in Season 10 but never enters into any group himself. Thus, Joey brings the two together while remaining somewhat connected to Phoebe.

As noted in the penultimate shot of the 266th episode with the characters present, the dichotomies return: Monica and Chandler are stage left holding their twins, so the dichotomy is actually doubled. Stage right, there is Ross and Rachel hugging and kissing each other. In the back of the shot near the window, there is Joey and Phoebe with their arms intertwined. Mike is not present in the second half of the last episode at all. Joey and Phoebe physically complete the visual representation of the triangle. As such, their relationship as outsiders still completes the triangle. This visual pun is unique because in a certain regard there is closure and completion, but still Joey remains the only lonely soul, emotionally but also physically, as he is the only character to remain in the original building. From a geo-political reading, therefore, Joey is the only character truly outside of the dichotomy and can only exist within the triangle. In fact, he was to gift Monica and Chandler with Chick Jr. and Duck Jr. for a housewarming present, but ultimately Chandler suggests it best they reside with Joey. Chandler's gesture proposes two concepts: first, Chandler has grown up from farm animals to children and no longer wants animals in his new Westchester home and second, Chandler is afraid that Joey will be lonely so he leaves the animals with him. Even this aspect recalls a lack of growth on Joey's part, as he is uncoupled and a foster parent to a chick and a duck. It also retains Joey's ignorance as a chick and a duck are not even considered domestic animals.

CONCLUSION

In short, Joey Tribbiani's character fulfills a niche the show needed, primarily sex appeal. In the first episode, Joey's hair is long and in his eyes; his image is still that of Italian Stallion but a tad more feminine. From the second episode forward however, Joey's image becomes sexier and more masculine, focusing more on the brawny side. In fact, his character perpetuates the stereotypes already established on mainstream television beginning as far back as Arthur Fonzarelli from *Happy Days*. Joey is the only character that cannot flourish in a coupled relationship and must also rely on two other friends, underscoring his inept nature. Within Girard's theoretical triangle, Joey is never the couple; he remains stuck between the others and loses what essentially is his own persona. By examining the various aspects of Joey's character, it becomes evident that his role eternalizes early stereotypes, suggesting that the Italian American community, as represented through most individual mainstream television personas, has in fact not truly integrated into society, and remains marginalized, uneducated, and merely laughable. Whether conscious or unconscious, as an *inetto*, the Joey character is forced outside of the inner circle of friends in *Friends*.

NOTES

1. https://www.thesun.co.uk/fabulous/7526023/friends-leaving-netflix-soon-fans-devasta
ted/. December 18, 2018. https://www.vox.com/culture/2018/12/11/18131021/netflix-friends-
gone-streaming-cord-cutting. December 18, 2018.

2. Adam Sternbergh, "Is *Friends* Still the Most Popular Show on TV? Why 20-Somethings
Want to Stream a 20-Year-Old Sitcom about a Bunch of 20-Somethings in a Coffee Shop."
https://www.vulture.com/2016/03/20-somethings-streaming-friends-c-v-r.html. September 25,
2019.

3. Kelsey Miller, *I'll Be There For You: The One about* Friends, Toronto, Hanover Square
Press, 2018.

4. Jonathan J. Cavallero, among others, have argued for a study of this nature for some
time. See "Gangsters, Fessos, Tricksters, and Sopranos: The Historical Roots of Italian
American Stereotype Anxiety," *Journal of Popular Film and Television* (2004): 50–51.

5. See for example Robert Casillo's *Gangster Priest: The Italian American Cinema of
Martin Scorsese,* Toronto, University of Toronto Press, 2007, or Aaron Baker, *A Companion to
Martin Scorsese,* Oxford, Wiley-Blackwell, 2014, or Vito Zagarrio, *The "Un-Happy Ending"
Re-Viewing the Cinema of Frank Capra,* New York, Bordighera Press, 2011, Nick Browne,
Francis Ford Coppola's The Godfather Trilogy, Cambridge, Cambridge University Press,
1999.

6. See Jonathan Cavallero, *Hollywood's Italian American Filmmakers: Capra, Scorsese,
Savoca, Coppola, and Tarantino,* Urbana-Champaign: University of Illinois Press, 2011.

7. For an Italian perspective, see also Flaminio Di Biagi's *Italoamericani tra Hollywood e
Cinecittà.* Genoa, Italy, Le Mani, 2010 or Paola Casella, *Hollywood Italian: Gli italiani
nell'American celluloide,* Milan, Baldini & Castoldi, 1998.

8. See Edvige Giunta and Kathleen Zamboni-McCormick, *Teaching Italian American Literature, Film, and Popular Culture,* New York, The Modern Language Association of America, 2010. In this volume, two articles pertain to the topic: "A Contested Place: Italian
Americans in Cinema and Television" by Anthony Julian Tamburri and "Cultural Stereotyping
in *Happy Days* and The Sopranos" by Courtney Judith Ruffner.

9. See Massimo Zangari, *"Everybody Loves Raymond* and Sitcom's Erasure of Difference"
in *Racial and Ethnic Identities in the Media,* London, Palgrave Macmillan, 2016, 199–210.

10. I purposefully refer to Ross as Dr. Ross Geller to follow official protocol as his character
is written this way on IMDB and highlight the difference in status his character recalls.

11. In the first season of *Happy Days,* the Fonz only wore his leather jacket when pictured
with his motocycle to underscore his greaser look. Otherwise during that first season, he
actually wore a gray windbreaker. See "Why did the Fonz rarely wear a leather jacket during
the first season of 'Happy Days'?" https://www.metv.com/stories/why-did-the-fonz-rarely-
wear-a-leather-jacket-during-the-first-season-of-happy-days.

12. Ironically in 2011, Henry Winkler revealed that he used the "aaaaay" to "hide the
crippling undiagnosed dyslexia with which the Fonz star Henry Winkler was struggling." See
Lucy Buckland, "Unhappy Days: Fonz Star Reveals He Created 'aaaaay' Catchphrase to Cover
Up Misery of Undiagnosed Dyslexia." *Dailymail.com* October 13, 2011. https://www.
dailymail.co.uk/news/article-2048553/Unhappy-days-Fonz-star-reveals-created-catchphrase-
cover-battle-undiagnosed-dyslexia.html. Accessed 20 December 2018.

13. A thorough study of Fonzie's Italian Americanness is lacking in our field, especially
considering Garry Marshall, an Italian American is indeed the creator. Courtney Judith Ruffner's "Cultural Stereotyping in *Happy Days* and The Sopranos" is however a good place to
initiate research in the field.

14. Vanessa Golembewski, "The Success Rate of 'How YOU Doin?'" https://www.
refinery29.com/en-us/2015/09/93481/joey-friends-pick-up-lines. December 29, 2018.

15. Suzanne C. Ryan, (December 7, 2006). "Friendly art of funny." *The Age.* Melbourne,
Australia. Archived from the original on August 25, 2009. Retrieved December 30, 2008.

16. Gloria Nardini, Che Bella Figura! *The Power of Performance in an Italian Ladies' Club
in Chicago,* Albany, NY, State University of New York Press, 1999, 12.

17. Ibid., 18.

18. Ibid., 19.

19. Ibid., 4.

20. Jacqueline Reich, *Beyond the Latin Lover: Marcello Mastroianni, Masculinity, and Italian Cinema.* Bloomington and Indianapolis: Indiana University Press, 2004, 1.

21. Ibid., 8–10.

22. *Friends,* Season 1, Episode 1, "The One Where It All Began"/"The One Where Monica Gets a Roommate"/"The First One (The Pilot)."

23. *Friends,* Season 1, Episode 13, "The One with the Boobies."

24. There are a lot of connotations related to the "making of spaghetti sauce," including a way to catch a cheater, to make someone fall in love with you, to even a code-word for reproduction. The fact that Joey never cooks seems to suggest a hidden meaning for this episode in particular, most appropriately that of cheating.

25. See Anthony Julian Tamburri, 2017.

26. From a Gender Studies standpoint, I applaud Aurora and believe that her character attempts to push the bounds of dichotomy in our society. Yet from a cultural studies standpoint, particularly of Italian/Italian American studies, I find her character to be problematic and stereotypical.

27. See Leo Bersani, "Is the Rectum a Grave?"

28. http://www.cottet.org/girard/desir2.en.htm . December 31, 2018.

29. Lindsey Weber, "*Friends* Countdown: Is Rachel Green Jewish?" https://www.vulture.com/2014/12/friends-countdown-is-rachel-green-jewish.html. December 29, 2018.

30. This action also evidences my earlier argument that Joey is eye candy for both the characters on screen and the spectator. Charlie likes Joey because he is sexy, suave, and a good kisser, but he cannot even figure out how to woo her properly. This underscores his ignorant, uneducated character.

BIBLIOGRAPHY

Baker, Aaron. *A Companion to Martin Scorsese.* Oxford: Wiley-Blackwell, 2014.

Bersani, Leo. "Is the Rectum a Grave?" *October* 43 (1987): 197–222. doi:10.2307/3397574.

Browne, Nick. *Francis Ford Coppola's* The Godfather Trilogy. Cambridge: Cambridge University Press, 1999.

Casillo, Robert. *Gangster Priest: The Italian American Cinema of Martin Scorsese.* Toronto: University of Toronto Press, 2007.

Reich, Jacqueline. *Beyond the Latin Lover. Marcello Mastroianni, Masculinity, and Italian Cinema.* Bloomington and Indianapolis, Indiana University Press, 2004.

Cavallero, Jonathan. *Hollywood's Italian American Filmmakers: Capra, Scorsese, Savoca, Coppola, and Tarantino,* Urbana-Champaign: University of Illinois Press, 2011.

Di Biagi, Flaminio. *Italoamericani tra Hollywood e Cinecittà.* Genoa, Italy: Le Mani, 2010.

Flood, Rebecca. "OH MY GAWD *Friends* could be leaving Netflix soon—and devastated fans say they'll CANCEL their subscriptions in protest." 18 December 2018.

Friends, Season 1, Episode 1, "The One Where It All Began"/"The One Where Monica Gets a Roommate"/"The First One (The Pilot);" Season 1, Episode 6, "The One with the Butt;" Season 1, Episode 13, "The One with the Boobies;" Season 2, Episode 8, "The One Where Dr. Ramorary Dies;" Season 3, Episode 6, "The One with the Flashback;" Season 3, Episode 11, "The One Where Chandler Can't Remember Which Sister;" Season 5, Episode 19, "The One Where Ross Can't Flirt;" Season 6, Episode 25, "The One with the Proposal, Part 2;" Season 8, Episode 11, "The One with Monica's Boots;" Season 8, Episode 16, "The One Where Joeys Tells Rachel;" Season 9, Episode 20, "The One with the Soap Opera Party;" Season 9, Episode 23, "The One in Barbados, Part 1;" Season 9, Episode 24, "The One in Barbados, Part 2;" Season 10, Episode 1, "The One After Joey and Rachel Kiss;" Season 10, Episode 2, "The One Where Ross Is Fine;" Season 10, Episode 12, "The One with Phoebe's Wedding;" Season 10, Episode 15, "The One Where Estelle Dies;" Season 10, Episode 17, "The Last One, Part 1;" Season 10, Episode 18, "The Last One, Part 2."

Giunta, Edvige, and Kathleen Zamboni-McCormick. *Teaching Italian American Literature, Film,and Popular Culture.* New York: The Modern Language Association of America, 2010.

Golembewski, Vanessa. "The Success Rate of 'How YOU Doin?'" December 29, 2018.

Laurino, Maria. "From the Fonz to 'The Sopranos,' Not Much Evolution." December 24, 2000.

MeTV Staff. "Why did the Fonz rarely wear a leather jacket during the first season of 'Happy Days'?" February 20, 2017.

Miller, Kelsey. *I'll Be There for You: The One about* Friends, Toronto: Hanover Square Press, 2018.

Nardini, Gloria. *Che Bella Figura! The Power of Performance in an Italian Ladies' Club in Chicago.* Albany, NY: State University of New York Press, 1999.

Casella, Paola. *Hollywood Italian: Gli italiani nell'American celluloide.* Milan: Baldini & Castoldi, 1998.

Ruffner, Courtney Judith. "Cultural Stereotyping in *Happy Days* and *The Sopranos* in *Teaching Italian American Literature, Film, and Popular Culture,* Edvige Giunta and Kathleen Zamboni McCormick, eds. New York: The Modern Language Association of American, 2010, 231–236.

Ryan, Suzanne (December 7, 2006). *The Age.* Melbourne, Australia, from the original on August 25, 2009. Retrieved December 30, 2008.

Tamburri, Anthony Julian. "Italian Americans and Television," in *The Routledge History of Italian Americans.* William J. Connell and Stanislao G. Pugliese, eds. New York: Routledge, 2018.

———. "Il Sistema di segni del cinema italiano/americano: *code-switching* e la significabilità di *Mean Streets* di Martin Scorsese," *Ácoma* 13 (Autunno-Inverno 2017): 108–121.

———. "Chapter 1: Italian Americans and the Media: Cinema, Video, Television," in *Re-Viewing Italian Americana: Generalities and Specificities on Cinema.* New York: Bordighera Press, 2011.

———. "A Contested Place: Italian Americans in Cinema and Television," in *Teaching Italian American Literature, Film, and Popular Culture.* Edvige Giunta and Kathleen Zamboni McCormick, eds. New York: The Modern Language Association of America, 2010.

VanDerWerff, Emily Todd. "Why Netflix could have lost Friends - and what it means for the future of streaming." https://www.vox.com/culture/2018/12/11/18131021/netflix-friends-gone-streaming-cord-cutting. December 11, 2018.

Weber, Lindesey. "*Friends* Countdown: Is Rachel Green Jewish?" https://www.vulture.com/2014/12/friends-countdown-is-rachel-green-jewish.html. December 29, 2018.

Zagarrio, Vito. *The "Un-Happy Ending" Re-Viewing the Cinema of Frank Capra.* New York: Bordighera Press, 201.

Zangari, Massimo. "*Everybody Loves Raymond* and Sitcom's Erasure of Difference," in *Racial and Ethnic Identities in the Media*, London: Palgrave Macmillan, 2016.

Chapter Seven

Tony Soprano Meets Furio Giunta

Italian Americans and "Real" Italians in The Sopranos

Francesco Chianese

It has been twenty years since the first episode of *The Sopranos* aired in 1999, and film and television critics are still questioning whether this is the best TV series ever made, as was often stated while the show was being broadcast.[1] According to Peter Bondanella, *The Sopranos* "has changed the face of American television and has done more to popularize Hollywood's vision of Italian Americans than any single film or group of films since *The Godfather* trilogy."[2] This was Bondanella's reason behind the inclusion of this TV series in a volume devoted to Italian American cinema.[3] The news about New Line purchasing the screenplay of a prequel to the show, co-written by *The Sopranos* showrunner David Chase and Lawrence Conner, under the working title of *The Many Saints of Newark*, revived the feeling that nothing so complex and sophisticated has been seen on screen either before or afterward. Expectations could not be higher for this revival, despite the absence of the series' star James Gandolfini, who sadly passed away in 2013, but will be replaced somehow by his son Michael, starring as a younger version of protagonist Tony Soprano.

One of the most popular and critically acclaimed TV shows in the history of American television, *The Sopranos* ran for six seasons, over eighty-six episodes, from 1999 to 2007, winning twenty-one Primetime Emmy Awards, five Golden Globe Awards, and many other accolades. It has been described as one of the more sophisticated and realistic American TV productions, which has provided the most complex television representations of the Italian American character. While centered on the personal crisis undergone by mob boss Tony Soprano (James Gandolfini), it would be limiting to reduce the narrative of the series solely to the evolution of this storyline. In fact, the

141

development of Tony's plot is constantly intertwined with the events concerning both his personal family and criminal family, which often overlap in providing reasons for Tony's recurrent panic attacks. The large number of characters by whom Tony is constantly surrounded provide their own specific contribution to the complex picture defined by *The Sopranos*, which allows us to watch the series from a variety of viewpoints.

In this chapter I will not examine the series as a whole, but focus on Furio Giunta (Federico Castelluccio), appearing in a secondary role in only three seasons, for twenty-eight episodes in total. Furio migrates from Naples to join the Soprano crew in "Commendatori" (Season 2, Episode 4), and then returns to Naples in "Eloise" (Season 4, Episode 12). My aim is to demonstrate that while apparently a secondary character, Furio plays a significant role in the development of Tony's perspectives on gender, his family dynamics, and more broadly, in the framework of Tony's whole neighborhood, also influencing the storylines when he is not present on screen, and even after leaving New Jersey. In this contribution, I interpret Furio in the light of Lacanian psychoanalysis, and specifically, through Slavoj Žižek's and Fabio Vighi's reading of the Lacanian concept of the "Real." By embodying the Lacanian "Real," Furio obliges Tony to negotiate his myths about Italy and becomes a textual device that invites the audience to reconsider the romanticized image of Italy fed to the Italian American communities, as it has been handed down through generations.

By discussing the definition of "Real" in its specific meaning of the Lacanian Real, my argument seeks to dialogue with Fred Gardaphé's interpretation of *The Sopranos* in his wider consideration of the evolution of the representation of masculinity in Italian American culture.[4] It also engages with Laura E. Ruberto's and Joseph Sciorra's reflection on the "arrival of Real Italians" to the United States, by considering the case of Furio Giunta as exemplary of this more recent Italian flow of migration.[5] In fact, while in the world of television not much seems to have changed, the world around *The Sopranos* has undergone significant transformation, as has the field of Italian American studies. By challenging the delusions of his Italian American fellows, Furio may be considered as a representation on screen of the cultural clash highlighted by Ruberto and Sciorra, acted out when Italians migrating more recently to the Unites States meet the progeny of Italians who settled in the United States before World War II. Specifically, he questions their concept of masculinity and their view of gender roles. Overall, exemplifying Ruberto's and Sciorra's argument of a history of the Italian migration in constant evolution, Furio obliges his fellow mobsters to face the Lacanian "Real" of Italy as a country that has been transforming constantly in the decades they have spent in the United States, despite their expectations of a motherland that houses their origins.

THE SOPRANOS AND NAPLES:
"THE MOTHER COUNTRY, HERE THEY MAKE IT REAL!"

The discourse carried out in this context continues from a previous analysis of *The Sopranos* centered on "Commendatori," and concentrated on the first journey of the Soprano crew to Italy.[6] In that case, I addressed the portrait of Naples provided on screen and the implication of the journey in terms of expectations, especially how the experience of Italy challenged Tony's ideas about family dynamics and gender balance. Starting again from "Commendatori," and the specific moment when the men of the Soprano family meet Furio, my new analysis focuses on the implications of Furio's migration to the United States, as well as considering a number of subsequent episodes in which the character of Furio is central on the narrative of the TV series and the evolution of its leading characters.

In my previous work, I compared *The Sopranos* to a more recent, also internationally acclaimed Italian TV show, *Gomorrah—the Series* (2014–), which as I demonstrated previously, took some inspiration from the American TV show.[7] By contrast, inspired by Bondanella's cinematic reading of the TV series, I will return here to the most celebrated precedent of *The Sopranos* on the big screen: Francis Ford Coppola's monumental *The Godfather* trilogy (1972, 1974, 1990). Anyone who is familiar with *The Sopranos* surely recognizes Coppola's saga as a recurrent intertext—indeed the most important of the various influences feeding into it—and a constant topic of discussion between the mobsters in the show.[8] Multiple sources highlight this constant conversation between the TV show and Coppola's trilogy, leading many, such as writer Stephen Holden,[9] to state that the TV series should be viewed as a real sequel to the previous two chapters of the film saga, instead of the weaker and unsatisfying *Part III*. It is no surprise that, by following in Coppola's footsteps, Chase wanted to provide in *The Sopranos* characters who engage and question the stereotypes of the Italian American on screen, but also to go beyond them and challenge the Italian American film representations of Italians. In fact, the journeys to Italy undertaken by Don Vito Corleone (Marlon Brando) and his son Michael (Al Pacino) are the most recurrent references in the series: Don Vito's trip to Sicily in *Part II* is said to be Tony's favorite scene. It shows the ultimate object of fantasy for the offspring of Italian migrants fantasize the most: their homeland.

In "Commendatori," one can verify Yacowar's argument that Coppola's influence on *The Sopranos* ranges "from the passing to the profound."[10] The episode opens with a discussion on the film between Tony and the other members of the gang in Tony's office, located at the back of the nightclub, which is, not by coincidence, named "Bada Bing!" If the recurrent rite of the mobsters watching their beloved film appears "incidental" at the beginning, its development encourages a deep dialogue with the most profound meaning behind Tony's trip to Italy, officially organized to export to Naples a stolen car business.[11] More precisely, while the Soprano crew discusses Vito's journey to Sicily in *Part II*, it is rather Michael's journey to Sicily in *Part I* that Tony emulates in the narrative. In fact, Michael visits Sicily for the first time in a moment of personal emergency. He must leave the country after killing the assassins who shot his father, Don Vito, to save himself from the consequences of the "vendetta" between the families in charge of the crime business in New York City. The journey is organized to protect Michael, but behind this apparent reason lies Vito's idea that a journey to the idealized homeland would inspire Michael and bring him back to the family: a possibility to which, since the beginning of the film, Michael has proven particularly resistant. Introduced in the film as the member of the Corleone family most assimilated to American culture having attended college and served in the army, but also as Vito's preferred son, Michael needs to be exposed to an actual Italian experience to reclaim his family identity. So too in *The Sopranos*, the journey to Italy suggests to Tony a possible solution to solving the crisis affecting his criminal family since the first episode of the TV show, from which his unstable mental health partially originates. After attempting to sort out his personal crisis through psychoanalysis for the whole of the first season with no success, Tony assumes that a journey to Italy can introduce some ideas on how to handle more assuredly the issues that undermine his role as a father, as a husband, and as a mobster. His fantasy of Isabella (Maria Grazia Cucinotta), a beautiful, nurturing Italian exchange student met in the Cusamanos' garden, in "Isabella" (I, 12), also inspires Tony to visit his motherland.

But if the business trip is a success, "Tony's Italian experience does not live up to the *Godfather* model."[12] The arrival of the Soprano gang in Naples immediately introduces a tension between expectation and disillusionment that constitutes the main topic of the episode. The plane boarded by the Soprano men takes off at sunset, following a reunion of some of the Soprano women: Tony's wife Carmela (Eddie Falco), the widow Rosalie Aprile (Sharon Angela), and Angie Bonpensiero (Toni Kalem). Sitting in a restaurant, they have a tense discussion that ends with Angie declaring her intention to divorce Tony's associate Salvatore "Big Pussy" Bonpensiero (Vincent Pastore). On the soundtrack, Andrea Bocelli's romantic song "Con te partirò" opens on the frame of Carmela's puzzled face, continues on the plane taking off and the subsequent beautiful shot of the sunset on the sea with the Mont Vesuvio in the background, and fades to be replaced by the noises of the traffic jam when Tony and his men get out of their car on the *Lungomare*. Conceived as an escape from the domestic, troubled routine of their lives in New Jersey, the journey leads the Sopranos to the delusion of their Italian dream. Here it finds a deeper meaning in the statement of the enthusiastic

Paulie "Walnuts" Gualtieri (Gennaro Anthony Sirico), which can barely be heard over the street noise: "The mother country! Here they make it real." The "real" of Naples is presented as a dirty city, its streets in construction and congested with traffic, its old, beautiful buildings wrapped in scaffolding. After being introduced in the luxurious hotel that is waiting for them, the Soprano gang is welcomed by Furio, who informed Tony that Zi Vittorio (Vittorio Duse) is not there, substituted by the unknown Nino. At their first dinner, Tony is disappointed by Zi Vittorio's absence. Paulie does not appreciate the sophisticated dishes being served, and asks for "macaroni with tomato sauce;" then, he decides not to use the restroom due to its poor conditions. When Tony eventually meets Zi Vittorio, he is not the "the serious man" uncle Junior (Dominic Chianese) remembers anymore, but a wheelchair-bound invalid affected by dementia and visibly unable to run any business. On top of everything, what shocks Tony the most is the fact that Vittorio's daughter Annalisa (Sofia Milos) runs the family business while her husband, the boss in charge, is in prison: a woman boss. Nonetheless, there is one thing that does not disappoint Tony's expectations: Furio, who works as interpreter for the whole expedition, allowing the dialogue between the two families; he is revealed to be reliable and respectable, the actual "serious man" Junior expected.

As the most attentive viewers have noticed, Tony's journey to Italy does not end with a return to New Jersey. By escaping New Jersey, Tony only postpones the need to face the issues at the base of his panic attacks: his marital crisis; his dysfunctional family; his troubled relations with his extended family, significantly worsened after the arrival in Season 2 of Tony's sister Janice (Aida Turturro), adding new issues to the existing trouble with his mother and uncle; and his unstable leadership of his crew. He also brings home a new series of doubts that make him thoroughly question his beliefs, his values, his certainties, everything he identified as truth about Italy. Meanwhile, a revolution begins among the Soprano women, with Carmela questioning her marriage as a reaction to her friend addressing the possibility of a divorce, a solution that is taboo in the Italian community of North Jersey. Nonetheless, invited to solve Tony's troubles, Furio will actually make them worse: he introduces a silent time bomb, ready to detonate in Tony's world.

FURIO GIUNTA . . . WHO?

When he arrives in the Garden State in the subsequent episode, "Big Girls Don't Cry" (Season 2, Episode 5), both of the Soprano families—his extended, private family, and his criminal one—wonder: who is Furio? And why is he here?

Upon his arrival, the most interested in Furio seems to be Big Pussy Bonpensiero, who has good reasons to believe Tony does not trust him as much as before and is willing to replace him. Challenged by his addition to the crew, Pussy makes jokes about Furio's name, calling him "Foolio" or "Foodio." Equally suspicious, Chris seems mostly annoyed by the fact that nobody informed him of Furio's arrival. The viewer knows well that there are good reasons for Tony to trust neither his beloved associate Pussy, who is "wired" and has a deal with the FBI, nor Chris, who seems more interested in selling his family secrets to Hollywood than pursuing his criminal career.

Even more interesting is why Tony is so eager to have Furio in his crew, as we saw him in action just for an episode, and he does not strike us as a particularly imposing presence, despite Annalisa naming him as her best man. Tony is impressed by his seriousness, his devotion to his bosses, to the point of beating a kid simply for setting off some firecrackers nearby, and his loyalty to a woman as if she were a man. The answer is that Tony sees in Furio his myth of the "strong, silent type," who he has romanticized since the first scene of "Pilot" (Season 1, Episode 1); in fact, Furio embodies Tony's American myth of Gary Cooper, who was not "in touch with his feelings," and "just did what he had to do." Even though Tony's idealized expectations about Italy have failed, he finds in Furio an Italian equivalent of his greatest American hero.

Despite his limited exposure in the show, Furio is promptly introduced into a significant position in the Soprano crew: his main duties are to drive Tony and to personally take care of annoying issues related to money collection, to which Chris does not seem to pay enough attention. He responds directly to Tony, Paulie, and Silvio, who in the same episode are promoted to "consiglieri." Even though "Commendatori" has been cited as one of the major episodes of the series, it is in "Big Girls Don't Cry" that things start changing quite drastically. In fact, Tony informs Paulie of both the arrival of Furio and their promotion in the hierarchy of the family in one of the first scenes, set in the Lou Costello Memorial Park, in Paterson, New Jersey. Tony announces to Paulie: "I'm making some changes."

It is not coincidental that Tony communicates his intention to Paulie first. Fred Gardaphé uses this moment to introduce his analysis of how, through the character of Paulie, the show undertakes a critique of American culture.[13] Already in "Commendatori," Tony's perplexity is mostly represented through his troubled relationship with the stunning Annalisa, where he is caught between sexual attraction and skepticism over the possibility that a woman could lead a mobster family. By contrast, it is Paulie who shows most clearly to the audience the genuine disappointment of their Italian experience. The name of the episode encapsulates the idea through the honorific title of "commendatori," which is mentioned twice: the first time, when the hotelier in Naples addresses the Soprano gang in this way, which visibly pleases Paulie; the second, when Paulie uses it to address men in the streets, but is completely ignored by them.[14]

Gardaphé reads Paulie's character through the humoristic role of the "fool" or the "zanni" of the Italian *Commedia dell'arte*, as he is able to question the American establishment by saying things that nobody else dares to say. My reading of Furio is complementary to Gardaphé's reading of Paulie and is built on the idea that the development of these two characters is related in a deeper way than this career shift underlines. Not only is Paulie the first of the gang to be informed of the arrival of Furio, but Tony also asks him to pick Furio up at Newark airport, while Chris and Pussy meet him directly at the welcoming party, highlighting a fall in their place in Tony's esteem. If it is Silvio who reassures Pussy about Furio by informing him Furio is "the friend of ours from the other side," Paulie is the one to introduce Furio to their New York affiliate, Johnny "Sachs" Sacramoni, and asks Pussy to leave the table because he is not welcome in their conversation. Based on their closeness to Furio, Tony draws a line that places Paulie and Silvio on the side of the people he trusts, while Chris and Pussy are on the other side. Furio and Paulie also appear complementary in their attempts to tell Tony the truth, which Tony rejects with equal intensity: Paulie speaks with words, for example when he tries to reveal to Tony the disappointing truth about Italy in "Commendatori;" conversely, Furio does so with his silence, and Tony will discover at his own expense that there are many things a "silent type" can hide.

In a similar vein to "Commendatori," "Big Girls Don't Cry" shows the outcome of many issues introduced in the previous episode. If not exactly symmetrical, it contains several significant parallels. While in "Commendatori," Tony travels to Italy with Paulie and Chris and meets Furio, now Furio travels to New Jersey and meets Tony, while the roles of Paulie and Chris in Tony's business diverge: Paulie is in, Chris is out. Between Chris and Furio there is also a symmetrical relationship. At the opening of "Big Girls Don't Cry," Chris is unable to take care of the money collection from the owner of a brothel disguised as a massage parlor, who for the second week has given a "light envelope." The scene immediately brings us back to "Pilot," and to the first moment in the show where we witness Tony and Chris together, in the car, when Tony learns he needs to take care of his business himself. At the end of "Big Girls Don't Cry," Tony is in the car with Furio, who conversely is seen to know well how to handle the collection: Furio in fact becomes a replacement for Chris.

After providing many insights about his relevance in the series, at the end of "Big Girls Don't Cry" Furio slips into the background, silently taking care of his assignments in the following episodes: he is integrated in the crew, yet does not stand out for any specific reason. Nonetheless, his presence is very eloquent whenever he is around, and not only because he appears to be out of context in any situation but also because he impresses the women with his manners and he challenges the men by perfectly performing his job as a mobster. In fact, Furio embodies everything Tony and the men of his gang are not: he is always kind and respectful in relation to the women, he appears careful of their thoughts and feelings, and not patronizing at all. Gently but persistently, Furio undermines the balance in Tony's house and neighborhood by showing, spontaneously and without imposing, an image of Italy that contrasts with their beliefs. Chase aims to represent Furio as a challenge to all the stereotypes of Italian men: he is elegant, sophisticated, and polite; he never raises his voice or shows any gesture of disrespect; he is not a womanizer; he addresses his attraction to Carmela by engaging in appropriate conversations about houses and family. In this way, Furio raises questions over Tony and Carmela's relationship, leading them to a thorough reconsideration of their marriage, which instigates a separation at the end of Season 4.

After his introduction in Season 2, it is in Season 4 that Furio's role starts to become particularly relevant. In "Christopher" (Season 4, Episode 3), devoted to the never-ending controversy dividing Italian Americans and Native Americans about Columbus Day, Furio demonstrates crucial knowledge of specific issues of Italian history, explaining to the Soprano crew that Columbus was a Northern Italian, and as such, he despised Southern Italians as peasants. Shortly after, when he comes to pick Tony up from home, he brings some *struffoli*, a traditional dish from Naples, which immediately wins over Carmela. Despite the title suggesting a reference to Tony's nephew Chris, the focus of the episode, ironically, is on Furio. Conversely, a later episode in the season, "The Silent Type" (Season 4, Episode 10), presents a titular connection with Furio, as he returns to the United States after visiting Naples for his father's funeral. In the time that has passed from one episode to the other, the bond between Carmela and Furio has remarkably strengthened. After many moments of small talk while waiting for Tony, in "The Weight" (Season 4, Episode 4) Furio engages in a sensual, traditional dance with Carmela, in which she realizes what she is missing in her relationship with Tony: fun, elegance, attention, and understanding.

While Furio is shown to be a man who, rather than confining Carmela to the kitchen, would cook for her, Carmela demonstrates a progressive desire to be more independent—she wants to be considered as something more than a housewife. She becomes more attentive to Tony's habits, specifically to his manners toward her. Overall, she feels the right to contest her husband's infidelity, which has been a recurrent issue throughout the series. From the ashes of Furio and Carmela's never-consummated liaison, and after a long separation, carried out over the course of Season 5, Tony and Carmela build a new alliance on a different premise: no unfaithful behavior is to be accepted and Carmela is to have the space to develop her own business. The audience witnesses in Carmela a sense of pride and a confidence that one would hardly have expected from her character in the first season. Therefore, Furio announces a revision of the patriarchal family model in Tony's house, which cannot survive the rise of Carmela's consciousness as an emancipated woman. Furio's presence facilitates the emancipation process of the Soprano women by showing an alternative model of manhood that was previously absent from the series. In this way, paradoxically, he adds further disappointment to Tony's delusional expectations of Italy and pushes the Soprano family to become more like a mainstream American one, as they appear in the final scene of the show.

THE "WISEGUY" AND THE "WISE MAN":
TONY, FURIO, AND THE LACANIAN REAL

By facing Furio, Tony accepts the challenge of confronting his myth about Italy with what presents as an actual embodiment of Italianness: Furio is a migrant just like Tony's grandfather, imported to New Jersey from contemporary Italy. By inviting Furio into New Jersey, Tony accepts a bigger challenge than his journey to Naples: he decides to face his doubts about the reality of his home. This produces a thorough interrogation of Italian American beliefs about the actual Italian lifestyle in the whole community, as well as for the viewer of the show. But after reciprocating Carmela's feelings and planning to kill Tony, as the only possible way to celebrate their love, Furio leaves New Jersey and goes back to Italy in the same way he arrived: silently. By contrast, the Sopranos cannot stop talking about him, and their world is compromised forever. As in the myth of the Pandora's Box, when the Real enters the discourse, it cannot be avoided anymore, only denied. It will be useful, at this point, to turn to a wider reflection on the Lacanian Real.

The Real enters the Soprano neighborhood between "Commendatori" and "Big Girls Don't Cry," while Furio is traveling from Naples to New Jersey. Not coincidentally, those two episodes feature the deepest level of psychoanalysis in the show. *The Sopranos* has held the ability to produce the most unpredictable readings, including a series of psychoanalytical interpretations.[15] In fact, the series engages with psychoanalysis in many ways. One is more visible, on the surface, for example any time Tony sits with his psychiatrist, Dr. Jennifer Melfi (Lorraine Bracco), or when Melfi talks with other patients or with her fellow psychiatrists. In other cases, Tony's dreams and fantasies suggest a more sophisticated Freudian interpretation. So too, there is a more profound and subtle use of psychoanalysis, which recalls Lacanian theory and which, has not yet been fully explored. My analysis of the Real in the show contributes to a wider understanding of aspects of the series that in this way gain a more developed explanation.

We know that at the beginning of Season 2, Dr. Melfi refuses to see Tony, and he looks for a new therapist. If one considers a Freudian reading, the journey to Naples appears as an exit strategy from a situation that has become too complicated. Tony faces a situation of return of the "repressed," when Big Pussy and Richie Aprile come back to the "Sopranoland";[16] the eternal conflicts with his mother Livia and uncle Junior, who together attempted to end his life; his sister Janice's manipulations; his fights with Carmela; his children's unbearable teenage conflicts and existential crises. In "Big Girls Don't Cry," Tony seeks somebody to talk to, and the therapy session duplicates on screen. Tony confesses his health issues to Hesh (Jerry Adler), a Jewish associate who holds a recurrent role of consultant in the criminal business of the tristate area. At the same time, Dr. Melfi confesses to her analyst (Peter Bogdanovic) her guilt for having abandoned a patient to whom she feels a special attachment. Both Dr. Melfi and Tony tell their "analysts" their dreams, which always introduce fundamental revelations to the series. There is even a spectacular return of the ducks, while Tony is on his yacht with his "girlfriend" from Kazakhstan. This is another reference to the beginning of the series that makes us aware that Tony's crisis has found no solution since, as in his relationship with Chris.

In the two previously mentioned episodes, other psychoanalytical issues are related to gender relationships. In contrast to the title "Commendatori," which refers to a title of honor for men, "Big Girls Don't Cry" suggests a focus on the women of the Soprano family, insisting on the division between men and women in the previous episode. Surprisingly enough, it is one of the boys that cries: Chris, while performing a scene of *Rebel Without a Cause*, which brings back his father issues. In this case, Chris follows in Tony's footsteps, who also presents father issues, and exactly in this episode, thanks to Hesh, he discovers that his father suffered from panic attacks too. Again symmetrically, if in "Commendatori" the Soprano women were analyzed in their marital crises, now the men are to be analyzed: the focus is on Chris's relationship with Adriana La Cerva (Drea De Matteo). In the following episode, "The Happy Wanderer" (Season 2, Episode 6), the two couples Chris-Adriana and Tony-Carmela confront each other at the dinner table, confirming their respective couple crises. The meta-psychoanalytical discourse helps to shift from Freudian to Lacanian theory, and sets up the groundwork for the entrance of the Real in the Sopranos' community.

How does Furio perform the Lacanian Real? In Lacanian terms, the "Real" is what escapes the order of the "Imaginary," which is the view of the world that an individual creates; it is located beyond the order of the "Symbolic," which is the order that structures reality for us through a network we build up with language. To keep it simple, we can take the Real to mean everything one excludes or does not want to accept in order to keep on living an ordinary life in the happiest way. We see this in concrete terms when

Tony meets Furio: he is immediately fascinated by him. Tony's attitude is controversial: on the one hand, he views Furio as a model and trusts him; on the other, he tries to understand what is so different about this man from himself and his crew. While Tony questions Furio, Tony is constantly questioned by him: an interrogation which is also paralleled through Carmela, who questions Angie Bonpensiero about her decision to get a divorce. Tony and Carmela are mirroring a similar crisis, from different sides of the mirror.

It is through Žižek's interpretation of Lacan that my analysis of Furio as the Lacanian Real finds further insights and turns out to be decisive, if one considers my reading of *The Sopranos* through the crucial intertext of *The Godfather*. In fact, the Real is manifested as the inconsistency and incompleteness of the Symbolic, but insofar as it cannot be symbolized, the Lacanian Real cannot be incorporated into reality. Žižek has presented the perception of the Real in terms of a family narrative as a fundamental ideological operation undertaken by Hollywood cinema.[17] Conversely, Coppola uses a family narrative to describe the perception of the Real as a form of trauma, as in the case of "the traumatic encounter with the disavowed core of cinematic representation" that Vighi theorized as the "cinematic unconscious" in his elaboration on Žižek.[18] If one considers a specific application to *The Sopranos* that follows Coppola,[19] in their works Coppola and Chase agree on the impossibility of returning either to the roots of the traditional male model identified by the mobster, or to a traditional family model of masculinity.[20] In fact, Tony's journey to Naples follows closely Michael's journey to Sicily, in showing that the homeland where the traditional model of the Italian mob was created has introduced the impossibility of this typology of mob. In this case, the "Real" of both Tony's and Michael's journey to Italy highlights the fictional character of the myth that they have romanticized. The gap between the reality of the Italian mob and the myth fed by Italians in the United States corresponds to the Lacanian Real, and finds an equivalent in both *The Sopranos* and in the *Godfather*, where Michael's generation corresponds to Tony's father or his right arm Paulie. By further developing Coppola's image of the "Hollywood Italian" mobster to a "postmodern Hollywood Italian" mobster,[21] Chase portrays the Real as a specific character, Furio, who becomes the personification of what Tony aims toward but cannot become.

According to Vighi and Heiko Feldner, "the lesson of Lacanian psychoanalysis lies in locating the repressed nucleus of a given text."[22] Both Vighi and Žižek define the Lacanian Real as the direct experience against the ideology that keeps our social reality functional. The Lacanian Real uncovers the "deceptive layers" that ideology builds up. In fact, ideology works on this perception of the Real, which is not part of the Symbolic; it rather makes the Symbolic impossible, yet at the same time possible via the exclusion of the Real. This is portrayed by Furio, whose presence tells Tony the Real of Italy, which is an image of Italy Tony does not want to accept—because it chal-

lenges everything he believes as Italian and as part of his Italian education—
and especially, how to behave as an Italian man.

Before focusing specifically on Paulie, Gardaphé addressed the figure of
the gangster as a "suburban trickster" and analyzed how *The Sopranos* contributed to the rewriting of American masculinities on screen.[23] By opposing
the "wiseguy" portrayed by early representations of the Italian mobster in
film to the "wise man" of the more recent gangster cinema introduced by
Coppola, Gardaphé highlighted that a certain "macho behavior" was for a
long time "the only meaning of being an Italian-American man," because it
was the only way most Italian Americans knew how to be men.[24] Consequently, while meeting Furio, among other issues Tony also has to accept
new ways of being an Italian man. Not coincidentally, the arrival of Furio in
the Sopranos' world is anticipated by the first fight Carmela and Tony had
after the trip to Italy, in "Big Girls Don't Cry." Tony smashes the phone on
the floor, after an animated discussion with his sister Janice, in front of his
visibly shocked son. Carmela erupts and comments: "Why don't you grow
the fuck up?" Nonetheless, as Gardaphé highlights, Tony misses his chance
to grow up as a "wise man."[25] He rather pushes Furio out of his community,
even if unconsciously, to be once again the only man of the house. Furio and
Tony are revealed to be characters at odds through their relationship, from
any viewpoint. In fact, at his welcome party, Furio exhibits perfect manners
and the ability to entertain kids to his new community. By playing "the silent
guy" and the behavior at the base of the persecution of Italians in the United
States—their reserved manner, their silent attitude—he is at odds with Tony,
who is considered a traitor by the old generation of his family because he
talks too much, and, even worse, he talks to strangers in consulting a shrink.

By reading Gardaphé alongside Lacan, one can see the way that Furio, by
playing the Real, questions and then confirms Tony's crisis and his inability
to grow up throughout the series, even if his marriage to Carmela will find a
new balance on the basis of new promises that Tony seriously attempts to
respect, though they prove to be provisional and unstable. By accepting the
Real, Tony would have to cope with this new way of performing Italian
manhood and his role as a father in an Italian family, even his ways of acting
as a mobster in his Italian American gang. His Symbolic, which is the system
of values on which his behavior is based, is legitimated by the exclusion of
Furio; introducing Furio's reality challenges Tony and his fellows. Eventually, by rejecting Furio, Tony can again be the man he is used to being, by
excluding again the Real embodied by Furio, when Furio leaves New Jersey
at the end of Season 4. This implies that Tony's crisis has not found any
solution: this denial brings him back to the starting point of his crisis in the
first season of the show, when his marriage is somehow working with some
small adjustments. In the end, Tony's balance turns out to be even more
precarious, as now he has met the truth of the Real. He wants to be faithful to

Carmela, because he understands it is not fair to keep cheating on her. This costs him a great deal of effort, and ultimately, he fails. Even if Tony refuses the Real, even if the Real is no longer in evidence, it nonetheless acts on Tony, unconsciously undermining his behavior and decisions.

Even though "Commendatori" has been considered one of the major episodes of the series, it is in "Big Girls Don't Cry" that "big" changes happen. The passage of Furio from Italy to New Jersey functions as a catalyst: by quoting Paulie, Furio came "to make it real" over the Ocean. Or, to refer to Lacanian discourse, "Real," with a capital R. Paulie proclaims this phrase on their arrival in Naples, just as he reveals the disappointment of the experience of the Sopranos in Naples, in accordance with his role as the Shakespearean "fool" that Gardaphé attributes to him: "The role of the fool is to attract the audience's attention through his ability to say things that other characters can or would never say."[26] By performing this role, Paulie embraces the criticism on Italian American society, as well as on American society at large. By saying things that nobody else can say, Paulie demonstrates an ability to speak the impossible. He assumes the impossible of the Lacanian Real without other characters being shocked by him, in contrast with what happens to Tony. In the same scene, Tony says that Furio would respond to him and Silvio. It should be noted that Silvio was not in Naples with them. Only Paulie shares the complete experience of the Real with Tony and can tell Tony the impossible of the Real, as he has already tried to do in Naples, where an angry Tony rejected his truths to avoid being distracted from his business. By refusing to listen to Paulie, Tony decides to introduce the shock of the Real into his life, and to get exposed to him without "protection." Therefore, Paulie is shown to be the only actual ally Tony had in his crew, by telling the truth nobody wanted to tell. Once in New Jersey, Paulie again tries to explain the Real to Tony, but Tony refuses to accept it again. Tony opens up to Paulie only when it is too late, having already missed the opportunity to upgrade to the status of "wise man."[27] Furio, in turns, goes back to the place where the Real of Italy can be spoken without challenging Italian Americans: where this Real belongs, in Italy.

At the base of the discourse here addressed, there is a wider consideration of identity, and of how the representation of Naples matters in such a context. It is related to the "otherness" of Naples and implies a loss of identity. As for Coppola, Sicilian identity is a regional, traditional identity that Italians started losing from the 1950s, in the process of assimilation to a global, capitalist culture.[28] This culture defines a society deprived of specific qualities, which experiences a form of multiculturalism and otherness without an actual experience of the other. If one considers the wider picture, the implications are huge and concern reality itself as deprived of its substance. It means that Tony's neighborhood in New Jersey works as a "virtual reality," as in the Watchowskis's film *The Matrix* (1999), to provide a case addressed by

Žižek.[29] In Žižek's view, *"The Matrix* . . . functions as the 'screen' that separates us from the Real, that makes the 'desert of the real' bearable."[30] Virtual reality lets Tony and his fellows experience reality without the actual experience of the Real.

To cope with the Real, therefore, and wake up from virtual reality, one needs to experience the Real in its extreme violence, that is, the trauma of the Real.[31] This is the moment when Tony really understands what is going on between himself and Carmela, like when the characters awaken in *The Matrix*, after taking the red pill. Because the Real is Real, for its traumatic and excessive nature, we are unable to integrate it into our reality, and we are obliged to perceive it as anxiety, as a nightmare. To be accepted, the Real must be perceived as something unreal: as an Italian who looks different from their own representation of what is Italy. It is Paulie who experiences this Real in Naples, when he expresses his disappointment—the food, the restroom, the sexual adventure, the attempts to get in touch with Neapolitan people in the streets—while Tony tries to convince himself he is in the wrong and he has something to learn from them. Bringing the Real home would eventually provide him with a chance to grow up, as Carmela highlights in "Big Girls Don't Cry."

In this context, Michael's journey to Sicily again anticipates Tony's journey to Naples, though they feature a different trauma, yet a homologous outcome: they change his mode of living in the United States for the rest of his experience on screen. Nonetheless, differently than Michael, Tony does not evolve from the "wise guy" to a "wise man." The shock of the Real has an equivalent force, but which is opposite in direction: Michael rushes away from Sicily, just as Furio rushes away from New Jersey. Both Tony and Michael accept that they cannot escape to Italy, but have to learn how to sort out their family troubles in the United States. While Michael embraces his Real, Tony decides to go back to his virtual reality, instead of attempting to find a new and more stable balance, related to the awareness that his Italian American identity lies in a space that is neither Italian nor American, but the result of the merge of the two: a transnational and transcultural space that we can call Italian Americana. Consequently, the final scene of the entire series of *The Sopranos*, "Made in America" (Season 6, Episode 21), portrays Tony and his family as a mainstream American family: they eat onion rings in an American diner listening to "Don't Stop Believin'" playing on the jukebox. The events that happen after this are not relevant to my analysis. On this basis, Tony is indeed a moral figure and a contemporary, if not a postmodern, Hamlet: he does not avoid the contact of the Real, he brings his doubts and questions home with him and faces them, but he eventually fails to act and escapes in front of the truth. Whether the character dies or not, in Chase's narration, this model of manhood is in any case destined to disappear. His children will survive this model of masculinity and fatherhood. They will have a life outside the mob and the family business. In particular, Meadow will perform her modern Italian American identity as an independent woman, who is happy and proud of her Italian heritage, but free from any stereotype of being Italian in the United States.

CONCLUSION: A "REAL ITALIAN" OR THE ITALIAN "REAL"?

My last point is a reflection on the concept of the "real Italian," a "phrase that has been used repeatedly in popular parlance," which according to Ruberto and Sciorra, has often been employed as a "shorthand to explain the division between new Italian immigrants and the established Italian American community."[32] Ruberto and Sciorra highlight that "phrases such as 'real Italians' and 'Italian Italian' are commonly used to distinguish between postwar immigrants and pre-established Italian Americans."[33] The perception of new immigrants as "real Italians," resulting in "a particular Italian look or style more associated with the nation state as opposed to the *paese*" has operated as a divide between the two different experiences of Italian diaspora.[34] Consequently, "a narrative mindful of Italian postwar migration includes how migrants helped construct a contemporary *italianità* (italianness) with which pre-established Italian Americans had little or no connection," also reflecting the different features of Italians migrating in the last seventy years.[35] Those more recent Italians migrating to the United States are more educated than the previous waves who, conversely, are more easily identified with the values of the working-class—think of the phenomenon known as "brain drain"—thus encouraging the identification of the late migration to the United States as an "elite" migration, whose members rarely recognize themselves as immigrants. By moving to New Jersey at the beginning of the 2000s and leaving after three years, Furio demonstrates a strong case of new Italian migration highlighted by Ruberto and Sciorra. He embodies an "elite," as Tony personally asks him to join his crew because he is impressed by his skills, and he very likely represents one of the individual cases not legally enrolled in the United States, so as not to become part of the official statistics. When in their following volume, devoted to the cultural representation of Italians in the United States, Ruberto and Sciorra focus on the "dichotomy between those called 'real Italians' versus 'Italian Americans,' even as the two groups intermingled," we can again recognize *The Sopranos* as a case study.[36] In fact, Furio joins the gang as a legitimate part of it, with no difference from Chris and Pussy, who are born and raised in Tony's neighborhood. It is in the following episodes that we can identify a cultural clash between Furio and his mobster fellows and neighbors, and that Furio can be identified as the Italian "Real," and not only as a "real Italian," as explained previously: the element that challenges the expectations about being Italian held by Italian Americans.

Ruberto and Sciorra introduce their collection with an insightful reflection on Lawrence Ferlinghetti's poem "The Old Italians Dying" (1976), which highlights the difficulties of the older generation of Italian Americans in accepting the changes taking place in the community. By celebrating a requiem for a time and way of life that are disappearing, Ferlinghetti demonstrates a refusal of the possibility that Italian American culture can continue through the generational succession, or through the rejuvenating effects of new generations of immigrants. It also has to be taken into account that Italian culture in the Italian American communities after World War II was undergoing the same postwar propaganda the American allied countries like Italy were undergoing under the Marshall Plan, which was transforming Italian culture in Italy in similar ways. From this standpoint, Ferlinghetti could have been right to defend a culture that originated in Italy, or in several regions that were part of a patchwork called Italy at the end of the 19th century, which was disappearing in Italy too. Nonetheless, refusing the cultural transformations that Italy, together with the United States, was undergoing is like living in the "Matrix," as in the case made by Žižek: a nostalgic attachment to a world that does not exist anymore. This is the message Chase wanted to give by portraying Furio as an embodiment of the Real, while at the same time defining him as a cultural agent introducing a more authentic, or at least more up-to-date, Neapolitan culture in New Jersey. Chase's process was sophisticated and subtle: the way Furio introduces his culture in the New Jersey community is kind, polite, but nonetheless it intimidates and shocks his neighbors. One should also note that Chase represents the transformation introduced by Furio through a formal process that reconfigures the series: from the touristic postcard portrayed in "Commendatori," the representation of Naples and of Neapolitan culture becomes more realistic and accurate. This aspect appears to be true especially if one focuses on one issue in particular, that is, the specific regional heritage of the Italian characters represented. In fact, the Soprano family takes its origins from Naples—more accurately, from the surroundings of the closer city of Avellino, on the mountains—and they are shown to be attached to their specific Neapolitan features, in terms of habits, character, fashion, food, and language. Consequently, the Italian words in the script are actually in most cases taken directly from the Neapolitan dialect. The food, the music, the dance, the Southern Question: "struffoli" against "baked ziti," folk band Spaccanapoli's song "Vesuvio" against the popular Andrea Bocelli's "Con te partirò," the hostility to Columbus as a Northern Italian against his emulation by the Southern Italian from New Jersey. Any cultural issue introduced by Furio challenges his American neighbors and tells them the Lacanian Real of their distance from what is to be considered as Italian in contemporary Italy. This is another reason why, to allow Tony to reassemble his crew around him, Furio has to leave. And yet, his ghostly presence cannot be avoided, as Carmela cannot stop thinking about the Neapolitan music, once it is introduced in her head. Despite Tony's efforts to seduce her again with flowers, a beautiful vest that suits her perfectly, and elegant manners, it is Furio she fantasies about: once the Real has entered the Italian American community, it cannot be ejected.

To conclude, through his silent and discrete, but also shocking, presence, Furio provides the possibility for Tony to reconfigure Italian American identity and culture as something unique, which is not reducible to the categories of Italian or American, but rather to a transnational, transcultural space which is far more complex than the two viewed separately. From a certain standpoint, the very Italian American experience appears to become the Lacanian Real itself for mainstream Italian Americans, who must realize the impossibility of belonging to what they consider the true Italian experience in order to accept their own specific, and culturally remarkable character. By contrast, according to my reading of *The Sopranos* through the lens of Žižek's and Vighi's theories, Tony and his family miss their chance to "rejuvenate" or "reboot" the "dying" old Italian American culture.[37] They rather accept complete recognition of their family as a mainstream American family, at the end of the show, as a way to defend themselves from the Real: they decide to live in their delusional world. Hence, it has to be highlighted that Furio's contribution to the Italian American community was properly revolutionary, against the "reactionary" character of the evolution of Italian American culture in the 1960s, as highlighted by Gardaphé.[38] By confirming Gardaphé's thesis, Tony misses this chance. Nonetheless, the shock Furio introduces completely subverts Tony's behavior and beliefs, and despite Furio's ostracism from the New Jersey community, Tony's world has been transformed forever. A truth that, conversely, young Meadow appears to be ready to accept.

NOTES

1. See Maurice Yacowar, *The Sopranos on the Couch: Analyzing Television's Greatest Series* (New York, London: Continuum, 2002).

2. Peter Bondanella, *Hollywood Italians: Dagos, Palookas, Romeos, Wise Guys, and Sopranos* (New York: Continuum, 2004): 297.

3. Bondanella, 297.

4. See Fred L. Gardaphé, *From Wiseguys to Wise Men: The Gangster and Italian American Masculinities* (New York: Routledge, 2006).

5. See Laura E. Ruberto and Joseph Sciorra, "Introduction: Real Italians, New Immigrants," in *New Italian Migrations to the United States*, Vol. 1: Politics and History Since 1945 (Urbana: University of Illinois Press, 2017): 1–32.

6. Francesco Chianese, "About Family Reunions: When *The Sopranos* Met Their Cousins from Naples," in *Harbors, Flows, and Migrations: The USA in/and the World*, ed. Vincenzo Bavaro, Gianna Fusco, Serena Fusco and Donatella Izzo (Newcastle Upon Tyne: Cambridge Scholars, 2017).

7. Francesco Chianese, "Sicily as a Transnational Space of Cultural Resistance Against Assimilation to Consumerism in Pier Paolo Pasolini's *Teorema* (1968) and Francis Ford Coppola's *The Godfather* (1972)," in *Sicily and Cinema*, ed. Giovanna Summerfield (Jefferson: McFarland & Company, 2020).

8. Yacowar, 177.

9. Stephen Holden, "Introduction," in *The New York Times on the Sopranos* (New York: ibooks, 2000): IX.

10. Yacowar, 177.

11. Yacowar, 178–179.

12. Yacowar, 87.

13. Fred L. Gardaphé, "Running Joke: Criticism of Italian American Culture through Comedy in *The Sopranos*," *Between* 6, no. 11 (2016).

14. Yacowar, 179.

15. See Regina Barreca, ed., *A Sitdown with the Sopranos: Watching Italian American Culture on TV's Most Talked-About Series* (New York: Palgrave MacMillian, 2002); Glen O. Gabbard, *The Psychology of* The Sopranos*: Love, Death, Desire, and Betrayal in American's Favorite Gangster Family* (New York: Basic Books, 2002); and Yacowar.

16. Bondanella, 316.

17. Slavoj Žižek, "The Family Myth of Ideology," in *In Defence of Lost Causes* (London, New York: Verso, 2009): 52–94, and *Trouble in Paradise: From the End of History to the End of Capitalism* (London: Penguin, 2015).

18. Fabio Vighi, *Traumatic Encounters in Italian Film: Locating the Cinematic Unconscious* (Bristol: Intellect, 2006): 11.

19. See Chianese, 2020.

20. See Anthony E. Rotundo, "Wonderbread and Stugots: Italian American Manhood and *The Sopranos*", in *A Sitdown with the Sopranos*, 47–74.

21. Bondanella, 306.

22. Fabio Vighi and Heiko Feldner, *Žižek: Beyond Foucault* (Basingstoke: Palgrave MacMillan, 2007): 1.

23. See Gardaphé 2006.

24. Gardaphé, XII.

25. Gardaphé, 164.

26. Gardaphé, 10.

27. Gardaphé,164.

28. See Chianese, 2020.

29. See Slavoj Žižek, *Welcome to the Desert of the Real* (London, New York: Verso, 1992).

30. Žižek, 252.

31. Vighi, 11.

32. Ruberto and Sciorra, 2017a, 9.

33. Ruberto and Sciorra, 2017a, 9.

34. Ruberto and Sciorra, 2017a, 9.

35. Ruberto and Sciorra, 2017a, 10.

36. Ruberto and Sciorra, "Introduction: Rebooting Italian America," in *New Italian Migrations to the United States, Vol. 2: Art and Culture Since 1945* (Urbana: University of Illinois Press, 2017): 5.

37. Ruberto and Sciorra, 2017b, 5.

38. Gardaphé, XVI.

BIBLIOGRAPHY

Barreca, Regina, ed. *A Sitdown with the Sopranos: Watching Italian American Culture on TV's Most Talked-About Series*. New York: Palgrave MacMillian, 2002.

Bondanella, Peter. *Hollywood Italians: Dagos, Palookas, Romeos, Wise Guys, and Sopranos*. New York: Continuum, 2004.

Chianese, Francesco. "About Family Reunions: When *The Sopranos* Met Their Cousins from Naples." In *Harbors, Flows, and Migrations: The USA in/and the World*, edited by Vincenzo Bavaro, Gianna Fusco, Serena Fusco, and Donatella Izzo. Newcastle Upon Tyne: Cambridge Scholars, 2017.

Chianese, Francesco. "Sicily as a Transnational Space of Cultural Resistance Against Assimilation to Consumerism in Pier Paolo Pasolini's *Teorema* (1968) and Francis Ford Coppola's *The Godfather* (1972)." In *Sicily and Cinema*, edited by Giovanna Summerfield. Jefferson: McFarland & Company, 2020.

Gabbard, Glen O. *The Psychology of* The Sopranos*: Love, Death, Desire, and Betrayal in American's Favorite Gangster Family*. New York: Basic Books, 2002.

Gardaphé, Fred L. *From Wiseguys to Wise Men: The Gangster and Italian American Masculinities*. New York: Routledge, 2006.

Gardaphé, Fred L. "Running Joke: Criticism of Italian American Culture through Comedy in *The Sopranos*." *Between* 6, no. 11 (2016).

Holden, Stephen. "Introduction." In *The New York Times on* The Sopranos, IX. New York: ibooks, 2000.

Rotundo, Anthony E. "Wonderbread and Stugots: Italian American Manhood and *The Sopranos*." In *A Sitdown with the Sopranos*, 47–74. 2002.

Ruberto, Laura E. and Joseph Sciorra. "Introduction: Real Italians, New Immigrants." In *New Italian Migrations to the United States, Vol. 1: Politics and History Since 1945*, 1–32. Urbana: University of Illinois Press, 2017.

Ruberto, Laura E. and Joseph Sciorra. "Introduction: Rebooting Italian America." In *New Italian Migrations to the United States Vol. 2: Art and Culture Since 1945*, 1–31. Urbana: University of Illinois Press, 2017.

The Sopranos, Season 1, Episode 1, "Pilot;" Season 1, Episode 12, "Isabella;" Season 2, Episode 4, "Commendatori;" Season 2, Episode 5, "Big Girls Don't Cry;" Season 4, Episode 3, "Christopher;" Season 4, Episode 4, "The Weight;" Season 4, Episode 10, "The Strong, Silent Type;" Season 4, Episode 12, "Eloise;" Season 6, Episode 21, "Made in America."

Vighi, Fabio. *Traumatic Encounters in Italian Film: Locating the Cinematic Unconscious*. Bristol: Intellect, 2006.

Vighi, Fabio, and Heiko Feldner. *Žižek: Beyond Foucault*. Basingstoke: Palgrave MacMillan, 2007.

Yacowar, Maurice. *The Sopranos on the Couch: Analyzing Television's Greatest Series*. New York, London: Continuum, 2002.

Žižek, Slavoj. *Welcome to the Desert of the Real*. London, New York: Verso, 1992.

Žižek, Slavoj. "The Family Myth of Ideology." In *In Defence of Lost Causes*, 52–94. London, New York: Verso, 2009.

Žižek, Slavoj. *Trouble in Paradise: From the End of History to the End of Capitalism*. London: Penguin, 2015.

Part IV

Italian Newspapers, Italian Cinema, and 2.0 Media

Chapter Eight

Il Bambino in Pericolo

Serializing Italian American Futurity

Sarah H. Salter

The theoretical opposition between ethnicity as material or imagined association has long been meaningful for scholars of Italian American literature and
culture. Many describe a community unmoored from both ends of an ethnic
binary, adrift without a single organizing ethnic identity nor distinguishable
version of cultural hybridity. [1] While students of immigrant history use mass-
market genres such as newspapers and material studies of print to present
histories of ethnic assimilation, cultural theorists of identity often privilege
imaginative forms and aesthetic associations. On both ends of this spectrum
and from places in between, scholars explore the relation between identity
and the forms through which it is articulated and reiterated.

For both creators and consumers of Italian-language newspapers during
the era of mass migration, pressure to develop new forms of social coherence
(as a unified, participatory community within US public life) and to acknowledge a new nation's civic norms (as responders to US political logic) must
have seemed urgent. To address these connected impulses and illuminate
essential aspects of US civic imagination, newspapers engaged repetitively
with certain cultural events or arguments: discussions of American Independence Day, for example, remained a yearly ritual; articles examining the
similarities between American and Italian public or economic life recurred
across and among newspapers with frequency. [2] As newspapers exploited the
educational opportunities of seriality, they produced and reproduced social
values tied to civic norms. This process would have had especial utility in the
context of migration's assimilative demands: the ritualized repetition of
Fourth of July articles in Italian would have mirrored the day's ritualized
national meaning, preparing the way for broader civic participation.

Many have described the use of repetition—specifically the "everyday repetition" of serialized forms—as an important means for developing collective identity.[3] Often, seriality operated as both a generic context and a publication condition. The newspaper's structural dependence on (re)publication found conceptual echoes in imaginative literature of immigrant experience. Describing immigrant autobiographies, Jolie A. Sheffer claims that authors often "establish immigration as an experience akin to death and resurrection. The language of new beginning is familiar to readers of the bildungsroman, immigration narratives, and autobiographies."[4] Each of the genres Sheffer names could be considered realist: centered on particular persons and concerned with the details of daily lives being lived. Shannon Gannon points to a similar cycle of repetition in the romance: "sometimes in fantastic narrative or romance fiction, there is a haunting similarity between almost-identical episodes."[5] For both realism and romance, one important cultural goal of textual repetition is "to convey meaning . . . [Repetition is] a subtle way of conveying the moral logic of the action."[6] In the era of mass migration, Italian language newspapers used meaningful repetition—of tropes, of news features—to highlight particular elements of Italian American experience.[7]

The work of communal meaning-making also followed a repetitive frame imposed from without, with English-language newspapers iterating into stability the racialization of Italian immigrants as at once threatening and vulnerable, a collectivity outside the structures of US white civic life. Having already spent decades responding to United States cultural order and constructing well-developed, organized social support systems and economic exchange networks, Italian populations were reimagined as a novel foreign element during the final decades of the 19th century.[8] Freshly categorized in US newspapers, public reports, and even imaginative literature as ignorant and underdeveloped, Italians were often represented as a caretaking burden foisted upon America's commercial adulthood.[9]

Although they were victims of a distinct system of cultural othering, Italians in the United States were creating new forms of cultural awareness through symbolic cultural repetition internal to their community. For many, the particular ethnic association of Italian American developed through a mixture of temporally limited and politically useful textual genres, like newspapers. This was especially the case in the century's latter decades, when immigrant and labor papers offered a potent combination of economic and social organization.[10] Looking only at the late-century writing of Italian Americans, we imagine the literature of this emergent ethnic population to be realist in orientation; we imagine it to index the gritty reality of ethnicity.[11] In this essay, I explore the intersection of Italian and American cultural logic through one newspaper's hybridization of genre, its invocation of a romanticized cross-cultural collective through the realist details of a local scandal.

Navigating between imaginative sympathy and sensationalist revelation, *Il Progresso Italo-Americano* built for readers a sense of urban experience and civic responsibility partaking simultaneously of romantic association and realist intercession.

If the Italian homeland has been understood through romantic nationalism since Alessandro Manzoni's famous *I promessi spossi* (1827), Italian American media histories have more often explored the intersection of realist forms and individual realities. As other essays in *Italian Americans On Screen* ably illustrate, the visual vocabularies of Italian America offered contexts for articulating and restaging the struggles of migrant families across generations and national identifications. On one hand, the outsize importance of mid-20th-century Italian neorealism as a cultural aesthetic and critical touchstone offers a clear trajectory of political and social purpose for filmic realism in Italy, even as recent work has expanded the scope of Italian film studies.[12] On the other (Black) hand, mid-century films set in US cities proliferated depictions of Mafiosi and their spiraling social structures. As scholars like Robert Casillo have pointed out, such depictions depended upon a sustained cultural imaginary around the codes and conducts of Italian Americans.[13] However, the alignments and misrecognitions that have characterized cultural imaginaries of Italian American possibilities and dangers, as realist enterprises, have a longer history in the pages of serial publications. While the visual languages of gangsters, bicycle thieves, and urban spaces have overdetermined our sense of Italian American aesthetic history, the development of actual orthographic language—the standard Italian that unified US Italians into an increasingly coherent polity—has remained undertheorized.

Even before the mass migration era, imaginative coherence was sought through written language. Italian-language papers in the United States, which helped to establish a cross-regional community of immigrants, were most often published in the national language of Italy, a modification of Dante's Tuscan dialect. Robert Viscusi details a linguistic practice that drew a sharp distinction between Italian dialect as a private, spoken language and standard Italian as a public one: "People could read it [national Italian] in the numerous Italian journals or understand when they heard it on the radio, although few immigrants actually spoke it."[14] Not only were there fewer potential readers of standard Italian at mid-century than in the early days of radio Viscusi describes, Italian literacy rates remained quite low into the 20th century, except among the rich and educated classes. The Italian-language newspapers of mid-century, then, were always and already addressed to an immigrant public in implicitly politicized terms: printed in the single language of Italian nationalism, these community periodicals hinged on linguistic knowledge whose goal was a "seamlessness of identity"[15] as Italian, not Calabrian, Genoan, or Florentine. Thus, reading community news in these publications was both a local and a national act. Immigrant newspapers contained the highly specific news of neighborhood Italian associations, ran reports on the operations of American federal government, and included as dispatches from Europe. Linguistically, the very activity of reading in these papers produced a movement in readers away from the micro-collectives of dialect toward the broadly communal experience of national language.

Indeed, the common language through which Italians communicated in the United States was being at that time standardized in the pages of the locally published newspapers circulating around the country. As is well documented, emigrating Italians often spoke only a local dialect, which might vary widely not only by region but even by town; efforts to introduce a standardized Italian were politically popular during the *Risorgimento* and following Italian unification in 1861, but no standard language usurped spoken dialect in families and local settings for much of the 19th century. Moreover, a national education system, which would promote literacy in standard Italian, was sporadically enforced in Italian regions. Thanks to Italy's 1877 Coppino Law, "education was free and compulsory up to the age of nine, and strict provisions were in place for enforcing attendance."[16] Intended to bring about meaningful change in the number of Italian illiterates—in 1861, the national census estimated that 81 percent of females and 68 percent of males over the age of six was functionally illiterate—the institutionalization of educational laws did not result in significant changes until the 20th century.[17]

New York City's *Il Progresso Italo-Americano* (1880–1989), often characterized as one of the earliest Italian-language newspapers in the United States,[18] was a complex participant in the serialization of identity through language, as its standard Italian content was hastily produced and inconsistently regularized. In descriptions of "the most influential Italian daily paper in New York and the United States,"[19] scholars introduce its powerful editor, Carlo Barsotti, once a Tuscan *padrone*. Barsotti opposed labor unions, allowed "unscrupulous advertisers" to hawk patent medicines in his vast advertising section,[20] and hired "Italians who could [not] write their own language properly"[21] to produce the paper's content.

Yet the paper's role in producing communal meaning, and circulating that meaning even beyond the confines of the New York City *colonia*, was significant. By 1893, Rowell's *American Newspaper Directory* includes *Il Progresso Italo-Americano* (daily circulation "not exceeding 3,000," 535), San Francisco's *La Voce del Popolo* (circulation between 3,000–5,000, 82), and a Chicago paper, *L'Italia*, that claimed almost 20,000 readers alongside New York City's old standby, *L'Eco d'Italia*.[22] Thus, the cultural associations and descriptions in *Il Progresso* had an audience that was proportionately noteworthy; moreover, the newspaper was itself participating in a larger "culture of letters" developing for Italian readers in the United States.

The paper Barsotti founded (which ran for more than a century) reached thousands of Italians across the nation. In addition to the work of news circulation, *Il Progresso* built a community in its pages, publishing the names of newly arrived families, letters of solidarity from Italians around the nation, lists of local books for sale or rent on topics from agriculture and economics to anatomy, hygiene, foreign languages, and literature. Describing the appeal for recently immigrated Italians, Bénédict Deschamps claims, "Barsotti's editorial recipe[,] made of translated American news, a collage of imported Italian newspaper clippings, commercial ads . . . and regular columns dedicated to the life of the 'colonia'[,] could seduce an Italian population."[23] Part of the appeal of Barsotti's paper was the way it both recreated and altered the conventions of US newspapers for its Italian reading public, through the forms described by Deschamps. For example, the weekly feature "Di Qua e di La [Of Here And There]" offered short descriptions of local events and news, creating not just an Andersonian "imagined community" of far-flung readers but a tightly knit immigrant collective sharing the same streets and columns.[24]

When offering histories of "the immigrant press," scholars often develop a progress narrative. Deschamps characterizes New York City's *L'Eco d'Italia* (founded in 1850) as "a mediating agent in the process that drove Risorgimento émigrés from their condition of forced expatriation to that of chosen settlement."[25] She argues for the real capitalist function of even early Italian American newspapers, despite what might appear as "excessive" rhetorical tendencies. "There is no doubt that . . . the Italian-language press provided Italian ethnic businesses with a promotional space"; moreover, "those papers helped Italian immigrants *name* the surrounding reality and decipher its cultural codes."[26] In other words, the immigrant press helped readers learn to translate real events or circumstances into metaphor and back again, and into profit.

In *No Future: Queer Theory and the Death Drive*, Lee Edelman depicts this metaphoric work with greater force as "the domestication, the colonization, of the world *by* meaning."[27] In his foundational critique of US heteronationalism, Edelman is less concerned with bodies and pleasures than he is with alternatives to repressive social norms. Edelman theorizes the making of social meaning itself through the future-oriented figure of The Child, highlighting how citizens misunderstand imagined meaning as "social reality." At the bottom, the fantasy of social reality reproduces identity through the linear time of biological reproduction. Through an investment in the symbolic future order of "reproductive futurism . . . the subject's alienation would vanish into the seamlessness of identity at the endpoint of an endless chain."[28] Like the endless chain of a newspaper's daily issues, presumptively circulating into perpetuity, collective identity solidifies and sustains itself as a seamless repetition of individualized bodies with the same desires and sociopolitical

commitments.[29] In the symbolic logic of Italian romanticism, stock characters like the "perfect knight" (what Daniel Aaron calls "the militant") and the
"virtuous patriot" tended repetitiously to dramatize broad themes of "defiance in the face of oppression, and redemption" in the service of cultural (and
national) coherence.[30] In the colonization of Italian identity by US civic
pressure, the political system of US futurity and the symbolic order of Italian
romance sought common ground.

Through the imaginative repetition inherent in newspaper publication, *Il
Progresso* helped readers navigate US cultural rituals like Independence
Day. At the same time, the paper's investments in local coherence as a
familial project (as in the grandmotherly vigilance of "Di Qua e di La") was
creating a distinct set of imaginative codes that sought to inflect everyday life
for readers. Thus, the paper deciphered cultural and practical meaning, such
as the intention of US Independence Day, as both linguistic and cultural
translation. Simultaneously, it affirmed the values and practices of social
reproduction as an important avenue for civic virtue. Yet, what *Il Progresso*
presents as reality updates look different, unfamiliar, when we read them as
quasi-romantic dramatizations with particular political purpose. Across
weeks of columns during 1889, *Il Progresso* developed an aestheticized,
heightened reality of threatened children to illustrate the civic maturity of the
community it addresses. This romanticized vision of endangered futurity
offered readers of *Il Progresso* one place to participate imaginatively, in a
specific material context, in the political imagination of US heteronormative
capitalism. In the embrace of this logic, Italian readers could imagine themselves contributors to the happy polyglot celebrated every July Fourth. Yet
these columns also illustrate how the paper developed a distinct discursive
tradition and value system.

Il Progresso, with its forceful motto[31] and its investment in national
symbols that crossed US and Italian nationalisms, was contributing directly
to the creation of a recognizable ethnic collective in the United States. When
the paper took up subscriptions for a Christopher Columbus statue in New
York City, it published bilingual letters of support for the enterprise alongside fundraising updates (Figure 8.1). In the sample below, the paper includes the letter of an American (or at least English using) "Admirer," in
order "mostrare . . . gli americani ferve l'interesse il monumento a Cristoforo
Colombo [to illustrate . . . the intense interest of Americans]" in such a
monument.

Thus two cultural perspectives became increasingly connected through an
Italian/American imaginary,[32] where recognition of Columbus as both "il
Grande Genovese" and a symbol of "all America" was seamless and simultaneous.[33] Columbus allowed Italians to weave themselves into a holistic national fabric in the United States, where commemoration of the Italian ex-
plorer served a celebratory purpose, much like the Independence Day festi-

Figure 8.1. *Il Progresso Italo-Americano*. 27 October, 1889. Courtesy of Calandra.

vals described as part of the Italian language newspapers's civic lessons in Americanness.[34] Through a symbol like Columbus, Italian readers could imagine how the glorious past of Italian achievement had set the terms for the US future.

Edelman's doctrine of futurism insists upon a fantasy of social wholeness in the future, and unites that fantasy around a potent embodied symbol, what he calls "The Child." Edelman's imagined Child is intended both to defer and constantly to retain participatory political wholeness: there is always a fresh generation of children for whom the same social order must be preserved. In September of 1889, *Il Progresso* was one of many newspapers covering "a vile plot [una congiura infernale]" to defraud local Assemblyman Robert Ray Hamilton, a descendant of Alexander Hamilton, through a paternity scam. Invoking by association the American Founding Fathers, and including the Hamilton drama among other coverage, *Il Progresso* is actively helping to develop cross-cultural relations, and an Italian American identity, through sympathetic attachment to US children used up and discarded by the hoaxers.

This identity, like that characterized by Edelman, remains oriented toward a future inhering in the community's children. The Hamilton paternity story, spread across several weeks of reporting, employs the communal investment of *Il Progresso* in the service of children beyond the neighborhood scope.

Exploring the rhetorical register and political implications of *Il Progresso*'s Hamilton coverage highlights how the newspaper used a successful formula—local investment plus national imagination—to bring readers into the circle of hetero-nationalism described in Edelman's definition of national politics. "Politics," in Edelman's words, "works to affirm a structure, to authenticate social order, which it then intends to transmit to the future in the form of its inner Child."[35] This logic of reproductive futurism encourages citizens to invest in a fantasy of future social coherence instead of challenging oppressions in the present moment. Futurism, always tied to social reproduction by way of biological procreation, is for Edelman an aggressively repressive system of political control, naming a regime of social order that views the Child as the "universalized subject" for whom "social order is held in perpetual trust."[36] Italian-language accounts of the Hamilton-Mann paternity scandal and its most vulnerable victims straddle repressive political and empathetic affective registers. As a broader urban story developed beyond initial familial drama, the newspaper engages with increasingly seedy and sensationalist elements; through repetition-with-difference of the narrative of vulnerability, *Il Progresso*'s columns invite identification with a paternalistic social order of protection and surveillance.

In its uneven appeal to future-oriented social maintenance, *Il Progresso*'s sense of cultural futurity offers a contrast to Edelman's despotic sense of reproductive futurism. For postbellum Italian immigrants, the imperatives of cultural and political assimilation and the social flexibility such imperatives required might be more accurately understood through a provisional logic of "futurity" instead of the regime Edelman names "futurism." Italian American futurity appeals to a collective sense of human connection across sociopolitical identifications instead of dictating compulsory adherence to a single order, to one particular version of the future.

According to the *Oxford English Dictionary*, the suffix "ism" is most often employed when forming "the name of a system of theory or practice"; "ism" creates a "descriptive term for doctrines or principles." In contrast, the suffix appended to the word "future" in "futurity" offers a conceptually looser signification used to "express a state or condition." In this exploration of Italian-language newspaper stories about threats to children, I use "futurity" instead of Edelman's more particular "futurism" to register Italian-immigrant awareness of their contingent relation to US social order and its presumed generational consistency.

Moreover, characterizing this logic as one of civic "futurity" for Italian Americans distinguishes it from a near-concurrent aesthetic and political phenomenon in Italy, the radical doctrine of Futurism that would affect aesthetic and social imagination for subsequent decades. In 1909, F. T. Marinetti's "Manifesto del Futurismo" decried the old regime of "la mitologia e l'ideal mistico [mythology and mystical ideals]" as useless. The manifesto elevated instead a modernity of materialism: machines, militarism, masculinity all valorized against stuffy commitments to museums and morality.[37] Moreover, the rejection of inherited social codes and normative civic discourse in Marinetti's "Manifesto del Futurismo" may offer an Italian version of the social negativity and refusal Edelman calls for in his polemic. Such an exploration is outside the scope of this essay, but the overlaps between futurism's nihilism and Edelman's queer negativity are compelling.[38]

The belief in futurity expressed in *Il Progresso* is generally cast as a personal moral imperative, not a collective political one, a distinction exacerbated by the newspaper's tendency toward dramatic direct address. In the news stories discussed below, recently arrived Italians imagine affiliations across culture as they come to share with US readers the Child-oriented collective future Edelman is at pains to diagnose and challenge. The distinction between futurism and futurity undergirds this brief exploration of Italian American cultural adaptation; more broadly, I explore alternative modes for imagining cultural distinctiveness and correspondence.

These distinct perceptual registers, "futurism" vs. "futurity," align with discourse communities themselves connected to discrete collective identities. Futurism, addressing US readers of English, participates in the imposition of US social order; futurity, addressed to readers of Italian, solicits identification with a collective of children, from diverse communities, who request aid for a better future through an appeal to the future's contingency. We could consider the former an imposition upon political citizens: Edelman refers to reproductive futurism as a "constraining mandate" that conditions "every social structure or form," foreclosing refusal as "unthinkable."[39] As theorized through *Il Progresso*, Italian futurity is visible as a state or condition of hope, a recognition of the future's open-endedness: what is to come might be different from what is now. This sense of future possibility is also often a condition of immigration. The decision to emigrate might depend, in part, on belief in the personal and cultural differences available for the emigrating citizen. Furthermore, the logic of futurity as an open-ended proposition connects with a formal feature of newspapers: their seriality.

Across the unfolding details of the Hamilton scandal, attention to child safety and welfare encourage newspaper readers to share a social collectivity organized around children as "a fantasy of the future." However, differences of language and rhetoric, and subsequent perspectival distinctions, illustrate diverse relations to that future. To be more specific: the English periodical community, governed by the coercive logic of futurism, speaks for the Child in the voice of the regulatory adult. This voice compels moral and political adherence to existent cultural values. Writers for *Il Progresso,* by contrast, inhabit the voice of the Child, supplicating readers instead of mandating their acquiescence.

Involving several unclaimed children who died after being illegally purchased, an attempted murder, and the tantalizing prospect of bigamy, the Hamilton-Mann scandal was national news during the fall of 1889. Thanks to an intrepid Inspector Brynes, Eva Hamilton-Mann's jailhouse confession revealed a wealth of salacious details. After stabbing an Atlantic City nurse, Eva was arrested and a complex plot revealed. New York State Senator Robert Ray Hamilton, "head of a group that calls itself the virtuous ones [il capo di quell partito che s'intitola dei 'virtuosi],"[40] consented to marry Eva following the appearance of a baby. Eva, already married to one Joshua Mann, had purchased three illegitimate babies from underground midwives before the fourth, bought for $10, lived long enough to be presented to Hamilton as the fruit of his noble American loins.

Certainly, the story featured to excess the sexual deception, economic exploitation, and political intrigue required for juicy scandal. But why did *Il Progresso*, the "most influential" news provider among Italian American communities, devote front page inches to the scandal for weeks after the story broke? What need was being served in rehashing the sordid details of these badly-behaving Americans in place of more typical fare like the procedures for achieving citizenship, labor-union developments within the community, or uplifting social news from around Italian American neighborhoods?

The volume of *Il Progresso*'s coverage, and the tone of breathless distress everywhere evident within it, illustrate the newspaper's participation a collective future imagined for American politicians, Italian immigrants, and the children being born every day in 1889 New York City. This particular content was responding to a desire for cross-cultural understanding that seems to have been one of the paper's broader discursive goals. Expanding its focus from Italian offspring to a variety of the tenement's endangered babies, *Il Progresso* appealed to an Italian community in the voice of the many. Alongside notices of naturalization meetings and news from Italy, "la dramma" Hamilton-Mann-Swinton suggested to readers that a precarious relation to future stability was not limited to Italian experience.

One distinction of the Italian coverage is its appeal for sympathetic attachment in place of a US tendency toward censure. *The Chicago Tribune* claims the scandal as "a warning . . . for those who think they can defy the moral sentiment of the community" and chastises Hamilton for "the disgrace he has brought upon himself."[41] The social mandate of futurism is evident in the editor's aggressive impulse to shame, positioning Hamilton as well as the Manns against a "moral" community. The *New York Times* similarly glosses the scandal as a "crushing" revelation, and describes Hamilton's offer of marriage as "preposterous . . . he had no hesitation being seen with her in public places . . . where he was morally sure to meet some if his friends."[42] Yet appeals to personal morality are never connected explicitly to the lost child(ren) involved in the original scam. The paper highlights morality and marriage without attention to the institution's ostensible purpose, suggesting that a reproductive imperative escapes (or perhaps disappears into) the conceptual contexts in which it emerges.

Il Progresso's editorial voice instead invokes vanished children, describing the "no fewer than four babies" who "called Hamilton 'papa' [non meno di quattro bambini . . . che chiamavano 'papa' l'Hamilton]."[43] This report engages directly in a familial fantasy, imagining that any of these newborns ["i neonati"] understand their false father through the language of family affiliation and affection. Calling out to "papa," perhaps holding aloft their chubby arms for a paternal embrace, these children, all four dead or rejected, call out as well to readers of *Il Progresso*, who are repeatedly confronted with news of tragic death. An adjacent report on the mysterious suicide of a sixteen-year-old reminds readers that this lost girl—like all the lost and the dead—"merits the compassion of all who hold in their hearts a place for feelings of kindness and devotion [merita la compassione di ogni persona che abbia nel suo coure il posto per sentimenti gentili ed affetuosi]."[44]

Certainly, the relatively small community of New York City Italians had practical reasons to worry about endangered children: without a stable youth population, the community's shared future would become uncertain. However, this concern for a communal future increasingly operates beyond the bounds of national identity, encompassing a diverse range of New York City's youth. *Il Progresso* is as interested in memorializing the four "neonati" as in narrating the unfolding legal drama of Hamilton, his wife, his wife's husband, and his wife's husband's mother. Italian coverage of the scandal, in both its ethical stance and its language, demonstrates community investment in a shared, but unknown and uncertain, sense of the future. This appeal to individual compassion on behalf of the endangered operates in a rhetorical register I have referred to as "cultural futurity," distinct from reproductive futurism's imposed social compliance and mandated political agenda.

My final example comes from a seemingly unrelated article appearing a week after the scandal broke. It illuminates the slippery discursive ground of cross-cultural association, as the supplication of futurity becomes the moralizing assertiveness of Edelman's reproductive futurism. *Il Progresso* proclaims its ethical investment in the city's youth population by publishing an expose of "un mercato dei bambini" [a baby market] operating in the city, complete with names, addresses, and pricing. In the face of this concrete and multiethnic abomination, *Il Progresso* expresses forceful social judgment, approximating the regulatory tone of US newspapers and moving closer to a social program aligned with the censure of reproductive futurism.

The article lists several notorious commercial midwives, whose names (Koehler, Knapp, Schwab, O'Reilly, and Wemer) suggest a range of ethnic identities.[45] Closing with the kind of adult-oriented admonition we saw in English-language coverage, *Il Progresso* chastises the police, the church, and an adult social order for whom baby-markets should be of great concern. Indeed, the article's tone of astonished outrage proceeds from a hypocrisy identified as specific to US colonial and political history. This editorial disgust is prompted by the (perceived) acquiescence of local institutions which look the other way as "baby markets" ply human trade in the land of "republicanism and puritanism."

> And the police know all, understand all, and take no action; those vile cowards, these repulsive middle-men, these sellers of sainted children, responsible for pain, robbery, and evil, are touched by no one; they pursue their trade under the eyes of justice, in the midst of flourishing churches, missionaries, and other religious people, amid the languages of morality, republicanism, and puritanism.[46]

Il Progresso demands protection for the city's threatened children through reference to a broad domestic collective of religious followers, regulatory bodies, and proponents of a specifically republican, distinctly puritan moral virtue. The specificity of US political and social hypocrisy prompts the paper's intercession into a sensationalized horror of sheer neonatal innocence and utter capitalist degradation. In place of appeals to individuals "whose hearts hold a place for kindness and devotion," instead of requesting sympathy and aid for the endangered, these closing lines compel collective action by invoking a US sociopolitical order of police forces, missionaries, and outraged moral citizens. Children of diverse ethnic backgrounds, menaced by an assortment of "vile" "repulsive" abusers, become the protected province of an Italian American collective who sees clearly the disjunction between political ideals and local actions.

For Edelman, reproductive futurism is an insidious social evil. In the process I have traced here, the rhetorical and affective tendencies of an Italian community publication are modified through contact with a political order invested in reprimand and social control. Across this shifting discursive landscape, the figure of the Child organizes a relation to the future: as the Child blurs from a distinctly Italian offspring to an ethically indeterminate salable item, writers for *Il Progresso* become more strident, more assertive in their tone and politics. This rhetorical shift, this cultural hybridization between two versions of the future, is not necessarily an unquestionable good. In Edelman's analysis, the real cultural work of the Child is its invocation in the service of a stable, unified identity. Thus, the Child could also be perceived as a romantic figure, one who suggests an idealized potential for social unity and satisfaction.[47] Defining politics as "the social elaboration of reality," Edelman claims that the Child's purpose in the political arena (the entirety of social reality) is to "enac[t] a logic of repetition that fixes identity through identification with the future of the social order."[48]

Although the most politically charged erasures of Italian civic maturity occur in English-language writing such as other newspapers, ethnographic reports, and government documents, studies of Italian American writing (in English) also tend to reify commitments to realist imaginaries while de-emphasizing Italian America's more romantic visions. In conclusion, I identify some of the cultural functions of what might now be recognizable as a repetitive, ceaseless imperative for civic maturation, sketching out some of the implications for ethnic identifications and histories.

Scholars of migrant experience point to the circular or repetitive nature of migration and cultural assimilation. In the current historiography of Italian-America, too little attention is given to the immigrant communities preceding the mass migration "flood." Thus, we have lost sight of a long and important early stage of Italian migration in the US, overlooking those people and communities who, throughout the long 19th century, moved through the processes of cultural decoding and social recognition more typically understood to have come later in US history.

Folding this periodical romance into a larger story of Italian America, we might see two related things about the identity that history describes. Italian America lacks, in Anthony Julian Tamburri's terms, a sufficiently "tragic" history, in part because of its assertive normalization into a longer 19th century ethnic trajectory.[49] This is how romance conveys meaning through repetition, according to Gannon: "magical thinking uses cyclical repetitions . . . in attempts to bring about solutions to inner conflicts."[50] While the conflict explored here could not traditionally be understood as an "inner" (that is, personally interior) one, Tamburri's analysis implies that navigating between ethnic and national identity is best understood as a struggle interior to particular ethnic groups. We should continue to develop robust, imaginatively expansive ways to explore how multiethnic or cross-cultural experiences condition the presumptively interior experience of migrant communities.

Additionally, the progressive nature of these repetitive maturation cycles enables us to recognize how the collective history of Italian America "came-of-age" alongside the United States itself. The growth of American industry, urban space, and cultural customs is fully consistent with the growth of Italian American participation in US sociopolitical life. These conclusions suggest the productively dialectical nature of Italian experience in the United States, although they also imply the normalizing weight of such an identity. Donna R. Gabaccia's *Italy's Many Diasporas* points out that Italian migration was also characterized by a cycle of return back to Italy, as "50 percent of Italy's migrants returned to their country around the turn of the century."[51]

The cyclical and recursive development of Italian and Italian American national identification was thus complicated by the seemingly endless exchange between countries as people moved back and forth regularly.

In our contemporary moment, the aesthetic identity Thomas Ferraro describes as "feeling Italian" may be imaginable, even open for broader cultural affiliation, beyond genetic identity. In the historical moment of mass migration's horizon—the new beginning of the new Italian American history—US public writing often refused fully to appreciate or even to see immigrant maturation. Instead, many newspapers sought to represent these communities as made up entirely of fresh-off-the-boat arrivals, culturally unprepared and economically dependent. This cultural narrative also demonstrates the era's felt need to reassert the importance of civic maturity, to affirm the endlessness of a cultural assimilation cycle in which the ignorance of a recently arrived populace overwhelms the long-standing cultural awareness of a stable residential community. Recognizing this (re)assertion as historical repetition underscores the power of a certain national romance that imagines US progress and political maturity as conveying an ultimate moral logic. In the service of this essential lesson, immigrants cycle through hauntingly similar episodes, as they remain ever (or always newly) childlike.

NOTES

1. Robert Orsi characterizes the fin-de-siècle racial status of Italian Americans as one of "inbetweenness": "the issue of racial inbetweenness existed in the urban, industrial North as well, where most of the immigrants from Southern Italy settled. . . . The issue of the immigrants' place on the American landscape vis-à-vis other dark-skinned peoples fundamentally shaped not only the contours of their everyday lives at work and on the streets, but also the 'Italian-American' identity they crafted for themselves" (Orsi, "The Religious Boundaries of an Inbetween People," 314). See Anthony Julian Tamburri, *Re-Reading Italian Americana* (2014) and *A Semiotic of Ethnicity* (1998). In the latter, Tamburri imagines the literary history of "Italian/American" texts through what he calls a "cognitive" perspective, in which writers "represent different modes of being dependent on different levels of consciousness" (Tamburri, *A Semiotic of Ethnicity*, 12). See also Joseph Cosco, *Imagining Italians* (2003); Thomas Ferraro, *Feeling Italian* (2005); Robert Viscusi, *Buried Caesars, and Other Secrets of Italian American Writing* (2006); Lydio F. Tomasi, ed. *Italian Americans: New Perspective in Italian Immigration and Ethnicity* (1985).

2. As early the mid-1850s, New York City's *L'Eco d'Italia* was describing American Independence day as a celebration for a "population of heterogeneous elements. . . [within] which few fights occur [*una popolazione composta di tanti elementi eterogenei . . . non succede alcuna rissa*]" ("*Anniversario dell'Indipendenza Americana*"). All citations to *L'Eco d'Italia* come from holdings at the American Antiquarian Society, Worcester, Mssachusetts. All translations from original Italian are my own.

3. If Jean-Paul Sartre's *Critique of Dialectical Reason* (1976) offers a foundational theoretical vision of collectivity through seriality, scholarship in periodical studies engages the question of seriality across many sorts of imagined communities. As a start, see an overview in Faye Hammill et al., "Introducing Magazines and/as Media: The Aesthetics and Politics of Serial Form"; on seriality as a form of autobiographical meaning-making see Nicole M. Stamant, "Maya Angelou's Memoirs in the "Gastronomic Contact Zone" and David Scott Diffrient, "Autobiography, Corporeality, Seriality."

4. Sheffer "Recollecting, Repeating, and Walking Through," 141. Maria Lauret likewise highlights formal similarity in migration memoirs through structures of repetition: "Compared to other immigrant tales of the early 20th century, such as Mary Antin's *The Promised Land* (1912), Bok's is not only atypical in its subject matter but also in its style, which is anecdotal and repetitive" ("When's an Immigrant Biography Not an Immigrant Biography?" 7).

5. Gannon, "One More Time," 2.

6. Gannon, "One More Time," 2–3.

7. Indeed, the use of repetition for conveying political and social meaning was not developed during mass migration, but it remains where we have most commonly sought this story. A handful of Italian-language newspapers, including *L'Eco d'Italia* (1850–1896) and Chicago's *L'Unione Italiana* (1860s), interpolated Italian readers into serialized forms of citizenship decades earlier.

8. Most scholarship of Italian migration to the US emphasizes mass migration (1880s-1920s). For recent alternative histories, see Richard N. Juliana, *Building Little Italy* (2005); Justin Nystrom, *Creole Italian* (2018).

9. 19th century writers for United States newspapers often used the language of childishness and maturation to represent immigrant experience and acculturation. This was no different for late-century Italian immigrants, regularly constructed as helpless, unprepared, and childlike. In 1872, influential paper *The New York Tribune* describes them as "deluded" and unable to ensure their own survival: "During the winter, the Italians cannot sustain themselves, and how the immense numbers pouring in here are to be kept from starving remains to be settled" ("Deluded Italian Immigrants"). Twenty years later, the paper strikes the same tune, characterizing the prototypical immigrant thusly: "by nature ardently attached to whatever his affections incline toward, so that when his success weans his heart from Italy he generally gives the full measure of his love to the land of his adoption" ("Bad Italian Immigration"). The metaphoric system—terms like "weans" and "adoption," the figure of the "ardently attached" innocent—represents these immigrants as socially immature, claiming them "less intelligent than those of northern climates" but willing to perform the "unskilled cheap labor that has to be done and is unattractive to Americans" ("Bad Italian Immigration").

10. Humbert Nelli, *Italians in Chicago 1880–1930* (1970); Rudolph Vecoli, *Italian-American Radicalism* (1973); George Pozzetta, *Pane e lavoro* (1980).

11. Certainly, there was a robust national literary tradition in Italy as well as a wealth of Italian American literature today. For the Southern Italian immigrant population of the late 19th century, though, neither the linguistic nor the cultural context supported engagement with diasporic literary traditions. Classic studies include Tamburri, *To Hyphenate or Not to Hyphenate;* Fred Gardaphé, *Italian Signs, American Streets* (1996). Anthologies include Helen Barolini, *The Dream Book* (2000); Martino Marazzi, *Voice of Italian America* (2012); Francesco Durante and Tamburri, eds. *Italoamericana: The Literature of the Great Migration, 1880–1943* (2014).

12. For a foundational argument on the cultural influence and political value of Italian neorealism, see Millicent Marcus, *Italian Film in the Light of Neorealism* (1986); for a useful recent introduction to the genre and its critical history, see Mark Shiel, *Italian Neorealism* (2006); on Italian silent film, see Giorgio Bertellini, ed. *Italian Silent Cinema: A Reader* (2013).

13. Robert Casillo, "Moments in Italian-American Cinema: From Little Caeser to Coppola and Scorcese." Fred Gardaphé has been a prolific contributor to the recognition and refutation of these stereotypes in US media. See for example, "The Gangster Figure in American Film and Literature."

14. Viscusi, *Buried Ceasers*, 33.

15. Edelman, *No Future*, 8.

16. Duggan, *The Force of Destiny*, 276.

17. Figures on Italian literacy rates from "Literacy," *Encyclopedia of European Social History, vol. V.*

18. In a different version of this argument, Mangione and Morreale assert of *Il Progresso* that it was the "most successful of all the Italian-language newspapers [and]. . . the first to profit from the massive Italian immigration" (*La Storia,* 454). Several studies of Italian

American culture identify *Il Progresso* as a originary example of the Italian-language periodical. While it was certainly one of the earliest and most broadly circulated Italian-language *daily* papers, it was by no means an influential *early* one, as my work with numerous earlier papers illustrates. For versions of this claim about *Il Progresso's* temporal superiority, see Salvatore J. LaGumina et al., *Italian America Experience: An Encyclopedia* (2005) and Alexander De-Conde, *Half Bitter, Half Sweet* (1971).

19. Quoted from the paper's masthead, English in original. September 2–3, 1889. All citations from *Il Progresso Italo-Americano* are taken from the microfilm holdings at the John D. Calandra Italian American Institute, CUNY, New York City. All translations from original Italian are my own.

20. Mangione, *La Storia*, 454.

21. DeConde, *Half Bitter, Half Sweet*, 75.

22. Geo. P. Rowell & Co's American Newspaper Directory (1893 ed.), 150). Circulation figures for most foreign-language papers in the US did not reach the heights of nationally circulating periodicals in English. In 1873, for example, the *New York Herald* weekly edition was circulating to 88,000 people (Rowell, *Directory*, 238).

23. Deschamps, "The Italian Ethnic Press in a Global Perspective," 82. For more on serialization in Italian-language newspapers, see Dechamps, "Bernardino Ciambelli's Misteri Di Harlem: An Example of Serialized Fiction in the Italian American Press."

24. Benedict Anderson's influential description of newspaper's "imagined communities" still structures our understanding of how newspapers create collectivity: "the newspaper reader, observing exact replicas of his own paper being consumed . . . is continually reassured that the imaged world is visibly rooted in everyday life" (*Imagined Communities*, 36).

25. Deschamps, "The Italian Ethnic Press in a Global Perspective," 80.

26. Deschamps, "The Italian Ethnic Press in a Global Perspective," 83.

27. Edelman, *No Future*, 137.

28. Edelman, *No Future*, 8.

29. Edelman, *No Future*, 9.

30. Lucy Riall, *Garibaldi*, 26. Daniel Aaron's di-historicized yet progressive rubric employs generic language (the first stage of migrant writing is described as "local-colorist") in portraying the first stage of immigrant experience ("The Hyphenate Writer and American Letters"). Nancy Glazener makes a strikingly similar point in Anglo-American context, arguing that the shifting definitions and values associated with "the romance" and "the novel" in American periodical writing "identified the romance with earlier or less mature phases of a culture's development" (*Reading for Realism*, 60).

31. Beneath the title flag several mottos were printed in English and Italian: "Il Primo Giornale Quotidiano Italiano Fondato Negli Stati Uniti [The First Italian Daily Newspaper Founded in the United States]"; "The Most Influential Italian Daily Newspaper in New York and the United States"; "Having the Largest Circulation of Any Italian Paper in America."

32. In *To Hyphenate or Not to Hyphenate*, Tamburri offers the diacritical "slash" instead of the hyphen when describing US Americans of Italian descent. For Tamburri, the hyphen's ideological implications ("the distance created by the hyphen," 8) outweigh its grammatical utility. Instead, the slash "bridges the physical gap between the two terms, thus bringing them closer together" (47).

33. "Per Cristoforo Colombo."

34. The development of Columbus Day as an "international" US celebration was not confined to New York City. For a survey of the holiday's intracontinental history, see Gerald McKevitt "Christopher Columbus as a Civic Saint."

35. Edelman, *No Future*, 3.

36. Edelman, *No Future*, 11.

37. Marinetti, "Manifesto del Futurismo."

38. One can imagine Marinetti taking great pleasure in Edelman's most deliberately provocative formulation in *No Future*: "Fuck the social order and the Child in whose name we're collectively terrorized; fuck Annie; fuck the waif from Les Mis. . . ." (29).

39. Edelman, *No Future*, 4.

40. "Lo Scandalo Hamilton-Mann-Swinton."

41. "The Hamilton Case."
42. "Mrs. Hamilton in Prison."
43. "Una Congiura Infernale."
44. "Suicidio di una giovinetta italiana."
45. "Mercato di Bambini in N.Y."
46. "E la polizia sa tutto, e conosce tutto, e non provvede; quelle turpi femminaccie, quelle schifose mezzane, quelle mercantesse della santa infanzia, responsibili di dolori, di colpi e di mali, nessuno le tocca; seguitano il loro mestiere. . . sotto gli occhi della giustizia e in mezzo al fiorire di cheise, di missioni, di evvangelizzazioni, e di retorica morale, repubblicana, quaquera e puritana" ("Mercato di Bambini in N.Y.").
47. Margaret Hunt Gram posits a provocative connection between Edelman's notion of reproductive futurity and genre. Exploring the progressive commitments of Jonathan Frazen's *Freedom*, Gram argues that one narrative way around the problem of textual futurity is to imagine "forms better equipped for doing that imaginative work. Would exploring the limits of growth," she asks, "require, paradoxically, the creation of open-ended stories. . . . Stories that 'declin[e] to affirm as certain,' as Edelman puts it . . . 'any future at all'" ("Freedom's Limits," 312).
48. Edelman, *No Future*, 25.
49. Tamburri, *Re-Reading Italian Americana*, 3–4.
50. Gannon, "One More Time," 3.
51. Gabaccio, *Italy's Many Diasporas*, 94.

BIBLIOGRAPHY

Aaron, Daniel. "The Hyphenate Writer and American Letters." *Smith Alumnae Quarterly* 55, no. 2 (1964): 213–217.
Anderson, Benedict. *Imagined Communities: Reflections on the Origin and Spread of Nationalism.* New York: Verso, 2006 revised ed.
"Anniversario dell'Indipendenza Americana." *L'Eco d'Italia*, July 8, 1854. American Antiquarian Society.
"Bad Italian Immigration." *New York Tribune*, February 10, 1891. America's Historical Newspapers.
Barolini, Helen. *The Dream Book: An Anthology of Writing by Italian American Women.* New York: Syracuse University Press, 2000.
Bertellini, Giorgio, ed. *Italian Silent Cinema: A Reader* Herts: John Libbey Publishing, 2013.
Casillo, Robert. "Moments in Italian-American Cinema: From Little Caeser to Coppola and Scorcese." In *From the Margin: Writings in Italian Americana*, edited by Anthony Julian Tamburri, Paolo A. Giordano, and Fred L. Gardaphé, 394–416. Indiana: Purdue University Press, rev. ed. 2000.
Cosco, Joseph. *Imagining Italians: The Clash of Romance and Race in American Perceptions, 1880–1910.* Albany: SUNY Press, 2003.
Deschamps, Bénédict. "Bernardino Ciambelli's Misteri Di Harlem: An Example of Serialized Fiction in the Italian American Press." In *Transnationalism and American Serial Fiction*, edited by Patricia Okker, 148–161. *Routledge Transnational Perspectives on American Literature*: 16. New York: Routledge, 2012.
———. "The Italian Ethnic Press in a Global Perspective." In *The Cultures of Italian Migration: Diverse Trajectories and Discrete Perspectives*, edited by Graziella Parati and Anthony Julian Tamburri, 75–94. Lanham, MD: Fairleigh Dickinson University Press, 2011.
DeConde, Alexander. *Half Bitter, Half Sweet: An Excursion into Italian-American History.* New York: Scribner, 1971.
"Deluded Italian Immigrants" *New York Tribune*, December 11, 1872. America's Historical Newspapers.
Diffrient, David Scott. "Autobiography, Corporeality, Seriality: Nanni Moretti's Dear Diary as a Narrative Archipelago." *Journal of Film and Video* 61, no. 4 (2009): 17–30.

Duggan, Christopher. *The Force of Destiny: A History of Italy since 1796*. New York: Penguin Books, 2007.

Durante, Francesco, and Anthony Julian Tamburri, eds. *Italoamericana: The Literature of the Great Migration, 1880–1943*. New York: Fordham University Press, 2014.

Edelman, Lee. *No Future: Queer Theory and the Death Drive*. Durham: Duke University Press, 2004.

Ferraro, Thomas. *Feeling Italian: The Art of Ethnicity in America*. New York: New York University Press, 2005.

Gannon, Susan R. "One More Time: Approaches to Repetition in Children's Literature" *Children's Literature Association Quarterly* 12, no. 1 (1987): 2–5.

Gabaccio, Donna L. *Italy's Many Diasporas*. New York: Routledge.

Gardaphé, Fred L. *Italian Signs, American Streets*. Durham: Duke University Press, 1996.

———. "The Gangster Figure in American Film and Literature." In *Mediated Ethnicity: New Italian-American Cinema*, edited by Giuliana Muscio, Joseph Sciorra, Giovanni Spagnoletti, and Anthony Julian Tamburri, 55–63. Studies in Italian Americana: 2. New York, NY: Calandra Italian American Institute, 2010.

Geo. P. Rowell & Co's American Newspaper Directory containing accurate lists of all the newspapers and periodicals published in the United States and Territories, and the dominion of Canada, and British Colonies of North America; together with a description of the towns and cities in which they are published. New York: Geo. P. Rowell and Co., Publishers and Newspaper Advertising Agents, 1893.

Glazener, Nancy. *Reading for Realism*. Durham: Duke University Press, 1997.

Gram, Margaret Hunt. "Freedom's Limits: Jonathan Franzen, the Realist Novel, and the Problem of Growth" *American Literary History* 26, no. 2 (2014): 295–316.

Hammill, Faye, Paul Hjartarson, and Hannah McGregor. "Introducing Magazines and/as Media: The Aesthetics and Politics of Serial Form." *ESC: English Studies in Canada* 41, no. 1 (2015): 1–18.

Juliana, Richard N. *Building Little Italy: Philadelphia's Italians Before Mass Migration*. Pennsylvania: Penn State University Press, 2005.

LaGumina, Salvatore J., Frank J. Cavaiolo, Salvatore Primeggia, and Joseph A. Varacalli, eds. *Italian America Experience*: *An Encyclopedia*. New York: Routledge, 2005.

Lauret, Maria. "When's an Immigrant Biography Not an Immigrant Biography?: *The Americanization of Edward Bok*." *MELUS* 38, no. 3 (2013): 7–24.

"Literacy." *Encyclopedia of European Social History, vol. V*. New York: Scribner's, 2001.

Mangione, Jerre, and Ben Morreale. *La Storia: Five Centuries of the Italian American Experience*, 5th edition. New York: Harper Perennial, 5th edition, 1993.

Marazzi, Martino. *Voice of Italian America: A History of Early American Literature with a Critical Anthology*, translated by Ann Goldstein. New York: Fordham University Press, 2012.

Marcus, Millicent. *Italian Film in the Light of Neorealism*. New Jersey: Princeton University Press, 1986.

Marinetti, Filippo Tommaso. "I manifesti del futurismo." *Figaro*, February 20, 1909. Project-Guttenberg.org.

McKevitt, Gerald. "Christopher Columbus as a Civic Saint: Angelo Noce and Italian American Assimilation." *California History* 71, no. 4 (1992): 516–533.

"Mercato di Bambini in N.Y." *Il Progresso Italo-Americano*, 11 September 11, 1889. Calandra Italian American Institute.

"Mrs. Hamilton in Prison." *New York Times*, August 28, 1889. Newspaper Archive.

Nelli, Humbert. *Italians in Chicago 1880–1930. A Study in Ethnic Mobility*. New York: Oxford University Press, 1970.

Nystrom, Justin. *Creole Italian: Sicilian Immigrants and the Shaping of New Orleans Food Culture*. Athens: University of Georgia Press, 2018.

Orsi, Robert. "The Religious Boundaries of an Inbetween People: Street Feste and the Problem of the Dark-Skinned Other in Italian Harlem, 1920–1990." *American Quarterly* 44, no. 3 (1992): 313–347.

"Per Cristoforo Colombo." *Il Progresso*, 27 October, 1889. Calandra Italian American Institute.

Pozzetta, George. *Pane e lavoro*. Toronto: MHSO, 1980.

Riall, Lucy. *Garibaldi: Invention of a Hero*. New Haven: Yale University Press, 2007.

Sartre, Jean-Paul. *Critique of Dialectical Reason*. Translated by Alan Sheridan-Smith. Verso Books, 2010.

Sheffer, Jolie A. "Recollecting, Repeating, and Walking Through: Immigration, Trauma, and Space in Mary Antin's *The Promised Land*." *MELUS* 35, no. 1 (2010): 141–166.

Shiel, Mark. *Italian Neorealism: Rebuilding the Cinematic City*. New York: Columbia University Press, 2006.

Stamant, Nicole M. "Maya Angelou's Memoirs in the "Gastronomic Contact Zone": Seriality and Citizenship." *a/b: Auto/Biography Studies* 27, no. 1 (2012): 101–126.

"Suicidio di una giovinetta italiana," *Il Progresso Italo-Americano*, September 2–3, 1889. Calandra Italian American Institute.

Tamburri, Anthony Julian. *To Hyphenate or Not to Hyphenate: The Italian/American Writer: An Other American*. Ontario: Guernica Press, 1991.

———. *A Semiotic of Ethnicity: In (Re)cognition of the Italian/American Writer*. Albany: SUNY Press, 1998.

———. *Re-Reading Italian Americana: Specificities and Generalities on Literature and Criticism*. Madison: Fairleigh Dickinson, 2014.

"The Hamilton Case." *Chicago Daily Tribune*, September 3, 1889. American's Historical Newspapers.

Tomasi, Lydio F. ed. *Italian Americans: New Perspective in Italian Immigration and Ethnicity*. New York: Center for Migration Studies of New York, Inc., 1985.

"Una Congiura Infernale," *Il Progresso Italo-Americano*, September 5, 1889. Calandra Italian American Institute.

Vecoli, Rudolph. *Italian-American Radicalism: Old World Origins and New World Developments*. New York: American-Italian Historical Association, 1973.

Viscusi, Robert. *Buried Caesars, and Other Secrets of Italian American Writing*. Albany: SUNY Press, 2006.

Chapter Nine

Cinema Paradiso

*Toronto's Italian Language Cinemas
and Distribution Networks*

Jessica Leonora Whitehead and Paul S. Moore

After WWII, an influx of new immigrants to Canada arrived from Southern and Eastern Europe. Earlier Italian immigrants from the turn of the century were termed "sojourners" because the Canadian government discouraged permanent immigration from countries outside of Northern and Western Europe.[1] Italian immigrants in the 1950s, in contrast, more quickly adopted parts of mainstream Canadian consumer culture. This was largely due to immigration reforms after WWII, which facilitated immigrants from Italy to become permanent settlers, changing the ethnic mix of Canada and especially the metropolis of Toronto. These new immigrants—Italians, but also Germans, Hungarians, Portuguese, and many others—changed the demographics of the country and laid the groundwork for official multiculturalism to greet Chinese, South Asian, and other immigrants from outside Europe in later decades. Newly arrived Italian-speaking immigrants after WWII very quickly organized community institutions, both commercial and parochial. These new routines helped to reshape the face of Canada's commercial and cultural landscape, including the news and entertainment industries. Soon after the arrival of postwar Italian immigrants, for example, Toronto hosted Italian-language newspapers, radio shows, concert venues, book and music shops, as well as Italian as the vernacular in countless commercial and community spaces.

A flourishing film industry in Italy coincided with the relative decline of mainstream Hollywood moviegoing in Canada. Dozens of Toronto movie theaters closed or sought new audiences in the face of new competition from television, exactly as tens of thousands of people newly arrived from Italy were seeking entertainment in their mother tongue. Film distribution and exhibition in Canada's largest city was transformed. In total, more than two dozen Italian-language cinemas operated at least briefly in Toronto between the early 1950s and the late 1980s, a time when the proportion of people with Italian as mother tongue grew to more than 10 percent of the city's population (see figure 9.1).[2] While smaller cities had Italian films once a week, or at one location, many of the Italian cinemas in Toronto were long-standing, profitable businesses fully integrated into larger, mainstream cinema chains and corporate structures, in addition to small, entrepreneurial ventures. This essay analyzes entertainment advertising from three decades of the *Corriere Canadese* to demonstrate how Italian-language film exhibition provided a flourishing movie culture for Italian enclaves in Toronto. Part of a distinctly secular, commercial routine of middle-class consumption, moviegoing in Italian offered a type of unofficial multiculturalism allowing people to retain diasporic cultural ties to popular culture and mass entertainment.

Italian showmen had previously played a supporting role in the history of film exhibition in Canada, but only as purveyors of Hollywood movies. Starting in 1953, however, imported Italian-language films after WWII became an everyday staple for cinemas catering to the ethnic enclaves of Toronto.[3] Between 1963 and 1972, for example, five long-standing theaters coexisted exclusively screening Italian films: the Studio and Pylon on College Street in the heart of Little Italy, the St. Clair in the heart of the Corso Italia, the Radio City on Bathurst Street at St. Clair—a simple transit ride equal distance from both Little Italy and the Corso Italia—and the Paradise, sometimes advertised as the *Cinema Paradiso*, on the major midtown transit line of Bloor Street. The competing owners of these theaters also started distribution networks sending their imported Italian films across Canada and into the United States. In this essay, archived newspaper publicity helps confirm information from a partial sample of historical business records from one of these entrepreneurs, which altogether recounts what John Caldwell has called the para-industry, "the aggregate cultural dimensions" of media. The distribution of Italian films in Canada was not a simple business, and its history must be recovered from traces such as ephemeral remnants of microfilmed advertising and biographical stories of locally important, pioneering individuals.[4] Theories of migration networks further allows for examination of the mechanisms and processes that facilitated the development of so-called foreign-language cinemas catering to Italian speakers across Canada.[5] Ultimately, the influx of Italian immigrants after WWII allowed for a new industry to develop around imported, diasporic films. Italian film distribution networks were an early multicultural industry, which would help to influence later foreign language film distribution in the country.

ITALIAN POSTWAR MIGRATION IN CANADA

Despite the close proximity of Canada and the United States, the two countries historically had different immigration policies and practices, particularly in terms of Italian immigration. Starting in the 1890s until the First World War there was a large influx of Italian immigrants globally, and this has often been described as the largest mass migration in world history.[6] The United States was the destination of many of these immigrants and their migrant labor was key to building large cities like New York and Chicago, and they also worked in rural areas such as plantations in the Southern United States.[7] While Italian labor was also important in Canada, most Italian laborers stayed in the country temporarily due to policies from both the Canadian and Italian governments that discouraged permanent settlement.[8] One key commonality between Canada and the United States was the importance of the padrone system where Italian labor agents acted as community leaders and were both venerated and feared in Italian diasporic communities.[9] These padrone leaders essentially controlled aspects of life in many early Italian communities in both Canada and the United States.

Immigration has consistently been tied to labor and growth of the Canadian economy, but this was especially true immediately following WWII as an era of extended economic expansion. The Canadian government of William Lyon Mackenzie King acted upon lobbying from business and industry groups and began to slowly change immigration policies to accept postwar refugees from Europe to contribute to expanding the Canadian economy through their relatively unskilled and affordable labor.[10] Immigration reform in the 1960s in Canada shifted away from this preference for laborers. Mirroring aspects of the United States's Hart-Celler Act of 1965, Canada established a nondiscriminatory point system in 1967, which helped open up immigration to Asian and other non-European countries.[11] The resulting system, however, strictly limited the arrival of uneducated laborers, and has been criticized as a direct reaction against the influx of unskilled Italian workers of the 1950s and 1960s.[12] Despite limited Italian immigration in the earlier interwar period, the larger Canadian cities of Toronto and Montreal had already established Little Italy neighborhoods where new immigrants of the 1950s first settled.

Even before the postwar influx, Toronto had three distinct Italian-identified areas, first in The Ward at Centre Avenue and Elm Street within a tight mix of other immigrants, poor and racialized peoples; then the neighborhood eventually labeled Little Italy, a slightly more domestic area northwest of downtown, around College and Grace Streets; and yet further northwest, the area later known as the Corso Italia at St. Clair Avenue West from Dufferin Street (see figure 9.2). Although all three were somewhat Italian-identified by 1916, with churches, meeting halls, and businesses nearby, their relative importance shifted over time away from the city center, with post–WWII settlement in a suburban trajectory. [13] John Zucchi explains how the development of these neighborhoods "reflected two main factors: the padrone movement which supplied labor to Canadian capital projects, and chain migration from towns and regions in Italy to the Canadian city." [14] Italians in Canada, as in other host countries such as the United States and Argentina, developed close-knit communities following village and familial ties and reflecting the labor agent networks of the community padrone leaders. In the period after WWII, Italians first settled primarily in Little Italy on College Street, which overtook The Ward as the key landing ground for Italians. Little Italy's core reached a majority Italian "mother tongue" in the 1961 census, although the area had an ethnic mix and unclear boundaries with nearby neighborhoods receiving other nationalities of new immigrants. Many more Italians settled just outside the official city limits in the City of York in the area that gained the label Corso Italia for its strip along St. Clair Avenue West. The Corso anchored a large suburban swath where Italian was vernacular on the streets and at home. Several adjacent districts reported majority Italian "mother tongue" in the 1961 census (see figure 9.4), climbing to more than two-thirds Italian in the 1971 census (see figure 9.5).

Although the first wave of Italian immigrants also lived in Little Italy, many severed cultural ties because of relatively smaller numbers and systemic discrimination. During WWII, especially, Italy was an enemy nation of Canada's allies and all Italian born citizens were labeled "enemy aliens." Italians with alleged fascist and communist ties were arrested and interned, their business assets seized in trust, for the duration of the war. [15] In any case, movies and other forms of imported Italian entertainment were not readily available, and even locally printed Italian newspapers were banned during the strict censorship of WWII. There are clear differences between the degree of integration and diasporic ties of earlier and later generations of Italians in Toronto. The new wave of immigrants in the 1950s were more assertive in maintaining their ethnic differences from Canadian society, and were sometimes at odds with the older generation over cultural heritage and distinctiveness. [16] Never having known WWII internment and legalized discrimination, the postwar Italian immigrant community institutionalized ways to maintain their language and cultural practices, and diasporic media such as Italian films at community theaters were important to many new migrants—and profitable to several businessmen in the community, too.

Hollywood moviegoing was often modeled on middle-class bourgeois respectability, cited as a key means of integration into mainstream society and mass consumption, transforming how working-class people spent their leisure time. [17] This integration of immigrants into mainstream consumer culture—embourgeoisement—was not totalizing, as Lizbeth Cohen has shown for Chicago. [18] In her work, Cohen demonstrates how immigrant communities in Chicago's regular attendance at theaters screening Hollywood movies did not fundamentally change their behavior, largely because ethnic audiences would often watch these films in ethnic or working-class audience neighborhood theaters. Film historians have also looked at the integration of immigrant audiences but most of these studies have focused on early cinema and in particular New York City. Imagine how much less homogenizing the movies would be if the moderation of enclaves and neighborhood audiences happened while watching imported films together, as in Toronto during the postwar period?

Hollywood's founding myth is providing a way for immigrants to learn about the American dream.[19] As movie palaces transformed cinema-going into a respectable and mainstream popular pastime, the industry's hardscrabble origins at makeshift nickelodeons were romanticized for catering especially to immigrants in urban ethnic ghettoes: the silent drama as a school for Americanization. Important debates among film historians have qualified this generalization and decentered urban, immigrant audiences by cataloguing the breadth of locations and spectators and the depth of investments behind the scenes, to highlight the diversity of audiences—from the start—along racial, gendered, class, and geographic lines.[20] Even Manhattan movie theaters, Ben Singer argued, catered to middle-class audiences at uptown shopping districts earlier than the prominent nostalgia for Lower East Side nickelodeons recognized.[21] Within all this debate, only a handful of scholarship has considered the existence of immigrant audiences within ethnic enclaves and moviegoing as a factor in retaining cultural identity rather than as a force of integration.

Judith Thissen argues, for example, that embourgeoisement was a complicated process that is hard to clearly trace. She explained how, up until 1913, immigrant audiences tended to view cinema in mixed-billed shows that included traditional music and performances.[22] Thissen has shown that Jewish audiences maintained cultural practices attending Yiddish "vaud-pic" theaters, and Giorgio Bertellini similarly observed the same phenomenon at early Italian cafés-chantants in New York, where Italian plays, operettas, and circus acts were shown with films for predominantly Italian audiences.[23] In a similar vein, Jan Olsson found Mexican, Japanese, and Chinese audience members a significant part of early cinema-going in Los Angeles, relatively well documented because of racist concerns for public safety and heightened policing.[24] Finally, Jacqueline Stewart's studies of Black audiences in Chicago after the Great Migration of African Americans to northern cities describes "laughing at themselves" as a type of racialized modernity apart from the mainstream.[25]

These studies contribute to the history of immigrant groups mainlining cultural practices through specific types of cinema-going, but again this phenomenon has largely only been studied in the silent film era in large

American cities. Even for early cinema in the United States, moviegoing's role in integrating immigrants has not often been studied outside of metropolitan areas. An important research question remains in considering how this process occurred with more recent immigrant populations, migrating to other countries. In the case of postwar Italian immigrants to Toronto, the process of embourgeoisement was complex. Although Italians maintained their culture through Italian film imports, they still became part of the larger North American consumer culture because of the involvement of the mainstream industry. Members of the local community that ran the early ethnic theaters in New York were not part of large commercial enterprises. In contrast, with the case of postwar Italian cinemas in Toronto, the largest theater chain in Canada was involved, and Italian film was profitable to the larger movie theater industry.

The idea of Canada as a multicultural country is a central facet of Canadian identity. As Eva Mackey points out, the mythology surrounding Canada as a tolerant nation has its roots in the idea of multiculturalism, which is a key ideology and official citizenship policy in Canada, largely embraced as a factor to differentiate the country from the supposed American imperative of integration.[26] While the United States often claims to be a melting pot, Canada sees itself as a cultural mosaic. The idea of multiculturalism is of course intrinsically problematic as it others non-English Canadians. The official policy of multiculturalism was started in 1971 under Pierre Trudeau's government. As Dewing writes, multiculturalism policy can be viewed in three distinctive stages: (1) the incipit stage before 1971's official policy; (2) the formative stage from 1971 to 1981, before the encoding of the Charter of Rights and Freedoms; and (3) the institutional stage from 1982 on the basis of enshrined Charter rights.[27] The incipit stage can be traced back to both the influx of postwar immigrants but also the Canadian Citizenship Act of 1947, which deemed Canadians no longer British subjects, allowing for new Canadians to become Canadian citizens rather than subjects of the Queen. It also led to new debates surrounding previously restrictive immigration policies.

The demographics of Toronto demonstrate the burgeoning incipit stage of multiculturalism policy with a large change in the postwar period. The shift in demographics particularly was reflected in the changing Italian population of Toronto. As indicated earlier, Toronto did not have a large multicultural population until the postwar period with the exception of the Jewish community, which since the 1890s made up 5 percent of the city's population. Up until 1950, the Italian population was less than 2 percent of the city when it quickly skyrocketed to over 12 percent of the population in the 1960s. From 1911 to 1981, no other ethnic group had such a large growth rate. In fact, between 1951 and 1981, the Italian population increased tenfold and is estimated that by 1970, one in ten Torontonians were of Italian heritage.[28] Italian immigration to Toronto is distinctive when compared to other groups (see figure 9.1). Although there were other new immigrant groups to have growth in the postwar period like the Portuguese, whose population grew to 3 percent, and Polish, Ukrainian, Hungarian, Dutch, Finnish, and Russian, who all grew to less than 1 percent—Italians had the largest and fastest growth in this period. After the immigration reforms of the 1960s, Chinese and Indian immigrants began to comprise of 2–3 percent in the late 1970s while Arab, Latin American, Filipino, and Korean, all increased in the 1980s, but again there are no drastic increases like in the Italian case.

THE FIRST ITALIAN SHOWMEN IN TORONTO

Although Toronto's Italian population was minimal in the early days of movies, there were still some significant Italian showmen involved in the business. At least five theater owners in Toronto were confirmed as born in Italy, based on cross-referencing census information with a list of all Toronto theater operators in city directories from 1910 to 1920 (see figure 9.2). Census records note how many of these Italian showmen had been involved with the fruit selling business, which was an important industry for many early Italian immigrants in Toronto.[29] One theater owner, Antonio Bartello, came to Canada from Italy when he was fourteen years old with his family in 1892. In the 1900 census, both he and his father were listed as being fruiterers. In 1916, he took over the Willowvale in the Annex neighborhood, and in the

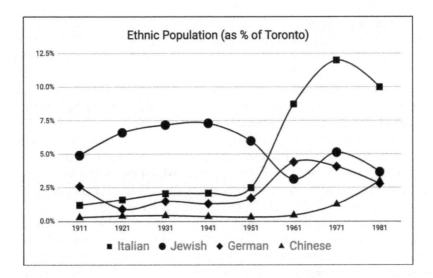

Figure 9.1. Toronto Ethnic Population Growth 1911–1981 based on "mother tongue," "religion," and "racial origins." Graph created by authors.

1920 census was listed as working in motion pictures. His time as a showman seems to have been short-lived and he left the theater business in 1922. He was a prominent member of the Italian community and his daughter married a popular downtown movie palace orchestra leader, Don Romanelli, in 1928; the Italian consul attended the ceremony.

Another fruiter involved in the movie business was Joe Cira who ran the empire on the east side of the city. Like Bartello, Cira's foray into the movie business was relatively short-lived and he ran the empire from 1912 to 1924; however, he continued in the fruit business until his death in 1949. Another fruiter involved in the movie business was Gian Garbarino who built the Odeon first in suburban Parkdale in 1914, later building another at a nearby location in 1932. He then expanded to a 765-seat theater. Garbarino ran the Odeon for twenty-five years until his death in 1939 at the age of sixty-two.[30] His son Joe Garbarino took over the theater after his father's death, along with several other neighborhood theaters, and was elected president of the Motion Picture Theatres Association of Ontario in 1946. Never part of the national chain of the same name, Garbarino's Odeon was later purchased by 20th Century Theatres in 1948 and closed in 1968.

There were two other Italian theater owners in Toronto who were not involved in the fruit business, Louie Mazza and John Taglietti. Louie Mazza operated the Classic on Gerrard Street in the east end from 1916–1921 with Jewish showman Joseph Coen as the manager. John Taglietti ran the Oriental on College Street in the west end from 1911–1919, until he sold the theater to another Jewish showman Jacob Goldstein. The relationship between Italian and Jewish showman would be important in the postwar period and there are indications that these relationships existed in the prewar period with these two examples. These intercultural ties were crucial for many Italian-Canadian theater owners because they connected them with what would become the larger business structures surrounding the film industry in Canada. The relationship between Jewish and Italian showmen would help forge important ties between distributors and theater owners that would later help to build foreign language film distribution in the country.

Outside of Toronto, in the province of Ontario, there are also other examples of the first wave of Italian immigrants involved in the theater business. One of the most prominent was Leo Mascioli, who started a chain of theaters in Northeastern Ontario with his first theater opening in 1912. Mascioli, like some of the Toronto showmen, also had a partnership with Russian Jewish businessman Charles Pierce. Another example from the same region was Anthony Giachino who had a small chain based in Cobalt, Ontario, and he opened his first theater in 1910. Giachino was a community leader as a member of the Cobalt city council and even produced his own films. The Giaschi family also owned and operated several theaters in what is known as cottage country in both the pre- and postwar eras. Joseph Giaschi built the

King George in Huntsville, Ontario in 1926 and would come to operate theatres in the towns of Bracebridge and Port Colborne. His sons and grand-sons took over the business and today his great-granddaughter, Gina Giaschi Mitchell continues to be involved with the Norwood in Bracebridge, Ontario.

These early examples of Italian showman have some similarities with their later counterparts but in other ways were very different. They were different in the sense that they had to appeal to a non-Italian audience to be successful, and there is no evidence that they screened Italian films in their theaters. The main similarity between the pre- and postwar period was the fact that many Italian showmen were community leaders. In the prewar war period, Antonio Bartello in Toronto, John and Tony Saso in Barrie, Joseph Giaschi in Huntsville, Leo Mascioli in Timmins, and Anthony Giachino in Cobalt were all prominent members of their communities. In fact, Leo Mas-cioli was even a padrone and used his role as a labor agent to help build his theater chain. The role of ethnic film exhibitors as community leaders are not unique to Italians, and this leadership role would later be repeated by Italian film exhibitors in the postwar period.[31]

IMPORTING ITALIAN FILMS TO CANADA

Starting in the 1950s, theaters in neighborhoods with significant Italian popu-lations began to exhibit Italian films. In 1951, brothers Lionel and Bob Lester acquired an old cinema which they rebranded as the Studio, an art house theater specializing in foreign films. They completely refurbished and redec-orated the theater, along with adding air-conditioning and new projectors. The Studio was located at College and Manning Streets in the vibrant mix of Little Italy, also not far from the University of Toronto. The *Globe and Mail* reported that they opened the theater with an Italian film, which the news-paper called *This Woman Is Mine*, starring Elli Parvo.[32] When the Studio first opened, it attempted to attract University of Toronto students interested in European art cinema. The school's student newspaper, the *Varsity,* had sev-eral articles on the theater and its films, often reviewed in the "Critic in the Dark" column. By the late 1950s the paper reported that the Studio now only played second- and third-rate Italian films that were no longer subtitled, and rarely still screened films that were of interest to the film society at the university.[33]

Another early theater to switch to Italian films was the Pylon, just a block away from the Studio in Little Italy. Jewish female exhibitor and film trade press editor Ray Lewis originally opened the Pylon in 1939, before the Lester brothers bought it after she died in 1954.[34] The Lester family had a long history with the theater business in Toronto. Like many Jewish showmen in the early 1900s, they were also involved in the garment industry; Sam Lester

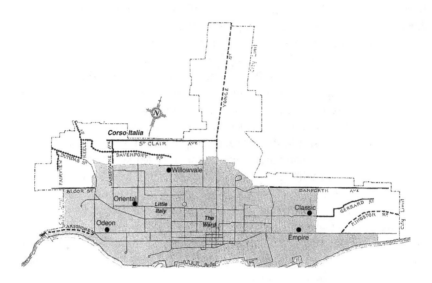

Figure 9.2. Italian-Owned Theaters in Toronto 1910–1920: Their names and available newspaper advertising indicate all appealed to a mainstream audience, and none are located near the Italian-identified area in The Ward and what would later be called Little Italy and Corso Italia.

originally operated a suit business by day and a theater by night.[35] Individually and together, Sam and his brothers would eventually come to own six theaters in Toronto. The second generation of the Lester family included Robert, who ran the Studio and Pylon and opened Italia Films distributors, and Lionel, who was a booking agent and national leader among Canadian independent theater owners. The Lester Brothers were two of many distributors in the 1950s and 1960s to take advantage of Toronto's changing demographics with German, Polish and Hungarian distributors starting businesses in the city. According to Lionel Lester in an interview with the *Toronto Star*, Italian films proved more popular because Italians "ghettoized" and wanted to maintain their culture while other immigrant groups like the Germans quickly integrated and were not as interested in media products from their homeland.[36] When the Lester brothers first started to screen Italian films in their theaters they were reliant on a local distributor called Alliance and would purchase fourteen Italian films a year, but soon they started their own distribution company, Italia Film, and by 1960 they distributed thirty Italian films yearly and obtained fifteen to twenty titles from other sources for their four theaters in Toronto and Hamilton.[37]

In 1954, there were five Italian film theaters regularly advertising in the new Toronto *Corriere Canadese* weekly newspaper. The Lester brothers' theaters—the Studio and Pylon in Little Italy, and the Continental on St.

Clair Avenue in the Corso Italia—as well as the independent Major St. Clair, just west of the Corso Italia, with frequent Italian films also playing at the Savoy downtown. These theaters were generally catering to a popular Italian-Canadian audience; only the Savoy was positioned as an art house for English-speaking crowds interested in European cinema. Indeed, art house cinema had proven to be unprofitable in Toronto. The University of Toronto's *Varsity* newspaper reported this was partly due to the failure of the Towne, which had a colossal flop when they screened *Bicycle Thieves*, and now European films needed to run twice as long as Hollywood films to be considered a success.[38] The newspaper also reported that European art cinema was not often screened because it was expensive and difficult to get from distributors in New York. The *Varsity* pointed out the only European films to be regularly screened in the city were on the Italian circuit, but only occasionally did they try to screen subtitled films that would appeal to an English audience. For example, in January of 1959, the Pylon showed Fellini's *I Vitelloni* with English subtitles, reported with excitement in the *Varsity*. And yet, Lionel Lester was quoted in the *Toronto Star* as saying that 99 percent of their audience was Italian with only 1 percent being from the university crowd.[39]

Italian theaters were not the only places to appeal to the Italian immigrant audience; mainstream theaters also advertised their Hollywood movies in the Italian newspaper. First-run downtown movie palaces such as the Odeon and the Imperial theaters advertised their premiere Hollywood movies, translating local information into Italian while keeping the movie advertising in its original English. Similarly, highbrow plays at the Royal Alexandra, the ballet, and opera all advertised directly to Italian readers. The Italian-language paper also had surprisingly prominent ads, translated into Italian, for the adult entertainment of burlesque at the Casino and the Lux. Although these risqué shows were advertised in the mainstream press, their relative size and prominence in the *Corriere Canadese* is notable. Less surprising, second-run double-bills were advertised by theaters located in Italian neighborhoods that were still playing Hollywood movies. Theaters also advertised Canada-wide promotions in the Italian newspaper. For example, the Paramount, on St. Clair Avenue in the Corso Italia, promoted their weekly contests called Foto-Nite, which was a popular lottery-like promotion held in Famous Players theaters across Canada; the cash prize contest would have had a special appeal even for audiences disinterested in the movies or unable to understand the English soundtracks.

Mainstream advertising in Italian newspapers became commonplace. By the late 1950s, all three of the mainstream chains—Famous Players, 20th Century, and Odeon—advertised in the Italian newspapers with partially-translated copy from their mass circulation displays (see figure 9.3). Similar Hollywood movie advertising appeared in translation in Greek, Ukrainian, and Portuguese newspapers, among others, and continued in the *Corriere Canadese* into the late 1980s. The widespread adoption of translated mainstream movie ads demonstrates the importance of the buying power of Italian and other immigrant communities to the movie business in Toronto. With the introduction of television, theater attendance in Canada was consistently declining; the outreach to new ethnic communities was a way to garner a new consumer base. That these ads were translated into Italian from the start in the mid-1950s also demonstrates a shift to embracing multiculturalism before official multicultural policy even existed.

In the 1960s, the mainstream press published several stories on the expansion of foreign language theaters. In 1966, the *Toronto Star* described the exotic scene of ethnic cinemas for its mainstream readership, focusing on the five Toronto theaters that played exclusively Italian films (as noted in the article, others showed Italian films on Sundays). The newspaper reported that it was an uncanny and strange experience to attend a Toronto Italian theater because there were loud and boisterous, largely male, audiences who yelled and whistled at the actresses on screen. According to the *Toronto Star* there were differences between the Italian theaters, the St. Clair, which was a Famous Players theater, attracted what the newspaper deemed a more refined upscale Northern Italian audience, while the Pylon, Studio, and Paradise attracted a more raucous Southern Italian crowd.[40] According to Lionel Lester in an interview with the *Toronto Star*, there were two types of theaters in the city, those south of Bloor Street, which catered to what he deemed the uneducated Sothern Italian immigrants and those North of Bloor Street, which attracted the more educated Northern Italian audience.

Italian cinemas were the first and the most ubiquitous among the trend of foreign-language theaters exclusively showing imported films for immigrant audiences in the postwar period. Mapping where the Italian cinemas were located, figure 9.4 shows census tract data from 1961 of proportion Italian mother tongue in each area. The Italian population was very concentrated in the city, clustered in a northwest fan from Little Italy out past the Corso Italia; only later did Italian speakers make up a majority of the population of distant suburbs in Downsview and Woodbridge. After the new immigration laws were enacted in the late 1960s, other immigrant populations grew to prominence in the city, including Chinese and Indian communities. While the key, older Italian cinemas in Little Italy and the Corso Italia remained open, their nearby competitors began to offer imported films from outside Europe. A first theater showing Hong Kong cinema opened in 1967 on College Street near Chinatown, while a first Bollywood cinema opened on Gerrard Street in 1973 in Little India. Meanwhile new Italian theaters opened in distant suburbs, east, north, and west as second-generation Italian communities expanded outside the old neighborhoods (see figure 9.5).

Figure 9.3. 1954 translated mainstream ads in the *Corriere Canadese.* Courtesy of *Corriere Canadese.*

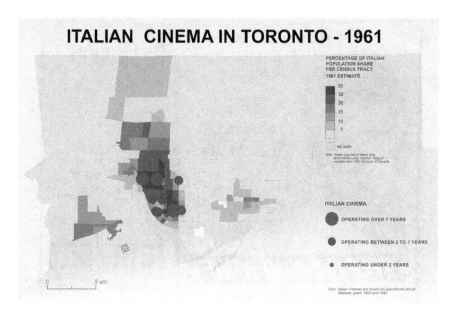

ITALIAN CINEMA IN TORONTO - 1961

Figure 9.4.   A total of sixteen Toronto theaters had featured Italian-language films and advertised in the *Corriere Canadese* by July 1961. The Studio and Pylon in Little Italy, and the Continental and Major St. Clair on the Corso Italia had already been operating as Italian cinemas for more than seven years. Map by Nebojsa Stulic, Ryerson University.

ITALIAN FILM DISTRIBUTION CIRCUITS IN CANADA

Rocco Mastrangelo was first of the second wave Italian immigrants to get involved with importing and screening of Italian films. Mastrangelo arrived in Toronto in 1957 and quickly made his mark on College Street's Little Italy with a variety of commercial ventures. In the 1960s, he purchased the Pylon from the Lester brothers (still open in 2019 as the Royal), operated the Radio City, and started the Radio City Film Exchange. While the Lester Brothers were first distributors to shift focus to imported Italian films, Rocco Mastrangelo was a pioneer for being himself a second-wave Italian immigrant. He also ran the Vogue in suburban Port Credit, and operated a distribution office in Montreal. Until the 1980s, Radio City Film Exchange supplied films to Italian communities in numerous cities across Canada and even in the United States. Mastrangelo's film exchange provided older movie titles to local multicultural television broadcasts and eventually transferred his films to video for home viewing, importing new tapes and discs to rent and sell even after his theaters closed.

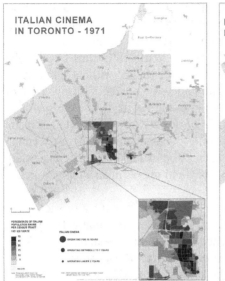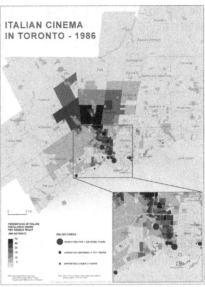

Figure 9.5. In the decade 1961–1971, over a dozen Italian-language cinemas operated and advertised in Toronto, including several in suburban areas. In the fifteen years 1971–1986, a total of sixteen Italian cinemas operated at least brief-ly, many of them in distant shopping plazas as Italian-speakers moved to new suburban homes. Maps by Nebojsa Stulic, Ryerson University.

One of the most important elements of our research into the Toronto Italian theaters is the availability of records from Rocco Mastrangelo who donated his entire film collection of over 1,800 titles to the University of Toronto Media Archives. Using his distribution records to map where many of the films screened, figure 9.6 demonstrates the wide appeal of Italian films in cities and smaller communities across Canada. The map shows two examples of films that were screened at Canadian theaters. *Le Belle Famiglie* was a 1964 Italian comedy, imported by Mastrangelo's distribution company in 1966. After opening first in Hamilton and Windsor, the film played at the St. Clair in Toronto and proved popular in larger cities across Canada, soon sent to Winnipeg and Vancouver, and eventually played also in smaller communities in Northern Ontario, Sault Ste Marie and Timmins. Continuing occasional screenings until 1973, many of the theaters that showed this film were part of the largest mainstream Canadian chain, Famous Players Canadian Corporation.

Another example *L'Amore Breve* was originally released in 1966 and imported to Toronto by Mastrangelo in 1970. The film was one of the many sexually explicit "art house" films from Italy, and starred Joan Collins, in her first nude scene. *L'Amore Breve* played at several Toronto theaters including the Studio, the St. Clair, and the suburban Crown Cinema in Downsview. Mastrangelo sent the film across Canada from Ottawa to Calgary and Vancouver, and it continued to be screened as late as 1985 before it was aired on CITY-TV and transferred to video. According to a Joan Collins fan site, the only available version is the Canadian one in Italian without subtitles, a reference to the copy in the Mastrangelo collection now at the University of Toronto. The most popular Italian films in Canadian theaters were spaghetti westerns and softcore sex films like *L'Amore Breve*. Imported Italian-made adult films and cheap westerns had some mainstream appeal in Canadian theaters. In an interview with the *Toronto Star* in 1976, Lionel Lester said, "Italy is now turning out sex films and spaghetti operas in an attempt to reach the world market."

Italian dubbed versions of Hollywood films were also a major success. A unique aspect of Toronto's Italian film scene was that many Hollywood features dubbed in Italian were screened at the Italian theaters. In 1959, an early dubbed Italian film, *The Bridge on the River Kwai*, premiered at the Pylon and gained attention to the film critic for the *Globe and Mail*, Stan Helleur. He wrote that the premiere of the film "was yet another indication of

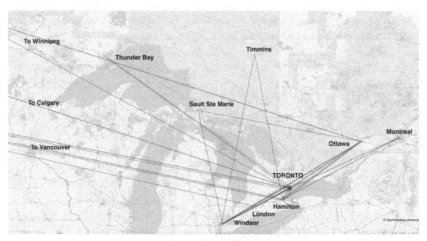

Examples of Italian Films Imported to Canada
Distributed by Rocco Mastrangelo

RED - Le Belle Famiglie (Dec 1966 to April 1978)
BLUE - L'Amore Breve (July 1970 to Sept 1986)

Figure 9.6.   Distribution routes for bookings across Canada of *La Belle Famiglie* (1966–1978) and *L'Amore Breve* (1970–1986) from lease information cards in the Rocco Mastrangelo Collection. Created with the *Atlasciné* cinematic cartography tool from Sébastien Caquard.

the increasingly important market represented by the local Italian colony."[41] There were many other examples of Italian-dubbed Hollywood features over the years, sometimes taking many years to debut. The 1951 MGM epic, *Quo Vadis* premiered in Italian at the St. Clair in January 1967, and advertised as being the first time the dubbed version had been shown in North America (see figure 9.7).

Although Hollywood films dubbed into Italian were common in Toronto, none drew quite as much attention and publicity as the "Prima Nordamericana di *The Godfather* in Italiano," or *Il Padrino*, as it was advertised to the Toronto Italian community (see figure 9.8). Toronto was an obvious choice for the North American premiere of the Italian-dubbed version because of its large Italian-speaking population and long-established Italian language theaters. The film premiered at the St. Clair in October 1972, just seven months after the original opened at the Imperial downtown. The St. Clair was an old 1920s movie palace, still owned and operated by the largest theater chain in Canada, Famous Players Canadian, in turn controlled by Hollywood's Paramount Pictures. Not coincidentally, Paramount was the distributor of the film. The *Corriere Canadese* reported that *Il Padrino* was a great success with eight thousand people in the city going to see the film in its first days (see figure 9.9). Many in the community were noted to have waited anxiously to see the movie until it was dubbed into Italian. According to the paper, the film did not disappoint and the newspaper interviewed some of the moviegoers who commented on the wonderful acting, especially of Marlon Brando, while others mentioned how the film was realistic.

The mainstream press also covered the phenomenon of the Italian-dubbed *Godfather* premiering in the city. The *Toronto Star* reported that over one thousand people attended the first screening of the film with the theater celebrating the event by providing floral bouquets while the manager dressed in a tuxedo. In its coverage, the paper focused on how dubbing the film in Italian made the film more raw and bawdy in its dialogue, and quoted theater-goers as saying that they attended the screening to hear the Sicilian slang. The St. Clair location was profitable enough for Famous Players that in 1974 the chain chose to completely renovate and divide the theater into a dual screen multiplex, making "*il primo 'twin cinema' italiano al mondo*." An early film at the St. Clair twin was the latest Oscar-winner for Best Picture, Paul Newman and Robert Redford in "*La Stangata: Il film piu atteso dell'anno*." Of course, *Il Padrino, Parte II* also played at the St. Clair 2 in its Italian dubbed version soon after it won the following year's Oscar.[42]

In the 1970s and 1980s, advertising in the *Corriere Canadese* for Toronto's Italian cinemas became more elaborate and highlighted the central importance of the theaters to the community. In these years, the list of Famous Players' Italian chain included the St. Clair and Studio, but also the Palace on the Danforth and the Playhouse in Hamilton, all together with other indepen-

PER LA PRIMA VOLTA IN AMERICA
PARLATO IN ITALIANO

"QUO VADIS"

A COLORI

CONTINUA CON SUCCESSO
PER LA

SECONDA SETTIMANA

*L'INSUPERATO COLOSSO DELLA
CINEMATOGRAFIA MONDIALE!*

ST. CLAIR

ST CLAIR angolo DUFFERIN   Telefono LE 3-3851

Figure 9.7.   The Ten Commandments "Parlato in Italiano" at the Pylon, *Corriere Canadese*. January 20, 1959. Courtesy of *Corriere Canadese*.

dent theaters labeled as "a strip of Italian culture in Canada." All provided regular Italian imported films, including those distributed by Mastrangelo, and dubbed Hollywood features, especially Paramount films that could sup-

Figure 9.8.   Ad for *Il Padrino* in the *Corriere Canadese*. October 23, 1972. Courtesy of *Corriere Canadese*.

port the Paramount-owned chain locations. The Italian dubbed version of Paramount's *Serpico* (1973), starring Al Pacino, was advertised as having simultaneous world premieres in Toronto and Milan. Another Paramount Christmas blockbuster, *King Kong* (1976), debuted in Toronto in "an international first," playing in three language versions simultaneously, all under one roof at the grand opening of a new suburban Famous Players multiplex: the original English played there, downtown and elsewhere, while audiences at this special location could also choose to see the film in French or Italian dubbed versions.[43] Other theaters went beyond films and regularly presented live acts from Italy and even screened live broadcasts of important soccer matches. For the 1976 World Cup, Rocco Mastrangelo arranged a live feed at the Radio City and St. Clair theaters. The *Toronto Star* reported that over two thousand members of the Italian community packed the theaters to watch Italy's victory in the qualifying match. The newspaper quoted Rocco Mastrangelo as saying "it was like everyone was in Rome watching the game

Battuto ogni record di pubblico durante il fine settimana

Grande successo al St. Clair di "Godfather" in italiano

Marion Brando protagonista del film "Il Padrino"

TORONTO - Serata di gala con pubblico delle grandi occasioni venerdi' sera al cinema St.Clair. Oltre mille persone sono intervenute alla prima nordamericana del film "The Godfather" in italiano.

"Il padrino", questo il titolo col quale il film e' presentato in lingua italiana, atteso con viva curiosita' da tutti, se non altro per i fiumi di parole dette e scritte su di esso da quando la produzione della Paramount e' stata presentata sugli schermi di tutto il mondo, non ha deluso le aspettative.

Tratto dall'omonimo libro di Mario Puzo, il film mette a nudo il mondo violento, brutale ed a volte patetico della criminalita' organizzata.

Diretto con mano sicura ed abile da Francis Ford Cop-pola "Il padrino" e' una pellicola di indubbio valore artistico e spettacolare. Ha un ritmo a volte travolgente a volte, volutamente lento, quasi sornione, poiche' il colpo di scena, e' sempre dietro la porta pronto a colpire gli spettatori con allucinante velocita' e brutalita'.

Marlon Brando e' veramente "il padrino"; la sua e' una interpretazione superba ed anche volendo porre obbiezioni sul valore morale o culturale del film, l'interpretazione di Brando vale da sola ad elevare il film a livelli artistici quanto meno notevoli. Brando ha posto una seria ipoteca sull'Oscar, quale migliore attore dell'anno, che verra' assegnato la prossima primavera.

Accanto a Brando, una folta schiera di famosi attori: Al Pacino Richard Conte, Richard Castellano, Robert Duvall e Diane Keaton, per nominarne soltanto alcuni.

Anche per loro, un'interpretazione perfetta. Ed e' questa forse una delle virtu' della pellicola : la finzione invade la realta', sia nei personaggi che nella trama. E non e' vero che "Il padrino" regala un volto di rispettabilita' al crimine organizzato, ne' tanto meno ne e' l'apologesi.

Tutta la malavita, le cosche, le "famiglie", sono presentate nel loro vero volto fatto di brutalita', di odii, di vendette e di omicidi.

"Il padrino" ha degli indubbi meriti artistici, oltre che trasmettere un messaggio eloquente sul pericolo che la criminalita' organizzata rappresenta per la nostra societa'.

La "prima" di venerdi' sera, ha lasciato il pubblico, vivamente soddisfatto e si prevede che il film si fermera' al cinema St.Clair per almeno un mese: "la pellicola - ci ha detto il manager del St.Clair, Pino Traversa- sara' in programmazione per un minimo di due settimane con la possibilita' di arrivare a sei". Il film comunque sta riscuotendo tale successo di pubblico e d'incasso che molto probabilmente "Il padrino" sara' al St.Clair per molte e molte settimane. Durante il fine settimana, da venerdi' a domenica, incluso lo spettacolo di sabato a mezzanotte, il film ha polverizzato ogni record esistente, sia d'incasso che di pubblico, in ciascuno dei tre giorni.

All'uscita del locale abbiamo intervistato alcune persone Nazzereno Colella ci ha detto:"Mi son piaciute soprattutto le interpretazioni degli attori. Brando e' stato bravissimo". Crescenzo Botticella ha affermato che il film "e' realistico";Filippo Lavecchia ha aggiunto "noi siamo italiani e certe usanze le conosciamo abbastanza bene." Abbiamo cercato di conoscere l'opinione di qualche signora" Io, io non so nulla" ci ha risposto frettolosamente.

Renato Ciolfi

Auguri a...

Lunedi' 23 ottobre

Domizio

Martedi' 24 ottobre

Raffaele

Mercoledi' 25 ottobre

Crispino

Giovedi' 26 ottobre

Folco

Venerdi' 27 ottobre

Fiorenzo

Sabato 28 ottobre

Simone

Domenica 29 ottobre

Massimiliano

Il vostro nome

SIMONE

deriva dall'ebraico *shime'on* che, collegandosi probabilmente alla radice *shm*, esaudire, significa « esaudimento ». Sarebbe quindi uno dei nomi che esprimono il ringraziamento dei genitori per l'esaudimento della preghiera fatta a Dio per avere un figlio.

SIATE GENEROSI con l'UNITED APPEAL E' UNA NOBILE CAUSA

La fila degli spettatori davanti al cinema St.Clair in attesa del loro turno per acquistare il biglietto.   (Astra Photo Studio)

Figure 9.9. *Corriere Canadese,* October 23, 1972, on the great success of *The Godfather* in Italian. Courtesy of *Corriere Canadese.*

live."[44] The longevity and popularity of Italian language theaters in Toronto demonstrate the consumer power of postwar Italian immigrants as well as their insistence on maintaining cultural ties through viewing Italian language films, cultural events, and Italian dubbed Hollywood features.

CONCLUSION: IMMIGRANT MIDDLE-CLASS CONSUMERS

By recovering the hidden relevance of immigrant entrepreneurs, we are able to connect early immigrant showmen to the late-20th century emergence of immigrant audiences and foreign-language film importing, in response to new waves of post–WWII immigration, which was largely focused in the Italian community. The early Italian film exhibitors in Canada may not have shown Italian films, but most had deep community ties and acted as leaders of the diasporic community. The pattern of community leaders becoming involved in the film business continued in the postwar period with men such as Rocco Mastrangelo making their mark on film exhibition in Canada. Mastrangelo was not only an important film exhibitor and distributor; he helped to shape Toronto's Little Italy and was involved in many businesses including restaurants and retail stores. Cinemas are cultural, community spaces, both public and personal, in ways that other diasporic and Italian-language media were not. Recorded music, books and magazines, television and radio, and the *Corriere Canadese* itself, all of these mediated the home and the homeland. As a gathering space, a cinema mediated the Italian-speaking community to the city and each other. Not only did people watch film at these theaters, they were regular meeting areas for community events such as world cup and live music presentations. The theaters also held political events and during the 1970s Italian construction workers had union meetings at the Lester-owned Lansdowne during labor strikes.

Another key aspect of this research is how the mainstream movie industry in Canada turned to diasporic audiences and imported films to support its sagging profits in the 1950s and 1960s. Thus, the case of imported Italian film is an example of an interaction between a subculture and the mainstream that was somewhat reciprocal because of the assurgency of immigrant populations happening concurrently with the decline of cinema-going as a mainstream pastime. Italian immigrants in the postwar period were treated as middle-class consumers with mainstream business directly appealing to the community through translated advertising. Starting as early as the 1950s, mainstream theaters translated their ads into Italian in Toronto's *Corriere Canadese*. The process of cultural integration of Italian postwar immigrants was complicated and allowed the community to maintain cultural ties while also becoming part of mainstream consumer culture. Even Hollywood films were dubbed into Italian to attract the Italian audience. In fact, Italian films became so popular that they were screened without subtitles by national chains. As cinema-going declined after the introduction of television, Canadian chains such as Famous Players and Odeon turned to diasporic audiences and Toronto's Italian language film exhibition and distribution would become a model for other diasporic groups.

NOTES

1. Robert F. Harney, *Italians in Canada*. Toronto, ON: Multicultural History Society of Ontario, 1978.

2. Population counts throughout the essay, charted in figure 9.1 and mapped in figures 9.4 and 9.5 are taken from Toronto and area census reports, 1911 to 1986. Ottawa: Statistics Canada. Note that the overall urban area expands to the new boundary of Metropolitan Toronto in 1951, and then further expands in 1981 to the Toronto Census Metropolitan Area. The best measure of ethnicity varies from one census to another, and from one group to another, encompassing such historical categories as "religious and racial origin," "ethnic origin," "mother tongue," "place of birth," and "home language."

3. Jessica Leonora Whitehead, "Cinema-Going on the Margins: Film Exhibition in a Company Town in Canada," in *Rural Cinema-going from a Global Perspective*, Daniela Treveri Gennari, Danielle Hipkins, and Catherine O'Rawe, eds., pp. 47–70. London: Palgrave, 2018. For an in-depth review of ethnic business relation to newspapers, see Mark Hayward, *Identity and Industry: Making Media Multicultural in Canada* (Montreal: McGill-Queen's University Press, 2019).

4. John T. Caldwell, "Para-industry: Researching Hollywood's Blackwaters." *Cinema Journal* 52, no. 3 (2013), pp. 159.

5. Ivan Light, Parminder Bhachu, and Stavros Karageorgis, "Migration networks and immigrant entrepreneurship," in *Immigration and Entrepreneurship: Culture, Capital, and Ethnic Networks,* Ivan Light and Parminder Bhachu (eds.), pp. 25–50. Abingdon, Oxon: Routledge, 2017.

6. Mark I. Choate, *Emigrant Nation: The Making of Italy Abroad* Cambridge, MA: Harvard University Press, 2008.

7. John V. Baiamonte, "Community Life in the Italian Colonies of Tangipahoa Parish, Louisiana, 1890–1950." *Louisiana History: The Journal of the Louisiana Historical Association* 30, no. 4 (1989), pp. 365–397; Jordan Stanger-Ross, *Staying Italian: Urban Change and Ethnic Life in Postwar Toronto and Philadelphia*. Chicago, IL: University of Chicago Press, 2010.

8. Robert F. Harney, *Italians in Canada*. Toronto: Multicultural History Society of Ontario, 1978.

9. Robert F. Harney, "Men Without Women: Italian Migrants in Canada, 1885–1930." *Canadian Ethnic Studies* 11, no. 1 (1979), pp. 29–47.

10. Franca Iacovetta, "Ordering in Bulk: Canada's Postwar Immigration Policy and the Recruitment of Contract Workers from Italy." *Journal of American Ethnic History* 11, no. 1 (1991), pp. 50–80; Harold Troper, "Canada's Immigration Policy since 1945." *International Journal* 48, no. 2 (1993), pp. 255–281.

11. Ceri Peach, "The Mosaic Versus the Melting Pot: Canada and the USA." *Scottish Geographical Journal* 121, no. 1 (2005), pp. 3–27.

12. Michael Buzzelli, "From Little Britain to Little Italy: an Urban Ethnic Landscape Study in Toronto." *Journal of Historical Geography* 27, no. 4 (2001), pp. 573–587.

13. John E. Zucchi, *Italians in Toronto: Development of a National Identity, 1875–1935*. Montreal, QU: McGill-Queen's University Press, 1988, pp. 65–68; John Lorinc, "Toronto's First Little Italy," in *The Ward: The Life and Loss of Toronto's First Immigrant Neighbourhood*, John Lorinc, Michael McClelland, Ellen Scheinberg, and Tatum Taylor, eds. pp. 181–183. Toronto: Coach House Press, 2015.

14. John E. Zucchi, *A History of Ethnic Enclaves in Canada 9 no. 3*. Ottawa, ON: Canadian Historical Association, 2007, pp. 9.

15. See: Jessica L. Whitehead, "The Italian-Canadian Internment: The Case of the Mascioli Brothers of Timmins, Ontario." *Italian Canadiana* 32 (2018), pp. 101–119.

16. Michael Di Giacomo, "Identity and Change: The Story of the Italian-Canadian Pentecostal Community." *Canadian Journal of Pentecostal-Charismatic Christianity* 2, no. 1 (2011), pp. 83–130.

17. Roy Rosenzweig, *Eight Hours for What We Will: Workers and Leisure in an Industrial City, 1870–1920*. Cambridge University Press, 1985.

18. Lizabeth Cohen, "Encountering Mass Culture at the Grassroots: The Experience of Chicago Workers in the 1920s." *American Quarterly* 41, no. 1 (1989), pp. 6–33.

19. Richard Sklar, *Movie-Made America: A Cultural History of American Movies.* New York, NY: Vintage, 1994; David Nasaw, *Going Out: The Rise and Fall of Public Amusements.* Cambridge, MA: Harvard University Press, 1993.

20. Gregory A. Waller, "Another Audience: Black Moviegoing, 1907–1916." *Cinema Journal* 31, no. 2 (1992), pp. 3–25; Giorgio Bertellini, "Shipwrecked Spectators: Italy's Immigrants at the Movies in New York, 1906–1916." *Velvet Light Trap* 44 (1999), pp. 39–53; Judith Thissen, "Charlie Steiner's Houston Hippodrome: Moviegoing on New York's Lower East Side, 1909–1913," in *American Silent Film: Discovering Marginalized Voices*, edited by Gregg Bachman and Thomas J. Slater. pp. 27–47. Carbondale, IL: Southern Illinois University Press, 2002.

21. Ben Singer, "Manhattan Nickelodeons: New Data on Audiences and Exhibitors." *Cinema Journal* 34, no. 3 (1995), pp. 5–35; Robert C. Allen, "Manhattan Myopia; or h! Iowa!" *Cinema Journal* 35, no. 3 (1996), pp. 75–103; Ben Singer, "New York, Just Like I Pictured It. . . ." *Cinema Journal* 35, no. 3 (1996), pp. 104–128; William Uricchio and Roberta E. Pearson, "Dialogue: Manhattan's Nickelodeons, New York? New York!" *Cinema Journal* 36, no. 4 (1997), pp. 98–102; Judith Thissen, "Oy, Myopia!" *Cinema Journal* 36, no. 4 (1997), pp. 102–107.

22. Judith Thissen, "Early Cinema and the Public Sphere of the Neighborhood Meeting Hall: The Longue Durée of Working-Class Sociability," in *Beyond the Screen: Institutions, Networks and Publics of Early Cinema*, Marta Braun, Charlie Keil, Rob King, Paul Moore, and Louis Pelletier, eds. pp. 297–307. London, UK: John Libbey, 2012.

23. Giorgio Bertellini, *Italy in Early American Cinema: Race, Landscape, and the Picturesque.* Bloomington: Indiana University Press, 2010, pp. 89 and 261.

24. Jan Olsson, *Los Angeles Before Hollywood: Journalism and American Film Culture, 1905 to 1915.* Stockholm: National Library of Sweden, 2008.

25. Jacqueline Stewart, "Negroes Laughing at Themselves? Black Spectatorship and the Performance of Urban Modernity." *Critical Inquiry* 29, no. 4 (2003), pp. 650–677.

26. Eva Mackey, *House of Difference: Cultural Politics and National Identity in Canada.* Toronto: University of Toronto Press, 2005.

27. Michael Dewing, *Canadian Multiculturalism.* Ottawa: Library of Parliament, Parliamentary Research Branch, 2013.

28. Michael Buzzelli, "From Little Britain to Little Italy: An Urban Ethnic Landscape Study in Toronto." *Journal of Historical Geography* 27, no. 4 (2001), pp. 576.

29. John E. Zucchi, *A History of Ethnic Enclaves in Canada.* Vol. 9. Canadian Historical Association, 2007.

30. Information about early Italian showman derives from annual Toronto City Directories, Building Permits, Municipal Tax Rolls between 1906 and 1921, and Census Registers in 1911 and 1921, in addition to press reports from the *Toronto Star* and film trade papers contained in the Media History Digital Library.

31. Ross Melnick, *American Showman: Samuel" Roxy" Rothafel and the Birth of the Entertainment Industry, 1908–1935.* New York: Columbia University Press, 2012.

32. Herbert Whittaker, "Show Business," *Toronto Star*, 1951, October 5, pp. 8. Both the *Toronto Star* and the *Globe and Mail* identified the opening film as *This Woman Is Mine.* Neither paper reported on the director of the film or release date but the *Toronto Star* reported that the film featured "a new Italian Glamour Girl Elli Parvo" and that the film had English subtitles. It appears this film was *Desiderio* released in 1946 and directed by Roberto Rossellini. In the United States, we found several advertisements from 1950 for a film called "Woman," which the papers reported starred Elli Parvo and Massimo Girotti and was directed by Roberto Rossellini. Elli Parvo and Massimo Girotti were the stars of *Desiderio*, so it is likely that this was the film that played at the opening of the Studio.

33. Warren Wilson, "Worth Watching," *Varsity*, 1958, March 4, pp. 5; Guy Green, *Varsity*, "Toronto Closed City," 1957, March 14, pp. 5.

34. Jessica L. Whitehead, Louis Pelletier, and Paul S. Moore. "The Girl Friend in Canada: Ray Lewis and Canadian Moving Picture Digest (1915–1957)," in Daniël Biltereyst and Lies Van de Vijver, eds., *Mapping Movie Magazines*. London: Palgrave Macmillan, forthcoming.

35. Hye Bossin, *Stars of David: Jewish Showmen in Canada's Film Industry*. Toronto: Canadian Jewish Congress, 1956.

36. "Newcomers invest in foreign films," *Toronto Star*, 1959, July 4, pp. 3.

37. Frank Morriss, "Film fans are jilting Hollywood to play the foreign field," *Globe and Mail*, 1960, June 4, pp. A10.

38. Guy Green, "Toronto Closed City," *Varsity*, 1957, March 14, pp. 5.

39. "Newcomers invest in foreign films," *Toronto Star*, 1959, July 4, pp. 3.

40. As Thomas Guglielmo points out in his chapter "Rethinking Whiteness historiography: The Case of Italians in Chicago, 1890–1945," the idea that Northern Italians are superior can largely be traced to Italian Sociologist and Statistician Alfredo Niceforo who argued in his work that Northern Italians were racially distinct from Southern Italians and were thus superior. There is a long tradition in both North America and Italy of proliferating this this racist notion and it was often repeated in the Toronto press in the wake of new Italian immigration in the postwar period.

41. Stan Helleur, "It's Entertainment," *Globe and Mail*, 1959, March 25, pp. 31.

42. Cinema St. Clair 2, *Corriere Canadese*, 1974, August 10, pp. 10; *Il Padrino, Parte II* in Italiano, *Corriere Canadese*, 1975, October 4, pp. 5.

43. Serpico, *Corriere Canadese*, 1974, April 27, pp. 9; King Kong, *Globe and Mail*, 1976, December 16, pp. 16.

44. Bob Graham, "Metro Italians Cheer Soccer Win," *Toronto Star*, 1976, November 17, pp. C2.

BIBLIOGRAPHY

Allen, Robert C. "Manhattan Myopia; or h! Iowa!" *Cinema Journal* 35, no. 3 (1996), pp. 75–103.

Baiamonte, John V. "Community Life in the Italian Colonies of Tangipahoa Parish, Louisiana, 1890–1950." *Louisiana History: The Journal of the Louisiana Historical Association* 30, no. 4 (1989), pp. 365–397.

Bertellini, Giorgio. "Duce/Divo: Masculinity, Racial Identity, and Politics among Italian Americans in 1920s New York City." *Journal of Urban History* 31, no. 5 (2005), pp. 685–726.

———. "Film, National Cinema, and Migration." In *Encyclopedia of Global Human Migration*, edited by Immanuel Ness and Marlou Schrover, pp. 1504–1509. Hoboken, NJ: Wiley-Blackwell, 2013.

———. "Historical Feature Films, and the Fabrication of Italy's. Spectators in Early 1900s New York." *Comunicazioni Sociali* 23, no. 2 (2001), pp. 152–168.

———. "Shipwrecked Spectators: Italy's Immigrants at the Movies in New York, 1906–1916." *Velvet Light Trap* 44 (1999), pp. 39–53.

———. *Italy in Early American Cinema: Race, Landscape, and the Picturesque*. Bloomington, IN: Indiana University Press, 2010.

———. "Manipulation and Authenticity: The Unassimilable Valentino in 1920s Argentina." In *Cosmopolitan Images: The Transnational Horizons of Latin American Film Culture, 1896–1960*, edited by Rielle Navitski and Nicholas Poppe, pp. 73–96. Bloomington, IN: Indiana University Press, 2016.

———. "Sovereign Consumption: Italian Americans' Film Culture in 1920s New York City." In *Making Italian America: Consumer Culture and the Production of Ethnic Identities*, edited by Simone Cinotto, pp. 83–99; 270–273. New York, NY: Fordham University Press, 2014.

Bossin, Hye. *Stars of David: Jewish Showmen in Canada's Film Industry*. Toronto, ON: Canadian Jewish Congress, 1956.

Buzzelli, Michael. "From Little Britain to Little Italy: An Urban Ethnic Landscape Study in Toronto." *Journal of Historical Geography* 27, no. 4 (2001), pp. 573–587.

Choate, Mark I. *Emigrant Nation: The Making of Italy Abroad* Harvard, MA: Harvard University Press, 2008.

Cohen, Lizabeth. "Encountering Mass Culture at the Grassroots: The Experience of Chicago Workers in the 1920s." *American Quarterly* 41, no. 1 (1989), pp. 6–33.

Caldwell, John T. "Para-industry: Researching Hollywood's Blackwaters." *Cinema Journal* 52, no. 3 (2013), pp. 157–165.

Dewing, Michael. *Canadian Multiculturalism*. Ottawa: Library of Parliament, Parliamentary Research Branch, 2013.

Di Giacomo, Michael. "Identity and Change: The Story of the Italian-Canadian Pentecostal Community." *Canadian Journal of Pentecostal-Charismatic Christianity* 2, no. 1 (2011), pp. 83–130.

Guglielmo, Thomas A. "Rethinking Whiteness Historiography: The Case of Italians in Chicago, 1890–1945." In *White Out: The Continuing Significance of Racism*, edited by Ashley W. Doane and Eduardo Bonilla-Silva, pp. 56–68. New York, NY: Routledge, 2013.

Harney, Robert F. *Italians in Canada*. Toronto ON: Multicultural History Society of Ontario, 1978.

———. "Caboto and Other Parentela: The Uses of the Italian-Canadian Past." In *Arrangiarsi. The Italian Experience in Canada, Montreal, Guernica*, edited by Roberto Perin and Franc Sturino, pp. 37–61. Montreal, QU: Guernica Editions, 1989.

———. "Men Without Women: Italian Migrants in Canada, 1885–1930." *Canadian Ethnic Studies* 11, no. 1 (1979), pp. 29–47.

———."Montreal's King of Italian Labour: A Case study of Padronism." *Labour* 4 (1979), pp. 57–84.

Iacovetta, Franca. "Ordering in Bulk: Canada's Postwar Immigration Policy and the Recruitment of Contract Workers from Italy." *Journal of American Ethnic History* 11, no. 1 (1991), pp. 50–80.

Iacovetta, Franca, Roberto Perin, and Angelo Principe. *Enemies Within: Italian and Other Internees in Canada and Abroad*. Toronto, ON University of Toronto Press, 2000.

Light, Ivan, Parminder Bhachu, and Stavros Karageorgis. "Migration networks and Immigrant Entrepreneurship." In *Immigration and Entrepreneurship: Culture, Capital, and Ethnic Networks*, edited by Ivan Light and Parminder Bhachu, pp. 25–50. Abingdon, Oxon: Routledge, 2017.

Lorinc, John. "Toronto's First Little Italy." In *The Ward: The Life and Loss of Toronto's First Immigrant Neighbourhood*, edited by John Lorinc, Michael McClelland, Ellen Scheinberg, and Tatum Taylor, pp. 181–183. Toronto: Coach House Press, 2015.

Mackey, Eva. *House of Difference: Cultural Politics and National Identity in Canada*. Toronto: University of Press, 2005.

Melnick, Ross. *American Showman: Samuel" Roxy" Rothafel and the Birth of the Entertainment Industry, 1908-1935*. New York: Columbia University Press, 2012.

Moore, Paul S. *Now Playing: Early Moviegoing and the Regulation of Fun*. SUNY Press, 2008.

Nasaw, David. *Going Out: The Rise and Fall of Public Amusements*. Cambridge, MA: Harvard University Press, 1993.

Olsson, Jan. *Los Angeles Before Hollywood: Journalism and American Film Culture, 1905 to 1915*. Stockholm: National Library of Sweden, 2008.

Peach, Ceri. "The Mosaic Versus the Melting Pot: Canada and the USA." *Scottish Geographical Journal* 121, no. 1 (2005), pp. 3–27.

Rosenzweig, Roy. *Eight Hours for What We Will: Workers and Leisure in an Industrial City, 1870–1920*. Cambridge University Press, 1985.

Singer, Ben. "Manhattan Nickelodeons: New Data on Audiences and Exhibitors." *Cinema Journal* 34, no. 3 (1995), pp. 5–35.

———. "New York, Just Like I Pictured It . . ." *Cinema Journal* 35, no. 3 (1996), pp. 104–128.

Sklar, Richard. *Movie-Made America: A Cultural History of American Movies*. New York, NY: Vintage, 1994.

Stanger-Ross, Jordan. *Staying Italian: Urban Change and Ethnic Life in Postwar Toronto and Philadelphia.* Chicago, IL: University of Chicago Press, 2010.

Stewart, Jacqueline. "Negroes Laughing at Themselves? Black Spectatorship and the Performance of Urban Modernity." *Critical Inquiry* 29, no. 4 (2003), pp. 650–677.

Thissen, Judith. "Jewish Immigrant Audiences in New York City, 1905–1914." In *American Movie Audiences: From the Turn of the Century to the Early Sound Era*, edited by Melvyn Stokes and Richard Maltby, pp. 15–28. London, UK: BFI, 1999.

———. "Oy, Myopia!" *Cinema Journal* 36, no. 4 (1997), pp. 102–107.

———. "Charlie Steiner's Houston Hippodrome: Moviegoing on New York's Lower East Side, 1909–1913," in *American Silent Film: Discovering Marginalized Voices*, edited by Gregg Bachman and Thomas J. Slater, pp. 27–47. Carbondale, IL: Southern Illinois University Press, 2002.

———. "Beyond the Nickelodeon: Cinemagoing, Everyday Life and Identity Politics." In *Audiences. Defining and Researching Screen Entertainment Reception*, edited by Gregory Waller and Ian Christie, pp. 45–65. Amsterdam: Amsterdam University Press, 2012.

———. "Early Cinema and the Public Sphere of the Neighborhood Meeting Hall: The Longue Durée of Working-Class Sociability." In *Beyond the Screen: Institutions, Networks and Publics of Early Cinema*, edited by Marta Braun, Charles Keil, Rob King, Paul Moore, and Louis Pelletier, pp. 297–307. London, UK: John Libbey, 2012.

Troper, Harold. "Canada's Immigration Policy since 1945." *International Journal* 48, no. 2, 1993, pp. 255–281.

Uricchio, William and Roberta E. Pearson, "Dialogue: Manhattan's Nickelodeons, New York? New York!" *Cinema Journal* 36, no. 4 (1997), pp. 98–102.

Waller, Gregory A. "Another Audience: Black Moviegoing, 1907–1916." *Cinema Journal* 31, no. 2 (1992), pp. 3–25.

Whitehead, Jessica Leonora. "Cinema-Going on the Margins: Film Exhibition in a Company Town in Canada," in *Rural Cinema-going from a Global Perspective*, edited by Daniela Treveri Gennari, Danielle Hipkins, and Catherine O'Rawe, pp. 47–70. London: Palgrave, 2018.

———. "The Italian-Canadian Internment: The Case of the Mascioli Brothers of Timmins, Ontario." *Italian Canadiana* 32 (2018), pp. 101–119.

Whitehead, Jessica Leonora, Louis Pelletier, and Paul S. Moore. "The Girl Friend in Canada: Ray Lewis and Canadian Moving Picture Digest (1915–1957)," in *Mapping Movie Magazines*, edited by Daniel Biltereyst and Lies Van de Vijver. London: Palgrave Macmillan, 2019.

Zucchi, John E. *Italians in Toronto: Development of a National Identity, 1875–1935.* Montreal: McGill-Queen's University Press, 1988.

———. *A History of Ethnic Enclaves in Canada.* 9, no. 31. Ottawa, ON: Canadian Historical Association, 2007.

Chapter Ten

Conversing about National Attributes Online

The Case of Italy and the United States

Giacomo Sproccati

Politics and war have traditionally been the primary two push factors that stimulated communication across national boundaries. However, "with the innovation of new information and communication technologies"[1] the free market entered the scene transforming it into a global communication infrastructure granting the possibility to communicate across boundaries not only for "government-to-government,"[2] but also for single individuals. Technological development shifted toward the creation of new media, which "are the result of technologies combining computers, laser discs, and telecommunications"[3] that allow users to interact in a "digitally linked globe"[4] because they "are fast, accurate, information rich, and responsive."[5] Thus, today communication takes place through new media several times within the same day, and online tools are used for many types of communication (i.e., personal and business related). Thereby the exchange of information beyond national boundaries becomes easy, instantaneous, and cheap.

Thanks to these new types of media, celebrities, news outlets, and a great amount of "common" users can express ideas, opinions, and questions in a creative way due to the availability of hyper-textual and multimodal content. As a result, the effects on intercultural dynamics so far have been disparate. Because new media are capable of bringing people together, these new platforms of communication contribute to the fast development of cultural traditions and national identities, which, as an example of collective identities, they "are constantly in the process of negotiation, affirmation or change."[6]

Before the advent of new media, scholars analyzed national identity through different perspectives such as imagined communities and banal nationalism. Among others, Anderson (1983) identified the factors which favored the birth of imagined communities. The philosopher and anthropologist Gellner "considered nationalism to be a function of modernity"[7] because in industrial societies "the work to be done is mostly semantic which in turn requires the development of standardized means of communication, that is, development of a uniform language."[8] Thus, Gellner highlighted the importance of the national language to create and maintain the feeling of belonging to a specific national group. The artifacts analyzed in this paper further corroborate such statements as Americans and Italians address each other in their native language to preserve the membership to their own national group.

Moreover, Billig (1995) coined the concept of banal nationalism and felt the need to analyze "what happened once the nation was established"[9] as opposed to "the emergence of the nation."[10] As a result, he "focused on the reproduction of nationalism in the established nations of the Western World."[11] For Billig, nationalism is banal as it happens in the daily routine. For instance, "the unwaved flag hanging limply on the public building we pass every day on our way to work; or the numerous forms of deixis ('we,' 'our,' 'here,' 'the') which populate daily conversations and the news we read, watch or listen to."[12] Once countries are created, they constantly change. Therefore, the aforementioned theories can be applied also to the more recent technological era as it is the case for this paper's artifacts.

Building on banal nationalism, for instance, Szulc (2017) studied "the role of the internet for the reproductions of nations and nationalisms."[13] She concluded that the internet gives minority groups the opportunity "to articulate and legitimize their distinct national identities or their denied belongings to a particular nation."[14] Szulc also argued that "online audiences often become not only receivers but also producers of content."[15] Indeed, her case study deepens the question of who produces the content as the clips she analyzes indicate that having the digital equipment allows one (the producer) to create content, which becomes part of the process that defines national identity, making the government only one of many actors in the process. Therefore, the internet created an additional channel to express national identity, and on this media stage, content competes for attention. The success depends on the producers' capability to make their artifact viral. The presence of large quantities of content keeps the negotiating process of national identity constantly active. Among these actors we find Buzzfeed, the newspapare, and *La Stampa*.

In 2006, Jonah Peretti founded BuzzFeed, a New York based online "cross-platform, a global network for news and entertainment." BuzzFeed produces videos, articles, and surveys to engage its followers on issues of national belonging. The questions BuzzFeed generally ask aim at clarifying the reasons behind a specific trait of the other country's national character. In 2015, BuzzFeed published an article entitled "24 Questions Americans Have for the British."[16] Later that same year, BuzzFeed also recorded a video entitled "Questions Americans Have for Italians," and this is one of the three videos this paper investigates as an example of the discussion of the continuous construction of national identity through new media.[17]

This paper examines three new media artifacts concerned with nationalism as case studies to understand how BuzzFeed and *La Stampa* stimulate a cross-cultural dialogue between two groups: Italians and Americans. As a result, the online outlets attempt to define the national character of Italy and the United States through the global media stage by calling into question stereotypes of each national group and by asking for clarifications about norms and habits that Italians and Americans usually take for granted. In addition to Italian and American habits, the online conversation outlines a third hybrid cultural group: Italian American. Both groups address each other in their own native language to reinforce the belonging to their own national group. These artifacts include one video from BuzzFeed[18] and two other videos, one in response to BuzzFeed's and the other is a follow-up conversation recorded by *La Stampa*, an Italian newspaper based in Turin, Italy.[19]

BuzzFeed published and first posted the video, "Questions Americans Have for Italians," on their Facebook page on October 8th, 2015. The post carried the message "Dear Italy, we have some questions for you. Please get back to us. Thanks! Sincerely, America" (see Appendix A). As of July 24, 2019, this BuzzFeed clip had 2.9 million views, 6.1 thousand comments, and over 32,000 shares. The numbers demonstrate that the video successfully attracted the attention of Facebook users, as well as *La Stampa*, one of Italy's leading newspapers. Indeed, the next day, October 9th, 2015, the Turin-based newspaper responded to the cross-cultural conversation with answers to clarify Italian identity, and added questions about the American way of life. *La Stampa* wrote an article on its website, which included the clips recorded in response to BuzzFeed. In addition to Facebook, both the Italian and American news outlets also posted their clips on their YouTube channels. Given the involvement of Italy and the United States and the intercultural conversation through online media, this case study combines the critical approach of Communication Studies with the question of national identity in Italy, which pertains to the field of Italian Studies.

Building on Smith's conceptions of national identity and Livolsi's definition of national character, this paper seeks to understand how BuzzFeed and *La Stampa* stimulate a cross-cultural dialogue between Italians and Americans by questioning stereotypes of both groups. Therefore, the current analysis delves into how the digital media stage provides a constitutive opportunity for the national sense of belonging, utilizing Harold Garfinkel's concept of ethnomethodology, and Erving Goffman's studies on personal and social identity.

THEORETICAL FRAMEWORK: NATIONAL IDENTITY, NATIONAL CHARACTER, AND INTERCULTURAL COMMUNICATION ONLINE

The question of "identity" is always evolving. Smith concentrated on national identity and argues for the coexistence of five features: "an historic territory, or homeland; common myths and historical memories; a common mass public culture; common legal rights and duties for all members; a common economy with territorial mobility for members."[20] The necessity for a multiplicity of features "reveals the complex and abstract nature of national identity."[21] As a result, "national identity is fundamentally multidimensional; it can never be reduced to a single element."[22] Smith's multidimensional view informs this study since the video discusses a variety of attributes which belong to the national character of Italian and American people.

Italian scholar Marino Livolsi has studied the conceptualization of national belonging in Italy. He distinguishes two concepts: national identity and national character. Livolsi posited that national identity existed if "those who share it are born (or at least have lived for a long time) in the same territory, speak the same language and share a common (and not too recent) history and culture."[23] Otherwise, the national character of a nation is "the product of some common sociopsychological traits which are either shared or eschewed, becoming a collective inheritance that is hard to ignore or reject."[24] Livolsi regards national character indispensable to explain "the deep essence of a population."[25] These videos focus mostly on the cultural dimension, which is composed of values, beliefs, customs, conventions, habits, languages, and practices specific of Italian, American, and Italian American culture. Therefore, just like national identity, national character is composed of a multiplicity of elements.

In "The Impact of New Media on Intercultural Communication in Global Context," Guo-Ming Chen began to set the frame for intercultural dialogue through online media. He argues that new media and globalization have brought the compression of time and space. As a result, he emphasizes Chen's and Zang's view that "globalization has changed the perception of what a community is, redefined the meaning of cultural identity and civic society, and demanded a new way of intercultural interaction."[26] Consequently, Chen believes that "new media continue to establish different kinds of new communities without the limit of time and space, which makes cultural identity more dynamic, fluid, and relativized, and imposes austere challenges to the autonomy and stability of cultural identity."[27] In addition to creating new communities, online media can work as a new platform to reinforce the sense of belonging within already existing communities, such as national groups. Therefore, such identities enter the new global media stage to claim their distinctiveness, and as culture is one of the dimensions of national identity, the videos are the example of Italian and American national identities being shaped in such a context through the discussion of their typically cultural practices. In his work, Chen sets the guidelines based on how future research in the field of new media should evolve. He identifies two components: first, "the impact of cultural identity on the use of new media;"[28] second, "the impact of new media on intercultural dialogue."[29] The present case study attempts to analyze these two components in relation to the online conversation between Italy and the United States.

Furthermore, Robert Shuter contributes to the growing field of intercultural communication by proposing new areas to explore. He proposes the establishment of Intercultural New Media Studies (INMS), which is divided into two subcategories. The first is concerned with how new media, which he calls Information and Communication Technologies (ICTs), "impact theories of communication between people who do not share the same cultural backgrounds, often defined as national culture (nation-state) and co-culture (i.e., ethnicity and race) in early intercultural communication research, but expanded contemporarily to include myriad cultures, both within and across geopolitical boundaries."[30] The videos are an example that fits into this category because the participants, who are shaping and discussing their cultural habits, are representatives of two different cultures located in two different locales and contexts.

By the same token, Pfister and Soliz posited that new media has changed the way in which intercultural communication takes place. They argue that "digital media fuel intercultural communication on a scale and of a kind that is a significant departure from mass-mediated contacts of the last several centuries."[31] Indeed, the difference between new media and traditional media is significant because the former allows users to comment on posts, as is the case of BuzzFeed and the *La Stampa*'s video since they received respectively 6.1K and 156 comments, which is a sign of empowering common users. Therefore, users have the opportunity to express their opinion regarding the content which they did not produce and possibly get a discussion started with the creators or other users.

The web is also an enormous archive of content, and it is easy for users to retrieve almost anything. Indeed, the BuzzFeed and *La Stampa* videos will be on the web forever, unless the creators decide to delete them. As a result, online media are the tools that Italians and Americans use to claim their distinctiveness on a global stage. One of the ways in which this can take place is by asking questions about the other culture acknowledging that the practices they are inquiring about are different from their own habits.

In summation, Livolsi's definition of national character and Smith's definition of national identity set the theoretical framework for the current study. This analysis also contributes to research in the field of intercultural communication on online media starting from Chen, Shuter, Pfister, and Soliz. I will now turn to analyzing two of three artifacts.

THE ARTIFACTS: "QUESTIONS AMERICANS HAVE FOR ITALIANS" AND "OUR ANSWERS TO BUZZFEED'S QUESTIONS ON ITALIANS"[32]

Before examining the attributes of national identity in the videos, this first part of the paper provides a brief overview of BuzzFeed and *La Stampa* as well as a summary of the content of each clip. On October 8th, 2015, Buzz-Feed started the intercultural conversation with Italy by posting a video on its Facebook page in which a group of Americans asked an array of questions, which included:

Do you ever get sick of eating pasta?

Why do you speak with your hands? It's really hard to concentrate when you're doing it. Do you all hate Olive Garden? Or do you feel like you have to [hate Olive Garden] just because you're Italian?

In Italy, are there any road rules? And if there are, why does nobody follow them?

Why do you guys have so many dialects?

How can I marry a man like Claudio Marchisio?

What's the deal with "prego"?

The "actors" who were asking these questions within the videos were being very sarcastic in tone and expression.

In response, a shorter video produced by *La Stampa*, aired within twenty-four hours and kept the conversation on the same sarcastic level, answering in the following way about dialects: "We have a lot of dialects because we are a super old country." In response to speaking with hands, a dark-haired woman ironically said, "You say we gesticulate a lot. Come on! That's not true! We gesticulate to place greater emphasis on the concept we are trying to express." She punctuated her words with hand gestures. An Italian journalist said, "no, we never get tired of eating pasta. Maybe it's because we can eat Trofie, Cannelloni, Fusilli . . . Farfalle . . . Spaghetti, Mezze Penne." The answer continued, spaced out between other answers, to convey the idea that Italians have a large variety of pasta they can choose from. Regarding Super Mario, *La Stampa* replied, "I'd be surprised if met you him on the street. Maybe Luigi." As far as Olive Garden is concerned, an Italian journalist said "we don't hate Olive Garden. What is Olive Garden, actually?" Those interested in marrying Marchisio need to "start cheering for Juve." To respond to the road rules, a journalist exclaimed, "let's be honest: road rules were made for the weak." Finally, "thank you for your attention! Prego."

From this first example, three important elements can be noted and analyzed. Humor is inherently cultural. In this vein, the brief questions asked online in a humorous way actually carry a deep cultural meaning. The questions demonstrate the interest in a more precise understanding of what it means belonging to the Italian and the American national group. Such comprehension goes further than the stereotypes for which these groups are often understood. For Americans, comprehending the external national group (Italians) facilitates the understanding of their own national group of belonging. Such a process also works the other way around. In the case of Italy and the United States, the cross-cultural dialogue analyzed shows the existence of an Italian American culture, a hybrid of Italy and the United States. The responses rhetorically construct the boundaries of all three cultures. Through BuzzFeed's and *La Stampa*'s clips, new media do augment intercultural communication within limits since the conversation is left unfinished as it is constantly evolving and expanding. In this specific case, BuzzFeed did not respond to *La Stampa*'s questions, leaving the cross-cultural dialogue incomplete. Consequently, new media become the platform on which the identity of single nations is continuously played out in the rapidly changing global media stage.

FUNNY QUESTIONS, DEEP MEANINGS OR LAYERED MEANINGS

Francesco Zaffarano, social media manager at *La Stampa*, believes that the videos have a serious cultural connotation. In my interview, he asserted,

> We found BuzzFeed's idea very funny, but we realized that they were not only asking funny questions. They were asking deep and real questions, things that those *people* who do not live in Italy have a hard time understanding. Italy is in many ways a strange country, and that's also its beauty, but telling others about it is not easy. Stereotypes can be a good starting point to tell others about Italy without using a rhetorical attitude, but a simple and funny one. So, we decided to realize a video to respond to BuzzFeed's, one that involved the journalists at *La Stampa* but, above all, without taking it too seriously. (*my emphasis*)

Zaffarano agrees that the videos were enjoyable, but that they also held a deeper meaning related to culture. In terms of choosing how to respond and before shooting the video, the editorial staff at *La Stampa* discussed what kind of content should be included in it. *La Stampa* decided to follow up by asking questions about American stereotypes. Such an approach shows that *La Stampa* noticed that online media can be used as tools for intercultural dialogue. As an example of online media which carry a deep cultural meaning, I will now discuss the issue of body language.

To expand on the reasons why Italians use body language while speaking, the documentary "The Voice of the Body," which discusses Italian body language with a special focus on Sicily, and the participatory-observation of director's Luca Vullo's interactive workshop that typically takes place immediately following the film screening, offer interesting insights.[33] Vullo's argument is that Sicilians are passionate people, and they communicate both through words and gestures. Interestingly, they use 250 hand and facial meaningful gestures whereas the British use 30. According to Vullo, this is part of who Sicilians are, and it dates back thousands of years. During his presentation, Vullo also explained that gestures vary across Italian regions, which means that there are many nuances of body language within the peninsula. This distinction is not present in the videos because the actors only ask about "Italian gestures," assuming that body language is the same all over the country.

Another important question is the one about dialects. The response "We have a lot of dialects because we are a super old country" brings up the history of Italy, made up of many little kingdoms that were only unified in 1861. This is indicative of Italy's diversity. Nevertheless, regions maintain their specific traditions still today as evidenced in the typical food products which vary in every part of the country. A question such as this raises an important issue about Italy's history, and thus creates the opportunity for a longer answer than the one provided by *La Stampa*. However, this conversation through digital media allows brief responses.

ITALIAN AMERICAN: A HYBRID CULTURE?

Intercultural exchange often takes place through foodways. Indeed, when Italians were asked if they ever get tired of eating pasta, they responded by listing the diverse kinds they can select from every day. Although an answer such as this does not make specific reference to the sauces (of which there is equal variety), it definitely goes beyond spaghetti and meatballs and Fettuccine Alfredo, which is the most common Italian pasta in the United States, thus an example of Italian American food.

As a scholar studying intercultural communication on virtual media, Camir developed the concept of third culture, which refers to the idea that individuals with different cultural backgrounds can get together in a comprehensive culture "that is not merely the result of a fusion of two or more separate entities, but also the product of the harmonization of composite parts into a coherent whole."[34] This concept highlights an interesting aspect of what intercultural communication is, and it links to the question about the Olive Garden commercials, which raises the issue of Italian American food culture. Nonetheless, in all clips the cultural boundaries are well defined. The two cultural groups are separated, and they ask each other questions, which contribute to reinforcing the differences between the two.

One of the journalists from *La Stampa* revealed that Italians, "Do not hate the Olive Garden. . . . But wait. . . . What is Olive Garden?" This statement is significant since it brings up the issue of the hybridization of Italian food with American food. As a land of immigrants, American food culture has been and continues to adapt and change, but newly arrived immigrants had to earn their credibility in the food sphere because "fear was the American primary response (sic) towards ethnic food."[35] Nevertheless, with time ethnic food paved its way in the American eating scenario, but "what was originally Italian food eaten by Italian immigrants within Italian communities in the United States has gradually become Italian American food, influenced by local and other ethnic cultures' traditions, consumed by larger and non-Italian origins groups (sic) in local restaurants."[36] Nonetheless, corporate production absorbed Italian food tradition in the United States and "has started to mass produce it, erasing culinary boundaries. Canned spaghetti, packed lasagna, and microwavable pasta have been present in American houses for so long."[37] According to Muccini, the mass production of Italian food has led to the loss of its authenticity and distinctiveness, and it has become "one of many American products; in many cases, it preserved an exotic name just to increase the sales, because after all, diversity is exciting."[38] Studying in the United States after having grown up in Italy made me realize that Muccini had a point. Italy becomes a brand able to attract customers, but the quality of the food served in Italian chains in the United States is lower than "one-of-a-kind" restaurants.

As an example of the Italian American corporate food restaurant, the Olive Garden (a chain founded in 1982 and currently owned by Darden Restaurants) is a "prototypical or emblematic Italian dining experience."[39] Despite the Olive Garden's claim to be an authentic Italian restaurant by using Italian language in their menus and defining themselves as eating establishments with "home-like settings," "the restaurant sells what is generally depicted as Italian food because that is what customers demand."[40] However, this chain does not exist in Italy, so Italians are not familiar with it unless they visit the United States. The absence of the Olive Garden in Italy's food landscape questions its capacity to produce authentic Italian food. Indeed, the young man who asked about the Olive Garden presented the question in a way that made him seem aware of the fact that the Olive Garden does not serve authentic Italian food. Such a question and its response, which asked what the Olive Garden was, indicates the existence of two different food cultures: Italian and Italian American.

ITALIAN CULTURE AND AMERICAN CULTURE

If pieced together, many of the attributes discussed in the clips create the puzzle which equals *italianità*, which I regard as the sense of belonging to Italian culture. Among others, Viscusi (1994), Gentile (2009), Patriarca (2010), Garau (2015), Pelizzari (2018), and Giovinazzo (2018) studied the concept of *italianità*. Gardaphé asserts *italianità* "is an invention, a construction"[41] and by discussing elements of *italianità* such as food, road rules, and body language, the artifacts provide the opportunity to reinforce such construction.

As the actors in the videos ask each other questions about their cultural habits, they talk about something that the other cultural group takes for granted. According to Garfinkel (1967), our actions make sense in the context within which we carry them out. This implies that there is no need for Italians to explain to other Italians the reasons for their actions because they are already aware, as they share the same knowledge and the same frames in which they act are all taken for granted. As a result, Garfinkel refers to ethnomethodology as "the investigation of the rational properties of indexical expressions and other practical actions as contingent ongoing accomplishments or organized artful practices of everyday life."[42] Indexical expressions are conventions with a shared meaning by members of the same group, and its connotation varies depending on the context.

Indeed, in the BuzzFeed video, an American asked, "What is up with your dinner structure? I don't understand how a human being can put so much food inside himself." This statement outlines the differences between Italian and American meal structures. In the first case, the meal is long in terms of time and amount of food; in the second case, Americans consume food more quickly and they pile it all together on the same plate. As a result, Italians and Americans have two different perspectives on meal structure, and among compatriots these characteristics can be taken for granted. If this discussion was not taking place, both Italians and Americans would not need to explain out loud this habit of theirs. Yet the new media stage affords the platform to engage in an intercultural discussion along with the opportunity to clarify practices which are usually considered "obvious."

To continue further with the videos' discussion, the national character is consistently negotiated through sets of different practices, and such procedures may also be interpersonal. To this extent, Goffman believed in the importance of seeking "the symbolic meaning of any given social practice and for the contribution of the practice to the integrity and solidarity of the group that employs it."[43] As a result of his studies, Goffman determined different forms including deference and demeanor which he elaborated upon in *Interaction Ritual* (1967). Although he reached this conclusion after studying individual and social identity in interpersonal communication, his analysis can also be applied to the construction of identity within a broader context. Goffman posits that there is a set of rituals which allows individuals to shape their identity when they interact with others. He also argues that when they interact, individuals perform rituals that celebrate themselves and their belonging to a specific group. As the Americans and Italians speak, they are becoming more aware of their cultural identity, and by clarifying their habits out loud, they also contribute to shaping their national distinctiveness on the global media stage.

Indeed, when a young American woman asked "In Italy, are there any road rules? And if there are, why does no one respect them?" She provided the opportunity to distinguish how Italians and Americans differ in respecting road rules. Such question leads to conclude that in the United States drivers tend to respect road rules, whereas in Italy the same happens rarely. One of *La Stampa*'s journalists said, "road rules are for the weak." Indeed, Italian drivers seldom grant pedestrians the right to cross the street, and for Italians, jay-walking is a common practice. Thus, this question brings up two different cultural approaches to road rules. As such questions are asked on videos through new media, they contribute to clarifying Italian and American cultural habits on the global media stage.

THE THIRD ARTIFACT: QUESTIONS ITALIANS WOULD ASK AMERICANS[44]

La Stampa also recorded another video in which the Italian journalists asked Americans to clarify some of their cultural habits. The questions included,

> You have a strong tie to your national flag. Where does your sense of patriotism come from?
> Why are you convinced that we (Italians) live the same way as we did in the fifties, or maybe the sixties if we're pushing it?
> Why are you so obsessed with air conditioning?
> Why do you think that America is only the United States? America also includes Argentina, Brazil, Mexico, Canada, Honduras, Guatemala, Chile, Colombia, and Venezuela.
> How can you guys make such awesome TV shows?
> Ok, I'll introduce you to Claudio Marchisio, but can you explain to me how to get a man like Patrick Dempsey?

These questions would have allowed Italians to have a clearer understanding about American routines and beliefs, but in my interview with Zaffarano, he declared that the Italian newspaper has yet to receive an answer from Buzz-Feed. The lack of a response leads one to deduce that even though online media are easy to access, they are low-cost, and can reach a wide global audience that engages in some degree of intercultural exchange, they also make it easy for users to leave interactions unfinished or ignored.

Despite being brief and entertaining, the videos offer a foundation to discuss the two cultures because they raise some interesting flash points such as diet, food, language, road rules, and soccer celebrities that can lead to a deeper cultural analysis. In addition, the videos provide a limited view of Italian and American culture because they tackle only certain aspects of these cultures. The videos, for example, did not mention national holidays in the countries, nor their political situation. As a result, the videos may become the only source on which many viewers base their understanding of the two cultures, and this would be dangerous because there are many more avenues to be explored in both cases but avoiding to discuss other cultural aspects in the videos could keep many unaware of other realities in Italy and the United States, unless new clips are shot.

Another risky aspect is the virality of the videos. BuzzFeed's video was shared on Facebook almost 33,000 times, but just a few days later it was left critically unanalyzed, and this is a typical phenomenon of new media. Companies such as BuzzFeed focus the users' attention on one topic and for a few hours, that is what the discussion is all about, but a few days later the topic of the discussion changes because the old content has been replaced by new content that is more successful in attracting the user's attention. This aspect underscores the great amount of content that flows on new media as well as its ephemerality. This is part of the potentially negative aspects of new media. However, this ephemeral content is archived, and thus preserved. Therefore, users may come across these videos three years from now hopefully engaging in more critical analysis.

In terms of percentages of usage of new media platforms, Statista, an American technology website that publishes news, reports, and interviews, found that in the announcement of the last quarter of 2015, Facebook had 1.59 billion monthly active users.[45] In its statistics report, YouTube declared to have over one billion users last year, and 80 percent of its views of its videos came from users outside of the United States.[46] These figures lead one to conclude that these large numbers demonstrate the extensive use of online media, and how much these tools are an appropriate platform to participate in the process of building and maintaining national identity. By the same token, the high number of users makes it possible for a large percentage of the world population to see this material independent of their being either Italian or American. Though coming from different backgrounds, these viewers can still be impacted by such cultural expressions because they contribute to constructing their understanding of Italian, American, and Italian American cultural habits.

The videos contribute to defining Italian and American character and its differences on the global media stage by discussing cultural habits. Consequently, this way of shaping national character differs from what happened prior to the birth of new media for two reasons. First, the videos under discussion were created by a group of journalists, and as viewers, we do not know any of their names; they are not cultural or political icons such as the prime minister, the captain of the national soccer or football team, or well-known actors and celebrities. Second, while the videos examine cultural habits that Italians or Americans employ in their lifestyle twenty-four-seven, they do not reference any national celebrations on a macro scale such as June 2nd in Italy or July 4th in the United States. Such celebrations offer an opportunity to reinforce the sense of national belonging. Traditional media coverage of such festivities supports such reinforcement.[47] New media has not replaced the traditional rituals which construct and reinforce national character; instead, they have added to them, and in some cases adjusted and redefined them, and continue to do so.

For instance, posts on new media may entail topics related to national pride, putting users in the position of participating in the process of constructing national identity. New media then, with its instant and global audience, can and do invite Italians, for example, to share and perhaps identify in some fashion with a major American sporting event such as the Super Bowl. New media can also invite Americans to participate in and perhaps identify with the Italian celebration day of liberation such as April 25th or June 2nd (Republic Day). Both cultures historically have had sporting events as well as liberation celebrations. New media, unlike former media, have developed an intercultural exchange, thereby increasing or expanding cultural globalization. But, of course, the negative effect is present: the potential erosion of traditional cultural identity and preservation.

CONCLUSION

Based on this study, new media stimulate intercultural communication. As actors engage in their native language, the videos definitely generate cross-cultural dialogue, and they can and do allow participants to carry out the conversation in a fun and entertaining way since they are inventive means of expression. Both groups address each other in their own native language, thus reinforcing the sense of belonging to the respective national group. However, communicating through online media easily allows for leaving the dialogue incomplete, as evidenced when *La Stampa* asked BuzzFeed questions, and BuzzFeed did not respond. This is due to the fact that, despite their dialogue format, new media allow communication mostly through mediated interaction, which is slower than face-to-face correspondence, since it is asynchronous. As a result, new media leave the discussion incomplete because participants fail to critically complete the conversational cycle. In addition, because of the high number of users, online media become part of the already existing group of institutions in charge of constructing and maintaining national character on the global media stage. As BuzzFeed's and *La Stampa*'s videos demonstrate, the construction of a national sense of belonging is possible because online media can be used as tools to explain the reasons behind cultural habits, providing opportunities for understanding the kind of logic that fosters intercultural comprehension and acceptance because it allows users to explain, clarify, and challenge cultural habits.

NOTES

1. Thussu, Daya Kishan. *International Communication: Continuity and Change*. Arnold; Co-Published in the United States of America by Oxford University Press, 2000, 82.

2. Ibid., 82.

3. Ripley, Casey. *The Media & the Public*. Reference Shelf; v. 66, No. 5. New York: H.W. Wilson, 1994, 187.

4. Thussu, Daya Kishan. *International Communication: Continuity and Change*. Arnold; Co-Published in the United States of America by Oxford University Press, 2000, 82.

5. Ripley, Casey. *The Media & the Public*. Reference Shelf; v. 66, No. 5. New York: H.W. Wilson, 1994, 187.

6. Wodak, Ruth. "Discourses about Nationalism." *The Routledge Handbook of Critical Discourse Studies*. Ed. John Flowerdew, and John E. Richardson. Routledge Handbooks in Applied Linguistics. Taylor and Francis, 2017, 405.

7. Gellner, Ernest. *Nations and Nationalism*. Second Edition. Blackwell Publisher: Cornell University Press. Ithaca, NY, 2006, xx.

8. Kumar, D. V. "Gellnerian Theory of Nation and Nationalism: A Critical Appraisal." *Sociological Bulletin* 59, no. 3 (2010): 397.

9. Skey, Michael. *Everyday Nationhood: Theorising Culture, Identity and Belonging after Banal Nationalism*. 2017,1.

10. Ibid., 1.

11. Ibid., 2.

12. Ibid., 2.

13. Szulc, Lukasz. "Banal Nationalism in the Internet Age: Rethinking the Relationship Between Nations, Nationalisms and the Media." *Everyday Nationhood: Theorising Culture, Identity and Belonging after Banal Nationalism*. 2017, 55.

14. Ibid., 68.

15. Ibid., 68.

16. https://www.buzzfeed.com/javiermoreno/we-need-to-know. Moreover, BuzzFeed wrote an article to ask twenty-one questions to Australia (https://www.buzzfeed.com/awesomer/wtf-australia). Also, in 2015 BuzzFeed published a survey which assessed "how stereotypically Swedish" a respondent was (https://www.buzzfeed.com/violag2/how-stereotypically-swedish-are-you-fj6w).

17. BuzzFeed also wrote another article addressed to the French in 2016 (https://www.buzzfeed.com/fr/awesomer/hard-questions-for-france). In 2018 BuzzFeed recorded a one-minute and a half video asking questions to the Russians (https://www.facebook.com/watch/?v=10154185199800329).

18. According to successstory.com, a website which aims at inspiring others by telling successful stories of people and companies, "one of the major reasons for the success of BuzzFeed is due to the fact that their content is enjoyable and simple to read," which makes it an example of infotainment, the hybrid genre of information and entertainment. Indeed, the same approach is visible also in the video, "Questions Americans Have for Italians." The infotainment orientation also explains why BuzzFeed's clips have easily become a viral phenomenon on the web. Despite having some history of plagiarism, BuzzFeed relies on millions of views every month from users all over the world, and thanks to advertising last year, these views turned into a thirteen-million-dollar a month revenue.

19. *La Stampa* was founded in 1987 in Turin, Italy, and started as a traditional printed newspaper with a centrist political stance. It joined the web later in the same way as other traditional newspapers did. It is now owned by the publisher Editrice S.p.A., which is part of Fiat Chrysler Automobiles. To advance its leadership position in the newspaper industry, two months ago *La Stampa*, Il Secolo XIX and *La Repubblica* signed a memorandum to create a publishing group that would be more competitive on the news market, since the new media conglomerate strives to own 20 percent of the Italian publishing industry.

Gruppo Espresso and Itedi stipulated the agreement on March 2nd, 2016. Gruppo Espresso is an Italian media company listed on the stock exchange, and it operates in different media areas including television, radio, and advertising. Gruppo Espresso is owned by the holding company Compagnie Industriali Riunite (CIR) group, whose chairman and CEO are respectively Rodolfo De Bendetti and Monica Mondarini. The memorandum grants Gruppo Espresso the acquisition of Italian Editrice S.p.A, also known as Itedi, which is a media company controlled by Fiat Chrysler Automobiles (FCA). Itedi was founded in 2014 as a result of the alliance between two master heads—La Stampa and Il Secolo XIX. Thanks to this memorandum, FCA is leaving the Italian publishing industry to take over the British weekly newspaper *The Economist*. Despite the fact that this memorandum, *La Stampa*, Il Secolo XIX, and *La Repubblica* are maintaining their editorial independence.

20. Smith, Anthony D. *National Identity*. Reno: University of Nevada Press, 1991, 14.

21. Ibid., 14.

22. Ibid., 14.

23. Livolsi, Marino. *Chi Siamo: La Difficile Identità Nazionale Degli Italiani*. Franco Angeli, 2011, 12.

Tr. "chi la condivide sia nato (o almeno viva da tempo) in uno stesso territorio, usi una medesima lingua e condivida una comune (e non troppo recente) storia e cultura."

24. Ibid., 11.

Tr. "*il prodotto di alcuni tratti sociopsicologici comuni che si possono condividere o da cui si possono prendere le distanze, ma che sono un'eredità collettiva difficile da ignorare o negare.*"

25. Ibid., 12.

Tr. "l'essenza profonda di un popolo"

26. Chen, Guo-Ming. "The Impact of New Media on Intercultural Communication in Global Context." *China Media Research* 8, no. 2 (2012):1.

27. Ibid., 5.

28. Ibid., 7.

29. Ibid., 7.

30. Shuter, Robert. "Intercultural New Media Studies: The Next Frontier in Intercultural Communication." *Journal of Intercultural Communication Research*. 41, no. 3 (2012): 220.

31. Smith Pfister, Damien, and Jordan Soliz. "(Re)conceptualizing Intercultural Communication in a Networked Society." *Journal of International and Intercultural Communication* 4, no. 4 (2011): 246.

32. Le nostre risposte alle domande di BuzzFeed sugli Italiani

33. I gathered the following data on at the movie screening and interactive workshop held by Luca Vullo at California State University, Long Beach on April 21, 2016. Vullo was invited by CSULB Club Italia, and the title of the event was "Italian Gestures: Exploring Stereotypes, Language, and Culture."

34. Camir, Fred L., and Nobleza C. Asuncion-Lande. "Intercultural Communication Revisited: Conceptualization, Paradigm Building, and Methodological Approaches." *Communication Yearbook* 12 (1989): 294.

35. Muccini, Francesca M. *From Italian "cibo" to American Food: The Construction of the Italian American Identity Through Food.* ProQuest Dissertations and Theses (2006), 176.

36. Ibid., 174–175.

37. Ibid., 175.

38. Ibid., 175.

39. Ibid., 199.

40. Ibid., 201.

41. Gardaphé, Fred. "Identical Difference: Notes on Italian and Italian American Identities." In Janni, Paolo, and George F. McLean. *The Essence of Italian Culture and the Challenge of a Global Age.* Washington, D.C.: Council for Research in Values and Philosophy (2003), 104.

42. Garfinkel, Harold. *Studies in Ethnomethodology.* Englewood Cliffs, N.J.: Prentice-Hall, 1967, 11.

43. Goffman, Erving. *Interaction Ritual: Essays on Face-to-Face Behavior.* Garden City, N.Y.: Doubleday, 1967, 47.

44. Le domande che gli italiani farebbero agli americani

45. In the third quarter of 2018 Statista reported that Facebook had 2.32 billion monthly active users worldwide (https://www.statista.com/statistics/264810/number-of-monthly-active-facebook-users-worldwide/). After monitoring the number of monthly active users since 2008 (100 in the third quarter), the trend has increased steadily every quarter.

46. YouTube, 2015.

47. See Boni, Federico. *Nel fantastico mondo di Oz: La costruzione dell'identità mediatica australiana a Sydney 2000.* Milan, Italy: Edizioni Unicopli, 2003.

Pappas, Peter. "America on Parade: Thrill's Affect-Zone and The 2012 NBC Super Bowl Broadcast." *Canadian Review of American Studies* 44, no. 3 (2014): 426–449.

Gavrila, Mihaela, and Mario Morcellini. "RAI narrates Italy: Current Affairs, Television Information and Changing Times." *Journal of Italian Cinema & Media Studies* 3, no. 1 (2015): 81–97.

BIBLIOGRAPHY

Anderson, Benedict R. O'G. *Imagined Communities: Reflections on the Origin and Spread of Nationalism.* Revised ed., 2006.

Billig, Michael. *Banal Nationalism.* Sage, 1995.

BuzzFeed. "Questions Americans Have for Italians." October 2015. YouTube video, 1:31. Posted in October 2015.

Camir, Fred L., and Nobleza C. Asuncion-Lande. "Intercultural Communication Revisited: Conceptualization, Paradigm Building, and Methodological Approaches." *Communication Yearbook* 12 (1989): 278–309.

Chen, Guo-Ming. "The Impact of New Media on Intercultural Communication in Global Context." *China Media Research* 8, no. 2 (2012): 1.

Garfinkel, Harold. *Studies in Ethnomethodology.* Englewood Cliffs, N.J.: Prentice-Hall, 1967.

Garau, Eva. *Politics of National Identity in Italy: Immigration and "Italianità."* Routledge Studies in Extremism and Democracy. Routledge Research in Extremism and Democracy; 20, 2015.

Gardaphé, Fred. "Identical Difference: Notes on Italian and Italian American Identities." In Janni, Paolo, and George F. McLean. *The Essence of Italian Culture and the Challenge of a Global Age.* Washington, DC: Council for Research in Values and Philosophy, 2003.

Gellner, Ernest. *Nations and Nationalism.* Second Edition. Ithaca, NY: Cornell University Press, 2006.

Gentile, Emilio. *La Grande Italia: The Myth of the Nation in the Twentieth Century.* George L. Mosse Series in Modern European Cultural and Intellectual History. Madison, WI: University of Wisconsin Press, 2009.

Giovinazzo, William A. *Italianità: The Essence of Being Italian and Italian-American*. Dark River, 2018.

Goffman, Erving. *Interaction Ritual: Essays on Face-to-Face Behavior*. Garden City, NY: Doubleday, 1967.

Halliday, Josh. "11 Things You Need to Know about BuzzFeed." *The Guardian*. January 6, 2013. http://www.theguardian.com/media/2013/jan/06/buzzfeed-social-news-open-uk.

Kumar, D. V. "Gellnerian Theory of Nation and Nationalism: A Critical Appraisal." *Sociological Bulletin* 59, no. 3 (2010): 392–406. http://www.jstor.org.csulb.idm.oclc.org/stable/23620890.

La Stampa. "Le nostre risposte alle domande di BuzzFeed sugli italiani." October 2015. YouTube video, 0:53. *LaStampa.it*. Posted October 2015. http://www.lastampa.it/2015/10/09/societa/le-nostre-risposte-e-domande-al-video-di-buzzfeed-sugli-italiani-nJ8fuJYCMwc0R1TUUwdnJO/pagina.html.

Livolsi, Marino. *Chi Siamo: La Difficile Identità Nazionale Degli Italiani*. Franco Angeli, 2011.

Muccini, Francesca M. *From Italian "cibo" to American Food: The Construction of the Italian American Identity Through Food*. ProQuest Dissertations and Theses, 2006.

Patriarca, Silvana. *Italian Vices: Nation and Character from the Risorgimento to the Republic*. Cambridge, UK; New York: Cambridge University Press, 2010.

Pelizzari, Maria Antonella. "Italianita O Cosmopolitanismo?" *Rivista Di Studi Fotografia*, no. 8 (2018): 124.

Szulc, Lukasz. "Banal Nationalism in the Internet Age: Rethinking the Relationship Between Nations, Nationalisms and the Media." *Everyday Nationhood: Theorising Culture, Identity and Belonging after Banal Nationalism*. 2017: 53–74.

Skey, Michael. *Everyday Nationhood: Theorising Culture, Identity and Belonging after Banal Nationalism*. 2017.

Smith, Anthony D. *National Identity*. Reno: University of Nevada Press, 1991.

Smith Pfister, Damien, and Jordan Soliz. "(Re)conceptualizing Intercultural Communication in a Networked Society." *Journal of International and Intercultural Communication* 4, no. 4 (2011): 246–251.

Shuter, Robert. "Intercultural New Media Studies: The Next Frontier in Intercultural Communication." *Journal of Intercultural Communication Research* 41, no. 3 (2012): 219–237.

Ripley, Casey Jr. *The Media & the Public*. New York: H.W. Wilson. 1994.

SuccessStory. "BuzzFeed Success Story." Successstory.com.http://successsstory.com/companies/buzzfeed (May 1, 2016).

Vullo, Luca. *The Voice of the Body*. DVD. Directed by Luca Vullo. Italy: Ondemotive Production, 2011.

Thussu, Daya Kishan. 2000. *International Communication: Continuity and Change*. London; New York: Arnold; Co-published in the United States of America by Oxford University Press.

Viscusi, Robert. "24: The Future of Italianità: The Italian Commonwealth." *Center for Migration Studies Special Issues* 11, no. 3 (1994): 483–90.

Wodak, Ruth. "Discourses about nationalism." *The Routledge Handbook of Critical Discourse Studies*. 2017: 403–420.

YouTube. "Statistics." Youtube.com.https://www.youtube.com/yt/press/en-GB/statistics.html (May 1, 2016).

Zaffarano, Francesco. Personal Interview. February 25, 2016.

Index

8½, 22, 88
12 Years a Slave, 83, 84, 85, 91n11, 91n12, 93

Aciman, André, 81
African Americans, 4, 5, 27, 53, 56n49, 56n50, 60, 61, 62, 63, 65, 66, 68, 70, 71, 72, 73, 74, 81, 83, 84, 87, 89, 91n4, 91n10, 91n13, 187
Afteb, Kaleem, 27, 28
AIDS, 87, 132
Alba, Richard, 15, 31n13, 31n14
Allen, Woody, 81
American cinema, 40, 52, 81, 92n17, 206n24
American Dream, 5, 16, 29, 31n11, 43, 63, 83, 90, 91n7, 187
Americanization, 99, 187
American myth, 146
American Newspaper Directory, 166, 178n22
Americans, 6, 41, 42, 43, 49, 50, 51, 52, 56n57, 83, 90, 99, 106, 108, 117, 125, 168, 172, 177n9, 178n32, 212, 213, 215, 216, 217, 220, 221, 223, 225n18
Anderson, Benedict R, 167, 178n24, 212
Anthony, Marc, 43
Antonioni, Michelangelo, 24, 32n38, 81, 91n5
Appiah, Kwame Anthony, 110, 111, 112n16

Aprile(April; movie), 88
Aprile, Richie, 150
Aprile, Rosalie, 144
Asuncion-Lande, Nobleza C, 226n34
auteurism, 28
Avellino, 103, 105, 156
Avildsen, John G., 4, 59, 74

Babette's Feast, 39
Bada Bing!, 143
Badham, John, 40
Baker, Aaron, 69, 76, 76n32, 137n5
Barolini, Helen, 13, 30n6, 30n7, 177n11
Barone, Raymond, 119, 125, 137n9
Barsotti, Carlo, 166, 167
Bartello, Antonio, 189, 190, 191
Bathurst Street, 184
Battipaglia, Amedeo, 101
Baudo, Pippo, 95, 111n1
Baywatch, 133
Beguiled, The, 13, 25, 26, 27, 28, 31n18, 33n41, 33n42, 33n43, 33n45
Bello Onesto Emigrato Australia sposerebbe Compaesana Illibata, 101
Benigni, Roberto, 90
Benton, Robert, 37
Bergman, Ingrid, 81
Bertellini, Giorgio, 3, 177n12, 187, 206n20, 206n23
Beyond the Latin Lover, 22, 32n34, 125, 138n20

Bianco, Rosso e Verdone, 98
Bicycle Thieves, 47, 86, 87, 89, 90, 192
Big Night, 5, 37, 38, 39, 40, 41, 44, 45, 46,
    47, 49, 50, 51, 52, 53, 54n3, 54n5,
    54n7, 54n13, 54n15, 55n19, 55n20,
    55n21, 55n31, 55n32
Billig, Michael, 212
Billy Bathgate, 4, 37
Bitter Rice, 47
Black Lives Matter, 61, 63
Black Panther, 63, 76n24, 77
Black, Todd, 83
Bling Ring, 27, 30n2, 31n18, 33n42
Bloor Street, 184, 194
Blow-Up, 81
Bocelli, Andrea, 144, 156
Bollywood, 194
Bona, Mary Jo, 13, 18, 29, 30n6, 30n7,
    32n30, 33n47
Bondanella, Peter, 1, 3, 8n7, 9, 54n17, 119,
    141, 157n2, 157n3, 157n4, 158n16,
    158n21
Bongiorno, Marylou Tibaldo, 29
Boni, Federico, 226n47
Bonpensiero, Angie, 144, 150
Bonpensiero, Salvatore "Big Pussy", 144,
    146
Bourdieu, Pierre, 110
Bracco, Lorraine, 48, 149
Bronx, 47
Brooklyn, 103, 104
Bruni, Michael, 100
Brusati, Franco, 98
Burstow, Bonnie, 73, 76n45
Buzzfeed, 6, 33n43, 212, 213, 215, 216,
    217, 220, 222, 223, 224n16, 224n17,
    225n18, 225n32

Cabiria, 81
Cage, Nicolas, 40
Caldwell, John, 184, 205n4
Call Me by Your Name, 81
Camaiti Hostert, Anna, 39, 54n3, 55n30
Camir, Fred L, 218, 226n34
Cammareri, Ronny, 40
Campbell, Fiona Kumari, 9n13, 61, 75n12
Campbell, Jane, 32n29
Canada, 6, 180, 183, 184, 185, 188, 189,
    190, 191, 193, 196, 197, 198, 199, 204,

205n1, 205n2, 205n3, 205n8, 205n9,
    205n11, 205n14, 206n26, 206n29,
    207n34, 221
Canadian Citizenship Act of 1947, 188
Cannell, Stephen J., 37
Caple Jr., Steven, 5, 59, 60, 61, 62, 63, 65,
    68, 70, 71, 72, 73, 74, 75n8, 75n9,
    75n17, 75n18
Capra, Frank, 8, 15, 31n12, 137n5
Cardinale, Claudia, 101
Carilli, Theresa, 18, 32n29
Carosone, Renato, 99
Caserta, 103, 105
Casillo, Robert, 1, 2, 8n1, 15, 31n10,
    31n12, 31n13, 31n14, 34, 53, 56n63,
    59, 75n1, 96, 111n4, 165, 177n13
Castorini, Cosmo, 40
Castorini, Loretta, 40
Catholic guilt, 127
Cavallero, Jonathan, 3, 4, 18, 32n26,
    55n35, 137n4, 137n6
CBS, 37, 40, 56n44
Chase, David, 6, 141, 143, 148, 151, 154,
    156
Chen, Guo-Ming, 6, 214, 216, 224n16
Cher (Cherilyn Sarkisian), 40
Chianese, Francesco, 6, 157n6, 158n7,
    158n19, 158n28
Chicago Tribune, The, 172
Chinatown, 95, 111, 194
Ciarrapico, Maddalena, 100
Cimino, Michael, 17
Cinema Paradiso, 6, 184
cinepanettoni, 102, 112n11
Cira, Joe, 190
Classic Theater, 190
Clayman, Mark, 83
Cocola, Jim, 60, 75n6
Coen, Joseph, 190
Cohen, Lizbeth, 186, 206n18
College Street, 184, 186, 190, 194, 196
Collodi, Carlo, 125
colonia, 6, 166, 167
Columbo, 8
Columbus Day, 148, 178n34
comedy, 41, 55n22, 81, 100, 101, 102,
    112n11, 112n12, 117, 118, 158n13, 197
*Commedia dell'arte/Commedia
    all'italiana*(comedy Italian style), 100,

102, 125, 147

Conner, Lawrence, 141

Conrad, Steven, 83, 89

Continental Theater, 192, 196

Conway, Brett, 60, 75n4

Coogler, Ryan, 5, 59, 60, 61, 63, 65, 67, 69, 70, 71, 73, 74, 75n6, 75n7, 75n8, 75n9, 76n24, 76n31, 76n35

Cooper, Gary, 146

Copacabana, 49

Coppino Law (Italy, 1877), 166

Coppola, Agostino, 14

Coppola, Carmine, 14

Coppola, Eleanor, 14, 30n8

Coppola, Francis Ford, 2, 8, 9, 31n10, 31n13, 32n27, 39, 56n63, 74, 75n1, 111n4, 137n5, 137n6, 143, 151, 158n7, 177n13, 179

Coppola, Sofia, 4, 13, 14, 15, 16, 24, 29, 30, 30n1, 30n3, 30n4, 31n18, 33n40, 33n41, 33n43, 33n44, 33n45

Corleone, Don Vito, 69, 143, 144

Corleone, Mary, 13

Corleone, Michael, 14

Corriere Canadese, 6, 183, 192, 193, 195, 196, 199, 200, 201, 202, 204, 207n42, 207n43

Corso Italia, 184, 185, 192, 193, 194, 196

The Cosby Show, 63, 64, 73

Coyle, Margaret, 43, 52, 55n20, 56n62

Crane, David, 117

Creed

Creed, Adonis/Johnson, Donnie, 4, 59, 60, 61, 62, 63, 65, 66, 67, 68, 69, 70, 71, 72, 73, 74

Creed, Amara, 4, 60, 61, 71, 72, 74

Creed, Apollo, 59, 60, 61, 63, 65, 66, 67, 68, 69, 71, 72, 73, 74

Creed, Bianca, 4, 60, 61, 62, 63, 65, 67, 68, 69, 70, 71, 72, 73, 74

Creed, Mary Anne, 63, 66, 67, 68, 71, 73

Creed, 4, 59, 60, 61, 62, 63, 65, 66, 67, 68, 69, 70, 71, 72, 73, 74, 75n6, 75n7, 76n31, 76n35

Creed II, 4, 59, 61, 63, 66, 67, 68, 70, 71, 72, 74, 75n9, 75n18

Crialese, Emanuele, 110, 112, 113

Cristiano, 38, 43

Cullinan, Thomas P., 25, 29

cult of the Madonna, 18, 19

cultural constriction, 99

Cuomos, 97

Dalla, Lucio, 103

Daniels, Lee, 81, 86, 87, 88, 91n4, 92n17, 92n18

D'Azeglio, Massimo, 111

De Marco, Giuliana, 107

Demarco, Steven, 37

DeMichiel, Helen, 29

Denby, David, 49, 55n40

De Niro, Robert, 3, 97

de Palma, Brian, 17

De Santis, Giuseppe, 46, 47

Deschamps, Bénédict, 167, 178n23, 178n25, 178n26

De Sica, Vittorio, 46, 47, 81, 86, 87, 88, 89, 90

diaspora, 2, 17, 18, 75n19, 96, 155, 175, 179n51

Di Biagi, Flaminio, 3, 8n9, 137n7

Dolnick, Edward, 73, 76n44

Don Salvatore, 95

Don Siegel, 25

Downsview, 194, 198

Drago, Ivan, 61, 68

Drago, Viktor, 4, 61, 66, 68, 70, 73

Driver, Minnie, 41

Dylan, Bob, 81

Eastwood, Clint, 25, 26

Edelman, Lee, 6, 167, 169, 170, 171, 173, 174, 177n15, 178n27, 178n28, 178n29, 178n35, 178n36, 178n38, 178n39, 179n47, 179n48

Emmy Awards, 141; winner, 50

English-language newspaper(s), 164

essentialism, 110

Eugenides, Jeffrey, 19, 31n18, 32n32, 32n38

Everybody Loves Raymond, 40, 119, 125, 137n9

Facebook, 213, 216, 222, 224n17, 226n45

Famous Players Canadian (theater chain), 197, 199

Farnsworth, Martha, 25, 26

Farrell, Collin, 26

Fascism, 97, 99, 109
Feldner, Heiko, 151, 158n22
Fellini, Federico, 17, 24, 37, 46, 49, 81, 92n21
Ferlinghetti, Lawrence, 156
Ferraro, Thomas, 1, 15, 29, 31n16, 33n48, 34, 52, 56n60, 57, 176, 176n1, 180
Fierro, Aurelio, 156
Fonzarelli, Arthur ("Fonz"/"Fonzie"), 8, 119, 120, 121, 122, 125, 133, 136, 137n11, 137n12
foodways, 50, 51, 218
"fool", 147, 153
foreigners, 103, 110
Foundas, Scott, 88, 92n17, 92n21
Franzina, Emilio, 97, 111n5, 111n6
Friends, 4, 6, 23, 32n35, 117, 118, 119, 120, 122, 124, 128, 130, 131, 132, 133, 136, 137n1, 137n2, 137n3, 137n14, 138n21, 138n22, 138n23, 138n29; friends, 6, 22, 101, 118, 123, 124, 129, 130, 131, 132, 133, 134, 135, 136, 172; friendship, 41, 45, 69, 107, 118, 130, 135
futurism, 6, 167, 169, 170, 171, 172, 173, 174; futurity, 167, 168, 170, 171, 173, 179n47

Gabaccia, Donna R., 51, 56n57, 62, 75n19, 175
Gabriella, 41, 45, 48
Gandolfini, James, 141
Gangster Priest, 1, 8n1, 31n13, 137n5
gangster(s), 4, 9n12, 37, 39, 40, 41, 52, 137n4, 165
Gannon, Shannon, 164, 175, 177n5, 177n6, 179n50
Gans, Herbert, 15
Garau, Eva, 220
Garbarino, Gian, 190
Garbarino, Joe, 190
Gardaphé, Fred, 1, 18, 31n10, 32n29, 40, 54n14, 56n63, 65, 75n1, 76n26, 111n4, 142, 146, 147, 152, 153, 157, 157n4, 158n13, 158n23, 158n24, 158n25, 158n26, 158n27, 158n38, 177n11, 177n13, 220, 226n41
Gardner, Christopher, 83, 89, 90, 91n3, 92n23

Garfield, Sally, 106
Garfinkel, Harold, 220, 226n42
Gavrila, Mihaela, 226n47
Gazzo, 65, 69
Gellner, Ernest, 212, 224n7
gender, 2, 4, 13, 14, 16, 18, 19, 21, 29, 30, 30n4, 30n7, 33n43, 76n22, 103, 108, 128, 130, 131, 138n26, 142, 143, 150, 187
Gentile, Emilio, 220, 226
Germi, Pietro, 109
Gerrard Street, 190, 194
Giachino, Anthony, 190, 191
Giaschi, Gina, 190, 191
Giaschi, Joseph, 190, 191
Giovinazzo, William A, 220, 227
Girard, René, 118, 132, 135, 136, 138n28
Girl in Australia, 101
Girotti, Massimo, 24, 206n32
Giunta, Edvige, 13, 30n6, 34, 137n8
Giunta, Furio, 6, 142, 143, 144, 145, 146, 147, 148, 149, 150, 151, 152, 153, 154, 155, 156, 157
Godfather, The, 14, 62, 69, 137n5, 144, 151, 158n7, 199, 202
Godfather Trilogy, The, 17, 28, 49, 137n5, 138, 141, 143; *Part II*, 143; *Part III*, 13, 14, 143
Goffman, Erving, 220, 226n43, 227
Golden Door, 110
Golden Globe Awards, 141
Goldstein, Jacob, 190
Gomorrah – the Series, 143
Good, the Bad, and the Ugly, The, 26
Goodfellas, 48, 49, 127
Gordon, Andrew M., 66, 76n29
Grace Street, 185
Gramsci, Antonio, 28
Grassi, Giovanna, 13, 30n5, 32n37
Grateful Dead, 81
Grey, Harry, 81
Griffith, D. W., 81
Grisham, John, 37
Guadagnino, Luca, 3, 81, 93
Gualtieri, Paulie "Walnuts", 69, 74, 144, 146, 147, 151, 152, 153, 154
Guglielmo, Thomas A., 64, 75n8, 76n25, 207n40

Halliday, Josh, 227
Hamilton, Alexander, 169, 170, 172
Hamilton, Canada, 191, 197, 199
Hamilton-Mann scandal, 170, 171, 172, 178n40, 179n41, 179n42
Hamiliton, Robert Ray, 169, 170, 172, 173
Handyside, Fiona, 16, 17, 30n1, 30n4, 31n19
Happy Days, 6, 119, 120, 121, 136, 137n8, 137n11, 137n12, 137n13
Hart-Celler Act of 1965, 185
Hastie, Amelie, 60, 77
HBO, 3, 4, 49, 105
Helleur, Stan, 198, 207n41
Hill, Henry, 48, 127
Hock, Stephen, 60, 77
Holden, Stephen, 143, 158n9
Hollywood, 3, 5, 6, 8n3, 8n9, 13, 14, 15, 18, 21, 22, 28, 29, 30, 30n5, 31n18, 37, 45, 53, 55n35, 57, 60, 75n3, 76n39, 81, 85, 96, 137n7, 146, 151, 183, 184, 186, 192, 193, 198, 199, 200, 201, 204, 206n24, 207n37
Hollywood Italians, 3, 8n7, 54n17, 57, 119, 157n2
Hoods, The, 81
hooks, bell, 63, 76n22, 77
Hudson, Kate, 88
Hundred-Foot Journey, The, 50
Huston, John, 37

Iammarino, Sarah, 39, 54n3, 54n10, 57
Il fu Mattia Pascal, 125
Il Padrino, 199, 201, 207n42
Il Progresso Italo-Americano, 6, 164, 166, 167, 168, 169, 170, 171, 172, 173, 174, 177n18, 178n19
Imperioli, Michael, 49, 56n44
inetto, 6, 23, 124, 125, 136
Information and Communication Technologies (ICTs), 211, 215
Intercultural New Media Studies (INMS), 215, 225n30
Intolerance, 81
I promessi sposi, 165
Italian American, 1, 2, 3, 4, 5, 6, 8, 8n3, 9n11, 13, 14, 15, 19, 20, 21, 23, 29, 31n10, 31n11, 37, 40, 41, 45, 46, 47, 49, 50, 51, 52, 53, 55n20, 55n43,

56n63, 59, 60, 65, 69, 74, 75n1, 75n2, 76n32, 81, 96, 97, 99, 100, 103, 104, 105, 106, 108, 109, 111n4, 118, 119, 121, 124, 125, 127, 128, 130, 136, 137n13, 141, 142, 143, 149, 152, 153, 154, 156, 157, 163, 164, 165, 169, 170, 172, 174, 175, 176, 176n1, 177n10, 177n13, 214, 217, 218, 219, 222
Italian Americana, 4, 6, 8n3, 8n4, 8n6, 9n11, 31n10, 31n15, 32n29, 54n3, 56n63, 60, 75n1, 75n6, 75n20, 111n4, 112n10, 154, 176n1, 179n49
Italian-dubbed, 198, 199
Italian-language cinema(s), 6, 183, 197
Italian-language newspaper(s), 6, 163, 165, 166, 170, 177n7, 177n18, 178n23
Italian neorealism, 37, 48, 55n34, 57, 88, 91n4, 165, 177n12
Italianness/*italianità*, 5, 18, 24, 29, 32n29, 95, 106, 125, 131, 155, 220
Italian Stallion, 60, 61, 62, 65, 67, 68, 69, 70, 74, 120, 121, 123, 125, 126, 133, 136
Italy's Many Diasporas, 75n19, 175, 179n51
I Vitelloni, 192

Jacobson, Matthew Frye, 61
Jenkins, Barry, 85, 86, 89, 92n15
Jersey Shore, 119
Jewison, Norman, 40
Jones, Claireece "Precious", 87, 88
Jordan, Michael B., 60, 76n35

Kauffman, Marta, 117
Keitel, Harvey, 48
Kelsch, Ken, 38
Khaled, 37
King George Theater, 190
King, Rodney, 60, 63
Kumar, D. V., 224n8

la bella figura, 18, 19, 23, 26, 32n29, 121, 123, 128, 137n16
Lacanian Real, 6, 142, 149, 150, 151, 153, 156, 157
La Ciociara, 81, 87
LaGravenese, Richard, 81
Lady Liberty, 100

La Mortadella, 100
La notte, 24
La Repubblica, 85, 92, 225n19
Lassiter, James, 83
La Stampa, 6, 213, 215, 216, 217, 218, 219, 221, 223, 225n19
La Strada, 49
La terra trema, 47
La vità è bella, 90
La voce del Popolo, 166
L'avventura, 24
Law & Order, 124
Lawton, Ben, 1, 8n4, 32n29, 63, 75n20
L'eclisse, 24
L'Eco d'Italia, 166, 167, 176n2, 177n7
Leisure Seeker, 81
Leone, Sergio, 81
Lester Brothers, 191, 192, 196
Lester, Bob, 191, 192
Lester, Lionel, 191, 192, 194, 198
Lester, Sam, 191, 192
Levy, Emanuel, 83, 93
Lewis, Ray, 191, 207n34
Lies that Bind, The, 110, 112n16
Life is Beautiful, 90
Lindenfeld, Laura, 50, 51, 52, 54n9, 55n33, 56n45, 56n46, 56n48, 56n52, 56n54, 56n56, 56n61
Liotta, Ray, 48, 127
Lisbon, Bonnie, 19
Lisbon, Cecilia, 19, 20, 32n31
Lisbon, Lux, 21, 25, 26
L'Italia, 30n5, 111
Little Italy, 54n14, 95, 111n1, 177n8, 184, 185, 186, 191, 192, 194, 196, 204, 205n12, 206n28
Livolsi, Marino, 6, 213, 214, 216, 225n23
Lodge, Guy, 28, 33n40, 33n45
Loren, Sofia, 3, 87, 100
Los Angeles Times, 88, 92n22
Lost in Translation, 13, 17, 30n2, 31n18
Lucky Luciano, 4, 37
L'ultimo bacio, 83
Lunchbox, The, 50, 56n47
Lupo, Frank, 37

Mackenzie King, William Lyon, 185
Mackey, Eva, 188, 206n26
Madonna, 18, 19, 41, 52

Madonna (complex), 52
mafia, 3, 37, 40, 62, 81, 107
mafiosa, 108
mafiosi, 39, 105, 165
mammone, 124, 128
Mancuso, Salvatore, 110
Manero, Tony, 21, 40
Manfredi, Nino, 98
Manifesto del Futurismo, 170, 178n37
Manning Street, 191
Maradona, 95, 111n2
Marco, Cleo, 25
Marco, Johnny, 21, 22, 23, 24
marginalization, 4, 65, 74, 86, 99
Marie Antoinette, 27, 30n2, 31n18, 33n42, 34
Marinetti, F. T., 170, 178n38
Marshall, Penny, 4, 18, 29
Marshall Plan, 156
Martin, Joel W., 60, 75n5
Marty, 1, 47, 55n35, 57
Mascioli, Leo, 190, 191, 209
masculinity, 6, 21, 32n32, 32n34, 45, 60, 76n32, 117, 118, 125, 130, 138n20, 142, 151, 154, 170
Maslin, Janet, 39, 54n8
Maslow, 135
Mastrangelo, Rocco, 196, 197, 198, 199
Mastroianni, Marcello, 22, 32n34, 125, 138n20
Matrix, The, 153, 154
Matthews, Peter, 44, 46, 55n21, 55n24, 55n28, 56n55
Maucione, Jessica, 60
Mazza, Louie, 190
McAdams, Rachel, 105
McBurney, John, 25, 26, 27
McCraney, Tarrell Alvin, 85
McDonald Carolan, Mary Ann, 3, 5, 9n10, 40, 54n16, 81
Mean Streets, 48, 49, 139
Mediated Ethnicity, 75n2, 111n5, 112, 180
Melfi, Dr. Jennifer, 91n10, 149, 150
MGM, 54n7, 55n19, 55n31, 57, 71, 77, 198
Miami Vice, 37
Micelli, Tony, 119
Mirren, Helen, 81
Molise, 105

Moltisanti, Christopher "Chris", 49
Monicelli, Mario, 5, 100, 102, 109, 113
Mo'Nique, 86, 87
Montreal, 55n43, 185, 196, 205n13
Moonlight, 85, 86, 89, 90, 91n14, 92n15, 92n16
Moonstruck, 40, 54n16
Morrow, Edwina, 25
Morcellini, Mario, 226n47
Moretti, Nanni, 88, 179
mortadella, 100
Mosco, Frank, 37
Muccini, Francesca M, 219, 226n35
Muccino, Gabriele, 3, 5, 81, 83, 86, 89, 90, 91n2, 91n6
multiculturalism, 6, 18, 49, 55n42, 58, 77, 153, 183, 188, 206n26
Muscio, Giuliana, 1, 75n2, 111n5, 180
Museum of Modern Art, 39
My Name is Tanino, 105, 108
My Voyage to Italy, 81

Naples, 6, 14, 91n5, 111n2, 142, 143, 144, 146, 148, 149, 150, 151, 153, 154, 157n6
Nardini, Gloria, 32n29, 123, 137n16
Native Americans, 148
Neapolitans, 95, 111n2
Negra, Diane, 50, 51, 54n4, 56n53, 56n58, 56n59
neorealism, 37, 48, 55n34, 57, 88, 91n4, 165, 177n12
neorealists, 46, 47, 81, 86, 87, 90
New Jersey, 6, 38, 142, 144, 145, 147, 149, 152, 153, 154, 155, 156, 157
New York City, 14, 100, 102, 143, 166, 167, 168, 172, 173, 176n2, 178n19, 178n34, 186
New York Film Critics Circle, 39
New York Times, 37, 39, 84, 86, 172
New York Times Magazine, The, 37, 54n1
Nights of Cabiria, 81
Nine, 88, 92n21, 92n22
No Future: Queer Theory and the Death Drive, 167, 177n15, 178n27, 178n28, 178n29, 178n35, 178n36, 178n38, 178n39, 179n48
Notti di Cabiria, 81
Nuovomondo, 110, 112n10

Odeon Theater, 190, 193, 204
Old World, 51, 56n54, 56n55, 181
Olive Garden, 51, 56n59, 216, 218, 219
omertà, 18
Ommobono, Buddy, 107
Once Upon a Time in America, 81
Ontario, 190, 197, 205n8, 205n15
On the Rocks, 13
Oriental Theater, 190
Orsi, Robert, 69, 76n34, 176n1
Overbrook Entertainment, 83

Pacino, Al, 97, 124, 143, 199
Paisan, 47
Pakula, Alan J., 37
Palace Theater, 199
Palazzolo, Dominic, 20, 32n31
Pandora's Box, 149
Pane e cioccolata, 98
Pappas, Peter, 226n47
Paradise, 38, 44, 45, 46, 54n8, 56n49, 184, 194
Paradise Theater "*Cinema Paradiso*", 6, 183, 184
Paramount, 84, 193, 199
Pascal, 38, 40, 44, 45, 46, 47, 48, 54n7, 55n27, 56n55
Pasolini, Pier Paolo, 24, 158n7
Pasquale, 47, 95, 98
Pastrone, Giovanni, 81
pater familias, 24
Patriarca, Silvana, 220, 227
Pavese, Cesare, 98, 100, 109, 112n7
Pelé, 95, 111n2
Pelican Brief, The, 4, 37
Pelizzari, Maria Antonella, 220
Perry, Tyler, 86
Pfister, Damien S, 215, 216, 225n31
Phyllis, 41, 47, 55n27
Pierce, Charles, 190
Pinocchio, 125
Pinzolo, Rick, 37
Pirandello, Luigi, 123, 125
Playhouse Theater, 199
Pope John Paul II, 103
Precious: Based on the Novel *Push* by Sapphire, 81, 86, 87, 88, 89, 90, 91n4, 92n20
Prima, Louis, 38, 44, 45

Primo, 38, 41, 42, 43, 44, 45, 46, 47, 48, 49, 50, 55n37
Prizzi's Honor, 37
Proietti, Gianni, 100
psychoanalysis: Lacanian psychoanalysis, 6, 142, 149, 150, 151, 153, 157; "Real", 6, 142, 149, 150, 151, 152, 153, 154, 155, 156, 157, 157n5, 158n29; "Symbolic", 150, 151, 152
Pursuit of Happyness, The, 5, 81, 83, 84, 86, 89, 90, 91n2, 91n3, 91n7
Pylon Theater, 184, 191, 192, 194, 196, 198, 200

queer theory, 167, 180
Quo Vadis, 198

race, 2, 3, 4, 5, 8n8, 27, 28, 33, 33n42, 33n44, 50, 53, 60, 63, 64, 75n2, 76n22, 76n25, 81, 97, 102, 109, 111n3, 179, 206n23, 215
Radio City Film Exchange, 184, 196, 199
Rafferty, Terrence, 44, 45, 55n22, 55n23, 55n26
RAI, 88
Rashad, Phylicia, 63, 76, 77
Rebel without a Cause, 21, 122, 150
Reich, Jacqueline, 22, 32n34, 60, 75n2, 123, 125, 132, 138n20
Remember Me, My Love, 83
Re-Reading Italian Americana, 176n1, 179n49
Ricordati di me, 83
Ripley, Casey, 224n3, 224n5
Risorgimento, 110, 166, 167, 227
Roberts, Doris, 40
Rocky (movie series/character): *Rocky*, 4, 59, 60, 61, 62, 65, 66, 67, 69, 70, 73, 74, 75n2, 75n3, 75n4, 75n5, 75n9, 75n18, 76n35
Rocky II, 59, 62, 67, 69, 71, 73
Rocky III, 59, 67, 68, 73
Rocky IV, 59, 61, 68, 73, 74
Rocky V, 59
Rocky Balboa, 59, 60, 62, 74
Rocky Balboa/Rocky, 60, 61, 62, 63, 64, 65, 66, 67, 68, 69, 70, 71, 72, 73, 74, 103
Rogers, Backman, 16, 30n4

Roma città aperta, 87
Romanelli, Don, 189
Rome, Open City, 87
Rose Tattoo, The, 1
Rosi, Francesco, 109
Rossellini, Isabella, 41
Rossellini, Roberto 46, 47, 55n34, 57, 81, 90, 206n32
Ruberto, Laura E., 142, 155, 156, 158n32, 158n33, 158n34, 158n35, 158n36, 158n37

San Gennaro, 95, 111n2
Saso, John, 191
Saso, Tony, 191
Saturday Night Fever, 20, 40
Savoca, Nancy, 4, 18, 29, 32n27, 34, 137n6
Savoy Theater, 192
Schultz, Jamie, 62, 75n17
Schwable, Michael, 75n13, 75n14, 75n16
Sciorra, Joseph, 111n5, 142, 155, 156, 157n5, 158n32, 158n33, 158n34, 158n35, 158n36, 158n37
Scola, Ettore, 5
Scorsese, Martin, 1, 2, 4, 8, 8n1, 8n3, 17, 31n10, 31n13, 32n27, 37, 39, 46, 48, 49, 56n63, 62, 74, 75n1, 96, 111n4, 137n5, 137n6
Scott, Campbell, 4, 37, 38, 39, 42, 44, 45, 47, 48, 53, 54n3
Secondo, 38, 40, 41, 42, 43, 44, 45, 46, 47, 48, 55n27, 55n30, 55n31
Shalhoub, Tony, 38
Sharkey, Betsy, 88
Sheffer, Jolie A., 164, 177n4
Shoeshine, 47
Shohat, Ella, 49, 55n42
Shuter, Robert, 6, 215, 216, 225n30
Sicilians, 62, 64, 218
Sicily, 92, 92n19, 106, 143, 151, 154, 158n7, 218
Singer, Ben, 187, 206n21
Skey, Michael, 224n9
Smith, Anthony D, 213, 214, 216, 225n20, 225n21, 225n22
Smith, Will, 83, 84, 85, 90
Sofia Coppola: A Cinema of Girlhood, 16, 30n1

Sofia Coppola: The Politics of Visual Pleasure, 16, 30n4
Soliz, Jordan, 215, 216, 225n31
Somewhere, 15, 21, 22, 23, 24, 29, 30n2, 31n18, 32n28, 32n33, 32n38
Soprano, Carmela, 6, 144, 145, 147, 148, 149, 150, 152, 154, 156
Soprano, Corrado John "Uncle Junior", 144, 150
Soprano, Janice, 145, 150, 152
Soprano, Meadow, 154, 157
Soprano, Tony, 6, 141, 142, 143, 144, 145, 146, 147, 148, 149, 150, 151, 152, 153, 154, 155, 156, 157
Sopranos, The, 3, 6, 49, 56n44, 57, 105, 119, 137n8, 137n13, 141, 142, 143, 144, 149, 150, 151, 152, 153, 154, 155, 157, 157n1, 157n6, 158n9, 158n13, 158n15
Soul Food, 50, 56n50
Southern Italians, 62, 97, 105, 111n6, 148, 207n40
Spaghetti Western, 26, 197, 198
Stallone, Sylvester, 59, 60, 61, 62, 63, 65, 66, 68, 72, 75n6, 76n28, 76n30, 76n33, 76n35, 103
Stam, Robert, 49, 55n42
Statista, 222, 226n45
St. Clair Theater, 184, 185, 192, 193, 194, 196, 198, 199, 207n41
Stewart, Jacqueline, 187, 206n25
Stromboli, terra di Dio, 81
struffoli, 148, 156
Studio Theater, 184, 191, 192, 194, 196, 198, 199, 206n32
Sundance Film Festival, 39
Sutherland, Donald, 81
Szulc, Lukasz, 212, 224n13

Tamburri, Anthony Julian, 1, 2, 8n3, 8n6, 8n9, 9n11, 31n10, 32n29, 44, 48, 54n3, 54n5, 55n25, 55n37, 55n38, 55n39, 56n54, 75n1, 75n2, 78, 111n4, 111n5, 112n10, 119, 137n8, 138n25, 176n1, 177n11, 178n32, 179n49
Tanino, 105, 106, 107, 108
Tarantino, Quentin, 2, 4, 32n27, 34, 84, 137n6
Telegatto Award, 22, 23, 32n36

Teorema, 24, 158n7
"The Child", 167, 169, 170, 171, 174, 178n38
"The Old Italians Dying", 156
Thissen, Judith, 187, 206n20, 206n21, 206n22
Thompson, Tessa, 60, 77
Thussu, Daya Kishan, 224n1, 224n4
Toby Dammit, 24
To Rome with Love, 81
Toronto, 6, 183, 184, 185, 186, 187, 188, 189, 190, 191, 192, 193, 194, 196, 197, 198, 199, 204, 205n2, 205n7, 205n8, 205n12, 205n13, 206n28, 206n30, 206n33, 207n38, 207n40
Toronto Star, 191, 192, 194, 199, 206n30, 206n32, 207n37, 207n39, 207n44
Tortilla Soup, 50, 56n48
transatlantic, 9n10, 81, 91n4
Travolta, John, 3, 20, 40
triangle of desire, 132, 134, 135
Tribbiani, Joey, 6, 23, 32n35, 118, 119, 120, 122, 125, 128, 129, 130, 136
Troisi, Massimo, 95, 96, 111, 111n1
Tropiano, Joseph, 39, 40, 44, 47, 50, 54n3, 54n13, 54n15, 56n55
Tsuda, Takayuki, 17, 32n25
"Tu vuo' fa' l'americano", 99
Tucci, Stanley, 4, 37, 38, 39, 42, 44, 45, 47, 48, 50, 53, 54n3, 54n7, 54n12, 55n19, 55n20, 55n31, 56n51, 56n55
"Two Italies", 5, 96, 97, 108, 109
Two Women, 81, 87, 92n18, 103

Umberto D., 47, 86
Unification of Italy (see *Risorgimento*), 110, 166, 167, 227
United States/US, 8n3, 22, 29, 32n36, 50, 51, 54n3, 54n9, 57, 63, 64, 69, 76n23, 76n25, 78, 81, 83, 85, 86, 88, 89, 90, 91n5, 91n10, 96, 97, 99, 100, 102, 104, 105, 106, 109, 142, 143, 148, 151, 152, 154, 155, 156, 157n5, 158n36, 164, 165, 166, 168, 175, 177n9, 178n31, 184, 185, 188, 206n32, 213, 214, 217, 219, 221, 222, 223, 224n1, 224n4
University of Toronto, 8n1, 31n13, 34, 137n5, 138, 191, 192, 197, 198, 206n26

Valentino, Rudolph, 3, 207
Vanzina, Carlo, 5, 102, 103, 112n12
Varsity, 191, 192, 206n33, 207n38
Vecoli, Rudolph, 15, 31n15, 177n10
Vera, Hernán, 66, 76n29
Verdone, Carlo, 98
Vesuvio, 144
Vighi, Fabio, 142, 151, 157, 158n18, 158n22, 158n31
Village Voice, 88, 92n21
Virgin Suicides, The, 13, 17, 19, 21, 25, 26, 29, 30n2, 31n18, 32n38
Virzì, Paolo, 81, 105, 106, 107, 108
Visconti, Luchino, 46, 47, 81, 90
Viscusi, Robert, 165, 176n1, 177n14, 220
Vittorio, Zi, 144
Vitullo, Juliann, 69, 76n32
Vullo, Luca, 218, 225n33

Ward, The, 185, 192, 205n13
Webb, Lawrence, 60, 66, 75n3, 76n27
Wheeler, Charlie, 120
White, Red and Verdone, 98
whiteness, 21, 30, 54n4, 58, 60, 61, 77, 100, 112n9, 205n4
Who's the Boss?, 119

Williams, Tennessee, 1
Willowvale Theater, 189
Windsor, 197
Winfrey, Oprah, 86
wiseguy, 152, 158n23
Wiseguy, 37, 149
wise man, 149, 152, 153, 154
Wodak, Ruth, 224n6, 227
Woodbridge, 194
World War II, 38, 49, 55n43, 96, 97, 98, 99, 100, 108, 109, 142

Yacowar, Maurice, 143, 157n1, 158n8, 158n10, 158n11, 158n12, 158n14, 158n15
YouTube, 213, 222, 226n46

Zadoorian, Michael, 81
Zaffarano, Francesco, 217, 222
Zagarrio, Vito, 15, 31n11, 137n5
Zampa, Luigi, 100, 101, 102, 109, 113
zanni, 147
Zasa, Maria, 14
Žižek, Slavoj, 142, 151, 153, 156, 157, 158n17, 158n22, 158n29, 158n30, 159
Zucchi, John, 185, 205n13, 206n29

About the Contributors

Ryan Calabretta-Sajder is assistant professor of Italian at the University of Arkansas, Fayetteville, where he teaches courses in Italian, Film, and Gender Studies. He is the author of *Divergenze in celluloide: colore, migrazione e identità sessuale nei film gay di Ferzan Özpetek* (*Celluloid Divergences: Color, Migration, and Sexual Identity in the Gay Series of Ferzan Özpetek*) with Mimesis editore (2016) and editor of *Pasolini's Lasting Impressions: Death, Eros, and Literary Enterprise in the Opus of Pier Paolo Pasolini* with Fairleigh Dickinson University Press (2017), *Theorizing the Italian Diaspora: Selected Essays* (with Alan Gravano and Courtney Ruffner Grieneisen, 2018). His research interests include the integration of gender, class, and migration in both Italian and Italian American literature and cinema. In Spring 2017, he was a Fulbright Foundation of the South scholar at the University of Calabria, Arcavacata. He is currently working on two authored, book-length projects, one exploring the Italian American gay author Robert Ferro who died of AIDS complications in 1988 and the second on the Algerian Italian author Amara Lakhous. Calabretta-Sajder is currently Director of Communication for the American Association of Teachers of Italian, vice president of the Italian American Studies Association, president of *Gamma Kappa Alpha*, the Italian National Honors Society, and secretary/treasurer for the American Association of Supervisors and Coordinators.

Mary Ann McDonald Carolan is professor of Modern Languages & Literatures at Fairfield University where she directs the Italian Studies program and teaches in the American Studies graduate program. Carolan is the author of *The Transatlantic Gaze: Italian Cinema, American Film* (State University of New York Press, 2014) which documents the sustained and profound artistic impact of Italian cinema upon filmmakers in the United States from the postwar period to the new millennium. Working across a variety of film genres, she explores how and why American directors from Woody Allen to Quentin Tarantino have adapted certain Italian trademark techniques and motifs. Carolan has also published articles on Italian American comedies as well as on the encounter of Italian and American cultures in Nico Cirasola's docufiction *Focaccia Blues*. Her current project, tentatively entitled *Visions of Italy and America in Film,* extends the analysis presented in *The Transatlantic Gaze* to focus on race and class. She is also working on another cross-cultural study, *Orienting Italy: China through the Lens of Italian Filmmakers* that examines the ways in which Italian directors have employed documentary, historical fiction, and fictional narratives to represent China and its people both at home and abroad in Italy. In spring 2019 Carolan was the Tiro a Segno Fellow in Italian American studies at New York University.

Jonathan J. Cavallero is associate professor of Rhetoric, Film, and Screen Studies at Bates College. He is the author of *Hollywood's Italian American Filmmakers: Capra, Scorsese, Savoca, Coppola, and Tarantino* (University of Illinois Press, 2011), and co-editor (with Laura E. Ruberto) of *Italian American Review*'s special issue on "Italian Americans and Television." His research focuses on representations of race and ethnicity in film and television. His essays have appeared in numerous journals including *Cinema Journal, Journal of Film and Video, The Journal of Popular Culture, The Journal of Popular Film & Television,* and in several edited collections including *Mafia Movies* (edited by Dana Regna) and *A Companion to Martin Scorsese* (edited by Aaron Baker). He is director of the Bates Film Festival.

Francesco Chianese holds a PhD in Comparative Literature (Italian and US American Literature) from the University of Naples L'Orientale and is the author of *"Mio padre si sta facendo un individuo problematico": Padri e figli nell'ultimo Pasolini* (1966–1975) with Mimesis editore (2018). In 2018–2019, he was the Fulbright Scholar-in-Residence at California State University, Long Beach, where he taught Italian and Italian American culture. He has published on Don DeLillo, John Fante, F. S. Fitzgerald, Pasolini, Philip Roth, Walter Siti, and topics related to the representation of the Italian diaspora and the Italian American experience for the journals *Italian Studies, Il Mulino,* and *Between* and in the volumes *Pier Paolo Pasolini: Transmediality and Transhumanization—Transmedialità e Transumanizzazione* (forthcoming, 2019), *Sicily and Cinema* (2019), *Italia Transculturale: Il sincretismo italofono come modello eterotopico* (2018), *Harbors, Flows and Migrations: The USA in/and the World* (2017), *Scrivere tra le lingue* (2017).

Alan J. Gravano has an MFA in Poetry and an MA and PhD in English from the University of Miami in Coral Gables, Florida. His poems have appeared in many journals, including *Gulf Stream: South Florida's Literary Current*, *The Museum of Americana*, *Red Rock Review*, *Review Americana: A Literary Journal*, and *Voices in Italian Americana*. He has co-edited two collections of essays on Italian American culture, film, and literature and has published two essays on Don DeLillo: "New York in Don DeLillo's Novels" and "New York City as Place in Don DeLillo's Fiction." Gravano organized a MLA Working Group entitled "Italian Americans on Screen" for Chicago, 2019, and "Italian Americans on the Page" for Seattle, 2020. He is an MLA Delegate Assembly member and recently has been appointed to the Committee on Contingent Labor in the Profession, president of the Italian American Studies Association, and is the Writing Center director and assistant professor at Rocky Mountain University.

Paul S. Moore is associate professor of Communication and Culture at Ryerson University and past president of the *Film Studies Association of Canada/ l'Association canadienne d'études cinématographiques*. His media histories of cinema exhibition and newspaper distribution in North America have focused on the relation between audiences and publicity, appearing in *Canadian Journal of Film Studies*, *The Moving Image*, and *Film History*. Recent work maps early "circuits of cinema," also theme of the 2017 International Conference on the History of Movie Exhibition and Reception (HoMER), which he hosted in Toronto.

Colleen M. Ryan is professor of Italian at Indiana University, where she teaches courses on contemporary Italian and Italian American literature, film, and culture with focuses on gender and sexuality. She also teaches courses on Italian pedagogy and professionalization for graduate students. Ryan is the author of *Sex, the Self, and the Sacred: Women in the Cinema of Pier Paolo Pasolini*, and co-editor (with Nicoletta Marini-Maio) of two pedagogical volumes: *Set the Stage! Italian Language, Literature, and Culture through Theater—Theoretical and Practical Perspectives*. (Yale, 2009) and *Dramatic Interactions: Teaching Languages, Literatures, and Cultures through Theater—Theoretical Approaches and Classroom Practices* (Cambridge Scholars Press, 2011). She is also co-author (with Daniela Bartalesi-Graf) of an intermediate-level Italian program, *Caldeidoscopio* (Pearson 2015), and co-editor (with Lisa Parkes) of *Creative Thinking: Integrating the Arts in the Foreign Language Curriculum* (Cengage 2015).

Sarah H. Salter is assistant professor of English at Texas A&M University-Corpus Christi. Her current book manuscript uses literary texts, archival materials, and antebellum Italian-language newspapers to tell a prehistory of Italian migration in the United States. This work received the Italian American Studies Association Memorial Fellowship as a dissertation. In addition, the monograph project has been supported by the American Antiquarian Society, the National Endowment for the Humanities, and the Midlo Center for New Orleans Studies at University of New Orleans, where Salter is a Visiting Scholar. Articles on Italian translation and literary intimacy have appeared in the collection *Facing Melville, Facing Italy: Democracy, Politics, Translation* (University of Rome Sapienza Press) and in Italian in *Ácoma*; her scholarship on Italian-language newspapers in the United States has appeared in *American Periodicals*.

Giuseppe Sorrentino is a scholar of American and Italian American Studies, who worked as coordinator of the Italian Program at Wagner College and collaborated with other institutions in New York and New Jersey (College of Staten Island, Baruch College, and Ramapo College of New Jersey) as an adjunct professor. Born and raised in the province of Naples, Italy, Dr. Sorrentino obtained his PhD in American Studies from the University of Rome "Roma Tre" and moved to the United States as a Fulbright Foreign Language teaching assistant in 2009. He has taught courses on a variety of topics ranging from Italian language and Comparative Literature to American History and Italian Cinema. His research mainly focuses on Post-modern American Literature, Italian American Literature and Cinema, Mass Media, and Identity. Dr. Sorrentino also collaborates with various cultural organizations in the New York area, lecturing on Italian Culture and Cinema and he presented papers at international conferences in the United States and in Italy. In the field of Italian American studies, he particularly focuses on the Italian American poets of the Beat generation, on the interconnections between Italian and Italian American culture in cinema and literature, and on the question of national identity among Italians abroad.

Giacomo Sproccati holds a MA in Italian studies from California State University, Long Beach. His graduate studies focused on merging his Italian roots with the background in communications he developed in his undergraduate career. As an undergraduate, he earned a dual degree in Communications, a Laurea Triennale summa cum laude from the University of Milan, and a Bachelor of Arts from John Cabot University. His final MA thesis project studied how two TED Talks construct a sense of national belonging in Italy. While a graduate student, Sproccati also taught Italian language courses as a teaching associate both online and in the physical classroom and presented his research at two IASA Annual Conferences where he received constructive feedback from experienced scholars that helped him improve his academic work. Currently, Sproccati works at Florida State University International Programs—Italy as student services coordinator.

Jessica Leonora Whitehead holds a PhD in Communication and Culture from York and Ryerson Universities and is currently an Arts & Sciences postdoctoral fellow at the University of Toronto. Her dissertation, *Cinema-Going on the Margins: The Mascioli Film Circuit of Northeastern Ontario* was funded by a SSHRC Joseph-Armand Bombardier Canada Graduate Scholarship, and explored a regional chain of movie theaters built by an Italian labor agent whose theaters fell under government control when he was sent to an internment camp during WWII. Her current research recounts the history of Italian-Canadian film exhibition and distribution in postwar Toronto, supported by a 2018 Italian American Studies Association Memorial Fellowship. Past research has appeared in *Transformative Works and Cultures*, *Italian Canadiana*, the *Canadian Journal of Film Studies*, and chapters in the books *Rural Cinema-going from a Global Perspective* and *Mapping Movie Magazines*. She is co-editing an upcoming special issue on comparative histories of film exhibition for the journal *Tijdschrift voor Mediageschiedenis/ Journal for Media History*.

CPSIA information can be obtained
at www.ICGtesting.com
Printed in the USA
LVHW080749290822
726885LV00012B/310